DATE DUE			
May 16 '77 P			
Dec 13 7 7 0			
Nov 14 7 8			
Dec 2 7 8			
Dec 15 7 8 B			
Apr 26 7 9			
Nov 27 7 9			
Dec 14 7 9			
Aug 12 '80			
Oct 7 '82			

PROGRESS IN BEHAVIOR MODIFICATION

Volume 1

CONTRIBUTORS TO THIS VOLUME

D. A. Begelman
Curtis J. Braukmann
Joseph R. Cautela
John Davis
Richard M. Eisler
Dean L. Fixsen
Michel Hersen
Alan E. Kazdin
Peter M. Lewinsohn
Robert Paul Liberman
Isaac Marks
Peter M. Miller
Dennis Upper

PROGRESS IN BEHAVIOR MODIFICATION

EDITED BY

Michel Hersen
Department of Psychiatry
Western Psychiatric Institute and Clinic
University of Pittsburgh School of Medicine
Pittsburgh, Pennsylvania

Richard M. Eisler
Peter M. Miller
Department of Psychiatry and Human Behavior
University of Mississippi Medical Center
Jackson, Mississippi

Volume 1

1975

ACADEMIC PRESS NEW YORK SAN FRANCISCO LONDON
A Subsidiary of Harcourt Brace Jovanovich, Publishers

ACADEMIC PRESS, INC.
111 Fifth Avenue, New York, New York 10003

United Kingdom Edition published by
ACADEMIC PRESS, INC. (LONDON) LTD.
24/28 Oval Road, London NW1

LIBRARY OF CONGRESS CATALOG CARD NUMBER: 74-5697

ISBN 0-12-535601-3

PRINTED IN THE UNITED STATES OF AMERICA

CONTENTS

Behavioral Treatments of Phobic and Obsessive-Compulsive Disorders: A Critical Appraisal
Isaac Marks

Ethical and Legal Issues of Behavior Modification
D. A. Begelman

Behavior Modification with Delinquents
Curtis J. Braukmann and Dean L. Fixsen

Recent Advances in Token Economy Research
Alan E. Kazdin

The Process of Individual Behavior Therapy

Joseph R. Cautela and Dennis Upper

Drugs and Behavior Analysis

Robert Paul Liberman and John Davis

LIST OF CONTRIBUTORS

Numbers in parentheses indicate the pages on which the authors' contributions begin.

D. A. BEGELMAN (159), Division of Social Sciences, Kirkland College, Clinton, New York

CURTIS J. BRAUKMANN (191), Department of Human Development and Bureau of Child Research, University of Kansas, Lawrence, Kansas

JOSEPH R. CAUTELA (275), Department of Psychology, Boston College, Chestnut Hill, Massachusetts

JOHN DAVIS (307), Camarillo-Neuropsychiatric Institute (UCLA) Research Program, Camarillo State Hospital, Camarillo, California

RICHARD M. EISLER (1), Department of Psychiatry and Human Behavior, University of Mississippi Medical Center, Jackson, Mississippi

DEAN L. FIXSEN (191), Department of Human Development and Bureau of Child Research, University of Kansas, Lawrence, Kansas

MICHEL HERSEN (1), Department of Psychiatry, Western Psychiatric Institute and Clinic, University of Pittsburgh School of Medicine, Pittsburgh, Pennsylvania

ALAN E. KAZDIN (233), Department of Psychology, The Pennsylvania State University, University Park, Pennsylvania

PETER M. LEWINSOHN (19), Psychology Department, University of Oregon, Eugene, Oregon

ROBERT PAUL LIBERMAN (307), Camarillo-Neuropsychiatric Institute (UCLA) Research Program, Camarillo State Hospital, Camarillo, California

ISAAC MARKS (65), Institute of Psychiatry, De Crespigny Park, Denmark Hill, London, England

PETER M. MILLER (1), Department of Psychiatry and Human Behavior, University of Mississippi Medical Center, Jackson, Mississippi

DENNIS UPPER (275), Brockton Veterans Administration Hospital, Brockton, Massachusetts

FOREWORD

As I pen these words, I have a nightmarish vision of scores of determined writers sequestered in little cubbyholes, each grimly committed to produce a forward-looking foreword for yet another book on behavior modification which promises to deliver something different and innovative. In their common dedication to the production of novel books and clever forewords, impressive sounding—but empty—phrases are coined, non-ideas are embellished with fanciful language in the hope that this will give them the stamp of authenticity, and hoary old concepts are trundled out with an overlay of new synthetic window dressing, with the implication that here at last is something new. But when all is said, but seldom done, the promise is usually all that remains and the hapless reader is left with a disquieting feeling of *déjà vu,* and a sense of having been had.

And yet, among the literally dozens of books which come across my desk each month for some purpose or another, there is always at least one which does have something new to say, and says it well. The present volume falls squarely into this category, and so it is with considerable pleasure that I write this Foreword. When my friends Hersen, Eisler, and Miller first raised the feasibility of a series of specially commissioned articles reviewing progress in selected areas of behavior modification at regularly scheduled intervals, rather than reprinting selected key papers in full, I was sceptical. Who would write these articles? How would one ensure quality control? Does enough worthwhile new material appear in any 12-month period—let alone the three-month interval originally proposed —to warrant an entire book of substantive reviews spanning the many diverse areas now encompassed under the expanding umbrella of behavior therapy?

To find 45 or so articles of intrinsic merit for reprinting in our *Annual Review,* Terry Wilson and I have to survey upwards of a thousand publications. While most can be dismissed out of hand, the fact that our *Commentaries* are able to note at least one positive feature of substance in each of some 400 of these articles for each volume never ceases to amaze us. Each year there does seem to be a small but significant increase in the number of such articles. At least, this is my opinion. It is this trend—if it is a trend—that leads to the hope that Hersen, Eisler, and Miller's contributors will find adequate material to cover in the years ahead. In assembling this collection of outstanding reviews, covering the broad spectrum of what behavior therapy is all about, Hersen and his associates have more than allayed my original apprehensions. In so doing, they have inaugurated a potentially important new series which, if all goes as planned, will meet the needs of those who require critical in-depth reviews of subject areas in behavior therapy rather than a set of *Commentaries* woven around the reprinting in full of selected papers.

A decade ago, the renaissance man of behavior therapy, single-handed, could have easily covered the entire field in one comprehensive chapter. Now, a compendium of such chapters is required, and it is of interest to speculate how this came about. As recently as the late 50's and early 60's, the only widely accepted procedures for the treatment of so-called personality and emotional disorders were either pharmacologically or psychodynamically oriented. Systematic desensitization, recently introduced by Wolpe, was looked at by most psychiatrists either with suspicion or as a minor adjunctive technique which could possibly be used on occasion to expedite the "real" treatment. Conditioning was regarded as something which applied to much of animal behavior and perhaps the more directly physiological reflexes in man. But it was generally agreed that conditioning, either operant or classical, was, at best, too simplistic for meaningful applicability in modern society or, at worst, downright invalid. Behavior therapy—when it was viewed at all—was viewed as a grab bag of techniques to be employed either with mentally defective children or perhaps as a method for the temporary control of certain circumscribed symptoms under the ever watchful direction of a competent psychiatrist. Some misguided and antiquated psychiatrists and psychologists still harbor these quaint notions! But, in all fairness, it should be noted that, by their rigid adherence to mechanistic and clinically unrealistic formulas, certain "behavior therapists"—often excellent laboratory scientists but naive with respect to the ways of the world—unwittingly contributed to these potentially disastrous impressions.

Gradually, an almost inevitable progression occurred: As more and more data, experience, and wisdom accumulated, behavior therapy became less simplistic and rigid, and the nonbehavioral professional became more accepting and more understanding of what we were trying to accomplish. As behavior therapy became broader in its conceptualization—while still adhering firmly to a behavioral (not to be confused with behavioristic) model—it began to encompass an increasing range of topic areas, fields of endeavor, and facets of society. Feeling and affect, imagery, societal influences, and sociopolitical forces all came within the purview of the forward-looking behavior therapist. The emphasis was increasingly upon broad-spectrum behavior therapy, multidimensional strategies of intervention, rational and cognitive processes, social processes, self-control, and biofeedback mechanisms. Increasingly, the emphasis was, on the one hand, upon generalization from the laboratory and the clinic to the natural environment, and, on the other hand, upon internal mechanisms rather than the imposition of obvious and artificial external reinforcers.

Not surprisingly, these rapid advances brought with them equally rapid antagonisms. When behavior therapy was viewed as weak and ineffective it could be questioned, derided, and even dismissed, but not feared. As both the methodology and the specific techniques of behavior therapy became demonstrably more effective and increasingly accepted, so behavior therapy both as a body of knowledge and a series of procedures became worthy of both fear and attack. The days when either mental health specialists or the lay public questioned the validity of the principles of conditioning as applied to social and clinical problems were largely over. Instead, the last few years have seen a spate of heated objections to its deployment and its underlying conceptualizations rather than to conditioning as a viable mechanism. Sometimes these objections are temperate and closely reasoned, at other times they take the form of impassioned "Clockwork Orange"-type diatribes, stemming more from illogical fear than from data. In either case, as behavior modifiers, it should not be beyond our capacities to modify our own behavior as well as that of others, and thus to cope constructively with these developments. It is no matter of chance that we are now witnessing among behavior therapists a healthy concern with problems of ethics, accountability, responsibility, licensing regulations, and the rights of human beings. Behavior therapists—like concerned and responsible people everywhere, in these changing times—have no alternative but to concern themselves with human rights and all that this entails.

This, then, is briefly where behavior therapy stands at the present time. It is well established, it still maintains its experimental rigor and its conceptual integrity, and its practitioners are becoming finely attuned to social and ethical issues. And all of this is accomplished without behavior therapy relinquishing its unique identity and its underlying adherence to the strategies and methodology of the behavioral scientist. It is this, rather than our success or acceptance, which is what behavior therapy is really all about. Perhaps most encouraging of all, this conceptual integrity has been retained without the necessity for adherence to any one set of principles. We are students rather than disciples, advocating an open-minded spirit of enquiry rather than a closed shop.

When the *Association for Advancement of Behavior Therapy* was founded in 1966 the original name was *Association for Advancement of the Behavioral Therapies.* Due to the prompting of such discerning individuals as Wilson and Evans, writing in the *Newsletter* of our Association as early as 1967, the name of the organization was changed to its present form on the grounds that it was a common conceptualization which united us rather than adherence to common language. This point is even more compelling now that behavior therapy has burgeoned forth in so many seemingly disparate areas—but it is hardly necessary to reiterate this thesis to our present readers. Certainly the Editors and contributors to this brave new serial publication are clearly aware of this important point, and it is this theme which seems to permeate the chapters which follow. Skillfully, and with a delicate touch, the Editors and authors have managed to capture the very essence of these exciting and important new developments in the evolution of behavior therapy, and they are to be congratulated. As a bonus, the Editors' thoughtful and incisive overview has succeeded in placing this vast canvas in its historical and conceptual framework. If subsequent volumes are as good as the first one—and past and present behaviors are undoubtedly the best predictors of the future—this serial publication will be very good indeed.

Cyril M. Franks
Graduate School of Applied and Professional Psychology
Rutgers University
New Brunswick, New Jersey

PREFACE

Progress in Behavior Modification is a multidisciplinary serial publication encompassing the contributions of psychology, psychiatry, social work, speech therapy, education, and rehabilitation. In an era of intense specialization, it is designed to bring to the attention of all workers in behavior modification, in a yearly review format, the most timely issues and developments in the field. Inasmuch as several journals are presently devoted entirely to publishing articles on behavior modification, and in consideration of the fact that numerous other journals are now allowing an increased allotment of pages to articles dealing with behavioral techniques, even the most diligent reader will find it difficult to keep abreast of all new developments in the field. In light of the publication explosion in behavior modification, there is a real need for a review publication that undertakes to present yearly in-depth evaluations that include a scholarly examination of theoretical underpinnings, a careful survey of research findings, and a comparative analysis of existing techniques and methodologies. In this serial publication we propose to meet this need.

Theoretical discussion, research methodology, assessment techniques, treatment modalities, control of psychophysiological processes, and ethical issues in behavioral control will be considered. Discussions will center on a wide spectrum of child and adult disorders. The range of topics will include, but will not be limited to, studies of fear behavior, measurement and modification of addictive behaviors, modification of classroom behaviors, remedial methods for the retarded and physically handicapped, descriptions of animal analogs, the effects of social influences on behavior, the use of drugs in behavioral approaches, and the contribution of behavior therapy to the treatment of physical illness.

Progress in Behavior Modification will present a diversity of views within the field. We will, on occasion, solicit discussions from theoreticians, researchers, or practitioners not directly associated with behavior modification. Cross-fertilization of ideas, *when maintained at the empirical level,* can be most rewarding and often leads to refinements in theory, research, and practice. In short, we propose not only to review critically developments in behavior modification at a particular point in time, but also to identify new directions and point toward future trends at all levels of inquiry.

In the first article of this volume, Hersen, Eisler, and Miller discuss the evolution of behavior modification. Emphasis is placed on the rapidly increasing number of publications in the area and the distinguishing features of behavior modification as a methodological approach to the study and treatment of psychological disorders. In the next paper, Lewinsohn reviews his interpersonal analysis of depression from theoretical, research, and therapeutic standpoints. The need for further research on the efficacy of behavioral approaches to depression is indicated. In the third article, Marks examines the most recent developments in the behavioral treatment of phobic and obsessive–compulsive disorders. Although behavioral approaches to the treatment of these disorders have been extensive, the need for additional work with clinical populations is underscored. Next, Begelman discusses one of the most crucial issues facing behavior therapists today—the ethical and legal ramifications of their practices. The problems are presented in light of recent court decisions, the issue of patients' rights, and the efficacy of the behavioral approach vis-à-vis other systems of treatment. Braukmann and Fixsen document the contribution of behavior modification to the field of juvenile delinquency. Kazdin discusses recent advances in token economy research. The extended use of token economic techniques for the betterment of society is outlined. Cautela and Upper present a comprehensive description of the process of individual behavior therapy, from its inception to its termination. The practical problems faced by the behavior therapist in his daily clinical endeavors are carefully detailed. In the final article, Liberman and Davis examine the complementary roles of drugs and behavior modification. The experimental single-case strategy is recommended for assessing the individual and combined effects of pharmacological and behavioral treatments on designated responses.

Michel Hersen
Richard M. Eisler
Peter M. Miller

ACKNOWLEDGMENTS

Many individuals have been involved in the inauguration of this serial publication, and we would like to acknowledge their efforts.

We are deeply grateful for Dr. Cyril M. Franks' support, encouragement, and reinforcement throughout the developmental stages, and are honored that he has consented to write the Foreword. Not only has Dr. Franks been at the forefront of the behavior modification movement as one of its true leaders, but he has demonstrated the teacher's imperative of encouraging colleagues, young and old, regardless of whether their views are consistent with his own, to realize their potentialities.

We would like to acknowledge the full cooperation of our eminent contributors, who took "time out" from their crowded schedules to meet our publication deadlines without complaint. We would also like to acknowledge the assistance of our colleagues W. Stewart Agras, David H. Barlow, and Leonard H. Epstein, whose critical comments facilitated our editorial review of the manuscripts.

We thank Margie Leiberton and Janet Sue Noblin for typing the final manuscript, and Harriet F. Alford, Diana H. O'Toole, Susan G. Pinkston, and Laura S. Wooten for their assistance in preparing this publication. We are also grateful to Marcia Schwartz for last-minute help in compiling the Subject Index.

Finally, we extend our gratitude to our respective wives, Lynn, Terri, and Gabrielle, for their forbearance while we were engaged in a multitude of editorial chores.

M.H.
R.M.E.
P.M.M.

PROGRESS IN BEHAVIOR MODIFICATION

Volume 1

HISTORICAL PERSPECTIVES IN BEHAVIOR MODIFICATION: INTRODUCTORY COMMENTS

MICHEL HERSEN
Department of Psychiatry
Western Psychiatric Institute and Clinic
University of Pittsburgh School of Medicine
Pittsburgh, Pennsylvania
AND
RICHARD M. EISLER AND PETER M. MILLER
Department of Psychiatry and Human Behavior
University of Mississippi Medical Center
Jackson, Mississippi

I. INTRODUCTION

In this chapter we will very briefly trace the historical roots of behavior modification, examine the publication trends in the area, outline the distinguishing features of behavior modification as a systematic method of studying and treating behavioral problems, and discuss future directions. Although these issues have previously been given detailed and careful consideration elsewhere (e.g., Adams, Heyse, & Meyer, 1973; Agras, 1972; Franks, 1969a; Kanfer & Phillips, 1970; Krasner, 1971; Lazarus, 1971; Levis, 1970; Meyer & Chesser, 1970; Wolpe, 1969; Yates, 1970), the objectives of this overview are twofold: (1) to familiarize the relative newcomer to the field of behavior modification with the basic issues, and

(2) to refresh the memory of our more established colleagues as to the rapid historical course that behavior modification has taken.

II. IMPETUS

The application of behavioral principles to problems of psychopathology has increased dramatically during the last two decades. Part of the impetus for the shift from the "dynamic" to the behavioral position can be attributed to the fact that the presumed causal variables in the psychoanalytic model are nonquantifiable internal events whose effects are difficult to study. Indeed, they can only be evaluated *indirectly*. By contrast, the behavioral model focuses *directly* on quantifiable objective phenomena as measured verbally, motorically, and physiologically. A further impetus for the shift to behavior modification has been the growing dissatisfaction with clinical outcomes based on therapeutic procedures derived from "dynamic" models of psychopathology (e.g., Eysenck, 1952, 1965a, 1965b, 1966).

Probably the greatest contribution of the behavioral model has been the improvement in methodologies for the study of clinically relevant human behavior. Experiments within the behavioral context have endeavored to develop functional relationships between measurable environmental manipulations and specific observable behaviors, in addition to comparing behavioral and nonbehavioral treatments, and carefully evaluating follow-up status.

III. HISTORICAL COURSE

One of the foundations of what now is labeled as behavior modification can be traced back to the original work conducted by the physiologists Pavlov and Bekhterev in their animal laboratories at the beginning of this century in Russia. For almost three decades, these two reflexologists conducted numerous animal experiments showing that a previously neutral environmental stimulus (e.g., a bell) when temporally preceding a naturally occurring autonomic response (e.g., salivation in the presence of food) could acquire the power to elicit the autonomic reaction after many such pairings. This phenomenon was later described as "classical conditioning," and a number of the current treatment strategies used by behavior modifiers are derived from the principles of classical conditioning (see Franks, 1969a).

The American psychologist J. B. Watson shrewdly recognized the applicability of the Russian work to human problems, and he pioneered experimentation in the conditioning of child behavior among other areas. Specifically, Watson and Rayner (1920) demonstrated how a fear reaction to a nonfeared white rat could be acquired by pairing presentation of the rat with a fear-producing loud noise. Other milestones based on the application of classical conditioning methods at the human level were Jones' (1924) treatment of a phobic child, Dunlap's (1932) work on negative practice and extinction procedures for maladaptive habits (now reprinted, 1972), Max's (1935) treatment of a homosexual fetish by aversion therapy, Mowrer and Mowrer's (1938) bell-pad conditioning treatment for enuresis (still in use), the treatment of alcoholics through chemical aversion procedures (Lemere, Voegtlin, Broz, Hollaren, & Tupper, 1942), and Salter's (1949) book *Conditioned Reflex Therapy.*

A parallel line of animal experimentation, which may also be regarded as a precursor to behavior modification, came from the laboratories of E. L. Thorndike and then of B. F. Skinner. Thorndike (1932) confined food-deprived laboratory animals in a "puzzle box" from which they learned to escape by making a "correct" motor response in order to open a latch. Once out of confinement, the animals were rewarded with food, and gradually they learned to escape in progressively shorter periods of time. Thorndike argued that, if particular behaviors randomly emitted by an organism were followed by a "satisfying state of affairs" (i.e., positive reinforcement), then the connection between the behavior and environmental event was "strengthened." If, on the other hand, the behavior were followed by an "annoying state of affairs" (i.e., punishment), then the connection between the behavior and environmental event was "weakened." These two relationships comprise Thorndike's (1933) famous "law of effect."

Skinner (1938), in his book *The Behavior of Organisms: An Experimental Analysis,* distinguished between respondent and operant behavior, the former referring to the Pavlovian model and the latter following Thorndike's system. In his discussion of operant conditioning, Skinner (1938) pointed out that the rate of a particular response could be controlled by its relation to environmental events (i.e., its consequences). He specifically described the process of positive reinforcement, wherein a particular response followed by a contingent (reinforcing) environmental event resulted in a high probability of that response being emitted in the future. By contrast, in the case of punishment, if the same response were followed by a contingent (punishing) environmental event, the probability of the behavior being emitted was decreased in the future. These two relationships comprise the "empirical law of effect."

Skinner (1938) argued against the need for postulating intervening processes (e.g., mediating states) to explain occurrence and changes of the rate of behavior. Indeed, the direct application of environmental contingencies to modify simple motor behaviors of hospitalized psychotics was first evaluated by one of Skinner's students (Lindsley, 1956, 1960; Lindsley & Skinner, 1954). These initial studies paved the way for applications of contingent reinforcement to clinically relevant behavioral problems by Ayllon and his colleagues (Ayllon, 1963; Ayllon & Azrin, 1964, 1965; Ayllon & Haughton, 1962, 1964; Ayllon & Michael, 1959). Finally, with publication of *The Token Economy: A Motivational System for Therapy and Rehabilitation,* Ayllon and Azrin (1968) illustrated the use of reinforcement techniques in structuring an in-patient psychiatric setting, both in terms of behavioral management and modification.

In the late 1940s and early 1950s, attempts were also being made to recast aspects of psychoanalytically oriented therapies into learning theory parlance (e.g., Dollard & Miller, 1950; Shoben, 1949). Thus, terms such as "reinforcement," "conditioning," "generalization," "discrimination," and "extinction" were used to describe various processes within the traditional therapeutic relationship. However, the results of these attempts, although exciting at the time and of interest historically, generated few improvements in traditional therapeutic strategies or developments of new ones. To the contrary, only a translation of psychoanalytic jargon into behavioral language was achieved (Ullmann & Krasner, 1965).

Also beginning in the 1950s and extending through the 1960s and early 1970s were the several hundred studies conducted in the area of verbal conditioning (reviewed by Greenspoon, 1962; Hersen, 1968, 1970; Krasner, 1958, 1962; Salzinger, 1959; Speilberger, 1962; Staats, 1961; Williams, 1964). Hersen (1968) pointed out: "At first these laboratory techniques seemed to serve as a bridge between experimental and clinical psychology in that the verbal interaction between *E* and *S* was construed as a model of the patterns of verbal behavior that occur during therapy [p. 287]." Here too, other than attuning therapists of varying persuasions as to their potential power as dispensers of social reinforcement, analyses of the traditional therapeutic relationship within the framework of verbal operant conditioning did not lead to significantly improved care of those evidencing behavioral disorders. However, when verbal reinforcement techniques are used systematically in a therapeutic context, marked changes in both verbal (e.g., Ayllon & Haughton, 1964) and nonverbal behaviors (e.g., Hersen, Gullick, Matherne, & Harbert, 1972) of patients become apparent. Thus, the planned use of verbal reinforcement techniques has gained its place in the armamentarium of behavior modifiers and certainly cannot be discounted as an agent of behavioral change.

One of the most significant contributions to behavior modification in the early 1950s was Joseph Wolpe's development of systematic desensitization as a treatment for phobic disorders (Wolpe, 1954). Based on his earlier work in the modification of experimentally induced neurotic reactions in cats, Wolpe (1952) identified principles (i.e., reciprocal inhibition) that could be used in the clinical treatment of phobia. He found that a hierarchical imaginal presentation of the phobic object under conditions of deep muscle relaxation led to remission of symptomatology in a high proportion of his phobic patients (Wolpe, 1954, 1958).

Publication of Wolpe's initial findings resulted in controversial reactions in the psychiatric world. While recent experiments questioned the initial theoretical rationale for his technique, with a resulting alteration in parts of the procedure, systematic desensitization is still considered to be one of the standard methods of treating clinical phobias. Many variants of the original technique have appeared and their relative merits were examined in several reviews (see Brady, 1972; Paul, 1969a, 1969b).

We should underscore at this point that behavior modification when first practiced clinically, and to a much lesser extent today, represented an enormous challenge to the psychological and psychiatric communities. However, behavioral techniques are now routinely used in many clinical settings. When examined from an operant perspective, it is not too difficult to understand why the earlier behavior modifiers met with such stiff "resistance" on the part of their colleagues. Indeed, that there should be the need for the *Progress in Behavior Modification* series is a testimonial to the pioneering efforts of such individuals as Sidney W. Bijou, Hans J. Eysenck, Cyril M. Franks, H. Gwynne Jones, Leonard Krasner, Arnold A. Lazarus, Ogden B. Lindsley, B. F. Skinner, Leonard P. Ullmann, Joseph Wolpe, and Aubrey Yates.[1] Beginning in the 1950s, these "early" behavior modifiers displayed the courage of their convictions and the ultimate in scientific integrity in challenging the existing psychological and psychiatric "establishments." They often suffered contempt and criticism, in press and professionally, at the hands of antagonistic colleagues. However, they persisted in their efforts and, through clinical and empirical demonstrations, began to influence their contemporaries by drawing adherents to their positions. The development of behavior modification as a clinical and scien-

[1] Obviously many other individuals contributed to the enormous growth of behavior modification, but space will only permit our listing *some* of those whose work began in the 1950s.

tific discipline since 1958 is perhaps best traced through an examination of publication trends.

IV. PUBLICATION TRENDS

The main impetus for the current interest in behavior modification stems from publication of Wolpe's (1958) *Psychotherapy by Reciprocal Inhibition* and Eysenck's (1960) *Behaviour Therapy and the Neuroses.* Shortly thereafter young psychologists and psychiatrists and converts from psychoanalysis on both sides of the Atlantic, Australia, and South Africa began expanding the use of behavioral techniques both at the clinical and experimental levels. This necessitated an outlet for their work, and in 1963 the first issue of *Behaviour Research and Therapy* appeared under the editorial direction of Hans J. Eysenck.

As has been described elsewhere: "That the field of behavior modification has grown enormously in the last decade is attested by: 1) the burgeoning numbers of publications . . . concerned with the behavioral approach; 2) the increased number of journals devoted entirely to behavior modification; 3) the increased use of behavioral principles in classrooms, schools, clinics, institutions, and hospital settings; and 4) the increased number of courses and programs devoted in part or entirely to behavior modification in graduate schools . . . [Hersen, 1973a, p. 373]."

In addition to *Behaviour Research and Therapy,* there are three other major journals whose function is to publish articles dealing with various aspects of behavior modification (*Journal of Applied Behavior Analysis*—first volume in 1968; *Behavior Therapy,* edited by Cyril M. Franks—first volume in 1970; and *Journal of Behavior Therapy and Experimental Psychiatry,* edited by Joseph Wolpe—first volume in 1970). Differences in editorial policies for these three journals have been documented by Agras (1973). The *Journal of Applied Behavior Analysis* is aimed primarily at the researcher, while the *Journal of Behavior Therapy and Experimental Psychiatry* appears to be directed more toward the practitioner. Articles published in *Behavior Therapy,* on the other hand, reflect a closer balance between practical application and research.

A fourth journal devoted to behavior modification is currently in the process of being established (*European Journal of Behaviour Analysis and Modification*). Furthermore, the marked linear increase in the number of papers representing the behavioral viewpoint that are appearing in the nonbehavioral journals (both psychological and psychiatric) was depicted graphically by Brady (1971) in his presidential address to the Association for Advancement of Behavior Therapy. Indeed, journals usually not associated with the behavior modification position have recently devoted entire editions to behavioral issues (e.g., Hersen, 1973a).

The number of books published in behavior modification between 1948 and 1971 similarly has increased dramatically (Ernst, 1971, presents a cumulative growth curve). There are presently four comprehensive overviews of the field (Bandura, 1969; Franks, 1969b; Kanfer & Phillips, 1970; Yates, 1970) and numerous shorter works and descriptions of more specialized areas. Publication of the *Advances in Behavior Therapy,* based on the proceedings of the yearly meeting of the Association for Advancement of Behavior Therapy, represented the first attempt to have a nonjournal annual series in the field (Rubin, Brady, & Henderson, 1973; Rubin, Fensterheim, Lazarus, & Franks, 1971; Rubin, Fensterheim, Ullmann, & Franks, 1972; Rubin & Franks, 1969). In addition, the field advanced to a point where the need for reprinting selected articles yearly, with editorial commentaries on these papers and the field at large, became apparent (Franks & Wilson, 1973). Finally, a *Handbook of Behavior Modification* is currently in preparation (Leitenberg, in press).

Not only has there been a tremendous increase in publications relating to behavior modification in the last decade and a half, but the tenor of the writing has changed over the years. That behavior modification is now truly reaching its adult status is underscored by the absence of acrimonious attacks on other schools of thought, so prevalent in the writings of the earlier behaviorists. This, however, does not mean that most behavior modifiers are willing to compromise and merge their views with nonempirical disciplines, although this merger has been suggested (e.g., Feather & Rhoads, 1972; Lehrer & Kris, 1972). But it does indicate that the scope of behavior modification has increased and that influences from other empirical approaches are being considered. For example, the importance of physiological processes, the use of drugs as adjuncts to behavior therapy, and the role of social psychological factors in the treatment process are subjects for both research and clinical application.

The full impact of behavior modification (with respect to theory, research, practice, and training) was recently acknowledged in the Task Force Report 5 (1973) on *Behavior Therapy in Psychiatry.* In this report it was concluded that, "The work of the task force has reaffirmed our belief that behavior therapy and behavioral principles employed in the analysis of clinical phenomena have reached a stage of development where they now unquestionably have much to offer informed clinicians in the service of modern clinical and social psychiatry [p. 64]." This represents a landmark endorsement on the part of the American Psychiatric Association, particularly as behavior modification poses a direct challenge to the medical model of behavioral disorders.

V. PROFESSIONAL SOCIETIES AND BEHAVIOR MODIFICATION

A separate index of the growth of behavior modification is reflected in the founding of professional societies concerned with the promotion of the behavioral position (e.g., Association for Advancement of Behavior Therapy; Behavior Therapy and Research Society). The memberships in these organizations and in the Society for the Experimental Analysis of Behavior have grown enormously in the last few years. For example, while there were 712 members in the Association for Advancement of Behavior Therapy in 1971, membership almost doubled to 1421 in 1973. An outgrowth of the development of some of these societies involves discussion on the issues of certification for behavioral therapists (e.g., Agras, 1973).

As noted earlier, curricula in a number of separate disciplines have also reflected, in part, the growth of behavior modification (e.g., Agras, 1971; Allen, 1970; Benassi & Lanson, 1972; Brady, 1973; Ernst, 1971; Gelfand, 1972; Shorkey, 1973). However, here the growth has been less spectacular inasmuch as "resistance" has been considerable at the faculty level. By contrast, students have insisted that certain courses in behavior modification be a part of their professional training. Further inroads are obviously warranted (Brady, 1973), especially in psychiatric residency training.

VI. RECENT ADVANCES

In our opinion, the most noteworthy contribution of behavior analysis and change to the social and behavioral sciences is its emphasis on the empirical-evaluative approach. This approach, which combines objectivity of measurement with experimental methods, is inherently atheoretical. Behavior modification may be regarded as more than merely a technology. In this sense, technology involves the application of a standard set of procedures for altering behavior patterns. The goal of a technological orientation is frequently the development and proliferation of therapeutic strategies that are linked by a common theoretical bond. By contrast, emphasis on methodology implies the systematic evaluation, refinement, and reevaluation of therapeutic procedures irrespective of their theoretical bases. Thus, clinical procedures are under constant scrutiny and revision in a methodological orientation. Early behavior modifiers identified with the technological approach through their universal emphasis on learning theory. Various techniques (e.g., aversion therapy) based on principles of conditioning derived from laboratory animal studies were applied to clinical disorders and compared with more traditional therapeutic modalities.

Two major problems are inherent in this early position. First, identification with a theoretical position tends to solidify the various orientations into yet another "school" of therapy. Such schools typically develop a cultism that is rigidly defined and closed to new experimental findings that might deviate from theoretical underpinnings of the orientation. The second problem with the early behavioral positions relates to its "learning theory" origins. In this respect Breger and McGaugh (1965) criticized the early behavior therapists for attributing the origin of their techniques to learning theory, arguing that there is no basis for positing a unified learning theory approach. While a number of laws of learning have been consistently demonstrated in laboratory studies, no theory of learning has as yet been formulated that can accommodate all the diverse findings. In their enthusiastic support of learning theory, early behavior therapists erroneously and prematurely adapted clinical procedures directly from experimental studies of animal behavior. It was assumed that the principles of reinforcement governing the modification of simple motor responses of animals in highly controlled laboratory settings could be applied directly to clinical disorders in humans.

On the basis of this reasoning, behavior modifiers have applied such procedures as electrical aversion therapy to alcoholism, sexual deviations, stuttering, and drug abuse. Successful clinical use of this therapeutic technique has been accompanied by claims that conditioning factors per se were responsible for its efficacy. This explanation has been generally accepted over the past 30 years, in which this technique has been widely used. Only recently have behaviorists experimentally evaluated the process of electrical aversion therapy in clinical settings. Contrary to previous notions, recent experimental evidence (Hallam, Rachman, & Falkowski, 1972; Miller, Hersen, Eisler, & Hemphill, 1973; Wilson, 1973) supports the contention that the clinical effects of this procedure are not necessarily related to autonomic conditioning processes, but rather to such general factors as therapeutic instructions, expectancy, specificity of the procedure, and therapeutic demand characteristics. Thus, directly generalizing principles of learning from animal conditioning studies to clinical human problems, without further experimentation, has the potential of seriously hindering progress in the behavioral sciences. Acceptance of the efficacy of therapeutic procedures on theoretical as opposed to empirical grounds leads to an inflexible and often doctrinaire position.

Fortunately, behavior modification has matured into a more broadly conceived methodological approach. The widening conception of behavior modification as a methodological approach as opposed to a series of technical operations derived from learning theory is most apparent in Yates' proposed definition. He argues: "Behavior therapy is the attempt to utilize systematically that body of empirical and theoretical knowledge which has resulted from the application of the experimental method in psychology and its closely related disciplines (physiology and neurophysiology) in order to explain the genesis and maintenance of abnormal patterns of behavior; and to apply that knowledge to the treatment or prevention of these abnormalities by means of controlled experimental studies of the single case, both descriptive and remedial [Yates, 1970, p. 18]."

In accordance with the above definition, any clinical issue is relevant to behavior modification if the conditions under which it occurs can be specified and the phenomenon itself can be objectively measured. Thus, this approach cuts across theoretical positions and opens up a multitude of therapeutic variables for the behavior modifier to investigate. Within this approach the distinction between clinician and researcher becomes meaningless. Ideally, behavioral practitioners examine the efficacy of their procedures as rigorously as the researcher within both the experimental single case paradigm (Barlow & Hersen, 1973; Hersen & Barlow, in press) and with respect to long-term results (Lazarus, 1973). Along these lines, the term "behavior modification" may be a misnomer. Certainly all clinicians, regardless of theoretical orientation, are attempting to modify the behavior of their clients. Perhaps the more general label of "behavioral scientist" might better convey the empirical underpinnings of behavior modification.

Although the thrust of behavior modification is inherently empirical, researchers and clinicians do not necessarily share identical theoretic positions. The fact that diversity of opinion exists within behavior modification can be used to advantage when lively debates stimulate new research, clarify theoretical expositions, and improve existing technologies. The empirical approach leaves no room for a doctrinaire position. When that happens all objectivity is lost and the "cultism" associated with nonscientific systems is approached. On the other hand, debate among proponents of differing positions within behavior modification is useful *only* when the issues at stake are discussed in terms of their scientific merit.

In recent years behavior modifiers sharing an operant orientation have focused on the socioenvironmental variables in the planning and implementation of their treatment approaches. Within the framework of be-

couraged. The modification of entire social systems represents a parsimonious application of behavioral principles in which large numbers of individuals are able to receive positive benefits. Moreover, in the future a preventive approach will undoubtedly prevail, and should result in greater benefits to society than behavior modification applied to selected individuals.

Behavior modification is both rapidly expanding and constantly changing. Since changes within the behavioral orientation are based on new experimental data, predictions regarding the future course of the field are highly speculative. However, current trends indicate that behavior modification is evolving into a most comprehensive approach to clinical and societal problems in which a large variety of social, emotional, physiological, cognitive, and environmental factors are objectively investigated. A result of these investigations is the subsequent application of empirically based techniques.

REFERENCES

Adams, H. E., Heyse, H., & Meyer, V. Issues in the clinical application of behavior therapy. In H. E. Adams & I. P. Unikel (Eds.), *Issues and trends in behavior therapy*. Springfield, Ill.: Thomas, 1973. Pp. 5–27.

Agras, W. S. The role of behavior therapy in teaching medical students. *Journal of Behavior Therapy and Experimental Psychiatry,* 1971, **2,** 219–221.

Agras, W. S. The behavioral therapies: Underlying principles and procedures. In W. S. Agras (Ed.), *Behavior modification: Principles and clinical applications.* Boston: Little, Brown, 1972. Pp. 1–26.

Agras, W. S. Toward the certification of behavior therapists. *Journal of Applied Behavior Analysis,* 1973, **6,** 167–173.

Allen, R. A resident's view of an ideal psychiatric training program. *Journal of Behavior Therapy and Experimental Psychiatry,* 1970, **1,** 323–324.

Ayllon, T. Intensive treatment of psychiatric behavior by stimulus satiation and food reinforcement. *Behaviour Research and Therapy,* 1963, **1,** 53–61.

Ayllon, T., & Azrin, N. H. Reinforcement and instructions with mental patients. *Journal of the Experimental Analysis of Behavior,* 1964, **7,** 327–331.

Ayllon, T., & Azrin, N. H. The measurement and reinforcement of behavior of psychotics. *Journal of the Experimental Analysis of Behavior,* 1965, **8,** 357–383.

Ayllon, T., & Azrin, N. H. *The token economy: A motivational system for therapy and rehabilitation.* New York: Appleton, 1968.

Ayllon, T., & Haughton, E. Control of the behavior of schizophrenic patients by food. *Journal of the Experimental Analysis of Behavior,* 1962, **5,** 343–352.

Ayllon, T., & Haughton, E. Modification of symptomatic verbal behavior of mental patients. *Behaviour Research and Therapy,* 1964, **2,** 87–97.

Ayllon, T., & Michael, J. The psychiatric nurse as a behavioral engineer. *Journal of the Experimental Analysis of Behavior,* 1959, **2,** 323–334.

Baltes, M. M. Operant principles applied to acquisition and generalization of non-littering behavior in children. *Proceedings of the 81st Annual Convention of the American Psychological Association,* 1973, **8,** 889–890.

Bandura, A. *Principles of behavior modification.* New York: Holt, 1969.

Barlow, D. H., & Hersen, M. Single-case experimental designs: Uses in applied clinical research. *Archives of General Psychiatry,* 1973, **29,** 319–325.

Benassi, V., & Lanson, R. A survey of the teaching of behavior modification in colleges and universities. *American Psychologist,* 1972, **27,** 1063–1069.

Brady, J. P. Behavior therapy: Fad or psychotherapy of the future. Presidential address delivered to the Association for the Advancement of Behavior Therapy, Washington, D.C., September, 1971.

Brady, J. P. Systematic desensitization. In W. S. Agras (Ed.), *Behavior modification: Principles and clinical applications.* Boston: Little, Brown, 1972. Pp. 127–150.

Brady, J. P. The place of behavior therapy in medical student and psychiatry resident training: Two surveys and some recommendations. *Journal of Nervous and Mental Disease,* 1973, **157,** 21–26.

Breger, L., & McGaugh, J. Critique and reformulation of learning theory approaches to psychotherapy and neuroses. *Psychological Bulletin,* 1965, **63,** 338–358.

Burgess, R. L., Clark, R. N., & Hendee, J. C. An experimental analysis of anti-litter procedures. *Journal of Applied Behavior Analysis,* 1971, **4,** 71–75.

Clark, R. N., Burgess, R. L., & Hendee, J. C. The development of anti-litter behavior in a forest campground. *Journal of Applied Behavior Analysis,* 1972, **5,** 1–5.

Cohen, H. L., & Filipczak, J. *A new learning environment.* San Francisco: Jossey-Bass, 1971.

Dollard, J., & Miller, N. E. *Personality and psychotherapy.* New York: McGraw-Hill, 1950.

Dunlap, K. *Habits: Their making and unmaking.* New York: Liveright, 1932. (Reprinted: Liveright, 1972).

Eisler, R. M., & Hersen, M. Behavioral techniques in family-oriented crisis intervention. *Archives of General Psychiatry,* 1973, **28,** 111–116.

Ernst, F. A. Behavior therapy and training in clinical psychology: A student's perspective. *Journal of Behavior Therapy and Experimental Psychiatry,* 1971, **2,** 75–79.

Everett, P. B. Use of the reinforcement procedure to increase bus ridership. *Proceedings of the 81st Annual Convention of the American Psychological Association,* 1973, **8,** 891–892.

Everett, P. B., Hayward, S. C., & Meyers, A. W. The effects of a token reinforcement procedure on bus ridership. *Journal of Applied Behavior Analysis,* 1974, **7,** 1–9.

Eysenck, H. J. The effects of psychotherapy: An evaluation. *Journal of Consulting Psychology,* 1952, **16,** 319–324.

Eysenck, H. J. (Ed.) *Behavior therapy and the neuroses.* Oxford: Pergamon, 1960.

Eysenck, H. J. The effects of psychotherapy. *International Journal of Psychiatry,* 1965, **1,** 99–142. (a)

Eysenck, H. J. The effects of psychotherapy: A reply. *International Journal of Psychiatry,* 1965, **1,** 328–335. (b)

Eysenck, H. J. *The effects of psychotherapy.* New York: International Science Press, 1966.

Feather, B. W., & Rhoads, J. M. Psychodynamic behavior therapy. *Archives of General Psychiatry,* 1972, **26,** 496–511.

Franks, C. M. Behavior therapy and its Pavlovian origins: Review and perspectives. In C. M. Franks (Ed.), *Behavior therapy: Appraisal and status.* New York: McGraw-Hill, 1969. Pp. 1–26. (a)

Franks, C. M. (Ed.) *Behavior therapy: Appraisal and status.* New York: McGraw-Hill, 1969. (b)

Franks, C. M., & Wilson, G. T. (Eds.) *Annual review of behavior therapy: Theory and practice.* New York: Brunner/Mazel, 1973.

Gelfand, S. G. A behavior modification training program for residents. *Journal of Behavior Therapy and Experimental Psychiatry,* 1972, **3,** 147–151.

Geller, E. S., Farris, J. C., & Post, D. S. Prompting a consumer behavior for pollution control. *Journal of Applied Behavior Analysis,* 1973, **6,** 367–376.

Greenspoon, J. Verbal conditioning and clinical psychology. In A. J. Bachrach (Ed.), *Experimental foundations of clinical psychology.* New York: Basic Books, 1962. Pp. 510–553.

Hallam, R., Rachman, S., & Falkowski, W. Subjective, attitudinal and physiological effects of electrical aversion therapy. *Behaviour Research and Therapy,* 1972, **10,** 1–13.

Hauserman, N., Whalen, S. R., & Behling, M. Reinforced racial integration in the first grade: A study in generalization. *Journal of Applied Behavior Analysis,* 1973, **6,** 193–200.

Hermann, J. A., de Montes, A. I., Dominguez, B., Montes, F., & Hopkins, B. L. Effects of bonuses for punctuality on the tardiness of industrial workers. *Journal of Applied Behavior Analysis,* 1973, **6,** 563–572.

Hersen, M. Awareness in verbal operant conditioning: Some comments. *Journal of General Psychology,* 1968, **78,** 287–396.

Hersen, M. Controlling verbal behavior via classical and operant conditioning. *Journal of General Psychology,* 1970, **83,** 3–22.

Hersen, M. Developments in behavior modification: An editorial. *Journal of Nervous and Mental Disease,* 1973, **156,** 373–376. (a)

Hersen, M. Self-assessment of fear. *Behavior Therapy,* 1973, **4,** 241–257. (b)

Hersen, M., & Barlow, D. H. *Single case experimental designs: Strategies for studying behavior change.* Oxford: Pergamon, in press.

Hersen, M., & Eisler, R. M. Behavioral approaches to study and treatment of psychogenic tics. *Genetic Psychology Monographs,* 1973, **87,** 289–312.

Hersen, M., Gullick, E. L., Matherne, P. M., & Harbert, T. L. Instructions and reinforcement in the modification of a conversion reaction. *Psychological Reports,* 1972, **31,** 719–722.

Jones, M. C. A laboratory study of fear: The case of Peter. *Journal of Genetic Psychology,* 1924, **31,** 308–315.

Jones, R. J., & Azrin, N. H. An experimental application of a social reinforcement approach to the problem of job-finding. *Journal of Applied Behavior Analysis,* 1973, **6,** 345–354.

Kanfer, F. H., & Phillips, J. *Learning foundations of behavior therapy.* New York: Wiley, 1970.

Kohlenberg, R., & Phillips, T. Reinforcement and rate of litter depositing. *Journal of Applied Behavior Analysis,* 1973, **6,** 391–396.

Kohlenberg, R. J. Operant conditioning of human anal sphincter pressure. *Journal of Applied Behavior Analysis,* 1973, **6,** 201–208.

Krasner, L. Studies of the conditioning of verbal behavior. *Psychological Bulletin,* 1958, **55,** 148–170.

Krasner, L. The therapist as a social reinforcement machine. In H. H. Strupp & L. Luborsky (Eds.), *Research in psychotherapy.* Washington, D.C.: American Psychological Association, 1962. Pp. 61–94.

Krasner, L. Behavior therapy. *Annual Review of Psychology,* 1971, **22,** 483–532.

Lazarus, A. A. *Behavior therapy and beyond.* New York: McGraw-Hill, 1971.

Lazarus, A. A. Multimodal behavior therapy: Treating the "BASIC ID." *Journal of Nervous and Mental Disease,* 1973, **156,** 404–411.

Lehrer, P. M., & Kris, A. O. Combined use of behavioral and psychoanalytic approaches in the treatment of severely disturbed adolescents. *Seminars in Psychiatry,* 1972, **4,** 165–170.

Leitenberg, H. (Ed.) *Handbook of behavior modification.* Englewood Cliffs, N.J.: Prentice-Hall, in press.

LeLaurin, K., & Risley, T. R. The organization of day-care environments: "Zone" versus "man-to-man" staff assignments. *Journal of Applied Behavior Analysis,* 1972, **5,** 225–232.

Lemere, F., Voegtlin, W. L., Broz, Q. R., Hollaren, P., & Tupper, W. E. The conditioned reflex treatment of chronic alcoholism. VIII. A review of six year's experience with the treatment of 1,526 patients. *Journal of the American Medical Association,* 1942, **120,** 269–270.

Levis, D. J. Behavioral therapy: The fourth therapeutic revolution? In D. J. Levis (Ed.), *Learning approaches to therapeutic behavior change.* Chicago: Aldine, 1970. Pp. 1–35.

Lindsley, O. R. Operant conditioning methods applied to research in chronic schizophrenia. *Psychiatric Research Reports,* 1956, **5,** 118–153.

Lindsley, O. R. Characteristics of the behavior of chronic psychotics as revealed by free-operant conditioning methods. *Diseases of the Nervous System,* 1960, **21,** 66–78.

Lindsley, O. R., & Skinner, B. F. A method for the experimental analysis of psychotic patients. *American Psychologist,* 1954, **9,** 419–420.

Max, L. W. Breaking up a homosexual fixation by the conditioned reaction technique: A case study. *Psychological Bulletin,* 1935, **32,** 734.

Meyer, V., & Chesser, E. S. *Behavior therapy in clinical psychiatry.* New York: Science House, 1970.

Miller, P. M., Hersen, M., Eisler, R. M., & Hemphill, D. P. Electrical aversion therapy with alcoholics: An analogue study. *Behaviour Research and Therapy,* 1973, **11,** 491–498.

Mowrer, D. H., & Mowrer, W. A. Enuresis: A method for its study and treatment. *American Journal of Orthopsychiatry,* 1938, **8,** 436–447.

O'Leary, K. D., & Drabman, R. Token reinforcement programs in the classroom: A review. *Psychological Bulletin,* 1971, **75,** 379–398.

Paul, G. L. Outcome of systematic desensitization. I. Background, procedures, and uncontrolled reports of individual treatment. In C. M. Franks (Ed.), *Behavior therapy: Appraisal and status.* New York: McGraw-Hill, 1969. Pp. 63–104. (a)

Paul, G. L. Outcome of systematic desensitization. II. Controlled investigations of individual treatment, technique variations, and current status. In C. M. Franks (Ed.), *Behavior therapy: Appraisal and status.* New York: McGraw-Hill, 1969. Pp. 105–159. (b)

Rubin, R. D., Brady, J. P., & Henderson, J. D. (Eds.) *Advances in behavior therapy.* New York: Academic Press, 1973.

Rubin, R. D., Fensterheim, H., Lazarus, A. A., & Franks, C. M. (Eds.) *Advances in behavior therapy 1969.* New York: Academic Press, 1971.

Rubin, R. D., Fensterheim, H., Ullmann, L. P., & Franks, C. M. (Eds.) *Advances in behavior therapy.* New York: Academic Press, 1972.

Rubin, R. D., & Franks, C. M. (Eds.) *Advances in behavior therapy 1968.* New York: Academic Press, 1969.

Salter, A. *Conditioned reflex therapy*. New York: Creative Age Press, 1949.
Salzinger, K. Experimental manipulation of verbal behavior: A review. *Journal of General Psychology,* 1959, **61,** 65–94.
Shapiro, D., Barber, T. X., DiCara, L. V., Kamiya, J., Miller, N. E., & Stoyva, J. (Eds.) *Biofeedback and self-control 1972*. Chicago: Aldine, 1973.
Shoben, E. J. Psychotherapy as a problem in learning theory. *Psychological Bulletin,* 1949, **46,** 366–392.
Shorkey, C. T. Behavior therapy training in social work education. *Journal of Behavior Therapy and Experimental Psychiatry,* 1973, **4,** 195–196.
Skinner, B. F. *The behavior of organisms: An experimental analysis*. New York: Appleton, 1938.
Skinner, B. F. *Walden two*. New York: Macmillan, 1948.
Skinner, B. F. *Science and human behavior*. New York: Macmillan, 1953.
Skinner, B. F. *Contingencies of reinforcement*. New York: Appleton, 1969.
Skinner, B. F. *Beyond freedom and dignity*. New York: Knopf, 1971.
Skinner, B. F. *Cumulative record: A selection of papers*. New York: Appleton, 1972.
Speilberger, C. D. The role of awareness in verbal learning. In C. W. Eriksen (Ed.), *Behavior and awareness*. Durham, N.C.: Duke University Press, 1962. Pp. 73–101.
Staats, A. W. Verbal habit-families, concepts and the operant conditioning of word classes. *Psychological Review,* 1961, **68,** 190–204.
Task Force Report 5. *Behavior therapy in psychiatry*. Washington, D.C.: American Psychiatric Association, 1973.
Thorndike, E. L. Reward and punishment in animal learning. *Comparative Psychology Monograph,* 1932, **8,** No. 39.
Thorndike, E. L. A proof of the law of effect. *Science,* 1933, **77,** 173–175.
Ullmann, L. P., & Krasner, L. (Eds.) *Case studies in behavior modification*. New York: Holt, 1965.
Watson, J. B., & Rayner, R. Conditioned emotional reactions. *Journal of Experimental Psychology,* 1920, **3,** 1–14.
Weisberg, P., & Waldrop, P. B. Fixed-interval work habits of Congress. *Journal of Applied Behavior Analysis,* 1972, **5,** 93–97.
Williams, J. H. Conditioning of verbalization: A review. *Psychological Bulletin,* 1964, **62,** 383–393.
Wilson, G. T. Aversive control of drinking by chronic alcoholics in a controlled laboratory setting. Paper read at the Association for Advancement of Behavior Therapy, Miami, December, 1973.
Winkler, R. C. The relevance of economic theory and technology of token reinforcement systems. *Behaviour Research and Therapy,* 1971, **9,** 81–88.
Winkler, R. C. A theory of equilibrium in token economies. *Journal of Abnormal Psychology,* 1972, **79,** 169–173.
Wolpe, J. Experimental neurosis as learned behaviour. *British Journal of Psychology,* 1952, **43,** 243–268.
Wolpe, J. Reciprocal inhibition as the main basis of psychotherapeutic effects. *Archives of Neurology and Psychiatry,* 1954, **72,** 205–226.
Wolpe, J. *Psychotherapy by reciprocal inhibition*. Stanford, Calif.: Stanford University Press, 1958.
Wolpe, J. *The practice of behavior therapy*. Oxford: Pergamon, 1969.
Yates, A. J. *Behavior therapy*. New York: Wiley, 1970.

THE BEHAVIORAL STUDY AND TREATMENT OF DEPRESSION

PETER M. LEWINSOHN
Psychology Department
University of Oregon
Eugene, Oregon

I. INTRODUCTION

The purpose of this chapter is to review the current empirical and theoretical status of behavioral approaches to depression and to suggest future directions for research and clinical application. During the past decade, there has been an upsurge in the number of biologically focused studies of depression. This rise has not been paralleled by a corresponding increase of interest in the behavioral aspects of depression. The current behavioral literature on depression is dominated by conceptual papers and by single case reports. Empirical studies aimed at the identification of critical socioenvironmental antecedent conditions for the occurrence of depression are scarce. Clearly, there is a need for more *empirical* research on the behavioral aspects of depression.

Since the term "depression" has many different meanings, an operational definition of the term is crucial. As Klerman (1972) has suggested, some of the confusion in the depression literature may derive from divergent concepts of what constitutes "depressive behaviors." A large number of psychological and physical symptoms have been included under the term depression by various authors (e.g., Schwab, Bialow, Clemmons, & Holzer, 1966; Schwab, Clemmons, Bialow, Duggan, & Davis, 1965) and these symptoms occur with considerable frequency in all psychiatric and medical patients. In view of this variegation of depression symptomatology, it is not surprising that considerable effort has been expended in attempts to establish a depression typology.

The original Kraepelinian formulation stipulated two types, manic-depressive depression and psychogenic depression. The former assumed psychotic proportions, and seemed unrelated to the patient's environment or life style. Its etiology was thus thought to be rooted in heredity, constitution, or metabolism. Psychogenic depression was an extreme reaction, in terms of intensity and especially duration, to occurrences in the patient's life. It ordinarily remained on a neurotic level. Depressive typology in American Psychiatry has thus evolved over the years into a binary system of psychotic and neurotic types, and factor analysis has been employed as the mathematical avenue along which to verify the binary theory. Mendels and Cochran (1968) reviewed the findings of seven-factor analytic studies. The first factor typically is a "general" factor on which all symptoms have a positive loading, indicating that they are properly classified as belonging to the depressive syndrome. The second factor, which is typically bipolar, is defined by symptoms that are relatively consonant with the endogenous-reactive concept.

The endogenous-reactive dichotomy (dimension) is felt by many to be important. Perhaps the clearest statement of the concept and its historical antecedents is presented in a paper by Rosenthal and Klerman (1966), while its operational referants are identified in a study by Mendels and Cochran (1968). The latter compared seven-factor analytic studies in which the endogenous-reactive factor was identified. There was *perfect agreement across studies* in identifying the following characteristics of endogenous depressives: psychomotor retardation, deeply depressed, lacking in reactivity to environmental changes, showing a loss of interest in life, having visceral symptoms, lacking a precipitating stress, having middle of night insomnia, and *not* showing self-pity. Characteristics among which there was fair agreement across studies showed the endogenous to be older, to have a history of previous episodes, weight loss, early morning awakening, showing self-reproach or guilt, and not showing personality traits of hysteria or inadequacy. However, there are several problems with the endogenous-reactive dichotomy: (a) In some studies there is a tendency for it to be confounded with depth of depression and with chronicity—the endogenous have been more depressed for a longer period of time; (b) few "pure" types exist; and (c) the distinction between endogenous and reactive depressions is based largely, although not entirely, upon the presence or the absence of a precipitating stress—reactive depressions being those which follow stressful environmental events. The endogenous-reactive depression dichotomy has implications for behavioral approaches in that environmental conditions and the manipulation of environmental conditions should be more effective with reactives. Its main value at this point seems to be in the reported prognosis for shock treatment, which is said to be better for the endogenous types.

A different depression typology has been presented by Winokur (1973). His classification is based on studies of family constellations of patients with affective disorders. Winokur distinguishes between two types of "primary affective disorders": manic depressive disease (bipolar) and depressive disease (unipolar). The bipolar type may either show a clinical picture of mania and depression, or the patient shows a clinical picture of depression only; but the patient comes from a family where mania exists. The unipolar-bipolar dichotomy has been used in a number of different studies, and clinical, genetic, biochemical, pharmacological, and neurophysiological differences have been reported to support the unipolar-bipolar dichotomy (Akiskal & McKinney, 1973). Bipolar depressives, as compared with unipolars, are reported to be more retarded in psychomotor activity, to have a higher genetic loading for affective disorder, to be more likely to have postpartum affective episodes, and to have a larger number of previous episodes.

The current, rather unsettled, status of depression classification has two implications: (1) A very large number of behaviors (symptoms) are subsumed under the term depression. Thus, two patients, both clinically diagnosed as being depressed, are likely to manifest different symptoms, and no single symptom is sufficient to diagnose a patient as depressed. (2) No generally accepted typology for depressive disorders exists. Hence, it is very important for the depression researcher to have a clear operational definition of how he/she is using the term depression so that his/her results can be replicated by other investigators.

A. Constituents of the Depression Syndrome

In spite of the ubiquitousness of the term "depression," there is very good agreement about the behaviors (symptoms) that characterize depressed individuals. These behaviors have been identified in descriptive studies of depressed individuals based on interview ratings, self-report measures, and observation of the behavior of depressed individuals. These studies have typically started with a fairly large number of relatively specific behaviors to be coded. Attempts were then made to reduce these to a smaller number of clusters through factor analysis. While studies have differed in regard to the kinds of observations used and, hence, with the kinds of factors finally derived, there is considerable agreement as to the constituency of the depression syndrome that extends across studies. Table I is a listing of the behaviors typically observed in depressed patients. It is important to note, however, that the correlation between these symptoms, while usually statistically significant, is not high enough to allow one to predict the presence of a given symptom on the basis of the occurrence of another symptom. Depressed patients manifest *different combinations* of the symptoms (target behaviors) shown in Table I.

B. An Operational Definition of Depression

In committing himself/herself to an operational definition of the term depression, the behavior therapist faces a major choice point. Consistent with the general (and well founded) tendency on the part of behavior therapists to avoid diagnostic labels because they typically lack precise behavioral referants, he/she may choose to concern himself/herself with the occurrence of specific behaviors in the individual depressed patient such as a low rate of social behavior, verbal expressions of guilt and personal inadequacy, sadness, etc. A major goal is to identify the socioenvironmental contingencies that control these particular behaviors, and which can be modified in order to produce the desired behavior change. This option, which is a very legitimate one, denies the existence of a unique syndrome (or symptom cluster) for which a special term ("depression") is needed. The specific behaviors shown by "depressed" patients (see Table I) are presumed to be explicable within the general framework of social learning theory and schedules of reinforcement. This alternative has the virtue of simplicity since

TABLE I

Symptoms of Depression

Dysphoria	Behavioral Deficits	Behavioral Excesses	Somatic Symptoms	"Cognitive" Manifestations
Feelings dominated by sadness and blueness	Minimal social participation—"I do not like being with people."	Complaints about: Material problems—money, job, housing Material loss—money, property The demands of others Noise Memory, inability to concentrate, confusion Lack of affection from others—"No one cares about me." Being lonely	Headaches	Low self-evaluation: feelings of failure, inadequacy, helplessness and powerlessness
Loss of gratification—"I no longer enjoy the things I used to."	Sits alone quietly, stays in bed much of time, does not communicate with others, does not enter into activities with others	Expresses feelings of guilt and concern about: Making up wrongs to others Suffering caused to others Not assuming responsibilities Welfare of family and friends Indecisiveness—"I can't make up my mind anymore."	Sleep disturbances: restless sleep, waking during night, complete wakefulness, early morning awakening	Negative expectation—"Things will always be bad for me."
Professes to have little or no feeling	Inability to do ordinary work	Crying, weepy, screaming	Fatigue—"I get tired for no reason."	Self-blame and self-criticism—"People would despise me if they knew me."
Feels constantly fatigued—"Everything is an effort."	Decreased sexual activity	Suicidal behavior—"I wish I were dead." "I want to kill myself."	Gastrointestinal-indigestion, constipation, weight loss	
Loss of interest in food, drink, sex, etc.	Psychomotor retardation: speech slow, volume of speech decreased, monotone speech, whispering; gait and general behavior retarded		Dizzy spells	
Feeling of apathy and boredom	Does not attend to grooming; neglect of personal appearance		Loss of libido	
	Lack of mirth response		Tachycardia	
			Chest sensations	
			Generalized pain	
			Urinary disturbances	

it does not require any new assumptions beyond those which are usually encompassed by such terms as learning theory and principles of behavior. Various depression typologies (unipolar versus bipolar; endogenous versus reactive) become irrelevant. "Depressed" individuals, like other patients, are defined in terms of specific behavior deficits and behavioral excesses, whereas behavioral intervention strategies are designed to modify these behavioral deficits and excesses.

The second option assumes a common antecedent (e.g., low rate of positive reinforcement or learned helplessness) to be causally related to all depressions, even though the behavioral manifestations of depression differ from one case to the next. This position, which does not deny the importance of schedules of reinforcement, or of the operant characteristics of depressive behaviors, views depression as a *psychopathological condition* whose existence can be defined in terms of the occurrence (frequency and intensity) of certain kinds of behaviors and symptoms. It also assumes that certain general therapeutic considerations are relevant to all depressed patients, and that a category of depressives (i.e., individuals with common characteristics and similar reinforcement histories) can be defined in spite of the known heterogeneity of such patients.

The present author subscribes to this second option and, hence, an operational definition for depression follows.

The two positions differ in that investigators who assume the second option (e.g., Lewinsohn and Seligman) find it necessary, and important, to have a "theory" or a "hypothesis" around which to organize what is known about the symptoms and causes of depression. It is on the basis of the "theory" that predictions about the cure and prevention of depression are then made. For the investigator in the former tradition, it becomes imperative, but sufficient, to clearly specify the exact behaviors he/she is attempting to modify (e.g., low rate of verbal behavior); for the second type of investigator it is also important to provide a general definition of depression so that other investigators can select similar depressives. *Neither* position justifies the all too common practice of defining depressives as "patients who were diagnosed as depressed."

In the studies done by Lewinsohn and his associates, many of which are reviewed in this chapter, a patient is defined as "depressed" if he/she meets certain experimental criteria (e.g., Lewinsohn & Libet, 1972) based on selected Minnesota Multiphasic Personality Inventory (MMPI) scales *and* on the interview factors defined by Grinker, Miller, Sabshin, Nunn, and Nunally (1961). The selection procedure is intended to yield a sample of "pure depressives," that is, individuals in whom depression is present to a clinically significant degree and where being depressed constitutes the major presenting psychopathology.

C. Measurement of Depression

Since the constituent behaviors of the depression syndrome are so very diverse, it is reassuring to know that the behavioral characteristics of depressed individuals, or what have been called the phenomena of depression, can be measured (counted, coded, rated, etc.) with considerable accuracy and reliability. Measurement instruments and behavior coding systems are available that allow one to quantify the specific symptoms manifested by a given depressed patient. Investigators have tended to rely on interview-based ratings, on self-report measures, and on behavior observations.

1. Interview Rating Scales

These scales have typically been constructed by incorporating items reflecting characteristic attitudes and symptoms associated with depression. Among the better known ones are the Hamilton Rating Scale for Depression (Hamilton, 1960; Mowbray, 1972), the Feelings and Concerns Check List (Grinker *et al.,* 1961), and the Psychiatric Judgment Depression Scale (Overall, 1962), the Depression Rating Scale (Wechsler, Grosser, & Busfield, 1963), and the PPH Depression Rating Scale (Friedman, Cowitz, Cohen, & Granick, 1963). On the basis of an interview, the professional judge rates each item on three- or four-point scales. Summing the items yields a measure of intensity of depression. Some of these scales have been factor analyzed. It is, thus, possible to compute factor scores for the various subareas of the depression syndrome (e.g., somatic complaints, guilt, dysphoria, etc.). When used by well trained raters, these scales possess high interrater reliability. They differentiate significantly between depressed and nondepressed patients, and between patients varying on the basis of intensity of depression.

2. Self-Report Measures

A number of excellent self-report measures for depression are available. The best known is the Depression (D) Scale of the MMPI which has been widely used for the measurement of depression for clinical and research purposes. The disadvantage of the D Scale is that it is highly correlated with the other "neurotic" scales of the MMPI (e.g., Hypochondriasis and Psychasthenia). Thus, neurotic patients in whom depression is not the major presenting symptom also tend to attain high D Scale scores.

Much easier to administer and more closely related to the clinical definition of depression are two self-report measures, the Beck Depression Inventory (Beck, 1967) and the Self-Rating Scale (Zung, 1965). The Beck

Depression Inventory consists of 21 items, there being 4–5 alternative statements for each item. The patient selects the one statement in each item group that best describes the way he/she feels. The Self-Rating Scale consists of 20 statements which are rated on a four-point frequency of occurrence scale going from "none or little of the time" to "most or all of the time."

In a class by themselves are the Depression Adjective Check Lists (DACL) developed by Lubin in 1965. The DACL (Lubin, 1965, 1967) consists of seven parallel lists of adjectives designed to provide a measure of what has been called *state* depression, that is, the individual's mood at a particular moment in time. The subject is asked to "check the words which describe how you feel now—today." The main advantage of the DACL is that it can be used to measure day-to-day fluctuations in mood level.

All the self-report measures described above have been shown to possess excellent internal consistency (split-half reliabilities tend to be in the high 80's), concurrent validity (they discriminate between depressed and nondepressed patients at a high level of significance), and convergent validity (they correlate with each other very substantially). Adequate normative data are also available.

3. Behavioral Observations

For obvious reasons, direct observation of the behavior of depressed patients is of greatest interest and relevance to behavioral approaches to depression. Several behavior coding systems have been developed which differ in the precision (specificity) with which the behaviors to be observed are defined.

An early attempt to quantify the behavior of depressed individuals in the hospital is represented by the Current Behavior Check List (Grinker *et al.,* 1961). It samples a continuum of relatively specific behavior categories (e.g., isolated and withdrawn, clean and neat, communicates with men) to much more inferential ones (e.g., denies need for help, tries to impress others with his/her talents).

Another attempt to develop a behavior coding system for depressed patients in the hospital is represented by the "Bunney-Hamburg 15-Point Scale" (Bunney & Hamburg, 1963). This scale consists of 24 items to represent six broad areas of behavior—depression, anger, anxiety, psychotic behavior, somatic complaints, and pacing.

A behavioral rating scale has been developed by Williams, Barlow, and Agras (1972). This scale includes only simple, easily observable behaviors like talking, smiling, patient takes a shower, etc. The presence or the absence of the behaviors is rated by aides using a time sampling procedure (e.g., one per hour). Excellent interrater reliability is reported for this scale which also correlated substantially with the Hamilton Rating Scale for Depression and the Beck Depression Inventory.

There have also been several attempts to count specific target behaviors in depressed patients. Liberman (1970), in the treatment of a depressed female, distinguished between "depressive" behavior (defined by behaviors like crying, complaining about somatic symptoms, pacing, and withdrawal) and "coping behavior" (defined by adaptive actions as housewife and mother like cooking, cleaning house, attending to the children's needs). Robinson and Lewinsohn (1973a) describe a method for counting of verbal rate which was used to increase the speech rate of a 50-year-old chronically depressed man in whom reduced rate of speech constituted one of the major presenting problems. "Crying" and "smiling" can also be counted with excellent interrater reliability (Reisinger, 1972).

Johansson, Lewinsohn, and Flippo (1969) and Robinson and Lewinsohn (1973b) used a coding system to partition verbal behavior into discrete response categories in their attempts to increase specific low rate verbal responses of depressed individuals.

Perhaps the most elaborate attempt to code the verbal-interpersonal behavior of depressed individuals has been developed by Lewinsohn *et al.* (1968). The system is shown schematically in Table II. Behavior interactions are seen as having a "source" and an "object." "Actions" are followed by "reactions" which can be coded as either positive (i.e., expressions of affection, approval, interest) or negative (criticism, disapproval, ignore, etc.). A simplified illustration of an interaction involving four people mght be as follows: A makes a statement (an action) which is responded to by B (a reaction). B continues talking (an action), and this is followed by a reaction on the part of C, which in turn is followed by some new action on the part of D, etc. Data so generated allow one to focus on any one individual in terms of the actions that he emits and the kinds of reactions that he elicits. Two observers code all interactional behaviors. The observers pace themselves with an automatic timer which delivers an auditory and visual signal simultaneously every 30 seconds. Differences between raters are conferenced. Interjudge agreement for the major scoring categories has been quite high (Libet & Lewinsohn, 1973). A manual for the coding system has been developed (Lewinsohn *et al.,* 1968). This system has been used extensively in coding the behavior of depressed individuals in their own home and in the group therapy situation. The system has also been used to derive a number of measures of social skill. The results of a rather extensive study

TABLE II

Behavior Rating Schedule

Action		Reaction			
Interactional Categories		Positive		Negative	
Psychol. complaint	Psy C	Affection	Aff	Criticism	Crit
Somatic complaint	Som C	Approval	App	Disapproval	Disapp
Criticism	Crit	Agree	Agr	Disagree	Disagree
Praise	Pr	Laughter	L+	Ignore	Ign
Information request	I−	Interest	Int	Change topic	Ch T
Information giving	I+	Continues talking about topic	Con T	Interrupts	Inter
Personal problem	PP	Physical affection	Phys Aff	Physical punishment	Pun
Instrument problem	IP				
Other people's problems	OP				
Talking about abstract, impersonal, general, etc.	Ta				

Content—Topics	
School	Sch
Self	X, Y, Z
Other people (group, family)	X, Y, Z
Treatment	Rx
Therapist	T
Sex	Sx

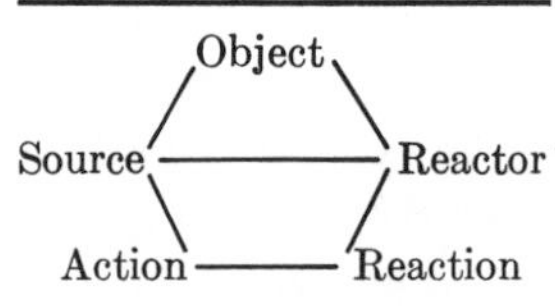

to evaluate the temporal stability, validity, dimensionality, and situational generalizability of the social skill measures are reported elsewhere (Libet, Lewinsohn, & Javorek, 1973).

It might, thus, be suggested that the methodology needed to operationalize the constituents of the depressive syndrome exists to a sufficient degree to permit investigators and therapists to describe the specific symptoms and behaviors shown by a given depressed patient and to make quantitative pre- and posttreatment comparisons.

II. BEHAVIORAL THEORIES OF DEPRESSION

Depression has been relatively neglected by behavior therapists. The first applications of behavioral treatment to depressed individuals were reported by Lazarus (1968), Burgess (1969), and Lewinsohn, Weinstein, and Shaw (1969). Since then a number of formulations have been presented and corresponding treatment strategies have been devised.

The first attempt at a functional analysis of depression is contained in Skinner's (1953) book *Science and Human Behavior* in which depression is described as a weakening of behavior and loneliness as due to the interruption of established sequences of behavior which have been positively reinforced by the social environment. The conceptualization of depression as an extinction phenomenon has been central to all behavioral positions.

Ferster (1965, 1966) provided more details of a functional analysis of depression. He considered depression to be characterized (defined) by retardation of psychomotor and thought processes and by a reduction or absence of previously successful behaviors. Thus, the *essential* characteristic of a depressed person is a reduced frequency of emission of positively reinforced behavior. Ferster listed diverse factors such as: (a) sudden environmental changes; (b) punishment and aversive control; and (c) shifts in reinforcement contingencies, which can give rise to depression, i.e., a reduced rate of behavior. Ferster also noted that some depressed individuals are strikingly restricted in the range of persons with whom they interact, in some cases there being only one person. This makes the depressed person especially vulnerable since the absence of that person, or drastic change in his/her behavior, brings about drastic changes in the depressed person's behavior. In his most recent article Ferster (1973), while continuing to view the frequency of depressed person's performance as *the* datum for research and therapy, extends his earlier statements. He sees the bulk of the depressed person's activity as being *passive*, i.e., as being reactive to the environment, derived from prompts, commands, or other aversive initiatives from other persons rather than freely emitted activities. Hence, the reinforcer in the interaction is more likely to be appropriate to the other person's repertoire than to the depressed person.

Ferster (1973) also sees failure to deal with, avoid, or escape from aversive social consequences as an antecedent for depression. Two kinds of actions may occur when a person faces an aversive situation: direct action, which can alter it; or indirect activity such as complaints, which simply acknowledges it. The indirect actions are passive because there is little chance that they will influence the aversive situation very much. Ferster also sees the very passive character of the depressed person's repertoire as leading to a lack of clarity about the social environment. Depressed individuals are said to have: (a) a limited view of the world (depressed individuals do not actually see very many of the features of the social world); (b) a lousy view of the world—the aversive consequences of not avoiding aversive situations; and (c) an unchanging view of the world (depressed individuals have a developmental history with diminished normal exploration of the environment and the clarification and expansion of the repertoire that comes from such exploration). Thus, Ferster's most recent position while still emphasizing low rate of emission of positively reinforced behavior also emphasizes the depressed individual's *passivity,* as well as perceptual and cognitive traits stemming from his/her developmental history.

Lazarus (1968, p. 84) views depression as a "function of inadequate or insufficient reinforcers." The depressed individual is considered to be on an extinction schedule, with lack of reinforcement resulting in a weakened repertoire. The temporal sequence as conceptualized by Lazarus is as follows: First, a significant reinforcer is withdrawn. The person enters a state of grief which lifts when he/she recognizes and utilizes other reinforcers at his/her disposal. If he/she lacks the ability, opportunity, or capacity to recognize and to utilize other available reinforcers, "a chronic and/or acute non-reinforcing state of affairs can result in a condition where the person becomes relatively refractory to most stimuli and enters a state of 'depression' [Lazarus, 1972, p. 249]."

Lewinsohn *et al.* (1969; Lewinsohn, 1974) also hypothesize that low rate of response-contingent positive reinforcement constitutes a sufficient explanation for parts of the depressive syndrome, such as the low rate of behavior, i.e., the depressed individual is assumed to be on a prolonged extinction schedule. They also introduce several additional hypotheses (assumptions): (1) A low rate of response-contingent positive reinforcement acts as an eliciting (unconditioned) stimulus for some depressive behaviors such as the feeling of dysphoria, fatigue, and other somatic symptoms. (2) The social environment provides contingencies in the form of sympathy, interest, and concern which strengthen and maintain depressive behaviors. These reinforcements are typically provided by a small segment of the depressed person's social environment (e.g., his immediate family). However, since most people in the depressed person's environment (and eventually even his family) find these behaviors aversive, they will avoid him/her as much as possible, thus decreasing his/her rate of receiving positive reinforcement and further accentuating his/her depression. (3) The total amount of response-contingent positive reinforcement received by an individual is presumed to be a function of three sets of variables: (a) the number of events (including activities) which are potentially reinforcing (PotRe) for the individual; PotRe is assumed to be a variable subject to individual differences, influenced by biological (e.g., sex and age) and experiential factors; (b) the number of potentially reinforcing events which can be provided by the environment, i.e., the availability of reinforcement in the environment (AvaiRe); (c) the instrumental behavior of the individual, i.e., the extent to which he/she possesses the skills, and emits those behaviors that elicit reinforcement for him/her from his/her environment. Social skill, defined as the emission of behaviors which are positively reinforced by others, is seen as an area of deficit especially important in the development of depressive behaviors. The position of Lewinsohn and associates thus differs from the previous ones in its assumption of a causal relationship between low rate of positive reinforcement and the feeling of dysphoria; in its emphasis on the maintenance of depressive behaviors by the social environment; and in its emphasis on lack of social skill as one of the antecedents from a low positive reinforcement rate. A schematic representation of the position of Lewinsohn and co-workers is shown in Fig. 1.

Before proceeding to an examination of other behavioral positions, several additional clarifications and hypotheses are offered:

1. It is the degree to which the individual's behavior is maintained (followed) by reinforcement that is assumed to be the critical antecedent condition for the occurrence of depression rather than the total amount of reinforcement received. It is a well known clinical fact that "giving" (i.e., noncontingently) to depressed individuals does not decrease their depression. We assume that the occurrence of behavior which is followed by positive reinforcement is vital if depression is to be avoided. We predict depression when the probability that the individual's behavior will be followed by reinforcement is low, and also when the probability that the individual will

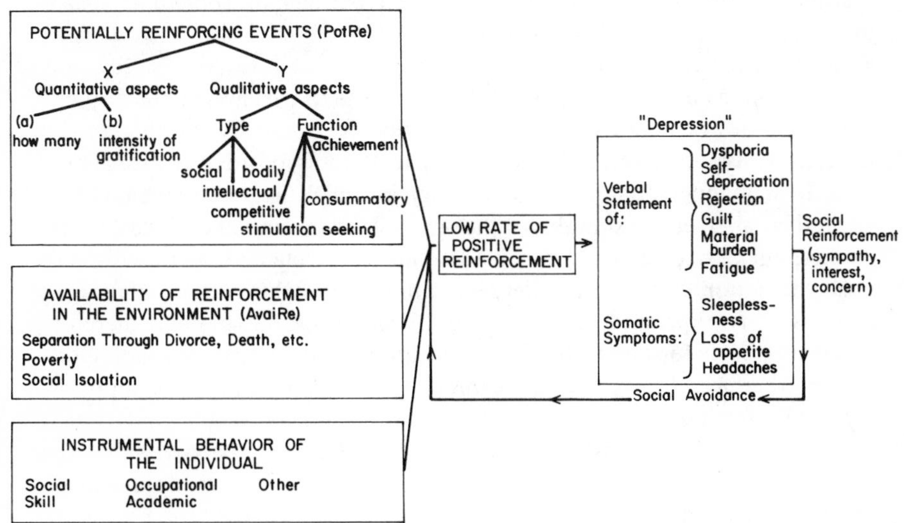

Fig. 1. Schematic representation of the causation and maintenance of "depressive" behavior.

be "reinforced" when he does not emit the behavior is high (e.g., the retired person receiving his paycheck regardless of what he does). Under both conditions the probability of the individual emitting behavior is reduced.

2. Low self-esteem, pessimism, and feelings of guilt are some of the cognitive (attitudinal) changes commonly observed in depressed individuals even though the specific manifestations vary considerably from individual to individual. Thus, there are depressed patients who do not have low self-esteem and there are many who lack feelings of guilt. Theorists such as Beck (1967) assign primary causal significance to these cognitive changes. Lewinsohn (1974) assumes these to be secondary elaborations of the feelings of dysphoria, which in turn is presumed to be the consequence of a low positive reinforcement rate. Initially the individual who becomes depressed experiences an unpleasant feeling state (dysphoria). The emotion of dysphoria is thus seen as the key phenomenon of depression. He *is* feeling bad. This feeling state is difficult for the individual to label, and a number of alternative "explanations" are available to him, including "I am sick" (somatic symptoms), "I am weak or otherwise inadequate" (low self esteem), "I am bad" (feelings of guilt), "I am not likable" (feelings of social isolation). The research of Stanley Schachter (Schachter & Singer, 1962) may contain important implications for this aspect of the behavior of depressed individuals and for treatment as well (cognitive relabeling). If the depressed individual can be helped to relabel his emotion (e.g., "I am worthless" into "I am feeling bad because I am lacking something that is important to my welfare") he may be in a much better position to do something about his predicament.

3. The role of hostility which is so central to psychodynamically oriented theories of depression (i.e., depression is caused by hostility turned inward) is hypothesized to be secondary to the low positive reinforcement rate. In a manner analogous to the way in which aggressive behavior is elicited by an aversive stimulus in the Azrin, Hutchinson, and Hake (1966) studies, aggressive behavior may be assumed to be elicited by a low rate of positive reinforcement in the depressed individual. When these aggressive responses are expressed, they serve to alienate other people and therefore contribute even further to the social isolation of the depressed individual. He/she therefore learns to avoid expressing hostile tendencies by suppressing (or repressing) them.

Costello (1972) disagrees with the view that depression results from loss of reinforcement and suggests instead that "a loss of reinforcer effectiveness causes depression." He suggests that such a loss can be due to either endogenous, biochemical, and neurological changes, or to the disruption of a chain of behavior.

Wolpe emphasizes the role of anxiety in the etiology of depression. Wolpe (1969) initially hypothesized that depression is merely a consequence of "protective inhibition where anxiety is very prolonged and intense [p. 24]." In his most recent statement (Wolpe, 1971), he postulates three sets of circumstances in which depression occurs: (1) as a consequence of severe and prolonged anxiety; (2) as a consequence of failure to control interpersonal situations—such failure being due to the inhibiting effects of neurotic anxiety; and (3) as an exaggeration and prolongation of the normal reaction to loss.

The key assumption of Seligman's theory of depression is that "if the symptoms of learned helplessness and depression are equivalent then what we have learned experimentally about the cause, cure, and prevention of learned helplessness can be applied to depression [Seligman, 1973b, p. 43]."

Learned or "conditioned" helplessness, a laboratory phenomenon first observed in animals, refers to the passive and helpless behavior shown by dogs subsequent to inescapable shock. The dogs were strapped into a Pavlovian harness and given electric shock from which they could not escape. That is, nothing they did, or did not do, affected their receipt of shock. Later the dogs were put into a two-compartment shuttle box where they could escape the shock by jumping across the barrier separating the compartments. Compared with nonshocked, experimentally naive dogs, the shocked dogs soon stopped running and howling, settled down and took the shock, whining quietly. Typically the shocked dogs did not cross the barrier and escape. Instead they seemed to give up. In succeeding trials, the traumatized dogs made virtually no attempts to escape. They passively took as much shock as was given.

The main psychological phenomena of learned helplessness are:

1. Passivity in face of later trauma, i.e., the organism is slower to initiate responses to alleviate trauma and may not respond at all.

2. The organism is retarded in learning that his responses produce relief, i.e., if he makes a response that produced relief, he may have trouble "catching on" to the response-relief contingency. Inability to control trauma not only disrupts shock escape, but also debilitates adaptive behavior in situations not involving shock.

3. Lack of aggressiveness and competitiveness.

4. Weight loss and undereating.

The generality of the facts of unescapable shock across species and across situations are discussed in greater detail by Maier, Seligman, and Solomon (1969), Seligman, Maier, and Solomon (1971), and Seligman (1974). There are obvious similarities between the symptoms of depression and the symptoms of learned helplessness.

The critical antecedent for learned helplessness is not trauma per se but not having control over trauma. The distinction between controllable and uncontrollable reinforcement is central to Seligman's position. The concept of control is defined within a two-dimensional training space. The x axis $(p(RFT/R))$ represents the conditional probability of reinforcement given the absence of *that* response $p(RFT/\bar{R})$. The points in this training space which are of special concern for learned helplessness are those that lie along the 45° line (where $x = y$). Whether or not the organism responds, it still receives the same density of reinforcement. Responding and reinforcement are independent. Depressed individuals are presumed to have been, or to be, in situations in which responding and reinforcement are independent. Recovery of belief that responding produces reinforcement is the critical attitudinal change for cure of depression.

The major strengths of the learned helplessness theory are: (1) In contrast to the earlier positions, which emphasize low positive reinforcement rate, it provides a plausible paradigm for how aversive events can result in depression. (2) It generates testable predictions about the behavior of depressed persons (Miller & Seligman, 1973).

Two criticisms can be leveled against the learned helplessness theory.

1. While the critical experiments on learned helplessness in dogs were done with aversive contingencies, the theory has been extended to situations that lack control over positive contingencies. Whether lack of control over positive contingencies can produce learned helplessness in animals (and depression in man) is an empirical, and as yet unanswered, question. Lewinsohn and the other low positive reinforcement rate positions would also predict the occurrence of depression along the 45° (no control) line because such a state of affairs would reduce the person's rate of emitting reinforceable behavior. By the same argument, however, the positive reinforcement theory would predict depression when $p\ (RFT/\bar{R}) > p\ (RFT/R)$, as exemplified, perhaps, by the elderly person with a high probability of receiving a pension for not working and a low probability of finding a job. For this type of situation the learned helplessness and low positive reinforcement positions lead to different, but testable predictions.

2. Its relevance to clinical depression rests entirely on the similarity of the symptoms of a laboratory animal phenomenon (learned helplessness) and depression in man. The direct link between uncontrollable trauma (the presumed cause of learned helplessness) and clinical depression remains to be demonstrated.

Beck (1963, 1964, 1967, 1970b) has advanced a "cognitive" approach to depression, which is included because it has much in common with behavior therapy (Beck, 1970a). In both systems of psychotherapy, the patient's presenting symptoms are formulated in highly specific terms; the goal of treatment is circumscribed; and perhaps most important, cognitive theory also assumes that the patient has acquired maladaptive reaction patterns that can be unlearned.

Beck's theory of depression assigns a primary (causal) position to a cognitive triad consisting of a very negative view of the self, of the outside world, and of the future. The depressed person's cognitions lead to misinterpretations of experiences and produce the phenomena of depression, such as the lack of motivation, the affective states, and other ideational and behavioral manifestations. The depressed patient's cognitions are distorted and unrealistic in that the patient tends to exaggerate his/her faults and the obstacles in his/her path. As this trait becomes increasingly dominant, the patient becomes progressively more depressed, i.e., the symptoms of depression become evident. The person believes that he/she has been rejected, hence, he/she feels sad. Because all tasks seem insurmountable and boring, he/she shows paralysis of the will and wants to escape. Beck sees the emotional, motivational, and behavioral changes of depression as flowing directly from the depressed person's perception that he/she is worthless, the world is barren, and the future bleak, no matter what he/she might do to improve it. In Beck's model, affect is intimately linked with cognition. Between an event and an individual's emotional reaction to it, a cognition, or "automatic thought" intervenes, which dictates the resulting affect. When this cognition represents an inaccurate or distorted appraisal of the event, the affect will be inappropriate or extreme.

III. EMPIRICAL STUDIES CONSISTENT WITH BEHAVIORAL HYPOTHESES

The term consistent is used to convey that while there are findings which are *consistent* with certain behavioral positions, the critical experiments which would allow one to accept or to reject specific hypotheses have yet to be performed.

A critical test of the hypothesis that positive reinforcement rate is less for depressed persons than for nondepressed persons requires a two-step strategy: (a) First, one must identify, functionally, events that act as reinforcement for individuals who may be characterized as either depressed or nondepressed. (b) Second, one must compute the rate of response contingent reinforcement for these subjects. The hypothesis predicts a lower rate of positive reinforcement for depressed individuals. This crucial test has not been performed so far. However, several studies have reported findings consistent with this hypothesis.

A. Depressed Individuals Elicit Fewer Behaviors from Others

The finding that depressed individuals elicit fewer behaviors than do control subjects (Libet & Lewinsohn, 1973; Libet *et al.,* 1973; Shaffer & Lewinsohn, 1971), assuming that it is reinforcing to be the object of attention and interest, suggests that depressed persons receive less social reinforcement.

B. Association between Mood and Pleasant Activities

There is a significant association between mood and number and kinds of "pleasant" activities engaged in (Lewinsohn & Graf, 1973; Lewinsohn & Libet, 1972). In these studies groups of depressed psychiatric controls and normal control subjects were used. An activity schedule was generated for each subject from his/her responses on the Pleasant Events Schedule (MacPhillamy & Lewinsohn, 1971). This is an instrument consisting of 320 events and activities which were generated after a very extensive search of the universe of "pleasant events." The subjects were asked to rate each item on the schedule on a 3- or 5-point scale of pleasantness. An activity schedule, consisting of 160 items judged by the subject to be most pleasant, was then constructed for him/her. The schedules were put on ditto masters, and the subject was asked to indicate at the end of each day which of the activities he/she had engaged in. In addition, subjects were asked to fill out the Depression Adjective Check Lists (Lubin, 1965) at about the same time of day. Each completed set was mailed to the experimenters the next day for 30 consecutive days. In both studies, the correlation between the mood and pleasant activities score was computed over days ($N = 30$) for individual subjects. The correlation between each individual item from the subject's activity schedule and his/her mood ratings was also computed over days ($N = 30$). Items with correlation coefficient greater than .30, which would be significant at the .01 level under conditions of independence of observations, were assigned a score of 1 (correlated items). Items with a correlation coefficient of less than .30 were assigned a score of 0 (uncorrelated items). Not only was it possible to examine the correlation between total pleasant activity scores and the mood ratings for the groups, but it was possible to identify the number of individuals out of the total sample for whom each activity was found to be associated with mood.

There was a substantial and statistically significant correlation between mood and pleasant activities level in both studies. Items which were found to be associated with mood for at least 10% of the subjects are listed In Table III. Inspection of the content of the items suggests that they fall into

TABLE III

Activities Associated with Mood for 10% of the Sample[a,b]

1. Laughing (IA)
2. Being relaxed (IA)
3. Being with happy people (S)
4. Eating good meals
5. Thinking about something good in the future (IA)
6. Having people show interest in what you have said (S)
7. Thinking about people I like (IA)
8. Seeing beautiful scenery (IA)
9. Breathing clean air (IA)
10. Being with friends (S)
11. Having peace and quiet (IA)
12. Being noticed as sexually attractive (S)
13. Kissing (S)
14. Watching people (S)
15. Having a frank and open conversation (S)
16. Sitting in the sun (IA)
17. Wearing clean clothes (IA)
18. Having spare time (IA)
19. Doing a project in my own way (E)
20. Sleeping soundly at night (IA)
21. Listening to music (IA)
22. Having sexual relations with a partner of the opposite sex (S)
23. Smiling at people (IA, S)
24. Being told I am loved (S)
25. Reading stories, novels, poems, or plays (E)
26. Planning or organizing something (E)
27. Going to a restaurant
28. Expressing my love to someone (S)
29. Petting, necking (S)
30. Being with someone I love (S)
31. Seeing good things happen to my family or friends (IA)
32. Complimenting or praising someone (S)
33. Having coffee, tea, a coke, etc., with friends (S)
34. Meeting someone new of the same sex (S)
35. Driving skillfully (E)
36. Saying something clearly (E)
37. Being with animals
38. Being popular at a gathering (S)
39. Having a lively talk (S)
40. Feeling the presence of the Lord in my life (IA)
41. Planning trips or vacations (E)
42. Listening to the radio (S)
43. Learning to do something new (E)
44. Seeing old friends (S)
45. Watching wild animals (IA)
46. Doing a job well (E)
47. Being asked for my help or advice (S)
48. Amusing people (S)
49. Being complimented or told I have done well (E, S)

[a] From Lewinsohn and Graf (1973).
[b] IA, incompatible affects; S, social interactional behaviors; E, ego supportive.

three categories. Many (21) involve social interactional behaviors (S) (e.g., being with happy people; having people show interest in what you have said). Another group (15) (incompatible affects—IA) involves affects and states which are presumed to be incompatible with feeling depressed (e.g., laughing, being relaxed). Another group of items (8) (ego supportive—E) involves activities which are presumed to lead to feelings of adequacy, competence, independence (e.g., doing a project in my own way; reading stories, novels, poems, or plays; planning or organizing something; doing a job well; learning to do something new, etc.). Yet others fall into more than one category (e.g., being complimented or told I have done well) or are difficult to categorize (e.g., being with animals).

The results suggest that certain kinds of activities, i.e., the ones shown in Table III, may be more efficacious in counteracting depression than other activities.

C. Total Amount of Positive Reinforcement Obtained

The total amount of positive reinforcement obtained is less in depressed than in nondepressed persons (MacPhillamy & Lewinsohn, 1973b).

The critical term (construct) in the behavioral position is "amount of response-contingent positive reinforcement" which is assumed to be an antecedent of depression. In nonlaboratory situations amount of response-contingent positive reinforcement would be very difficult to measure directly, and would require the continuous observation and coding over long periods of time of an individual's behavior and the stimulus events that influence it. The Pleasant Events Schedule was constructed to measure a closely related but more accessible variable, namely, the amount of pleasure obtained by the individual. "Pleasure" is defined as the occurrence of events to which an individual reports having experienced a positive affective response. It is assumed that such "pleasant events" are a major subset of all positive reinforcements and that, therefore, measurement of pleasant events may be used to approximate measurement of positive reinforcement.

Sample size for this study (MacPhillamy & Lewinsohn, 1972a) was 120, evenly divided between depressed, nondepressed psychiatric, and normal control groups. The depressed group was composed primarily of mildly and moderately depressed individuals. Each subject was administered the Pleasant Events Schedule, Form III-S. Subjects were instructed to respond to each item twice, first rating the frequency with which the event (activity) occurred during the past month and, second, rating its subjective enjoyability. Three scores were computed for each subject: the sum of his frequency ratings, the sum of his enjoyability ratings, and the sum of the products of the two sets of ratings. These scales are assumed to be measures of general activity level, reinforcement potential, and obtained pleasure. The *obtained pleasure* for any event was defined as the product of the frequency and enjoyability ratings for that event. A multiplicative function was chosen so that an activity of zero frequency or no enjoyability would yield a zero product score. Since an attempt had been made to sample exhaustively from the domain of "Pleasant Events," the average of the obtained pleasure scores (product scores) was asserted to be an approximation to *net obtained reinforcement*. The depressed group had a lower activities score, rated fewer items as pleasant, and had a lower net obtained pleasure value than either of the two control groups, and thus presumably were receiving lower levels of obtained positive reinforcement. Mean scores for the normal and psychiatric control groups were virtually identical, suggesting that the observed effect was associated uniquely with depression.

D. Loss of Reinforcer Effectiveness in Depressed Individuals

Costello (1972) has suggested that depression results when there is a "general loss of reinforcer effectiveness." This hypothesis stems from the reports of depressed individuals that they do not enjoy activities that were enjoyable for them before they became depressed. A direct experimental test of this important hypothesis has not been made. However, a prediction from the hypothesis, i.e., that the subjective enjoyability of pleasant events is lower in depressed than in nondepressed (normals and nondepressed psychiatric controls) persons has been confirmed in two studies (Lewinsohn & MacPhillamy, 1974; MacPhillamy & Lewinsohn, 1973b).

The question whether differences between depressed and nondepressed groups could also be demonstrated for groups differentiated on the basis of age formed the point of departure for the second study (Lewinsohn & MacPhillamy, 1974).

Sample 1. Three diagnostic groups were sought: depressed individuals, psychiatric controls (those experiencing psychological disorders other than depression), and normal individuals. A two-step classification procedure was used employing both selected MMPI Scales (Byrne, 1964) and the structured clinical interview rating form constructed and validated by Grinker *et al.* (1961). The criteria for classification have been presented elsewhere (Lewinsohn & Libet, 1972).

Subjects were also selected to form three age groups: Age I (18–29); Age II (30–49); and Age III (50 and over). Subjects who met all criteria were asked to complete the Pleasant Events Schedule.

Sample 2. Data on a larger sample of "normal" individuals were also collected. Each subject who successfully met the classification criteria described earlier was administered the Pleasant Events Schedule, Form III-S (MacPhillamy & Lewinsohn, 1971). The sum of the frequency ratings and of the enjoyability ratings was computed for each subject.

The results from Sample 1 were as follows: There was a significant decrease in the frequency ratings as a function of age and of depression. Thus, both the depressed and the elderly individuals engage with less frequency in potentially pleasant activities. While there was a significant decrease in the enjoyability ratings as a function of depression, no corresponding decrease in the enjoyability ratings of the elderly was obtained.

The results for the larger sample of "normal" individuals (Sample 2) were entirely consistent with those obtained with Sample 1 in showing a systematic decrease in the frequency ratings as a function of age without a corresponding decrease in the enjoyability ratings.

The major finding of this study is that while in depressed individuals a decrease in pleasant activity level *is* accompanied by a decrease in subjective enjoyability, no such decrease in subjective enjoyability was found to be associated with the decrease in pleasant activity level in the elderly subjects. The results are consistent with the hypothesis of Costello (1972) about a loss of reinforcer effectiveness in the depressed individual. Mean scores for the normal and psychiatric control groups were virtually identical, suggesting that the observed effect was associated uniquely with depression.

E. "Sensitivity" of Depressed Individuals to Aversive Stimuli

The hypothesis that depressed individuals are more sensitive to aversive contingencies has been tested and supported in three different studies (Lewinsohn, Lobitz, & Wilson, 1973; Libet *et al.*, 1973; Stewart, 1968).

Stewart (1968) hypothesized that "the behavior of depressed subjects is more influenced by the quality (positive or negative) of social reinforcement elicited than is the behavior of non-depressed subjects [p. 2]." Stewart found that depressed individuals generally had a longer latency of response, operationally defined as the amount of time between the reaction by another person to the subject's verbalization and a subsequent action by the subject in a group situation. As predicted, the largest differences between depressed and nondepressed subjects occurred following the incidence of a negative social reaction (e.g., being ignored, criticized, disagreed with, etc.). The subjects in Stewart's study were also asked to rate their liking or disliking for various kinds of positive and negative social reactions on a six-point scale. The depressed subjects reported disliking negative reactions more than did nondepressed subjects. However, these results did not attain statistical significance.

Libet *et al.* (1973) were also concerned with the social behavior of depressed individuals. The dependent variable was defined by a measure of the extent to which an individual's behavior is "turned off" by eliciting a reaction from the most "aversive" person in a group situation. The basic data in this study were constituted by the probability that the individual will emit another action following an action by another person. Base rate was defined as probability of emitting an action for the total situation, i.e., independent of whose action preceded it. An "aversive" person was defined as someone who significantly reduced the probability of the other persons in the group acting below the base rate. The behavior rate of depressed individuals was found consistently to be more attenuated by the "aversive" person than that of nondepressed subjects.

In a study in which autonomic response (GSR) to an electric shock of depressed subjects was compared with that of nondepressed subjects, depressed subjects were found to emit a larger autonomic response to the shock (Lewinsohn *et al.,* 1973).

The three studies provide strong support for the hypothesis that depressed individuals are more sensitive to an aversive stimulus. This finding would lead one to expect depressed individuals to show a greater tendency to avoid and to withdraw from unpleasant situations. The short-term consequence would be greater isolation, with the long-term consequence of less skill acquisition for the depressed individual.

F. Relationship between Social Skill and Depression

In contrast to the large amount of interest in the social behavior of schizophrenics, relatively few studies have been directed to understanding the interpersonal and family relations of depressives.

Lewinsohn and his associates have been interested in the social skill of depressed individuals because lack of social skill could be one of the antecedent conditions producing a low positive reinforcement rate. Social skill is defined as the ability to emit behaviors that are positively reinforced by others. This definition involves sequences of behavior consisting of actions emitted by an individual together with the reactions that he/she elicits from the social environment.

As a result of investigating the behavior of depressed and nondepressed persons in group therapy situations (Lewinsohn, Weinstein, & Alper, 1970; Libet & Lewinsohn, 1973; Libet *et al.,* 1973) and in their home environment (Lewinsohn & Shaffer, 1971; Libet *et al.,* 1973; Shaffer

& Lewinsohn, 1971), a number of different measures of social skill have evolved. The measures differ in that they focus on various aspects of an individual's interpersonal behavior. Nevertheless, they embody a common rationale. Consistent with the definition of social skill, each measure is assumed to be related to the amount of positive reinforcement an individual elicits from the social environment. The system for coding the interactional behavior of people described earlier (Table I) serves as an operational basis for the measures of social skill.

The definition of social reinforcement is critical to the model of social skill used by Lewinsohn and co-workers. Two approaches are utilized (Libet *et al.,* 1973). First, the definition of positive social reinforcement is made on "rational" grounds. In particular, it is assumed that it is "better" to be attended to than to be ignored, and, if one is attended to, it is better to elicit "positive" than "negative" reactions. The second approach is an empirical one which entails the analysis of social consequences of behavior and involves an examination of behavioral sequences that consist of actions emitted by an individual together with the reactions he/she elicits from the environment. The rate of positive reinforcement elicited is estimated by making an independent determination of what social consequences serve to increase the probability of antecedent behavior (reinforcers) and what social consequences serve to decrease the probability of antecedent behavior (aversive events).

As a result of an extensive analysis of the social-interactional data obtained in five therapy groups and 18 homes, several different aspects of social skill emerged as temporally stable and "valid." Temporal stability of each measure of social skill was determined by computing odd-even correlations since data on more than one observational period was available for each subject. The validity of the social skill measures was determined by correlating them (a) with rationally derived criterion measures: rate of behaviors elicited, rate of "positive" behaviors elicited, independent estimates (sociometric ratings) of social stimulus value, amount of interpersonal behavior estimated by self-report; and (b) with functionally derived criterion measures: rate of eliciting those social events which were found to significantly accelerate the base rate of emitted behavior. For the latter case, interpersonal behaviors were considered to be valid measures of social skill if they acted as discriminative stimuli for responses that had been independently shown to increase the probability of emitting an action.

The following social skill measures emerged as reliable ($r > .7$) and valid ($p < .02$) in either the group or home situation.

1. *Activity Level:* Total rate of behavior emitted expressed as the number of actions emitted per hour.

2. *Initiation Level:* Number of actions emitted per hour given that

the individual emitted neither an action or a reaction in the immediately preceding time interval. *Rationale:* A distinction is made between the initiation of interchanges and the maintenance of on-going exchanges. Initiation level yielded very high validity coefficients only for the groups. In the home situation, initiation level had a high positive relationship with the silence level measures and a negative correlation with the criterion variables, indicating that being socially skillful in a family situation consists of being nearly continuously involved.

3. *Silence Level 1:* Number of single time intervals per hour during which the individual is neither an actor nor a reactor.

4. *Silence Level 2:* Number of two consecutive time intervals per hour during which the person is neither an actor nor a reactor.

5. *Positive Reinforcement Level (PRL):* The number of times a functional positive reinforcing event is emitted per hour.

6. *Action Latency 1 (Action):* Probability of emitting an action in the same or next time interval subsequent to an elicited action. *Rationale:* Behaviors which an individual emits are not positively reinforcing for another unless the behaviors are emitted at the "appropriate time." Moreover, the greater the delay in emitting a behavior, the greater the likelihood of "losing the floor."

7. *Action Latency 2 (Reaction):* Probability of emitting an action in the same or next time interval subsequent to an elicited reaction.

8. *Action Latency 3 ("Positive" Reactions):* Probability of emitting an action in the same or next time interval subsequent to an elicited "positive" reaction.

9. *Action Latency 4 ("Negative" Reactions):* Probability of emitting an action in the same or next time interval subsequent to an elicited "negative" reaction.

10. *Sensitivity to an Aversive Reactor:* Measure of the extent to which an individual is "turned off" by eliciting any reaction from the most aversive person.

11. *Object—Reactor Discrepancy:* Ratio of the number of times the individual is the object of an action by another person but he/she does not react to the number of times he/she is the object of an action from another person. *Rationale:* Similar to Action Latency 1 and 2—the extent to which a person does not react to the behavior of others, he/she isolates himself/herself from the flow of interaction.

12. *Interpersonal Range:* The degree to which an individual distributes his/her actions equally to the other group members is expressed in terms of an information theory statistic, namely relative uncertainty value (R) (Attneave, 1959). If an individual emits actions only to one other group member, $R = 0$ (lower limit), this reflects minimum unpredictabil-

ity of the object of an action, or minimum interpersonal range. Conversely, if a person distributes his actions equally among his/her peers, $R = 1$ (upper limit), this reflects maximum unpredictability of the object of an action, or maximum interpersonal range. The computational procedures for determining R values are given in Libet and Lewinsohn (1973). Interpersonal Range emerged as a moderately valid measure only for the groups. Since the number of potential individuals with whom a person can interact is considerably less in the home than in a group situation, the critical factor here may simply be group size.

The results suggest that individuals who: (a) are active; (b) are quick to respond; (c) are relatively insensitive to an aversive person; (d) do not miss chances to react; (e) distribute their behaviors fairly evenly across members in group situations; and (f) emit the functional positive reinforcing events, maximize the rate of positive reinforcement elicited, i.e., are socially skillful.

Having established the reliability and validity of their social skill measures, Libet *et al.* (1973) then went on to compare depressed and nondepressed individuals on the measures.

The results may be summarized as follows:

a. In a small-group situation depressed males emit and initiate fewer actions, emit the positive reinforcing event at a lower rate, are more silent, have a delayed latency of response following a reaction, and are more sensitive to the "aversive person." In addition, depressed males elicit positive reinforcement at a lower rate than nondepressed males. Depressed males also describe themselves as less active socially and are rated by their peers as being less sociable. Consistent with the depressed males, depressed females are more sensitive to the "aversive person," describe themselves as being more socially isolated, emerge as less active, and elicit less positive social reinforcement.

b. In the home situation, depressed males emit fewer actions, initiate more actions (i.e., participate less in the on-going interchange), are more silent, have a delayed latency of response following a reaction, and elicit a lower rate of positive reinforcement. Consistent with the depressed males, the depressed females are less active, have a delayed latency of response, and elicit a lower rate of positive reinforcement. The conclusion that depressed individuals, in the home, elicit a lower rate of positive reinforcement than do nondepressed persons is also true when each home is treated as an individual social unit. Specifically, the rate of positive reinforcement elicited by the depressed person relative to that of the spouse was computed. Compared with his/her spouse, the depressed person was found to elicit significantly less positive reinforcement than the nondepressed spouse.

There have been several other studies on aspects of the social behavior of depressed individuals. Ekman and Friesen (1974) examined nonverbal communication in depressives. They identified two classes of hand motions which accompany conversation—illustrators, which are voluntary hand motions that assist in communicating the intent of the conversation, and involuntary adaptors which do not cohere with the conversation, e.g., nose picking and ear scratching. Illustrators were depleted in depressives whereas adaptors were more numerous. Furthermore, the number of illustrators increased and the number of adaptors decreased with clinical improvement.

Hinchliff, Lancashire, and Roberts (1971) found that depressed, compared with normal controls, spoke more slowly (words/minute). Samples of speech were tape recorded for 5 minutes. Subjects were instructed to verbalize on a topic of their choice without comment or interruption by *E*.

A related series of reports by Weissman, Paykel, Siegel, and Klerman (1971), Paykel, Weissman, Prusoff, and Tonks (1971), and Weissman, Paykel, and Klerman (1972) indicate impaired social performance on the part of depressed females. These reports are based on a comparison of 40 depressed female patients with 40 normal females matched for age and socioeconomic background. On basis of an interview the subjects were rated on a modified form of the Social Adjustment Scale (Gurland *et al.*, 1967). A factor analysis of the scale showed it to sample six areas of social adjustment (Paykel *et al.*, 1971): (1) work performance; (2) interpersonal friction; (3) inhibited communication; (4) submissive dependency; (5) family attachments; (6) anxious ruminations. The depressed subjects were significantly impaired on all factors. The interview ratings also included eight items concerned with maternal role performance. In two other reports (Weissman & Siegel, 1972; Weissman *et al.*, 1972) a much higher incidence of problems between the depressed mother and her children is reported. These reports can be criticized on two grounds. First, no nondepressed psychiatric control group was used. It is thus possible, indeed likely, that similar findings would have been obtained with nondepressed psychiatric patients; and second, the data are based on reports from the subjects themselves and are not supported by independent observations.

G. Environmental Factors and Life Events Preceding Depression

As indicated earlier, among the factors that on theoretical grounds would be expected to reduce the occurrence of behavior are changes in the environment which remove an important reinforcer or discriminative stimulus, introduction of aversive stimuli, or interruption of behavior chains. Hence, the examination of the types of events that precede depression is of relevance to the behavioral study of depression.

There have been a number of studies (e.g., Leff, Roatch, & Bunney, 1970) concerned with the relationship of life events and depression and with the descriptive characterization of those events occurring at the onset of depression. The best controlled of these is the study by Paykel *et al.* (1969) in which incidence of different, predominantly aversive, life events ($N = 33$) in the 6 months prior to the onset of depression in a sample of depressed patients was compared with the occurrence of these events in a matched control group. The overall incidence of events in the depressed group was nearly three times that in the control group during a comparable 6-month period. The study also indicates that certain kinds of events are more likely than others to precede depression. The individual events differing significantly in the two populations fell mainly into three groups: marital difficulties such as arguments and separations; deaths and illnesses; and work changes (demotion, being fired, starts new type of work). The findings of this study are, thus, entirely consistent with the hypothesis that a reduction in positive reinforcement rate constitutes a critical antecedent condition for the occurrence of depressions.

IV. BEHAVIORAL TREATMENT OF DEPRESSION

Over the past five years, a number of case reports describing the application of learning theory to the treatment of depression have appeared in the literature (Hersen, Eisler, Alford, & Agras, 1973; Lazarus, 1968; Lewinsohn & Atwood, 1969; Lewinsohn & Shaw, 1969; Lewinsohn & Shaffer, 1971; Lewinsohn *et al.,* 1970; Liberman & Raskin, 1971; Liberman & Roberts, 1974; Reisinger, 1972; Seitz, 1971; Stuart, 1967; Todd, 1972; Wanderer, 1972; Wolpe, 1971).

The guiding principle for the behavioral treatment of depressed individuals is to restore an adequate schedule of positive reinforcement for the individual through altering the level, the quality, and the range of the patient's activities and interactions. Because of the diversity and the multiplicity of the symptoms shown by depressed individuals, no *single* intervention strategy that is useful with all depressives exists or is likely to be discovered. Instead, a number of treatment techniques, which are derivable from the behavioral theory of depression, have evolved allowing the behavior therapist to select that combination of techniques which appears most suited and useful for the individual case. Thus, even though the *general* goal in all cases is the same (to restore an adequate schedule of positive reinforcement for the individual), *specific* intervention techniques are expected to vary from case to case, depending on the circumstances responsible for the patient's low rate of positive reinforcement.

A. Diagnostic Functional Analysis of Depressed Individuals

Because of the large individual differences between depressed individuals in regard to types of symptoms and problems manifested by them, a careful diagnostic evaluation is always needed. The goals of the diagnostic evaluation are 4-fold: (1) To evaluate the intensity of the depression including suicidal risk; (2) To pinpoint specific behavioral excesses and deficits; (3) To formulate a "behavioral diagnosis" in regard to causation and maintenance of the patient's depression; (4) To generate a treatment plan that includes specific behavioral goals and appropriate treatment procedures.

The beginning phase of treatment needs to be clearly defined for the patient as a diagnostic phase. During this phase the patient is told that he or she and the therapist will try to obtain as much information as possible about him/her and his/her behavior so that at the end of the diagnostic phase they (he/she and the therapist) can arrive at some mutually acceptable treatment recommendations for him/her. The importance of obtaining all kinds of data, such as observing him/her interacting with his/her family, filling out mood ratings, monitoring his/her activity level, finding out about his/her interests, etc., is emphasized.

During the initial phase, it is very important that there be concern for clarity of mutual understanding in regard to expectations, goals, time commitments, and other conditions. These need to be explicated as clearly, as concretely, and as concisely as possible to the patient.

In evaluating depression level, it is useful to follow some outline during the first interview so that information about the various manifestations of depression can be elicited.

The first interview typically identifies major problem areas for further exploration in future interviews. The following psychological tests are sometimes useful in helping to identify behavior problems and in measuring behavior change:

1. Minnesota Multiphasic Personality Inventory (MMPI)

This test not only provides a quantitative measure of intensity of depression, but also alerts the therapist to other possible areas of psychopathology. There are relatively few "purely" depressed people, and the MMPI allows the therapist to evaluate the relative importance of other symptoms (e.g., psychotic symptoms, confusion, anxiety level, etc.) vis-à-vis the depression.

2. Depression Adjective Check List (DACL) (Lubin, 1965)

Having the patient rate his/her mood at the end of each day on one of the alternate forms of the DACL helps to make the patient and the therapist aware of day-to-day fluctuations in mood and facilitates the identification of environmental changes and reinforcement contingencies correlated with the patient's mood (Lewinsohn, 1973).

3. Pleasant Events Schedule (PES) (MacPhillamy & Lewinsohn, 1971)

This schedule is useful in pinpointing specific activities and events which are potentially reinforcing for the patient. The schedule also usually helps to focus the fact that the patient is not engaging in many activities that are pleasant for him/her.

In administering these, or other diagnostic devices, it is important that the therapist: (a) not overwhelm the patient by giving him/her too many tests all at once. It has been useful with some patients to make the next appointment contingent on the patient's completing a diagnostic test; and (b) to include only those tests which the therapist feels can contribute to the diagnostic formulation and treatment of the particular case.

The diagnostic phase usually lasts 2 weeks. During the diagnostic phase, base level information is obtained with which to define treatment goals and with which to measure behavior change. The diagnostic phase is followed by one or more review sessions. The patient is told that at these review sessions the conclusions reached by the therapist will be presented to him/her. Behavioral terms, graphs, and other visual aids are used to present the "behavioral diagnosis" as clearly as possible. Several sessions, individual and joint, are sometimes necessary to present the information and to agree upon treatment goals. This process requires a great deal of skill and sensitivity on the part of the therapist and cannot be rushed. It involves considerable interaction between patient and therapist. The end product is a mutually acceptable "contract" (understanding) as to the nature of the client's difficulties and the desirable treatment goals and procedures.

Prior to describing specific treatment techniques, several general strategies might be mentioned.

1. Three-month time limit for treatment. Published case reports by behavior therapists all involve relatively short treatment periods. Lewinsohn *et al.* (1969) have been using a 3-month time limit which starts at the end of the diagnostic phase. The 3-month period is arbitrary, and if a time limit is used it should be determined for each individual patient on the basis of the nature of the treatment goals. The rationale for including a time limit is that it has a facilitative effect in that the provision of a definite period within which behavior change must occur can serve as a discriminative stimulus to avoid the aversive consequences of terminating treatment without improvement.

2. Use of home observations as an integral part of the treatment of depression. The treatment of depressed individuals suggests that many depressed individuals have serious marital problems. These problems are usually brought out and focused by the home observations. The home observations also provide a convenient way of involving the spouse.

The necessity of observing the depressed individual's interactions with his/her family in his/her own home as part of the diagnostic phase is stressed in the intake interview. The home visit typically becomes a focal point for discussion between therapist and client and requires the client to communicate and to plan with members of his/her family. The manner in which this is accomplished usually results in important diagnostic information. Home visits, lasting about an hour each, are scheduled around meal time when all members of the family are present. Observations are conducted during the beginning, middle, and ending phases of treatment. Interactions are coded in terms of the behaviors emitted by the client and the social consequences of his/her behavior. Other members of the family are also observed and their behavioral interactions are coded. The methodology and the behavioral categories used in quantifying these observations have been described earlier. The primary objective of the home observation is to obtain base level information with which to define treatment goals and to measure behavior change. On the basis of the home observations, the therapist identifies those interpersonal behavior patterns which he/she assumes to be causally related to the depression. These findings are presented to the client and his/her spouse in individual and joint interviews in close temporal proximity to the home visit. Interpersonal patterns which have emerged as critical from case to case range from the complete absence of any interaction between patient and spouse to very one-sided interactions. It has also been observed that the client does not reinforce behavior which is directed toward him/her, that only a small portion of time is devoted to topics of interest to the client, or that his/her only "topic" is his/her depression. Detailed case descriptions illustrating the use of the home visit as part of treatment are available elsewhere (e.g., Lewinsohn &

Shaffer, 1971). In addition to the above, the home visits appear to have the following beneficial consequences: (a) They immediately focus the therapist-patient interaction on behavioral and interpersonal problems. This is especially important since many depressed persons start out by defining themselves in a passive way, i.e., as having some kind of disease that they expect someone to treat. (b) The home observations constitute an easy way of involving a significant part of the patient's environment in the treatment process. The necessity of arranging for the home observation gives a natural opening for relating to the spouse, children, etc., in ways that are usually more productive than the usual information-gathering oriented kind of social history interview with the relative.

Behaviorally oriented treatment strategies for depression seem to fall into four categories, described in Sections B–E below.

B. Techniques Aimed at Increasing the Patient's Activity Level

Historically, the oldest approach with this goal in mind is the *antidepression milieu therapy* developed at the Menninger Foundation during the 1950s. The approach involved making the patients perform menial tasks, with the staff insisting upon a high level of performance. An approach similar to the "antidepression milieu therapy" was used by Taulbee and Wright (1971). They reported a series of studies comparing a number of "attitude therapy programs," i.e., every staff member who comes in contact with a given patient responds to the patient with a single prescribed attitude. Patients are dealt with in a kind but firm manner. The patients are required to complete menial and monotonous tasks assigned to them. Aggressive behaviors are encouraged and reinforced. When the patient emits depressed behavior, he/she is placed in the "sanding room." Here the patient engages in such tasks as sanding a small block of wood, counting tiny sea shells, and mopping floors. These activities are supervised by nursing assistants who forbid the patients to talk and who continually point out all imperfections in the patient's work. Within a few hours, the patient typically becomes overtly hostile and "blows up." The patient is then allowed out of the room and the staff responds to his/her aggressiveness with acceptance. A series of studies suggest that this antidepression program was more effective than the other treatment conditions with which it was being compared.

A more subtle approach to increasing the patient's rate for certain behaviors is to make use of the Premack Principle. The Premack Principle states that the occurrence of a high frequency behavior can be used to reinforce a low frequency behavior by making the occurrence of the high frequency behavior contingent upon the emission of the low frequency behavior. In many depressed patients, certain behaviors (e.g., verbal statements of dysphoria, guilt, self-depreciation, rejection, material burden) are emitted at a consistently high rate. Hence, according to Premack's Principle, the occurrence of these high frequency behaviors would have reinforcing value for other low frequency behaviors. In other words, it should be possible to reinforce low frequency behaviors in the depressed individual (e.g., self-assertive, realistic, constructive behaviors) by making high frequency (self-depreciatory statements for example) behaviors contingent upon them. The potential utility of the Premack Principle for the treatment of behavior disorders was first pointed out by Homme (1965). Homme used high frequency behaviors, such as smoking and drinking coffee, to reinforce low frequency behaviors such as thinking self-confident thoughts. Similarly, Seitz (1971) and Todd (1972) had their patients generate a list of positive thoughts and then instructed them to think about one or more items on the list before lighting a cigarette (which was a high frequency behavior). Lewinsohn *et al.* (1969), Johansson *et al.* (1969), and Robinson and Lewinsohn (1973b) have made use of high frequency verbal behavior categories (e.g., talking depression) to reinforce low frequency verbal behaviors in therapy as well as extra-therapy behavior. Liberman and Roberts (1974) used a high frequency behavior (nap time in bed) to reinforce desirable but low frequency behaviors (performing adaptive, constructive activities at home) with a 36-year-old female depressed patient.

Social reinforcement was used to increase constructive behaviors in depressed patients by Burgess (1969), Beck (1970a), and Liberman and Raskin (1971). Burgess (1969) used a graded task assignment procedure whereby the patient was first told to emit some simple behavior like making a telephone call. The task requirements were then increased. The patient was reinforced by the attention and interest of the therapist for successfully completing the tasks. The goal was to reinforce active and constructive behaviors.

Beck *et al.* (unpublished) also used a graded task assignment procedure on 24 hospitalized depressives. The patients were socially reinforced upon successful completion of each step.

Liberman and Raskin (1971) have applied reinforcement contingencies in the context of family therapy for the modification of depressed behaviors. Family members were taught to change their focus of attention and interest from "depressed" behaviors to more "coping and constructive" behaviors (cooking, cleaning house, tending to the children's needs). Therapists instructed the family to pay instant and frequent attention to coping behavior and to gradually ignore depressed behavior. Within one week the patient's "depressed" behavior decreased sharply while her constructive behavior increased.

Hersen *et al.* (1973) successfully used a token economy program to increase work behavior in three depressed patients. An increase in work behavior was associated with a diminution of depression.

It is a well established clinical and empirical fact that depressed individuals as a group engage in relatively few activities and in even fewer activities which are considered to be pleasant or rewarding by them. The practical question facing the therapist is what activities should the patient be encouraged to engage in? How are they to be selected? Should the goal be an increase in the quantity of behavior as against focusing on specific behaviors because they are assumed to be especially therapeutic?

Since 1968 (Lewinsohn *et al.,* 1969) Lewinsohn and his associates have used *Activity Schedules*, i.e., having the patient keep a daily record of behaviors which he or she enjoys, in the treatment of depression. Empirical support for this practice is represented by the existence of a rather substantial relationship between engaging in pleasant activities and mood state (Lewinsohn & Graf, 1973; Lewinsohn & Libet, 1972). The more a person engages in activities which are pleasant for him/her the better he/she feels. Activity Schedules are constructed for patients by using activities and events judged by the patient himself/herself to be pleasant. Initially patients were asked to list activities which had been enjoyable, pleasant, meaningful, or interesting for them in the past. Many depressed individuals find it difficult to think of more than a few pleasant activities and this often required considerable assistance from the therapist. More recently, Activity Schedules have been generated for each patient from his/her responses on the Pleasant Events Schedule. The items are put on a ditto master and the patient is asked to indicate at the end of each day which of the activities he/she engaged in. In addition, the patient is asked to rate his/her mood at the end of each day on one of the alternate forms of the Depression Adjective Check List developed by Lubin (1965). A total Pleasant Activities Score is then computed for each day and systematic efforts are made to increase the patient's activity level by introducing various kinds of contingencies.

At the end of a base level period (30 days) it is possible to compute the correlation between the patient's mood and his/her total pleasant activity level, and to identify individual activities which are correlated ($r > .30$) with his/her mood. The patient continues to monitor his/her activity level and mood throughout the rest of treatment. The ten most highly correlated activities can then be selected. In a study by Lewinsohn (1973) a formula was then developed for each patient whereby the patient would obtain so many minutes of therapy time as a function of how many activities he/she engaged in. The patients were told which activities would earn therapy time. At the beginning of each subsequent treatment hour, the patient returned his/her completed Activity Schedule and mood ratings to a technician. The technician then computed the amount of treatment time to which the patient was entitled. The procedure was quite effective in producing a significant increase in the frequency of the correlated activities. Considerable stability in the magnitude of the correlation between mood and total pleasant activity level was also demonstrated. The results of this study (Lewinsohn, 1974) seem to justify the use of *either* a small number of selected activities *or* of the patient's total pleasant activities level as legitimate goals for the purpose of modifying mood level.

A question can be raised about the honesty with which people fill out these activity schedules. Like other self-report measures, they are completely under the subject's control. In our experience with about 30 patients, we have questioned the truthfulness of three. Two of these were poorly motivated, missing many sessions, and were generally critical of the approach. The third patient immediately increased her activity level substantially when the contingency program was instituted to where she was earning 50 minutes of therapy time every session. However, the majority of depressed individuals seem to be quite conscientious about filling out these schedules. In another series of studies (MacPhillamy & Lewinsohn, 1973a) we have found subject's self-reports of the frequency with which they have engaged in various pleasant activities to possess good validity when compared with ratings made by both peers and independent observers.

C. Techniques Aimed at Reduction of Behavioral Excesses

In the case of depressed individuals, "behavioral excesses" take the form of obsessive ruminating or verbalizations about negative aspects of the self, the past, statements of guilt, somatic complaints, etc. The frequency of such behaviors can be reduced in a number of different ways. (1) The therapist can ignore them (Burgess, 1969); (2) the social environment can be reprogrammed to ignore them (Liberman & Raskin, 1971); (3) the patient is taught how to control them. Thus, Wanderer (1972) used "thought stopping" procedures (adapted from Wolpe, 1969). At the onset of a negative thought sequence (signaled by the patient) the therapist would pair a loud sudden noise with the word "stop"! After a few training sessions, the patient was able to interrupt quickly any negative thoughts by himself/herself. Using a somewhat different procedure with a similar goal, Lewinsohn *et al.* (unpublished) provided "discrimination training" for patients by providing them with consecutive 2-minute intervals during which they could or could not emit the high frequency behavior in the treatment hour. The intervals were signaled by means of a green light. The patients reported that this helped them to control their "thoughts" in extra-therapy situations.

D. Techniques Aimed at the Induction of Affects That Are Incompatible with Depression

In the same way that anxiety can be reduced by associating an incompatible response such as muscle relaxation with the anxiety-provoking stimulus, it can be suggested that there are affects which are incompatible with feeling depressed. This hypothesis has indeed been proposed by Lazarus (1968), and his use of *"affective expression"* is based on the premise that ". . . the deliberate stimulation of feelings of amusement, affection, sexual excitement, or anxiety tend to break the depressive cycle [p. 88]." Among the activities which were found to be associated with mood for a substantial proportion of people (Lewinsohn & Graf, 1973) were many which were categorized as "incompatible affects" (laughing, being relaxed, thinking about something good in the future, thinking about people I like, seeing beautiful scenery, having peace and quiet). Thus, being relaxed is one of the activities which has been found to be negatively correlated with being depressed. While being relaxed is probably more appropriately thought of as a state rather than as an activity, there are activities (behaviors) that a person can engage in which make him/her feel relaxed. Hence, *relaxation training,* i.e., teaching the patient to relax at will, is useful for patients who are characterized by "tension—anxiety," who are obsessively ruminating about their problems or who have difficulty in falling asleep at night. Relaxation training has also been used by Seitz (1971) and by Lewinsohn *et al.* (unpublished).

E. Techniques Aimed at Enhancing the Patient's Instrumental Skill

A frequent goal of therapy is to train the patient in those skills which are necessary for him/her to deal effectively with his/her environment, i.e., to be reinforced for his/her efforts. Included under this heading are such techniques as *assertive training* (Wolpe & Lazarus, 1966), *social skill training* (Lewinsohn *et al.,* 1970), and *desensitization* (Seitz, 1971; Wolpe, 1971). Where the patient has lost some important set of skills due to physical illness, more extended occupational and academic training may be indicated.

An interesting use of desensitization to increase a patient's activity level is reported by Wanderer (1972). The patient's phobias limited his ability to travel, particularly by airplane, and therefore restricted him from potential satisfactions. Overcoming the phobia allowed the patient to travel extensively by air, thus increasing the range of positive reinforcers that could operate on his behavior.

The use of systematic desensitization with depressives would seem especially useful in cases where the patient is avoiding fear-arousing situations (e.g., social interactions) which might otherwise be rewarding for him/her.

Since many depressed patients have few friends, live by themselves, and emit very few social behaviors when they are with people, the use of *social skill training* as part of the treatment of depression is often suggested. Lewinsohn *et al.* (1970) attempted to create a social environment, in the form of a group therapy group, for the depressed person where his/her behavioral difficulties could be identified and where he/she could acquire a new and more efficient pattern of interpersonal behavior. The main therapeutic strategy was to provide each patient with information about his/her own behavior and its consequences, to define behavioral goals with him/her, and to use the peer group and the therapist to reinforce behavior consistent with these goals in the group interaction.

The patient's participation in group sessions generate data about his/her interpersonal behavior which can be used to provide him/her with a great deal of specific feedback (what impact his/her behavior has on others and the impact of others' behavior on him/her) and to define behavioral goals with him/her. The second purpose of the group is to allow the patient to acquire new and more efficient patterns of interpersonal behavior. Specific goals vary with each patient, but they can be operationalized through the social skill measures mentioned earlier. (Examples: To increase his/her rate of positive reaction toward others, to increase his/her rate of behavior in the group, to respond more quickly after eliciting a negative consequence, etc.) The general goal is to help the patient emit those behaviors that elicit behavior from others which are reinforcing to him/her. The individual sessions vary in content but have the following common features. At the beginning of each session, the therapist presents the group with a task or skill exercise. Many of the exercises (Lewinsohn *et al.*, unpublished; Liberman, DeRisi, King, & Austin, 1973; Pfeiffer & Jones, 1971) are designed to facilitate interpersonal communication, to aid with the development of communication skills, or they address themselves to specific interpersonal problems. The sessions last for 2 hours. At the conclusion of the exercise (approximately 30–45 minutes) the therapist and the group debrief, and the rest of the session is used in a traditional group therapy fashion. During this time the participants are concerned with their feelings, with what is happening in the group, their expectations, dissatisfactions, etc. This is also the time that the individuals can practice new social skills. The therapist's role throughout is to focus on the qualitative and quantitative aspects of the interactions between the members in the group setting.

Some depressed individuals have difficulty asserting themselves in the face of a potentially hostile or critical audience reaction and the need for *assertive training* has to be ascertained for each patient by probing with relevant questions (Wolpe & Lazarus, 1966) during the diagnostic phase.

Since most depressed individuals have serious marital problems (e.g., Weissman *et al.,* 1971), *marital therapy* is often useful. The marital problems are usually identified and focused by the home observations. To the extent that marital problems exist and are felt to be contributory to the patient's depression, marital counseling (i.e., joint sessions with husband and wife) is indicated. This has been used by Lewinsohn and Shaw (1969), Lewinsohn and Atwood (1969), and Liberman and Roberts (1974). The sessions are guided by the general principle that a good marriage is based upon reciprocity, i.e., there must be an equitable exchange of reinforcements, so that both partners feel that they are receiving in proportion to what they are giving. The marital counseling thus aims at maximizing positive interchange between the spouses. This can be accomplished by focusing on mutual expectations, and on the kinds of behaviors that are experienced as positive and negative consequences. Where appropriate, contingency contracting (Liberman, 1970; Stuart, 1969; Weiss, Hops, & Patterson, 1972) can be used. It is useful to include instruction in basic communication skills, with guided practice at home, in the sessions.

The information that can be obtained through a vocational interest test is often useful with depressed patients who are undecided and ambivalent about their occupational and academic goals. Often they are "underemployed" relative to their capabilities, but it is difficult for them to commit themselves to a career plan. The data obtained from a vocational interest test can be used to assist the depressed individuals to make a decision, and to take appropriate action steps, in regard to an occupational and academic career. Depressed female housewives often seem to get very little satisfaction out of the housewife-mother role. One of the treatment goals in these cases has been to help the patient to find activities outside the home, e.g., employment or academic courses which are potentially more reinforcing for them.

F. Techniques Aimed at Changing Patients' Cognitions—Cognitive Therapy

This treatment approach to depression stems from the cognitive theory of depression proposed by Beck (1967), which assigns a primary role to the cognitive manifestations of depression. The treatment procedure involves the identification and modification of depressive's inappropriate and inaccurate cognitions. Case studies of cognitive therapy with depressives may be found in Beck (1967).

Cognitive therapy has been defined as "a set of operations focused on a patient's cognitions (verbal or pictorial) and on the premises, assumptions, and attitudes underlying these cognitions (Beck, 1970a, p. 187)." The cognitive therapist formulates the presenting symptoms in terms of basic misconceptions and thought patterns which become apparent as the patient reports his/her thoughts and experiences. Thus, the cognitive therapist is more concerned, but not exclusively so, with covert events. He/she trains the patient to become more aware of his/her "automatic thoughts" and chooses from a wide range of therapeutic techniques in his/her attempts to alter the maladaptive cognitions.

Beck's cognitive therapy proceeds as follows. On the basis of the patient's life history data and his/her verbalizations during the intake interviews, the therapist formulates the problem, defines goals, and devises specific operations to deal with each problem. Major maladaptive patterns are identified and the patient is told that these result from maladaptive attitudes (e.g., expecting to be rejected, overreaction to specific stresses, and traumatic events). Next, the patient is taught to focus upon and to identify depression-generating cognitions which Beck labels "automatic thoughts." A subsequent goal is to increase the patient's objectivity toward these depressive cognitions, which Beck labels "distancing." Distancing is accomplished by applying rules of logic to these cognitions, by having the patient check the observations on which the cognitions are based, and, more generally, by helping the patient to see that his/her depressive cognitions distort reality. The last stage of therapy is directed at "neutralization" of the depressive cognitions by having the patient recite the reasons that some of his/her cognitions are invalid. The goal of neutralization is the reduction in intensity and frequency of the cognition and the accompanying affect.

In working with a patient the cognitive therapist might select specific, narrowly selected "targets" for intervention such as getting the patient to read, trying to introduce the patient to volunteer work, employment, and more generally, to direct the patient into experiences in which he/she is likely to be successful. While many of the specific behavioral treatment goals of the cognitive therapist are similar to those of the behavior therapist, to the cognitive therapist the behavioral interventions are merely a means toward the more important goal of producing cognitive (attitudinal) changes in the patient.

V. OVERVIEW AND RECOMMENDATIONS FOR FUTURE RESEARCH

For many years the study of depression was dominated by psychoanalytic formulations (Abraham, 1911; Freud, 1917), which emphasized the internalization of hostility and other intra-psychic processes as the critical etiological mechanisms. These hypotheses have not been productive either in generating empirical research or in the development of specific treatment procedures. The behavioral formulations of depression provide a relatively simple framework within which to understand depression. Specific treatment strategies and hypotheses about antecedent socioenvironmental conditions have been derived from this framework.

The notion of a reduced positive reinforcement rate is central to most behavioral formulations of depression. While the results of several studies (e.g., Lewinsohn & Graf, 1973; Hersen *et al.,* 1973) are consistent with the major tenet of the behavioral theory of depression, i.e., that there is an *association* between positive reinforcement and depression, the crucial question as to whether a reduction in positive reinforcement is an *antecedent* for depression or simply a *concomitant* has not been resolved. It is on *a priori* grounds equally plausible for a person to be less depressed following an increase in response-contingent positive reinforcement as it is to assume an increase in behavior, which elicits positive reinforcement, to follow his/her being less depressed. Most likely causation can operate in both directions. Research to clarify this issue is needed.

An important and related issue concerns the extent to which the features which have been found to be associated with depression (e.g., reduced subjective enjoyability of pleasant events, increased sensitivity to aversive stimuli, low social skill) are characteristic of depressed individuals when they are not in the depressed state. The answers will have theoretical as well as clinical implications. For example, if depressed individuals manifest reduced subjective enjoyability of pleasant events even when they are not in the depressed state, it would be difficult for behavioral intervention techniques to produce lasting behavioral changes, because the reduced potency of reinforcers would make the individual prone to extinction in the future. On the other hand, if reduced reinforcer effectiveness is associated only with being in the depressed state, it would suggest that reduced reinforcer effectiveness may be a consequence of being in a depressed state.

Perhaps most urgently needed at this point are well controlled, systematic, outcome studies to evaluate the efficacy of behaviorally oriented treatment techniques with depressed individuals. Existing case studies indicate that behavioral treatment strategies *can* produce a significant reduction in depression. However, a systematic study of the efficacy of the behavioral techniques, which have been proposed, with appropriate controls and follow-up data has yet to be done. Such a study is vitally needed because, as is well-known, depressions are cyclical and usually self-limiting (Beck, 1967). The methodological problems of doing outcome research are formidable indeed. Summaries of the relevant issues are found in the writings of Paul (1967); Goldstein, Heller, and Sechrest (1966); Campbell (1963); Campbell and Stanley (1963); and Strupp (1971). Nevertheless, we badly need answers to the following kinds of questions:

1. Are behavioral techniques effective in reducing depression compared with: (a) base level (pretreatment) observations; (b) "traditional" psychotherapy; (c) somatic therapies—convulsive and psychopharmacologic; and (d) no treatment?

2. To what extent are the changes produced by behavioral techniques maintained after the termination of treatment?

REFERENCES

Abraham, K. Notes on the psychoanalytic investigation and treatment of manic-depressive insanity and allied conditions (1911). *Selected papers on psychoanalysis.* New York: Basic Books, 1960. Pp. 137–156.

Akiskal, H. S., & McKinney, W. T. Depressive disorders: Toward a unified hypothesis. *Science,* 1973, **182,** 20–29.

Attneave, F. *Application of information theory to psychology.* New York: Holt, 1959.

Azrin, N. H., Hutchinson, R. R., & Hake, D. F. Extinction induced aggression. *Journal of the Experimental Analysis of Behavior,* 1966, **9,** 191–204.

Beck, A. T. Thinking and depression: I. Idiosyncratic content and cognitive distortions. *Archives of General Psychiatry,* 1963, **9,** 324–333.

Beck, A. T. Thinking and depression: II. Theory and therapy. *Archives of General Psychiatry,* 1964, **10,** 561–571.

Beck, A. T. *Depression: Clinical, experimental and theoretical aspects.* New York: Harper, 1967.

Beck, A. T. Cognitive therapy: Nature and relation to behavior therapy. *Behavior Therapy,* 1970, **1,** 184–200. (a)

Beck, A. T. The core problem of depression: The cognitive triad. *Science and Psychoanalysis,* 1970, **17,** 47–55. (b)

Bunney, W. E., Jr., & Hamburg, D. A. Methods for reliable longitudinal observation of behavior. *Archives of General Psychiatry,* 1963, **9,** 280–291.

Burgess, E. P. The modification of depressive behaviors. In R. D. Rubin & C. M. Franks (Eds.), *Advances in behavior therapy, 1968.* New York: Academic Press, 1969.

Byrne, D. Repression sensitization as a dimension of personality. In B. A. Maher (Ed.), *Progress in Experimental Personality Research.* Vol. 1. New York: Academic Press, 1964. Pp. 169–220.

Campbell, D. T. From description to experimentation: Interpreting trends as quasi experiments. In C. W. Harris (Ed.), *Problems in measuring change.* Madison: University of Wisconsin Press, 1963.

Campbell, D. T., & Stanley, J. C. Experimental designs for research on teaching. In N. C. Gage (Ed.), *Handbook of research on teaching.* Chicago: Rand McNally, 1963. Pp. 171–246.

Costello, C. G. Depression: Loss of reinforcers or loss of reinforcer effectiveness? *Behavior Therapy,* 1972, **3,** 240–247.

Ekman, P., & Friesen, W. V. Non-verbal behavior in psychopathology. In R. J. Friedman & M. M. Katz (Eds.), *The psychology of depression: Contemporary theory and research.* New York: Wiley, 1974. Pp. 203–224.

Ferster, C. B. Classification of behavior pathology. In L. Krasner & L. P. Ullmann (Eds.), *Research in behavior modification.* New York: Holt, 1965. Pp. 6–26.

Ferster, C. B. Animal behavior and mental illness. *Psychological Record,* 1966, **16,** 345–356.

Ferster, C. B. A functional analysis of depression. *American Psychologist,* 1973, **28,** 857–870.

Freud, S. Mourning and melancholia (1917). *Collected papers.* Vol. 4. London: Hogarth Press, 1957. Pp. 152–170.

Friedman, A. S., Cowitz, B., Cohen, H. W., & Granick, S. Syndromes and themes of psychotic depression: A factor analysis. *Archives of General Psychiatry,* 1963, **9,** 504–509.

Goldstein, A. P., Heller, K., & Sechrest, L. B. *Psychotherapy and the psychology of behavior change.* New York: Wiley, 1966.

Grinker, R. R., Miller, J., Sabshin, M., Nunn, J., & Nunally, J. D. *The phenomena of depression.* New York: Harper, 1961.

Gurland, B., Yorkston, N., Frank, L., & Stone, A. *Structured and sealed interview to assess maladjustment.* New York: Biometrics Research, Department of Mental Hygiene, 1967.

Hamilton, M. A rating scale for depression. *Journal of Neurology, Neurosurgery, & Psychiatry,* 1960, **23,** 56–61.

Hersen, M., Eisler, R. M., Alford, G., & Agras, W. S. Effects of token economy on neurotic depression: An experimental analysis. *Behavior Therapy,* 1973, **4,** 392–397.

Hinchliffe, M. K., Lancashire, M., & Roberts, F. J. Depression: Defense mechanisms in speech. *British Journal of Psychiatry,* 1971, **118,** 471–472.

Homme, L. E. Perspectives in psychology: XXIV; Control of coverants, the operants of the mind. *Psychological Record,* 1965, **15,** 501–511.

Johansson, S., Lewinsohn, P. M., & Flippo, J. R. An application of the Premack principle to the verbal behavior of depressed subjects. Paper presented at the meeting of the Association for Advancement of Behavior Therapy, April 1969. (Mimeo, University of Oregon, 1969.)

Klerman, G. L. Clinical research in depression. In J. Zubin & F. A. Freyhan (Eds.), *Disorders of mood.* Baltimore: Johns Hopkins Press, 1972. Pp. 165–193.

Lazarus, A. A. Learning theory and the treatment of depression. *Behaviour Research and Therapy,* 1968, **6,** 83–89.

Lazarus, A. A. Some reactions to Costello's paper on depression. *Behavior Therapy,* 1972, **3,** 248–250.

Leff, M. J., Roatch, J. F., & Bunney, W. E., Jr. Environmental factors preceding the onset of severe depressions. *Psychiatry,* 1970, **33,** 293.

Lewinsohn, P. M. The use of activity schedules in the treatment of depressed individuals. Mimeo, University of Oregon, 1973.

Lewinsohn, P. M. A behavioral approach to depression. In R. M. Friedman & M. M. Katz (Eds.), *The psychology of depression: Contemporary theory and research.* New York: Wiley, 1974. Pp. 157–185. (a)

Lewinsohn, P. M. Clinical and theoretical aspects of depression. In K. S. Calhoun, H. E. Adams, & K. M. Mitchell (Eds.), *Innovative treatment methods of psychopathology.* New York: Wiley, 1974. (b)

Lewinsohn, P. M., & Atwood, G. E. Depression: A clinical-research approach. *Psychotherapy: Theory, Research and Practice,* 1969, **6,** 166–171.

Lewinsohn, P. M., Alper, T., Johansson, S., Libet, J., Rosenberry, C., Shaffer, M., Sterin, C., Stewart, R., & Weinstein, M. Manual of instruction for the behavior rating used for the observation of interpersonal behavior. Unpublished manuscript, University of Oregon, 1968. (Revised, 1971.)

Lewinsohn, P. M., & Graf, M. Pleasant activities and depression. *Journal of Consulting and Clinical Psychology,* 1973, **41,** 261–268.

Lewinsohn, P. M., & Libet, J. Pleasant events, activity schedules, and depression. *Journal of Abnormal Psychology,* 1972, **79,** 291–295.

Lewinsohn, P. M., Lobitz, C., & Wilson, S. "Sensitivity" of depressed individuals to aversive stimuli. *Journal of Abnormal Psychology,* 1973, **81,** 259–263.

Lewinsohn, P. M., & MacPhillamy, D. J. The relationship between age and engagement in pleasant activities. *Journal of Gerontology,* 1974, **29,** 290–294.

Lewinsohn, P. M., & Shaffer, M. The use of home observations as an integral part of the treatment of depression: Preliminary report and case studies. *Journal of Consulting and Clinical Psychology,* 1971, **37,** 87–94.

Lewinsohn, P. M., & Shaw, D. A. Feedback about interpersonal behavior as an agent of behavior change: A case study in the treatment of depression. *Psychotherapy and Psychosomatics,* 1969, **17,** 82–88.

Lewinsohn, P. M., Weinstein, M. S., & Alper, T. A behaviorally oriented approach to the group treatment of depressed persons: A methodological contribution. *Journal of Clinical Psychology,* 1970, **26,** 525–532.

Lewinsohn, P. M., Weinstein, M. S., & Shaw, D. A. Depression: A clinical-research approach. In R. D. Rubin & C. M. Frank (Eds.), *Advances in behavior therapy 1968.* New York: Academic Press, 1969. Pp. 231–240.

Liberman, R. P. Behavioral approaches to family and couple therapy. *American Journal of Orthopsychiatry,* 1970, **40,** 106–118.

Liberman, R. P., DeRisi, W. J., King, L. W., & Austin, N. A clinician's guide to personal effectiveness training. Unpublished manuscript, BAM Project, Dynard Mental Health Center, 1973.

Liberman, R. P., & Raskin, D. E. Depression: A behavioral formulation. *Archives of General Psychiatry,* 1971, **24,** 515–523.

Liberman, R. P., & Roberts, J. Contingency management of neurotic depression and marital disharmony. In H. J. Eysenck (Ed.), *Case histories in behavior therapy*. London: Routledge & Kegan, 1974, in press.

Libet, J., & Lewinsohn, P. M. The concept of social skill with special references to the behavior of depressed persons. *Journal of Consulting and Clinical Psychology,* 1973, **40,** 304–312.

Libet, J., Lewinsohn, P. M., & Javorek, F. The construct of social skill: An empirical study of several measures on temporal stability, internal structure, validity, and situational generalizability. Mimeo, University of Oregon, 1973.

Lubin, B. Adjective checklists for the measurement of depression. *Archives of General Psychiatry,* 1965, **12,** 57–62.

Lubin, B. *Manual for the Depression Adjective Check Lists.* San Diego: Education and Industrial Testing Service, 1967.

MacPhillamy, D. J., & Lewinsohn, P. M. The Pleasant Events Schedule. Mimeo, University of Oregon, 1971.

MacPhillamy, D. J., & Lewinsohn, P. M. The structure of reported reinforcement. Mimeo, University of Oregon, 1972. (a)

MacPhillamy, D. J., & Lewinsohn, P. M. Measurement of reinforcing events. *Proceedings, 80th Annual Convention, American Psychological Association,* 1972, **7,** 399–400. (b)

MacPhillamy, D. J., & Lewinsohn, P. M. A scale for the measurement of positive reinforcement. Mimeo, University of Oregon, 1973. (a)

MacPhillamy, D. J., & Lewinsohn, P. M. Studies on the measurement of human reinforcement and on the relationship between positive reinforcement and depression. Mimeo, University of Oregon, 1973. (b)

Maier, S. F., Seligman, M. E. P., & Solomon, R. L. Pavlovian fear conditioning and learned helplessness. In B. A. Campbell & R. M. Church (Eds.), *Punishment.* New York: Appleton, 1969. Pp. 299–343.

Mendels, J., & Cochran, C. The nosology of depressions: The endogenous-reactive concept. *American Journal of Psychiatry,* 1968, **124** (May Suppl.), 1–11.

Miller, W. R., & Seligman, M. E. P. Depression and the perception of reinforcement. *Journal of Abnormal Psychology,* 1973, **82,** 62–73.

Mowbray, R. M. The Hamilton Rating Scale for depression: A factor analysis. *Psychological Medicine,* 1972, **2,** 272–280.

Overall, J. E. Dimensions of manifest depression. *Journal of Psychiatric Research,* 1962, **1,** 239–245.

Paul, G. L. Strategy of outcome research in psychotherapy. *Journal of Consulting Psychology,* 1967, **31,** 109–118.

Paykel, E. S., Myers, J. K., Dienelt, M. N., Klerman, G. L., Lindenthal, J. J., & Pepper, M. P. Life events and depression. *Archives of General Psychiatry,* 1969, **21,** 753–760.

Paykel, E. S., Weissman, M., Prusoff, B. H., & Tonks, C. M. Dimensions of social adjustment in depressed women. *Journal of Nervous and Mental Disease,* 1971, **152,** 158–172.

Pfeiffer, J. W., & Jones, J. E. *Handbook of structured experiences for human relations training.* Iowa City, Iowa: University Associates Press, 1971.

Reisinger, J. J. The treatment of "Anxiety-Depression" via positive reinforcement and response cost. *Journal of Applied Behavior Analysis,* 1972, **5,** 125–130.

Robinson, J. C., & Lewinsohn, P. M. Behavior modification of speech characteristics in a chronically depressed man. *Behavior Therapy,* 1973, **4,** 150–152. (a)

Robinson, J. C., & Lewinsohn, P. M. Experimental analysis of a technique based on the Premack Principle changing verbal behavior of depressed individuals. *Psychological Reports,* 1973, **32,** 199–210. (b)

Rosenthal, S. H., & Klerman, G. L. Content and consistency in the endogenous depressive pattern. *British Journal of Psychiatry,* 1966, **112,** 471–484.

Schachter, S., & Singer, J. E. Cognitive, social and physiological determinants of emotional state. *Psychological Review,* 1962, **69,** 379–399.

Schwab, J. J., Bialow, M. R., Clemmons, R. S., & Holzer, C. E. The affective symptomatology in medical inpatients. *Psychosomatics,* 1966, **7,** 214–217.

Schwab, J. J., Clemmons, R. S., Bialow, M., Duggan, V., & Davis, B. A study of somatic symptomatology of depression in medical inpatients. *Psychosomatics,* 1965, **6,** 273–277.

Seitz, F. C. A behavior modification approach to depression: A case study. *Psychology,* 1971, **8,** 58–63.

Seligman, M. E. P. Fall into learned helplessness. *Psychology Today,* 1973, **7,** 43–49. (b)

Seligman, M. E. P. *Helplessness.* San Francisco: Freeman, 1974, in press.

Seligman, M. E. P., Maier, S. F., & Solomon, R. L. Unpredictable and uncontrollable aversive events. In F. R. Brush (Ed.), *Aversive conditioning and learning.* New York: Academic Press, 1971. Pp. 347–400.

Shaffer, M., & Lewinsohn, P. M. Interpersonal behaviors in the home of depressed versus nondepressed psychiatric and normal controls: A test of several hypotheses. Paper presented at the meeting of the Western Psychological Association, April 1971. (Mimeo, University of Oregon, 1971).

Skinner, B. F. *Science and human behavior.* New York: Free Press, 1953.

Stewart, R. C. The differential effects of positive and negative social reinforcement upon depressed and non-depressed subjects. Unpublished master's thesis, University of Oregon, 1968.

Strupp, H. H. *Psychotherapy and the modification of abnormal behavior.* New York: McGraw-Hill, 1971.

Stuart, R. B. Casework treatment of depression viewed as an interpersonal disturbance. *Social Work,* 1967, **12,** 27–36.

Stuart, R. B. Operant-interpersonal treatment of marital discord. *Journal of Consulting and Clinical Psychology,* 1969, **33,** 675–682.

Taulbee, E. S., & Wright, H. W. A psychosocial-behavioral model for therapeutic intervention. In C. D. Spielberger (Ed.), *Current topics in clinical and community psychology.* Vol. 3. New York: Academic Press, 1971. Pp. 53–94.

Todd, F. J. Coverant control of self-evaluative responses in the treatment of depression: A new use of an old principle. *Behavior Therapy,* 1972, **3,** 91–94.

Wanderer, Z. W. Existential depression treated by desensitization of phobias: Strategy and transcript. *Journal of Behavior Therapy and Experimental Psychiatry,* 1972, **3,** 111–116.

Wechsler, H., Grosser, G., & Busfield, B. The depression rating scale: A quantitative approach to the assessment of depressive symptomatology. *Archives of General Psychiatry,* 1963, **9,** 334–343.

Weiss, R. L., Hops, H., & Patterson, G. R. A framework for conceptualizing marital conflict. Paper presented at the fourth annual International Conference on Behavior Modification, Banff, Alberta, March 1972.

Weissman, M. M., Paykel, E. S., & Klerman, G. L. The depressed woman as mother. *Social Psychiatry,* 1972, **7,** 98–108.

Weissman, M. M., Paykel, E. S., Siegel, R., & Klerman, G. L. The social role performance of depressed women: A comparison with a normal sample. *American Journal of Orthopsychiatry,* 1971, **41,** 390–405.

Weissman, M. M., & Siegel, R. The depressed woman and her rebellious adolescent. *Social Casework,* 1972, **53,** 563–570.

Williams, J. G., Barlow, D. H., & Agras, W. S. Behavioral measurement of severe depression. *Archives of General Psychiatry,* 1972, **72,** 330–337.

Winokur, G. The types of affective disorders. *Journal of Nervous and Mental Disease,* 1973, **156,** 82–96.

Wolpe, J. *The practice of behavior therapy.* Oxford: Pergamon, 1969.

Wolpe, J. Neurotic depression: Experimental analog, clinical syndromes, and treatment. *American Journal of Psychotherapy,* 1971, **25,** 362–368.

Wolpe, J., & Lazarus, A. A. *Behavior therapy techniques.* Oxford: Pergamon, 1966.

Zung, W. W. K. A self-rating depression scale. *Archives of General Psychiatry,* 1965, **12,** 63–70.

BEHAVIORAL TREATMENTS OF PHOBIC AND OBSESSIVE-COMPULSIVE DISORDERS: A CRITICAL APPRAISAL

ISAAC MARKS
Institute of Psychiatry
De Crespigny Park, Denmark Hill
London, England

I. INTRODUCTION

This review deals mainly with developments from 1970 onward. Conceptual issues, terminology, and human analogue experiments are considered, and clinical treatment studies are described in detail. An overview of the present status of the field together with suggestions for future research is then presented. Animal work is omitted, as it will be described in Volume II of this series. The overall framework recognizes that, bar a few important exceptions, effective techniques to reduce fear usually involve exposure of the subject in some way to the distressing situation until he adapts, and that most distinctions between desensitization, flooding, and other methods of fear reduction are variations on the theme of exposure. The explosion of work in this field dictates selection of a small sample of experiments to illustrate the general trend, and many useful studies regrettably cannot be referred to here. The volume of experimentation can be judged from the fact that at least 30% of *all* reports on behavior therapy in several journals concern phobias and obsessions.

In this area terms like avoidance and fear are sometimes used interchangeably, whereas at other times fear refers solely to autonomic accompaniments of stress reactions. Avoidance is often assumed to follow the rules governing instrumental conditioning, and fear those of classical conditioning. Such a distinction is useful, but on the other hand a global term is also needed to describe the syndrome of withdrawal responses and their autonomic concomitants. This emotional response syndrome (Averill, Opton, & Lazarus, 1969) is commonly labeled as "fear" in animals and man. Fear, like other emotions, has many component reactions, which can occur concurrently or sequentially and are often poorly correlated with one another. It is an organized emotional response syndrome across three main dimensions—cognitive-subjective, motor-behavioral, and physiological (Lader & Marks, 1972).

Terminologically a distinction must be made between habituation, adaptation, and extinction of fear. Habituation is commonly used to describe response decrement after repeated presentation of the "to-be-conditioned" CS before conditioning. Adaptation commonly refers to the process by which one gets rid of undesirable responses to a stimulus by presenting it repeatedly. Both habituation and adaptation are usually thought of as short-lived effects. Extinction generally refers to more durable changes. Extinction is the process of taking a conditioned stimulus which had been previously paired with an unconditioned stimulus to produce a conditioned response, presenting that stimulus in the absence of the unconditioned stimulus, and observing the withering away of the conditioned response. In the clinical situation, where it is usually an unproved assumption that there has been any conditioning of fear, it is impossible to know which term is most appropriate to use in describing exposure treatment. Neither adaptation nor habituation need imply conditioning, but they usually describe more short-lived effects than the lasting improvements found after exposure treatments. Yet another problem applies to habituation. Response decrement to repeated phobic stimuli is directly proportional to stimulus strength instead of inversely proportional as for habituated responses (Van Egeren, 1971).

A. Exposure: Toward a Unifying Theory of Fear Reduction (Marks, 1973b)

There are numerous analogue therapeutic studies concerning fear, though hardly any deal with obsessions. Among the many techniques that reduce fear are desensitization, flooding (implosion), prolonged exposure, aversion relief, paradoxical intention, modeling, operant shaping, cognitive rehearsal, behavioral rehearsal, coping and self-instructional methods, and sedative drugs. When many methods appear to have a similar effect, it is natural to search for a common mechanism of action, and an important mechanism shared by all these methods is exposure of the frightened subject to a frightening situation until he acclimatizes, a process that could be called adaptation, but has also been termed extinction or habituation. The theory of reciprocal inhibition contains within it the principle of exposure, the essence of the method being approach to the phobic situation in fantasy or *in vivo* during a "counteracting" response such as relaxation. Flooding involves rapid approach into the phobic situation. Operant shaping or conditioning of fear reduction describes systematic reward of the subject's steady approach toward the frightening situation; it is obvious that during operant treatment the therapist does not shape behavior away from the phobic object. An integral part of operant shaping thus consists of graduated exposure.

The same applies to treatment by modeling. Studies such as those of Bandura, Blanchard, and Ritter (1969) and Ritter (1968) demonstrated that when a subject observes a model entering a frightening situation, either on film or in real life, he becomes more able to do so himself. As with operant shaping, the modeling procedure inevitably contains a crucial element of exposure. In the experiment by Bandura *et al.* the live model slowly approached a snake while being observed by a subject with a snake phobia, who was then encouraged and cajoled into executing the same task. The procedure was essentially one of exposure *in vivo* after a model. Procedures such as cognitive rehearsal also reduce phobic anxiety (Hart,

1966). Simply preparing a tape recording to instruct the patient how to overcome his fears can have therapeutic value. In this process, too, the patient rehearses imagery concerning phobias. Paradoxical intention (Frankl, 1974) is like exposure *in vivo,* in that the subject is asked to expose himself to precisely that situation he fears.

With aversion relief, shocks are associated with the offset of a period of exposure to a phobic object. In the use of sedative drugs, either intravenously with methohexitone (Friedman & Lipsedge, 1971; Mawson, 1970) or orally with diazepam (Marks, Viswanathan, & Lipsedge, 1972), the drug is used to relax the patient during exposure to phobic scenes or situations. Most drug effects in this area incorporate an element of exposure. Tricyclic drugs such as imipramine in agoraphobia (Klein, 1964) and school phobia (Gittelman-Klein & Klein, 1971) have also been combined with firm insistence on the patient contacting the phobic situation. A synergistic interaction was posited in which antidepressants relieve the affective component of the disorder and thus facilitate exposure to the phobic situation.

Although many of the newer methods of treatment can be seen as acting through a common mechanism, it is still by no means clear how best to apply this mechanism of exposure. We know that prolonged exposure *in vivo* for several hours at a time is usually effective in reducing phobias in durable fashion. It is possible that the important point about exposure treatments is the way they encourage the patient to interact with the phobic stimulus until he has learned to deal with it, whatever "learned to deal with it" implies operationally. Anxiety during exposure may simply be an inevitable and unfortunate by-product of contact rather than the prime cause of change. This is suggested by repeated failure to find that anxiety during flooding sessions facilitates improvement (Marks, Boulougouris, & Marset, 1971a; Mathews & Shaw, 1973; Watson & Marks, 1971).

On the other hand, it could be that anxiety evocation can enhance therapy under certain circumstances. It is unknown whether, if anxiety can be facilitatory, it should be relevant or irrelevant to the phobia. Watson and Marks (1971) demonstrated that both relevant and irrelevant fear cues significantly reduced phobias but that they seemed to act through different mechanisms. The experiments by Meichenbaum (1971a) with volunteers suggest that subjects might be immunized to stress, including phobias, by deliberately subjecting them to stresses that are not connected with their particular phobias. If this is substantiated in patients, then the most beneficial results in the long run might be through exposure, not simply to the phobic objects alone but also to other stresses, in a manner that teaches a general skill in coping with unpleasant experiences. It might be that the most wide-ranging improvement would be obtained not simply by confrontation with the phobic situation without allowing avoidance so that avoidance is extinguished, but also by adding deliberate anxiety concerning the phobic object. This serves to extinguish subjective discomfort as well as avoidance, and in addition by inducing irrelevant anxiety and other unpleasant emotions in order to teach the patient how to cope with other disagreeable affects. Phobic volunteers overcame their fear even better when desensitization was combined with deliberate attempts by the subject to manage the discomfort induced by electric shocks (Meichenbaum & Cameron, 1974b).

The message may be that the more discomfort the patient is exposed to, up to a certain point, the more he learns to tolerate. The boundary conditions under which this applies would require much work to delineate. Under certain conditions exposure sensitizes the subject instead of habituating him, of which one example is shell shock in soldiers under bombardment. Exposure to an event can be "traumatic" and induce a phobia, or it may lead a person to "gird his loins" and emerge strengthened. Our problem is to unravel the factors that make "one man's meat another man's poison."

The exposure hypothesis does not explain all phenomena concerning fears and obsessions. It raises the fundamental question of why exposure to noxious stimuli should lead to phobias under certain circumstances, but to elimination of those phobias under others. Duration of exposure is one crucial variable; other things being equal, very brief periods of exposure might actually be sensitizing and long periods most therapeutic. Another problem is that, during exposure, patients can rehearse internal avoidance responses and say to themselves, "I want to get out, I want it to end, help." However, *avoidance* alone clearly cannot sustain phobias, since the classic and effective desensitization procedure requires a subject to terminate (avoid) his fearful image as soon as he feels anxiety. During *in vivo* exposure by agoraphobics by shaping (successive approximation) subjects were told to escape when discomfort was minimal, yet improvement occurred (Crowe, Marks, Agras, & Leitenberg, 1972; Everaerd, Rijken, & Emmelkamp, 1973). If a simplistic model of response prevention had applied, such subjects should have worsened. That they did not implies a complex relationship between attitude and behavior. With the "right" cognitive set, exposure with avoidance can be therapeutic which with a different attitude could be disastrous.

The uncomfortable fact remains that a small minority of patients in the author's experience have exposed themselves to the phobic situation for many hours at a time without, as far as one could tell, rehearsing covert escape or avoidance, yet without any improvement at all. Clearly, exposure per se is not always sufficient, and other unknown influences are sometimes needed to transform exposure from a traumatic to a healing experience. The exposure hypothesis also does not explain another important set of phenomena—the relief of fears and other problems after abreaction, not only of fear, but also of anger, guilt, and other affects. Unfortunately experimental data in this area are sadly lacking.

Perhaps the reader will forgive an irreverent cartoon to illustrate the common pathway by which most methods of fear reduction seem to work. Our height-phobic gentleman in Fig. 1 ultimately has to climb to the top of the ladder to get his book—entitled "How to Overcome Your Fear of Heights." He can be asked to close his eyes and relax and imagine himself on the first rung of the ladder repeatedly until he gets used to it, after which he can relax once more and then imagine himself on the second rung of the ladder, until finally he has ascended the complete hierarchy of steps in his mind's eye (desensitization in imagination). This could be followed by further relaxation and carrying out in real life slowly what he has already accomplished in imagination (desensitization *in vivo*). He can try to do the same thing without relaxation both in fantasy and *in vivo* (cognitive rehearsal, *in vivo* facilitation, graded exposure, behavioral rehearsal). Each

Fig. 1. The common pathway for most forms of fear reduction.

time our man progresses up the ladder either in fantasy or in real life, we can praise him or give some other reward (operant shaping or conditioning, successive approximation, reinforced practice). He can watch a film of some other person slowly going up the ladder either relaxed (vicarious desensitization) or not (symbolic modeling), or have the therapist precede him slowly up the ladder while encouraging the patient to follow suit (participant modeling, contact desensitization).

Alternatively our height-phobic gentleman can be requested to imagine himself standing right at the top of the ladder while swaying, trembling, and feeling anxious, but remaining there until he feels better in fantasy (flooding or exposure in fantasy, implosion, high-intensity stimulation). While imagining the scenes, he can be asked to elaborate these aloud, with occasional prompts by the therapist (guided fantasy). He can be asked to summon up his courage, to take a deep breath and rush up the ladder, remaining at the top and sweating it out until he feels all right (flooding or exposure *in vivo,* paradoxical intention, Arugamama of morita psychotherapy, anxiety-provoking psychotherapy). One could bring many other height phobics into the same room, and ask them all to proceed steadily up other ladders (group exposure *in vivo*).

Yet another way for our man in Fig. 1 to be induced to climb the ladder is to give himself, or be given, shocks until he puts his foot on the first rung, at which point the shocks cease (aversion relief), the procedure being repeated until he ascends the entire ladder. Equally he can be taught to learn stoicism by shocking himself, enduring the pain, and then testing himself out in the stressful situation of ascending the ladder (coping, stress inoculation, anxiety management training), perhaps while telling himself that he can cope, that he can do it, that he must do it (self-instruction). The reader can doubtless conjure up many additional variations on the theme of persuading a phobic to approach his phobic situation.

B. Exposure Variants and Terminology

These were reviewed recently in detail elsewhere (Marks, 1972). A host of terms confuses the area, but exposure variants can be ordered along a continuum of approach to distressing situations. At one end is *flooding,* in which the confrontation tends to be more sudden, more prolonged, and with greater emotion. Although in flooding there is some grading of approach, this is less than in *desensitization.* When exposure to a phobic situation is slow, graded and brief, with but minimum tension and with some contrasting experience such as relaxation or meditation, then the term desensitization is more appropriate. Commonly the approach is somewhere between these two extremes, and the choice of terms such as flooding or desensitization becomes rather arbitrary, so that the label "exposure" is preferable. A summary of the main varieties of exposure treatment appears in Table I to provide a guide to the rest of this chapter. It displays at a glance the formidable number of research issues involved in this field. The babel of terms in the literature requires further clarification.

TABLE I

Forms of Exposure Treatment

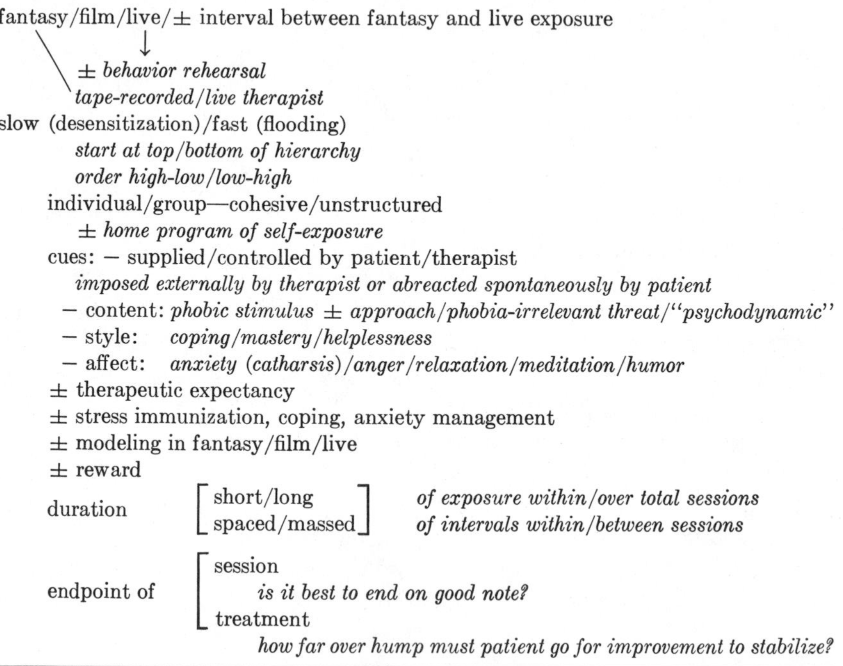

fantasy/film/live/± interval between fantasy and live exposure
↓
± *behavior rehearsal*
tape-recorded/live therapist
slow (desensitization)/fast (flooding)
start at top/bottom of hierarchy
order high-low/low-high
individual/group—cohesive/unstructured
± *home program of self-exposure*
cues: – supplied/controlled by patient/therapist
imposed externally by therapist or abreacted spontaneously by patient
– content: *phobic stimulus ± approach/phobia-irrelevant threat/"psychodynamic"*
– style: *coping/mastery/helplessness*
– affect: *anxiety (catharsis)/anger/relaxation/meditation/humor*
± therapeutic expectancy
± stress immunization, coping, anxiety management
± modeling in fantasy/film/live
± reward
duration [short/long — *of exposure within/over total sessions*; spaced/massed — *of intervals within/between sessions*]
endpoint of [session — *is it best to end on good note?*; treatment — *how far over hump must patient go for improvement to stabilize?*]

Exposure in REAL LIFE (*in vivo,* in practice) has assumed many forms. *Counter-phobic* treatment (Strahley, 1965) denoted a method of flooding in real life in which snake-phobic subjects were pressured into holding a live snake for two 6-minute periods without the benefit of successive approximation. Watson, Gaind, and Marks (1971) called a similar method *prolonged exposure,* during which a phobic patient was in continuous contact with the real phobic object for up to 2½ hours. When this occurs with several patients together, it is termed *group exposure in vivo* (Hand, Lamontagne, & Marks, 1974) or *group confrontation* (Zane, 1972).

Massed practice refers to repeated practicing of any behavior without much rest between trials. Flooding is sometimes described as a special form of massed practice. *Arugamama* (Kora, 1968) is a Japanese word for exposure to the real phobic situation without avoidance. *Paradoxical intention* (Frankl, 1974) indicates treatment in which the patient is asked to exaggerate his fears deliberately.

Exposure *in vivo* of a graded kind has been called *participation, participant modeling,* and *contact desensitization* (Bandura *et al.,* 1969; Lick & Bootzin, 1970; Litvak, 1969; Murphy & Bootzin, 1973; Rimm & Mahoney, 1969; Ritter, 1968). These refer to a subject slowly coming into contact with a real phobic situation, usually after watching a model, then doing the same himself. Without modeling, graded exposure *in vivo* has been called *practical retraining* or simply *practice* (Leitenberg, Agras, Edwards, Thomson, & Wincze, 1970). Graded exposure *in vivo* which is accompanied by contingent reward is termed *shaping, operant conditioning, reinforced practice* or successive approximation (Everaerd *et al.,* 1973; Leitenberg & Callahan, 1973; Crowe, Mark, Agras, & Leitenberg, 1972).

Deconditioning describes the reduction of anxiety in hospitalized soldiers who were subjected to repeated air raids (Rudolf, 1961). The soldiers were moved in stages from the more protected ground floor to the first and then the second floor of the hospital. Saul, Rome, and Leuser (1946) called a similar approach in soldiers with combat fatigue *desensitization;* patients saw graded war films using their own volume controls for sound.

Exposure IN FANTASY has also been very varied. *Implosion* refers to continuous prolonged exposure in fantasy, usually with much anxiety (Stampfl, 1967). An alternative term is *flooding in fantasy* or *in imagination. High-intensity stimulation* (de Moor, 1970; Rachman, 1969) denotes implosion in man and flooding in animals.

Reactive inhibition describes presentations to a patient of imaginal phobic stimuli from a hierarchy for 30 seconds at a time with the instruction that subjects attend to their sensations accompanying anxiety (Calef & MacLean, 1970). Similar procedures have also been called *catharsis* (Melamed, 1969), *programmed fantasy* (Crowder & Thornton, 1970), and *graduated extinction* (Guilani, 1972). In *prolonged exposure in fantasy* (D'Zurilla, Wilson, & Nelson, 1973) phobic scenes from a hierarchy were imagined for up to 8 minutes at a time with instructions to experience their feeling naturally. Repeated exposure to phobic slides has been called *cognitive desensitization* (Sushinsky & Bootzin, 1970). *Counter-conditioning* or *reciprocal inhibition* (Wolpe, 1958) usually implies intermittent imagining of phobic scenes while having a contrasting experience, such as relaxation or assertion; when the contrasting experience is a rewarding scene, this is called *covert reinforcement* (Blanchard & Draper, 1973; Wisocki, 1970, 1973).

With *induced anxiety* (Ascough, 1972; Noonan, 1971; Sipprelle, 1967), patients are relaxed under hypnosis and encouraged systematically to experience anxiety and other affects to the full, meanwhile associating these with past events. The process continues until the emotion subsides or, if time does not permit this, is terminated by suggestions to relax. The method seems a special form of catharsis or abreaction. Related approaches cited by Schutz (1967) include *guided fantasy, imagining or daydream* (Desoille, cited in Schutz, 1967; Wolpin, 1969), and initiated symbol projection (Leuner, cited in Schutz, 1967). In implosive-expressive therapy (Serber, Goldstein, Piaget, & Kort, 1969) the patient not only talks about his fantasies, but also acts them out in a controlled setting, a method that was also used by Lowen.

Other techniques that involve confrontation of the patient with real or simulated distressing situations are *assertive training, behavior rehearsal,* and *in vivo facilitation* of flooding (Stadter, 1973; Suinn, 1972). These methods are part of the traditional stock-in-trade of *psychodrama.*

Stress inoculation, stress immunization, cognitive modification and insight, and *anxiety management training* (Meichenbaum, 1971a,c; Suinn, 1974) are forms of coping training, or the learning of stoicism, either directly in the phobic situation or with another stressful experience.

C. Human Analogue Work

Analogue studies usually use volunteers who happen to have a fear for which they would not normally seek professional aid. The intensity of fear in these studies varies widely. Some select only those few who are most handicapped out of a large screened population, while others take almost all comers, most of whom have trivial or no fears. The greater the demands in a standard frightening task, the fewer will refuse and thus be called phobic (Miller & Bernstein, 1972). Reports usually concern psychology students, especially women, who appear to be the "white rats" of clinical psychology. These represent but a small section of the general population, i.e., intelligent, middle-class (usually white) students. This limits the conclusions that can be drawn. Moreover, volunteers who are not sufficiently distressed by a fear to seek treatment until sought out by a keen experimenter, differ in important respects from psychiatric patients with severe phobias or obsessions.

1. Differences between Volunteers and Patients

Volunteers usually have less intense and less extensive fears, more stable personalities, and fewer other psychiatric symptoms. Table II, from Marks (1969), summarizes some important differences between several patient populations and normals. Similar questionnaire data were also noted by Olley and McAllister (1974). Specific phobic patients are most like normal populations, but complex agoraphobic and obsessive-compulsive syndromes often differ greatly. Not only are their phobias likely to be more intense and extensive, but commonly associated problems like free-floating anxiety and disrupted social relationships confound treatment programs. In some patients their presenting psychopathology is the least of their difficulties. A phobia or obsession can simply be a respectable admission ticket for treatment of some other problem that only emerges later, e.g., frigidity, loneliness, or depression. Even specific phobics may present

TABLE II

Summary of Clinical and Psychophysiological Data[a,b]

	Anxiety States	Agoraphobias	Social Phobias	Animal Phobias	Normals
% Women	50	75	50	95	50
Onset age	25	24	19	*4	—
Treatment age	36	32	27	30	—
Overt anxiety (0–6 scale)	2.6	2.0	2.0	*0.4	0
Modified Cornell	—	34	21	*13	10
Neuroticism	**37	30	29	*21	20
Extroversion	**14	19	19	24	25
GSR					
Spontaneous fluctuations	36	32	33	*12	6
Habituation rate	29	39	39	*68	64
Resting forearm blood flow	**4.8	2.9	2.6	2.2	2.0
Eyeblink CR acquisition	11	15	19	***21	14

[a] From Marks (1969, p. 109). Data are composite of several studies, some unpublished. Main sources are:

Clinical variables: Gelder and Marks (1966), Lader (1966), and Kelly (1966).

Questionnaire scores: Gelder *et al.* (1967) and Kelly (1966).

Psychophysiological data: GSR: Lader *et al.* (1967) and Lader (1966).

Forearm blood flow: Kelly (1966).

Eyeblink conditioning: Martin *et al.* (1969) and Martin (unpublished).

[b] *n* Varies from 18 to 84 in different cells.

* = differs significantly from other psychiatric groups;

** = differs significantly from all groups;

*** = differs significantly from all groups except social phobias.

for treatment because they happen to be depressed at that time rather than because of their long-standing phobia. Similarly, homosexual men who seek help in changing their orientation tend to have other neurotic problems and in that respect resemble other neurotics more than nonclinical homosexuals (Feldman, 1973).

There are several reasons why controlled studies have been carried out more frequently with volunteers than with patients. It is obviously easier to study a captive volunteer student population with clear-cut isolated difficulties than it is to mount controlled treatment trials of psychiatric patients who have complicated problems. Furthermore, volunteer studies are usually completed in a much shorter time, especially since adequate follow-up is exceptional. Historically, many psychology training centers developed divorced from psychiatric clinics, making it difficult for psychologists to have access to severely disturbed populations. Finally, rivalries between the professions of psychology and psychiatry reduced access of psychologists to patients.

Granted these difficulties, the differences between patient and volunteer populations outweigh the overlap so much that analogue results cannot be assumed to apply automatically to patients. Progress in treating severe pathology would accelerate if more workers dealt with the sobering realities of clinical settings. Badly needed are more investigations on populations of psychiatric patients selected for homogeneity of problems, using closely defined techniques with adequate follow-up. Such studies are expensive in time, effort, and money. Fortunately, the false dichotomy of being *either* a researcher *or* a clinician is breaking down in a few centers, and more examples are appearing of that rare hybrid breed, the research-clinician.

Cautionary notes on the limited value of analogue studies were sounded by McGlynn, Williamson, and Davis (1973), who found that desensitization decreased avoidance in only two out of eight "genuinely fearful" subjects. Cooper, Furst, and Bridger (1969) found that some subjects would hold snakes after merely being told to hold them and to act unafraid, and argued that "treatments" for curing fears of snakes and rats might be irrelevant to the treatment of clinical phobias. In line with these warnings, McReynolds (1970) found no difference between the efficacy of desensitization, relaxation, and psychotherapy in the treatment of anxious psychiatric inpatients, while Watkins and Davidson (1970) found that cognitive rehearsal was ineffective in decreasing stress responses in psychiatric patients.

2. Problems in Experimental Designs

a. Avoidance Tests. A recurrent weakness in many designs is a failure to measure sufficient aspects of fear behavior. Many rely unduly on avoidance tests alone, even when other measures of fear may reveal different trends. Undue reliance on any one measure of fear can be misleading, and an avoidance test in an experimental situation is often but a poor guide to performance in more natural situations. Even chronically crippled patients can be induced to enter their phobic situation or to desist from rituals during a brief test, but this has debatable relevance to subsequent performance outside of the hospital. Of 21 severely agoraphobic patients, 7 managed to complete a stringent behavioral test task they had not done for years before, yet by 3 days later none had voluntarily exposed themselves to further similar situations in everyday life, and anticipatory anxiety remained as before (Hand *et al.*, 1974). Of 12 severely compulsive patients who failed a behavioral test before treatment, all passed the test after 2 hours of exposure *in vivo,* though improvement on other scales was highly variable (Lipsedge, 1974).

A noteworthy lack of correlation in obsessive-compulsive patients between outcome on behavioral avoidance tests and other measures was also noted by Rachman, Marks, and Hodgson (1973), though the fear thermometer during the test did correlate significantly with five other measures. This was also true in phobic patients (Gillan & Rachman, 1974). Treatment can improve uncomplicated behavioral avoidance without generalizing to more difficult situations. There is a need for both weak and strong behavioral avoidance tests, perhaps a weak one in hospital and the strong one alone in the patient's home environment. A behavioral checklist completed by a relative might be a time-saving compromise.

Change in performance on avoidance tests can occur without active treatment. In several analogue studies, control subjects who were simply given an avoidance test, sometimes followed by a procedure such as listening to music, were able to touch the phobic object after having previously failed to do so (Crowder & Thornton, 1970). Up to one-quarter did this in the studies of Fazio (1970)—6 out of 23; Layne (1970)—6 out of 24; and Barrett (1969)—3 out of 12. At times controls changed in other measures of fear; e.g., the controls of Willis and Edwards (1969) who were treated "by vague discussion" showed improvement in self report by follow-up, at which time they were not significantly different from the experimental groups treated by flooding and by desensitization. This emphasizes the importance of adequate measures of fear, both at the end of treatment and at follow-up. Confidence in experimental results in this area is possible only when there is a consistent pattern of change across measures and across time. This is all too rare in the literature.

b. Follow-up. Another defect in many studies is the absence of a reasonable length of follow-up. Often but a few minutes or, at most, weeks elapse before final testing, whereas reasonable stability of changes can be judged only after a minimum follow-up of 6 months, at which time measures are needed of several modalities of fear behavior. Sometimes interest centers on very short-term effects, or other constraints dictate a crossover design, in which follow-up is of limited value. These apart, most investigations adopt parallel designs, and conclusions from such studies would be strengthened by better follow-up measures.

c. *Control Groups*. A common misconception in analogue studies concerns the role of control groups. The term control simply implies a contrasting condition without the variable under consideration. It does *not* necessarily mean an untreated or a placebo group. What constitutes an adequate control group for one question is inappropriate for another. If the problem under examination is the role of relaxation, only two groups need to be contrasted, one with and one without relaxation. If the point at issue is the duration of exposure, then a minimum of two groups with varying durations are required. Untreated control groups are useful for answering questions about the role of therapeutic set, while placebo control groups help understanding of the part played by such factors as therapist attention and therapeutic commitment by the client. The more contrasting groups there are in an experiment, each designed to answer a specific question about a therapeutic ingredient, the more detailed the conclusions which might be possible from the study concerned. However, in an experiment on duration of exposure it would be meaningful to sacrifice a no-treatment control group for an extra group with a different duration of exposure, thus enabling more to be learned about that key variable, rather than about a factor which is peripheral for that particular experiment.

II. THERAPEUTIC COMPONENTS

Any treatment procedure contains several ingredients of varying importance for outcome. A major research thrust aims at a fractional distillation of treatments into their various components, some of which are inert, others facilitatory, and yet others crucial for the production of improvement. This section will review such work, only a small part of which has been with patients. Most research here concerns analogue studies of normal populations, and discussion in this area will thus deal with volunteers more than with patients. Survey of the literature is difficult primarily because it is so vast. However, reports at times bury straightforward ideas in abstruse argot and esoteric acronyms which stricter editorial control could help to simplify. Readers who are more interested in clinical than in research issues might prefer to skip this section and go straight to Section III: Studies in Patients on page 109.

A. Review of Controlled Exposure Studies in Volunteers

Tables IIIA and IIIB summarize most volunteer studies of fear reduction by exposure which included comparison with a control group. Excluded from these tables are groups which had systematic relaxation, modeling, or contingent praise together with the exposure. Two unavailable studies not in the table were mentioned by Jacobs and Wolpin (1971). In snake phobics, Donaldson (1969) found that implosion or coping imagery produced more approach than no treatment, whereas U. O. Evans (1968) noted that images of phobic approach, plus shocks to the hand, led to more approach than an untreated control condition.

The criterion for deciding whether exposure was effective in a given group varied of necessity. "Effective" indicates a significant or substantial improvement in that group. The chief criterion was the authors' report of a significant improvement from start to end of treatment, regardless of the comparison with control groups. Where this was unstated, other comments of the authors were taken as a guide, or the data were assessed arbitrarily; e.g., in the study by Mathews and Shaw (1973) the overall gain in hierarchy items was considered too small and transient to be of significance. The classification in these tables was made independently of the duration of treatment or other treatment variables. However, it can obviously be criticized because the data were sometimes unclear.

Granted some ambiguities in construction of these tables, they suggest several trends. First, the great majority of studies of exposure have been in fantasy. Only three were *in vivo,* and all these were effective in reducing fearful behavior. Seventeen studies of exposure in fantasy in Table IIIA and the two described by Jacobs *et al.* were effective in diminishing fear. Eleven reported that fantasy exposure was ineffective (Table IIIB). Second, duration of exposure seems important for outcome. On the average, compared to unsuccessful studies, effective exposure in fantasy had a much longer total duration of exposure across sessions (173 vs 70 minutes) and rather longer sessions (54 vs 33 minutes), but comparable durations of phobic scenes within sessions. Finally, most negative experiments utilized tape-recorded instructions (8 out of 11) while only 5 out of 17 successful studies had taped instructions.

An interactional model might reconcile many of these findings. The duration of exposure necessary to reduce fear might be increased when

TABLE IIIA

Controlled Volunteer Studies of Exposure, Excluding Groups with Relaxation, Modeling, or Contingent Praise
(STUDIES IN WHICH EXPOSURE WAS EFFECTIVE)

Author	Subjects: F = female, M = male	Phobia	Number Exposed	Scene Duration (min)	Session Duration (min)	Total Duration (min)	Treatment by Tape Recorder	Follow-up Duration (months)	Comments
In vivo									
Lopiccolo (1969)	F students	Snakes	24	1/3	30	14[a]	No	0	*In vivo* exposure superior to fantasy
Strahley (1965)	F students	Snakes	16	6	12	12	No	0	—
Sherman (1972)	F students	Swimming	27	10–20	10–20	60	No	1	—
In fantasy									
Wolpin and Raines (1966)	F inpatients	Snakes	2	2–30	30	90	No	1	Scenes re contact; not anxiety
Hogan and Kirchner (1967)	F students	Rats	21	40	40	40	No	0	—
Kirchner and Hogan (1966)	F students	Rats	16	40	40	40	Yes	0	—
Craighead (1971)	F students	Snakes	10	1/6	50	200	No	1	—
Crowder and Thornton (1970)	F students	Snakes	10		30	120	No	0	—
Hogan and Kirchner (1968)	F students	Snakes	10	60	60	60	No	0	—
Lott and Carrera (1971)	F students	Snakes	14	25	125	125	Yes	1	—
de Moor (1970)	M students	Snakes	9	20	20	80	No	6	Scenes re contact; not anxiety
Barrett (1969)	F, M students + public	Snakes	12	35–145 ($\bar{x}$ 75)	35–145 ($\bar{x}$ 75)	150	No	6	—

Schroeder and Hatzenbuehler (1973)	F students	Stage fright	11 −Shock, 11 +Shock,	50	50	200	Yes	0	+ Psychodynamic cues; implosion + shock = impl.
Calef and MacLean (1970)	M students	Stage fright	10	1/2	60	300	No	0	Scenes (very brief) = des. in
Mylar and Clement (1972)	M students	Stage fright	13	4	60	300	Yes	1	efficacy, very frightening
Prochaska (1971)	M students	Test anxiety	12 Symptom cues, 12 Dynamic cues, 12 Irrelevant anxiety cues	46	46	140	Yes	0	Test anxiety ↓ by symptom and dynamic cues, general anxiety ↓ by irrelevant anxiety cues
Dawley and Wenreich (1973)	M students	Test anxiety	12	30	30	150	No	1	Group implosion v. neutral scenes v. no treatment
D'Zurilla *et al.* (1973)	F students	Dead animals	9	8	60	240	No	0	Scenes re contact, not anxiety
Everaerd *et al.* (1973)	M, F phobic club members	Agoraphobia	7	5	90	540	No	3	—
Fazio (1970)	F public	Cockroaches	7	?	?	?	No	1	Implosion less effective than discussion + home *in vivo* experience
			MEAN:	26	54	173	5/17 taped		

[a] Exposure time.

TABLE IIIB

Controlled Volunteer Studies of Exposure, Excluding Groups with Relaxation, Modeling, or Contingent Praise
(STUDIES IN WHICH EXPOSURE WAS INEFFECTIVE)

Author	Subjects (students), F = female, M = male	Phobia	Number Exposed	Scene Duration (min)	Session Duration (min)	Total Duration (min)	Treatment by Tape Recorder	Follow-up Duration (months)	Comments
All in fantasy									
Hodgson *et al.* (1971)	F	Snakes	8	40	40	40	Yes	0	—
Hodgson and Rachman (1970)	F	Snakes	10	40	40	40	Yes	0	—
Lott and Carrera (1971)	F	Snakes	10	25	25	25	Yes	1	—
Mealiea and Nawas (1971)	F	Snakes	10	1–4	30	150	Yes	1	Every 1–4 min told to open eyes and see they had nothing to fear. *Ss* became less anxious
Rachman (1966)	F	Snakes	3	2	20	200	No	3	—
Kazdin (1973)	M, F	Snakes	16	1/4	15	30	No	3/4	Fantasy exposure + modeling more effective
Willis and Edwards (1969)	F	Mice	16	10–30	10–30 ($\bar{x}$ 17)	55	No	2	*Ss* improved, at follow-up not significantly different from desensitized or controls
Fazio (1970)	F	Cockroaches	6	29	29	87	Yes	2	—
Mathews and Shaw (1973)	F	Spiders	20	4 or 48	48	48	Yes	1	—
Layne (1970)	F	Rats	36	60	60	60	Yes	0	*Ss* became less anxious; suggestion had no significant effect
Orenstein (1972)	F	Rats	8	39	39	39	Yes	0	—
			MEAN:	25	33	70	8/11 taped		

treatment is in fantasy rather than in real life, by tape recorder rather than by a therapist, and intermittent rather than continuous. The shortest effective duration would then be associated with a combination of exposure in real life by a therapist who confronts the volunteer continuously with the phobic object, especially if the therapist models initial approach and praises the patient for progress achieved.

B. Duration of Exposure

Animal experiments (Baum, 1970; Rohrbaugh & Riccio, 1970; Rohrbaugh, Riccio, & Arthur, 1972) clearly indicate that duration of exposure to the CS is one crucial variable in the acquisition and extinction of fear. The same applies in man. Duration of exposure can refer to particular stimulus presentations, or to the total exposure time during any one session or over the whole course of treatment. Equally important might be the intervals between stimuli or between sessions. Another factor is the frequency of stimulus presentation. It is also relevant whether "longer" or "shorter" refers to seconds, minutes, hours, days, weeks, or months. Furthermore, there may be interactions between duration and intensity of fear during exposure. There are so many possibilities that only numerous systematic experiments can map out the area in detail. The scanty studies so far form but a rough guide.

Tables IIIA and IIIB indicated that controlled studies of exposure which produced significant fear reduction employed longer sessions and longer total time in treatment than did studies which were ineffective, but that duration of scenes within sessions seemed less important.

1. Spacing of Sessions

So far this has not seemed important for outcome. Spaced sessions of desensitization were not significantly different from distributed ones in test-anxious subjects (Marshitz, Almarza, Barra, & Medina, 1973) (two sessions daily over 5 days vs two sessions over 5 weeks). Over 2 days, longer sessions were not better than shorter ones in the test-anxious subjects of Hall and Hinkle (1972) (two 4-hour vs ten 45-minute sessions).

2. Within Sessions

a. Stimuli Longer Than 5 Minutes. Variations in visual exposure times to a phobic stimulus of less than an hour can significantly affect subsequent avoidance (B. V. Miller & Levis, 1971). Schoolgirls who were unable to touch a snake at pretest were assigned to either 0-, 15-, 30-, or 45-minute periods of live exposure, during which they were asked to record the snake's body and tongue activity as a device to focus their attention. At retest those who had received 15 minutes' exposure improved least in approach behavior. Exposure times of 30 and 45 minutes were more therapeutic.

An interaction between duration of exposure and level of arousing instructions was found by Mathews and Shaw (1973) in spider-fearful students. Over 72 minutes, six 8-minute sequences of taped exposure separated by 4-minute sequences of neutral material were better than a 48-minute identical sequence of exposure scenes. Massed exposure was only better when exposure scenes generated low rather than high arousal.

One report concerned exposure *in vivo* in agoraphobic patients (Stern & Marks, 1973a). Two hours of continuous exposure *in vivo* produced significantly greater improvement within and between sessions than did four half-hour sessions on the same afternoon which were separated by half-hours of neutral activity (see page 119). In uncontrolled studies of specific phobic patients (Watson *et al.,* 1971) 2–3 hours of continuous exposure *in vivo* were highly effective in reducing fear up to 3 months follow-up (see page 118).

b. Stimuli Shorter Than a Minute. Several stimulus durations of less than a minute were examined by Ross and Proctor (1973) during desensitization in fantasy of snake-phobic students. "Longer" durations of exposure scenes in fantasy producd the most effects posttest and at 1-month follow-up (30 vs 12 vs 3 seconds). Single 30-second exposures to hierarchy items appeared best for both avoidance and subjective anxiety, and better than shorter multiple exposures.

Similar stimulus durations were examined by Watts (1971, 1974) in mixed agoraphobic patients and insect phobic volunteers. Forty-five-second scenes were only slightly better than 15-second ones (Watts, 1974), but 30-second scenes were significantly better than 5-second scenes for high hierarchy items, the effect being both during treatment and for some days after treatment. In a similar population (Watts, 1973) short *interstimulus intervals* (15 vs 40 seconds) produced slower desensitization of high hierarchy items during sessions but did not affect long-term decrement over a week. Strong items thus desensitized faster if long imaginal presentations were used with longer interstimulus intervals. In contrast, in students, GSR adaptation to noise was faster with shorter interstimulus intervals (mean of 51 vs 96 seconds) (Glass & Singer, 1972).

In brief, many parameters still require systematic study, and fixed rules are premature. In patients, hours of exposure seem preferable to minutes, and half a minute to a few seconds.

3. Stimulus Termination

It is moot whether progress during exposure treatment is faster if the patient or the therapist controls the presentation of the phobic stimulus. In snake-fearful students progress occurred at the same rate whether or not the subject controlled his own presentation of phobic images (H. R. Miller & Nawas, 1970). In snake-fearful children during *in vivo* exposure with modeling, improvement was at similar speed whether the child performed each step after an experimental model or whether he remained still while the experimenter approached him with a snake in her hands (Murphy & Bootzin, 1973).

Another problem is whether there is an optimum point at which to terminate a given session; e.g., is it best to end on a "good note"? There are few data on this issue.

C. Flooding versus Desensitization

Comparisons of flooding with desensitization are not easy to interpret as they inevitably are confounded by at least three factors: (a) anxiety level during phobic approach, (b) the level of the hierarchy at which the approach begins and its gradation, and (c) the spacing or massing of approach trials. Each of these important variables requires separate assessment. Granted these reservations, several reports of the superiority of flooding exist. Barrett (1969) found that flooding in fantasy achieved a given criterion of improvement 55% more quickly than desensitization in fantasy, whereas Strahley (1965) noted that 12 minutes of flooding in real life was superior to more than 200 minutes of desensitization in fantasy (of which 30 minutes were spent in presentation of phobic scenes). D'Zurilla *et al.* (1973) observed that graded prolonged exposure in fantasy produced more behavioral improvement than desensitization in fantasy, but the latter group did not change more than the no-treatment control.

Three reports found desensitization and flooding variants in fantasy to be equally effective (Calef & MacLean, 1970; de Moor, 1970; Mylar & Clement, 1972). However, in three other studies in fantasy the desensitization package was more effective than flooding. In one of these (Willis & Edwards, 1969), the duration of desensitization was on average 2.5 times longer than that of flooding (Willis, 1968, p. 92); in the remaining two studies (Mealiea & Nawas, 1971; Rachman, 1966), desensitization and flooding were given for equal durations.

D. Effects of Relaxation

Past emphasis on pairing muscular relaxation with phobic exposure assumed that such pairing hastened the reduction of fear. This assumption involves at least three problems: (1) whether muscle relaxation reduces anxiety at rest, (2) whether it decreases initial and repeated responses to neutral and to stressful stimulation, and (3) whether relaxation has any therapeutic effect by the end of treatment and follow-up.

1. Background Activity

Lang (1970) cited results from relaxation that "may reflect no more than the lowering of background biological 'noise' through decreased muscle activity." In keeping with this, Butollo (1971) noted that softer background tones led to increased GSR responses to unconditioned tones of medium loudness, whereas loud background tones had the reverse effect. In normals both Burns and Ascough (1971) and Jordan and Sipprelle (1972) reported that contrasting periods with differential instructions to relax or to tense muscles could produce correspondingly different autonomic changes in respiration, heart rate, and GSR.

Less consistent differences have been found between training in muscle relaxation and neutral (as opposed to tensing) conditions. In anxious students Edelman (1971) found equal reduction in autonomic response [electromyogram (EMG), skin conductance (SC), pulse rate] or subjective anxiety to fearful scenes, whether taped instructions concerned progressive muscular relaxation or simply told the students to relax. Similarly, Davidson and Hiebert (1971) found equal decrease in physiological arousal of normals to a threatening film whether taped instructions simply told subjects to relax or gave brief training in muscle relaxation. Another study found no difference in subjective feelings after relaxation and after drug placebo conditions with instructions to keep still and quiet (Riddick & Meyer, 1973). Six weeks of relaxation training improved general anxiety in students (Sherman & Plummer, 1973), but there were few differences from a control condition. Although Paul and Trimble (1970) and Paul (1969) found that taped relaxation was inferior to live relaxation training, there was no difference between live relaxation and hypnotic instructions in their effect on autonomic responses (heart and respiration rate, muscle tension, and SC) at rest or to stressful imagery.

In 18 anxious patients, Lader and Mathews (1970) were unable to distinguish between the effect of taped neutral and muscle relaxation instructions on EMG, SC, heart rate, and forearm blood flow; the same occurred before and after an injection. In another 10 anxious patients, 6 hour-long sessions of untaped and taped relaxation instructions decreased SC activity equally by the end of the six sessions (Mathews & Gelder, 1969). In a second experiment 14 anxious patients were first trained in relaxation and then tested during a relaxation and a control condition. Total EMG and SC were significantly lower during relaxation than during the control condition, but heart rate and respiration rate were not.

Thus while differential instructions can sometimes produce differential levels of background activity, this effect is uncertain, and the evidence for the value of prolonging muscular relaxation training beyond a few brief instructions is unconvincing.

2. Response to Stimulation

That responses decrease or habituate more to repeated stimuli at lower levels of arousal is also unproved. In normals, Epstein and Fenz (1970) found less SC response and slightly greater habituation to a loud sound in subjects with low autonomic arousal on a questionnaire, but differences were negligible in subjects subdivided on a questionnaire about striated muscle tension. Also in normals, Ferstl (1972) noted that the rate of extinction of a conditioned aversive tone was similar whether subjects were relaxed or activated before and during the experiment.

Contrary to the predictions that follow from a maximal habituation model, in 30 phobic subjects Van Egeren (1971) failed to find the rate of habituation to be inversely proportional to SC activity during rest or arousal; on the contrary, habituation of SC was directly proportional to SC activity at rest, as was also found by Benjamin, Marks, and Huson (1972). In 8 phobic patients, Benjamin *et al.* (1972) found that the decrement of autonomic and subjective anxiety to repeated phobic images was the same in a relaxed and in a neutral condition, and failed to find significant negative correlations between levels of GSR arousal and rate of response decrement (see page 112). The same was observed in fearful students by Waters, McDonald, and Koresko (1972). Agras, Leitenberg, Barlow, Curtis, Edwards, and Wright (1971) reported 4 phobic patients whose progress in visualizing phobic scenes was not impaired by the removal of relaxation. These findings argued against ideas that habituation is greater under conditions of low arousal (Lader & Mathews, 1968).

In an analogue of desensitization (Lehrer, 1972), subjects were given slowly increasing intensities of shocks over 40 minutes as SC responses habituated. All subjects had an initial session of taped relaxation and were subsequently shocked under conditions of relaxation, increased muscle tension, unchanged tension, or no instruction. The relaxation showed no difference from the no-instruction group, though the increased tension group had a higher heart rate and more SC responses. There was no significant difference in pain threshold between groups. In spider phobics asked to approach a spider (Anthony & Duerfeldt, 1970), groups experiencing minimum tension showed more approach than those under maximum tension, but eating during approach facilitated approach only with maximum tension. The authors suggested their results favored an extinction hypothesis of fear decrement.

Investigations to date thus confirm Mathews' (1971) conclusion that "no direct evidence has been found for one of the central postulates of reciprocal inhibition theory, that relaxation reduces or prevents the autonomic anxiety responses associated with phobic imagery."

3. Outcome

Whatever the effect of relaxation during treatment, the crucial clinical question is its effect on outcome afterward. Of 19 controlled studies on the subject which the author has encountered from 1969 onward, 16 found no lasting value in trained muscular relaxation being added to exposure to the phobic stimulus, whether in fantasy, *in vivo,* or in the course of counseling techniques (Allen, 1973; Bellack, 1973; Benjamin *et al.,* 1972; Craighead, 1971; Crowder & Thornton, 1970; D'Zurilla *et al.,* 1973; Guilani, 1972; Jacobs, Edelman, & Wolpin, 1971; Jacobs & Wolpin, 1971; Lopiccolo, 1969; Marshall, Strawbridge, & Keltner, 1972; Perloff, 1970; Rimm & Medeiros, 1970; Sue, 1972; Vodde & Gilner, 1971; Waters *et al.,* 1972).

In a study of a laboratory conditioned fear, deep muscle relaxation had no advantage over the simple instruction to "relax and think of a pleasant scene" in conditioning a "safety response" to a conditioned stimulus (Bellack, 1973). Another study (Persely & Leventhal, 1972) found that the pairing of relaxation instructions with phobic imagery had but a slight effect. Although Nawas, Fishman, and Pucel (1970) found that relaxation training did have an additive effect to exposure, in a subsequent paper Nawas, Mealiea, and Fishman (1971) argued against the utility of relaxation and instead favored an extinction hypothesis. In the latter study an exposure condition that did less well than desensitization had only one-third the duration of sessions of the desensitized group. Farmer and Wright (1971) found that desensitization with muscular relaxation was effective in decreasing avoidance and subjective fear in both high and low Barrier scorers, but that desensitization with muscular activity was effective only for low Barrier scorers, the effects remaining at the 6-week follow-up.

The only recent report of lasting value from relaxation added to exposure was by Horowitz (1970), and in her study relaxation was simply by hypnotic suggestion, without training in muscular relaxation. She hypnotized snake phobics who were required to recall snake events while relaxed or while aroused, and found that relaxed subjects performed better than aroused ones at the end of nine sessions and at 9- to 34-day follow-up.

Psychophysiological as well as other criteria were used in two studies of process and outcome with relaxation. In an analogue report (Waters *et al.,* 1972) muscular relaxation was neither necessary nor facilitative for fear reduction in one session of desensitization. Forty female students with rat fear were divided into two groups which had relaxation training plus desensitization or comparable exposure without relaxation. All subjects were shown slides of girls approaching a rat and were told to imagine the scene without anxiety. The relaxed group was asked to practice relaxation at the same time. GSR, heart rate, and peripheral vasomotor responses were measured to the first 5 seconds of each slide. Immediately after treatment both groups decreased significantly and equally in avoidance of and physiological reactions to slides of rats, although desensitization subjects reached criterion in significantly fewer trials. During slide presentation, desensitization subjects showed less SC, though not heart rate activity, than the non-relaxation controls, yet both groups improved similarly in avoidance, GSR, and heart rate. Low arousal during treatment was thus not associated with better outcome.

In phobic patients, too, relaxation contributed nothing to desensitization in fantasy at outcome on clinical and physiological measures (Benjamin *et al.,* 1972). In obsessive-compulsive patients relaxation without exposure had no significant effect on outcome, while subsequent exposure *in vivo* with response prevention but no relaxation did reduce rituals significantly (Hodgson, Rachman, & Marks, 1972; Rachman, Marks, & Hodgson, 1971, 1973). These studies are detailed on pages 128–131.

Recent results from many quarters thus suggest that, to achieve fear reduction after treatment, systematic training in muscular relaxation is a redundant and time-wasting procedure, and that therapeutic time is better spent on straightforward exposure to the phobic stimulus, using any strategies that help the subject to remain in its presence and attend to it. While systematic training in muscular relaxation does seem unnecessary, more needs to be known about the effects of simple instructional sets to relax or tense up during exposure.

Questions also remain about the utility of related procedures like prolonged autogenic training and meditational techniques for anxiety reduction. Possibly if these methods were applied systematically over many weeks or months they might have a cumulative effect, but there are no controlled data on the topic, perhaps for the good practical reason that such research is so difficult to complete. Only brief case reports are available, like that of Boudreau (1972), who described one student whose phobias did not respond to desensitization but did to subsequent transcendental meditation, and a woman whose chronic hyperhydrosis was improved after 3 months of yoga.

E. Effects of Tension/Catharsis

Several workers observed that muscle tension during fantasy exposure did not hinder outcome. In students with snake or rat fear, Jacobs *et al.* (1971) found that fantasy desensitization led to similar approach whether students were asked to maintain muscle tension at high, medium, or very low levels during treatment. Jacobs and Wolpin (1971) reported that Myerhoff (1967) found a muscular-tension high-anxiety condition at least as effective in reducing fear and more effective in reducing avoidance as a simple cognitive rehearsal, no motor performance, condition. They also cited U. O. Evans' (1968) finding that when a group which received electric shock at the point of visualizing picking up a snake was compared to a no-treatment control, both groups decreased in anxiety, but there was more approach in the shocked group. In students with snake fear, desensitization in fantasy worked as well under muscle tension as with neutral tasks (Nawas *et al.,* 1970) or muscle relaxation (Sue, 1972).

Less clear-cut results were obtained by other authors. In nursing students, 20 minutes of jaw clenching had variable immediate effects on subjective anxiety depending upon its starting level, increasing initially low and decreasing initially high anxiety; auditory feedback of breath sounds helped to diminish initially high anxiety (Grim, 1971). In one brief session Anthony and Duerfeldt (1970) asked spider-phobic students to pull a tarantula toward them either to the point of maximum or of minimum tension. Groups experiencing more tension showed less approach immediately after the session.

With rat-fearful students, one session of muscle tension while watching 20-second film strips of the phobic object was better than no treatment, but this produced slightly less approach and fear decrement than in groups which had been relaxed, rewarded, or instructed to watch the same films (Vodde & Gilner, 1971). In snake-fearful students, desensitization during muscle activity produced equal results to those with relaxation in low Barrier scorers but less in high Barrier scorers, effects persisting to 6-weeks follow-up (Farmer & Wright, 1971).

Evidence was cited earlier (Burns & Ascough, 1971; Jordan & Sipprelle, 1972; Lang, 1970) that anxiety induction, as opposed to muscle tension, increases background autonomic activity when compared to relaxation instructions. In snake-fearful students, cathartic instructions led to less approach or fear decrement posttreatment and at follow-up than did hypnotic relaxation or suggestion about decreased fear during recall of snake-related events (Horowitz, 1970).

The effects of high- or low-arousing taped instructions in spider-fearful students during flooding scenes were examined by Mathews and Shaw (1973). Their experimental manipulation was only partly successful in producing differential arousal. Subjects had greater behavioral and attitude change immediately after low-arousing material, but this did not endure at 1-month follow-up.

In agoraphobic patients who were exposed *in vivo* while the therapist either raised their anxiety deliberately or simply emphasized the importance of contact without avoidance, both groups improved comparably. In other agoraphobics treated by group exposure *in vivo,* phobic outcome was worse in those who had experienced more panics during exposure treatment (Hafner & Marks, 1975).

In summary, while muscle tension or arousing instructions can increase anxiety and autonomic responses at rest and during exposure to a phobic stimulus, effect on outcome is variable. There is no clear evidence that anxiety provocation per se is helpful during exposure either in fantasy or *in vivo.*

F. Gradual versus Sudden Exposure

Few have compared the effect of presenting hierarchy items from the top or lower down the hierarchy while keeping other conditions constant. All reports have been of exposure in fantasy, not *in vivo.* Cohen (1966) noted that progress in desensitization was equally fast whether subjects had only the four most aversive hierarchy items or were presented with a traditional hierarchy, though Cohen and Dean (1968) observed that subjects who had a progressive graded hierarchy required significantly more trials than those desensitized to items at the top of the hierarchy. During prolonged desensitization in fantasy with relaxation, 4 hours of graded imagery led to similar improvement as 2 hours using items from the top of the hierarchy (Suinn, Edie, & Spinelli, 1970). Krapfl and Nawas (1970) reported that desensitization was equally effective whether stimulus presentation proceeded from the least to the most aversive items or the reverse, while Welch and Krapfl (1970) noted that desensitization was equally effective whether the scenes were presented going up, down, or randomly across the hierarchy. Exposure in fantasy without relaxation has yielded similar results whether images were graded or from the top of the hierarchy (Guilani, 1972). Fantasy exposure thus appears at least equally and rarely more effective when it starts at the top of the hierarchy and works down rather than the reverse. The issue still requires investigation during *in vivo* exposure.

Some evidence suggests that starting with scenes high on the hierarchy and then going onto low items is superior to the reverse order in flooding in fantasy (Mathews & Shaw, 1973). A similar result in desensitization was reported by Lang (1970) from the work of Melamed. When graded films were presented in a high-low or low-high order more rapid habituation and decreased fear resulted in subjects who had seen the films in the high-low order. This was attributed to contrast effects.

G. Fantasy versus Live (in Vivo) Exposure

Although many have compared fantasy with live exposure indirectly, conclusions are usually difficult because of confounding influences like duration and gradient of exposure, or accompanying relaxation, praise, or modeling. Graded exposure *in vivo* ± contingent reward but without modeling (reinforced practice, successive approximation, shaping) or with modeling (contact desensitization, participant modeling) has often been helpful in reducing fear (Bandura *et al.,* 1969; Crowe *et al.,* 1972; Emmelkamp & Ultee, 1974; Everaerd *et al.,* 1973; Leitenberg & Callahan, 1973; O'Connor, 1972; Perloff, 1970; Ritter, 1968; Strahley, 1965). All found significant effects from some form of real-life exposure to the phobic situation.

Two studies compared live with fantasy exposure without the confounding variables mentioned above. Lopiccolo (1969) demonstrated that two sessions of graded exposure *in vivo* produced marked improvement in snake-fearful volunteers. Relaxation training did not add to the efficacy of graded exposure *in vivo,* which was significantly more effective than systematic desensitization in fantasy on subjective, behavioral, and physiological measures.

Careful investigation of this issue was also made by Sherman (1972). Fifty-four female sudents with swimming fears had one of six treatments individually in a 2 × 3 factorial design. The factors were (a) desensitization in fantasy ± live exposure, (b) pretreatment discussion of swimming fear and its treatment ± live exposure, and (c) neither desensitization nor pretreatment discussion, ± live exposure. *In vivo* exposure consisted of graded water activities in a swimming pool, done with a minimum of tension in a total of three weekly sessions. Follow-up was after a 2-week swimming course that followed the end of treatment. Results showed that repeated live exposure produced the best results for performance anxiety, questionnaire reports and overall improvement, and this gain endured at 2 weeks follow-up. Those who were desensitized only in fantasy showed little transfer of improvement to the real situation. Furthermore, desensitization in fantasy required 7 hours of treatment whereas live exposure required only 1 hour.

Comparison of *in vivo* with fantasy exposure is also possible in a third study by Bandura *et al.* (1969) which examined modeling. Forty-eight adult volunteers with snake phobias had either (a) self-regulated symbolic modeling—subjects watched a film of models engaging in gradually bolder interactions with the same snake, were taught to relax throughout the procedure, and also controlled the rate of presentation of the film sequence (vicarious desensitization by film alone), or (b) live modeling with contact desensitization (vicarious desensitization plus desensitization in practice)—subjects watched models engaging in gradually bolder interaction with the snake in real life instead of in a film, and then were brought into gradual physical contact with the actual snake itself. Both these groups were thus controlled for the presence of modeling. (c) A third group had symbolic desensitization in which subjects were desensitized in fantasy in the usual way. (d) A fourth group had no treatment. Results showed that the desensitization and symbolic modeling groups improved equally and more than the untreated control group. The live modeling group did best of all, and better than the symbolic modeling or desensitization groups. Although the authors interpret their results as demonstrating the effect of modeling, in fact it argues more powerfully for the role of *in vivo* exposure, since of the two groups which both had modeling (a and b) that which also had live exposure did much better. An argument for a modeling effect could only be sustained by a superiority of modeling plus exposure over exposure alone in either the fantasy or the *in vivo* modality, and the design did not allow such comparisons.

These results all support the strong indirect evidence from earlier experiments cited with volunteers, and also with patients (Stern & Marks, 1973a; Watson & Marks, 1971; Watson *et al.,* 1971) that real-life exposure is the most powerful therapeutic factor so far identified.

A relevant issue is whether preceding fantasy treatment can potentiate subsequent exposure *in vivo* either immediately afterward or after a delay. There may be a refractory period after fantasy treatment which might facilitate subsequent real-life exposure.

H. Expectancy and Instructions

A large but inconclusive literature has accumulated on this topic (Borkovec, 1973b; Emmelkamp, 1974). Of at least 27 studies in the area from 1970 onward, 19 were reviewed by Borkovec (1973b). In 10 experiments of "crossed expectancy" where the treatment groups were matched except for expectancy level, desensitization was equally effective with or without therapeutic instructions. Nine other reports found that positive therapeutic expectancy led to a superior effect in desensitization, implosion, and operant shaping. Within a session, there is some evidence that cognitive rehearsal of an expected unpleasant task induces anxiety and later adaptation to the situation (Foxman, 1972).

Conflicting findings might partly reflect the great variability across experiments in the timing and frequency of expectancy manipulations and the differing ways in which those manipulations might have been perceived by experimental subjects. It might make a difference whether the manipulation of expectancy or therapeutic instruction is carried out just once before treatment, before every session, or even more frequently. Moreover, expectancies are not necessarily dependent primarily on what the therapist says, and perception of the procedure itself can influence expectations. Seventeen out of 20 fearful nonpsychology students said that though they knew desensitization was generally effective, neither the standard treatment nor its variations would work for them personally (Powell & Watts, 1973). Another problem is that expectations of treatment can change in a subject and in his therapist from the start to end of treatment, and thus reflect efficacy as well as determine it.

In agoraphobic patients Stern and Marks (1973a) found no correlation between outcome and patients' expectation of improvement at the start of treatment. Gelder, Bancroft, Gath, Johnston, Mathews, and Shaw (1973) attempted to manipulate patients' therapeutic expectancies by an induction interview before treatment but obtained few differences between experimental groups in expectancy levels, and little relationship between these and subsequent outcome. Results going in the opposite of *therapist* expectations were noted in school phobic children (Barrett, 1972) and in adult phobic patients (Watson & Marks, 1971).

It seems obvious that the more a patient cooperates in a difficult treatment the better the outcome might be, and that greater efforts to cooperate will be made if they are expected to bear tangible fruit. However, current understanding of this factor is confounded by methodological problems, and further progress depends upon clearer operational definitions of expectancy in the way it is applied and received by both parties in the therapeutic transaction throughout its various phases.

I. Feedback

A related murky area is *false* feedback. Since Valins and Ray (1967) reported that avoidance could be diminished by false feedback of low heart rates during "phobic" exposure, several experimenters observed conflicting results (Borkovec, 1973a; Gaupp, Stern, & Galbraith, 1972; Kent, Wilson, & Nelson, 1972; Koenig, 1973; Rosen, Rosen, & Reid, 1972; Sushinsky & Bootzin, 1970). Some boundary conditions to the value of false heart rate feedback were suggested by Borkovec and Glasgow (1973); they interpreted their results to indicate that its effects in modifying avoidance behavior were weak, and limited to situations where there is a high demand for subjects to perform well in situations that are not very frightening. Where fear is great, however, situational demands may have little effect, as was found by Foxman (1972). This accords with the student, quoted by Kent *et al.* (1972), who said that she "knew" she was "paralyzed by fear" of spiders, and so discounted information about her heart rate.

The foregoing also fits this author's experience with *true* feedback to a specific phobic patient during exposure *in vivo*. When praised because her true heart rate had slowed after prolonged exposure, she simply retorted "Yes, I know my heart is beating more slowly, but that does not help me—it's what I feel up here in my head that is important." The question therefore is how much false or true feedback of behavior and physiology can promote therapeutic advance. Physiology and behavior appear easier to influence than subjective feelings. During rapid exposure *in vivo* of specific phobic patients, Nunes and Marks (1975) found that pulse rates were significantly reduced over exposure periods containing visual feedback of true pulse rate, plus instructions to lower it, compared to controlled exposure periods without such feedback. However, this did not affect the rate of decline in subjective anxiety during the 2-hour session of treatment. Similarly, in rat-fearful students who were asked to look at a rat as long as possible (Rutner, 1973), true feedback of their times produced significantly longer looks compared to controls who looked at a rat without feedback, but did not affect subjective anxiety significantly; improvement continued to 2-weeks follow-up, at which point differences were not significant. In yet another study, subjects found it easier to keep still while relaxing if they heard a bell whenever they moved (Riddick & Meyer, 1973).

True feedback is not always helpful. In juvenile delinquents, videotaped feedback of boys' attempts to emulate sociable behavior of models actually impaired outcome when subjects were dependent (Sarason, 1968, 1971). Obvious failure can discourage some people from trying again, perhaps especially when they have a background of learned helplessness instead of learned resourcefulness.

Rutner (1973) posed the pertinent question: "What else does systematic desensitization do for the patient other than present him in some manner with a phobic object in a gradually increasing anxiety hierarchy and give him feedback of his behavior whenever the therapist proceeds up the hierarchy?" Like expectancy, true feedback seems a useful adjunct to exposure, in that patients can cooperate better when given accurate information about their progress in the desired direction. Successful completion of a task like fear reduction requires accurate monitoring of one's progress, and to that extent true feedback can be construed as an aid to self-control.

J. Self-Regulation, Coping, and Anxiety Management (Stress Immunization)

Whether a subject will expose himself to distressing stimuli partly depends on his capacity for self-control, a process which is popularly called "psyching oneself up" or "applying the power of cosmic consciousness." The scientific approach to willpower is only just beginning.

A large section is devoted to this "cognitive" area because of the recent ferment of research. Self-control techniques include labels like anxiety management training (Suinn & Richardson, 1971; Suinn, 1974; Ferstl, 1972), self-instruction or cognitive modification (Meichenbaum, 1972), stress inoculation (Meichenbaum & Cameron, 1974), behavior rehearsal (Suinn, 1972), and attentional training (Wine, 1971). A helpful recent overview was made by Goldfried and Merbaum (1973).

A few elements in self-regulating processes were explored by Kanfer and Seidner (1973). One factor is distraction during stress. Students who were asked to keep a hand immersed in iced water as long as possible did this for longer if at the same time they were shown travel slides, and for even longer if they were allowed to advance these slides on their own. Subjects also found it useful to create their own controlling responses to prolong the time they could keep their hands in water, e.g., by naming numbers. In a further study Kanfer *et al.* (1975) found greater stress tolerance (length of time the hand was held in iced water) where subjects were committed to an explicit written contract rather than an oral agreement conveying the same content. After an interpolated experience subjects who believed they had failed to meet contract conditions tolerated iced water longer than those who believed the experimenter had failed to meet the conditions. Those who anticipated a reward for fulfillment of their contract also showed greater stress tolerance than those who were not rewarded, or whose reward was only contingent on making the contract. Commitment to carrying out the test was diminished when the iced water was visible before the experiment, and when there was a high chance of being selected to carry out the task. Stress tolerance thus depends upon demand and other characteristics of the situation, and on the subject's commitment to future action.

Control can be enhanced when subjects have an instrumental response which they perceive as terminating an aversive stimulus such as noise (Glass & Singer, 1972) or shock (Geer, Davison, & Gatchel, 1970). However, snake-fearful students improved equally after desensitization whether their relaxation was perceived as being self- or drug-induced (Wilson & Thomas, 1973). Similarly therapeutic changes in agoraphobic patients were comparable whether they attributed these to "drugs" or to exposure treatment (Johnston & Gath, 1973).

There is some evidence that more accurate expectations and knowledge about dealing with an impending stress can increase self-control and diminish the damage. Leventhal (1973) reported on medical patients who received one of four differing manipulations the night before they had a gastroscopy. One group was told what sensations to expect during the procedure, e.g., gagging, full stomach. The second group was not given sensory information but instead was instructed to act appropriately in cooperation with the procedure (e.g., when to mouth-breathe and when to swallow). A third group was given both sensory and motor instructional information. The fourth group received no information. When patients had their gastroscopy the next day, there was less gagging and tachycardia in subjects who had had either sensory information or appropriate motor instructions the night before, compared to those who received no information. Disturbance accompanying the gastroscopy was least when subjects had received both sensory information and instructions to act. Thus there is evidence that response to stress is more controlled and less disturbing when people know what stress to expect and are advised how to deal with it.

Few have studied anxiety reduction under the heading of self-regulation. Rehm and Marston (1968) treated male students with dating problems by self-reinforcement in which subjects were given graduated daily tasks to perform at home, e.g., to telephone a girl for a date, and to reward themselves with approval for tasks successfully completed. The procedure was thus self-rewarded gradual exposure *in vivo* at home. Compared to nondirective or no treatment, self-reinforced subjects improved significantly more on a behavioral and subjective measure, retaining this improvement to 9-months follow-up.

During traditional desensitization, subjects are taught to relax when they encounter their frightening stimuli in real life. To some extent relaxation is thus an exercise in self-control (Sherman & Plummer, 1973), and so is *covert reinforcement,* in which an imagined reward is used instead of relaxation (Blanchard & Draper, 1973; Wisocki, 1970). With covert reinforcement subjects list their desired activities and practice visualizing these. They are then asked to imagine their phobic situations up a hierarchy; when the subjects get an image, the therapist says, "Reinforcer," which is the cue to switch the scene from a fearful to a rewarding one. In subjects with test anxiety, Wisocki (1970) found this technique to be significantly better on self-report than a no-treatment control.

Elements of self-management are also present in *rational-emotive therapy*. During such treatment the irrational basis of fears is discussed, more rational behavior is described, and subjects rehearse how to deal better with future situations. Two studies of students with stage fright (Karst & Trexler, 1970; Trexler & Karst, 1972) found that rational-emotive therapy had superior effects to no treatment. However, the earlier study found that fixed-role therapy, during which subjects compared notes with one another about their roles during public speaking and practiced adopting alternative roles, had similar effects to rational emotive therapy. In one comparison with desensitization in fantasy, rational-emotive therapy was inferior (Diloreto, 1971).

Ways of coping with fear can be learned directly in the particular phobic situation or as part of a more general process of dealing with anxiety. The latter can be called stress inoculation or stress immunization. Prochaska (1971) compared the effects on test anxious students of three forms of implosion: (1) symptom cues specifically describing the problem; (2) "dynamic" cues thought to be related to it, e.g., rejection by parents or girlfriend, castration; or (3) general anxiety cues irrelevant to the test anxiety, e.g., seeing snakes, rats, spiders. After treatment, subjects imploded by symptom or dynamic cues improved more on test anxiety measures, while those imploded with general anxiety cues improved more on general anxiety. Implosion using irrelevant anxiety cues resembles the management of similar cues described by Suinn and Richardson (1971), although Prochaska did not deliberately promote coping responses. It is also similar to the irrelevant flooding in fantasy given by Watson and Marks (1971) to phobic patients, which improved their phobias as much as implosion with relevant phobic cues; however, in that study relevant and irrelevant flooding had different prognostic correlates, suggesting that differential processes were involved (see page 117).

Self-control techniques can utilize anxiety responses as discriminative stimuli, which clients can be trained to deal with in a variety of ways. Suinn (1974) gives anxiety-provoking cues to which the client has to learn to respond in a coping manner. Subjects imagine anxious scenes, then relaxing scenes and then competency scenes, and practice switching from one type of scene to another. An analogy is present here with thought-stopping techniques.

Anxiety management training on these lines has been found to be as effective as group desensitization in fantasy for the reduction of mathematics anxiety (Suinn & Richardson, 1971). What is noteworthy is that the anxiety scenes rehearsed during anxiety management training were irrelevant to mathematics anxiety, so that what appeared to be learned was skill in coping with anxiety in general, not any particular fear. Suinn (1974) cited findings by Nicoletti that anxiety management training reduced stage fright and general anxiety more than waiting-list control conditions. Suinn also cited Edie, who compared the effects of anxiety imagery alone, anxiety feelings without scenes, and anxiety imagery plus feelings; with all these methods anxious subjects improved on measures of general anxiety.

Similar results with "anxiety management training" were obtained by Ferstl (1972) in volunteers with stage fright who were asked to learn to relax during repeated countdown which terminated in shock unless relaxation was achieved. Anxiety management training subjects improved to a similar extent as those who were desensitized in fantasy.

Attentional training describes a self-regulatory technique in the treatment of test anxiety (Wine, 1971). This utilizes Sarason's (1972a, 1972b) observations that though test-anxious subjects predict failure to themselves, and emit irrelevant responses, they are more sensitive to task-related modeling cues, and can be trained to be more attentive to relevant task stimuli. Wine (1971) trained students to practice serial learning tasks and to attend fully while inhibiting irrelevant thinking. Beforehand, subjects watched video-taped models carry out task-relevant behavior while telling themselves what to do first in a nervous and then in an increasingly coping manner. After 6 hours of attentional training, subjects improved significantly more than those in a control group who simply focused on their own faults.

Further evidence that knowledge of what to do might help people solve anagram or serial learning problems was noted by Sarason (1972b). High test-anxious students did better after observing models who solved similar problems, while describing aloud the general principles they were working on—e.g., vary the approach, look for familiar groupings, resist reentry of blind alleys. Further factors that made them perform better (Sarason, 1973a, 1973b) were reassurance, task orientation, rapport-building, praise for performance, instructing them to focus on task-relevant cues and practice relevant behavior. Performance was worse under the threat of evaluation or if subjects saw a model failing; in contrast, students without test anxiety were not hindered by these influences. Relaxed therapists facilitated improvement more than anxious therapists in all subjects. Sarason suggested that different kinds of test anxiety might need different approaches; e.g., focal posttraumatic anxious subjects might do better with narrower methods like desensitization, while more diffusely anxious subjects with other problems might need a broader treatment program.

1. Work by Meichenbaum and Colleagues

This group reported several careful experiments into *coping self-instructional* techniques (Meichenbaum, 1971a). In an early study, speech-anxious volunteers, mainly students, were treated in groups by desensitization in fantasy, by "insight," or by combined desensitization and "insight" (Meichenbaum, Gilmore, & Fedoravicius, 1971). Insight subjects were instructed to become aware of the self-statements they made when anxious in interpersonal situations, and were taught to produce incompatible self-instructions and behavior. No behavioral rehearsal or assertive training was employed. These three groups were compared with one another and with attention-placebo and waiting-list control groups. Compared to controls, insight subjects improved as much as those who were desensitized on behavioral, subjective, and cognitive measures of speech anxiety at posttreatment and at 3-month follow-up. Desensitization was better than "insight" for subjects whose speech anxiety was confined to formal speech situations, whereas "insight" was better with subjects who suffered anxiety in many varied social situations.

In a subsequent report of test-anxious students, a combined desensitization and insight group was termed "cognitive modification" (Meichenbaum, 1971c). Subjects were first made aware of the things they said to themselves before and during test situations. They were then trained in coping behavior during desensitization imagery. Coping included slow deep breathing and self-instructions to relax, to be task-relevant, and to inhibit task-irrelevant thought. If the subjects continued to remain anxious they stopped the image and relaxed again. These students were compared with others who received standard desensitization, and with a waiting-list control. Results showed that cognitive modification was significantly more effective than standard desensitization in reducing test anxiety in an analogue test situation, on self-report, and grade-point-average. Furthermore, after cognitive modification, but not after other treatments, many subjects reported an increase in facilitative anxiety, i.e., when they felt anxious they took this as a cue to be task-relevant and improve their performance.

In another experiment, Meichenbaum (1971b) examined the influence of modeled coping behavior on fear reduction. Snake-fearful students observed films of models approaching a snake in 4 different ways: (1) mastery models approached the snake fearlessly in a competent and commonplace manner, (2) mastery-plus-verbalization models approached similarly but also described aloud their lack of fear during the process, (3) behavioral-coping models first showed much fear, hesitancy and withdrawal, then slowly became bolder in approaching the snake, taking deep breaths to calm themselves, and only at the end showed pleasure on completing the task, (4) behavioral coping-plus-verbalization models simulated fear as in (3), but in addition described aloud how anxious and sweaty they felt, that their heart and respiration rates felt rapid, uttering determination to forge ahead one step at a time while remaining relaxed by slow breathing, coping with the fear and talking themselves into handling the snake; e.g. "I am going to make a deal with you, if you don't scare or hurt me, I won't scare or hurt you."

Results showed that coping models were significantly better than masterful models in decreasing avoidance and subjective fear, regardless of overt verbalization. The addition of overt self-statements by the coping model produced further significant decrease in subjective anxiety during the more bold approach tasks and a greater readiness to perform them. The addition of overt verbalization by the mastery model did not help. Coping models might be superior because they are perceived as more appropriate models for fearful observers and because they show the subject in detail how to cope with fear.

Finally, three experiments from this group examined cognitive variables during anxiety-relief in snake-fearful students (Meichenbaum & Cameron, 1974a, 1974b). In the first of these experiments, treatment did not involve exposure to the phobic stimulus. In five half-hour sessions, given individually, subjects received shocks to the forefinger, which were terminated and eventually avoided by self-instructions to "relax" and be "calm." These were compared with unshocked subjects who gave themselves the same calming self-instructions, and with waiting-list controls. Anxiety-relief subjects did best, both on the avoidance test and on subjective anxiety, though the unshocked self-instruction group also did significantly better than the waiting-list control on the avoidance test.

A second experiment amplified the first by adding in fearful subjects' avoidant self-statements and also more elaborate self-instructions to terminate shock. In the first experiment the therapist had said, "Shock," then gave the shock, followed by the subject saying, "Relax," which terminated the shock. In this second experiment the therapist said, "Snake," the subject said, "Ugly, slimy, I won't look at it," etc., then got the shock. When the client said, "Relax, I am in control," the shock was stopped. This group was compared with another which made similar fear-reducing self-statements without shock. A third group was included which had the expanded anxiety-relief procedure, but with the contingencies reversed with respect to shock; i.e., when the subject said, "Relax," shock began, and shocks were terminated only after subjects said, "I'm afraid, I want to run away," etc. Surprisingly, both regular and reversed anxiety-relief groups improved significantly and equally, more than in the first study, and with no important difference between them. The unshocked cognitive rehearsal group improved less significantly. Thus, the addition of shock to self-instructions was helpful, but not because of conditioning, since the backward-conditioning paradigm was as helpful as the forward-conditioning one. Results continued to follow-up and were consistent across all behavioral and self-report measures.

A third investigation tested whether self-instruction led to more general improvement than treatment based on phobic imagery in volunteers who had fears both of snakes and of rats. In a desensitization-in-fantasy group, half were treated for fears of rats and the other half for snakes. A second group had the simpler anxiety-relief procedure of the second experiment. A fourth group had "stress inoculation" in which they were told that their cognitions led to emotion, were given practice in controlling this emotion by relaxation and deep breathing, rehearsed how to handle the feeling of being overwhelmed and to make positive self-statements, and finally were shocked while utilizing these anxiety-management procedures. After treatment and 4–6 week follow-up, stress inoculation subjects improved most for both snake and rat fears while desensitized subjects improved only for their treated fears. Coping instructions had helped to translate learned helplessness into learned resourcefulness. The anxiety-relief subjects improved for both fears, especially after expanded anxiety-relief. All treated groups improved significantly more than a waiting-list control.

In brief, the rank-ordering of treatment effectiveness was first stress inoculation, then expanded anxiety relief, anxiety relief and desensitization, all of which were significantly different from a waiting-list control, which showed minimal change. The authors concluded that treatment techniques which deal with common self-instructional coping processes led to greater generalization.

A problem in interpreting the outcome of these ingenious experiments is the lack of operationally defined criteria of "coping responses." It could well be that negative self-statements might be just as therapeutic as positive ones, since patients who are asked during flooding or paradoxical intention to get as frightened as possible usually improve at least as much as those who relax. This experiment with negative self-statements remains to be done. If negative self-statements and flooding also help subjects to cope, what then is a noncoping response? Further progress depends on a logical way being found out of this dilemma utilizing testable hypotheses.

2. Relationship between Self-Regulation, Oriental and Other Psychotherapies

Self-regulatory approaches seem to share some elements that also appear in meditational and allied procedures. Research into this has hardly dawned, so it is premature to judge which similarities are trivial and which important. Ikemi, Luthe, Akishige, Ohno, Ishikawa, and Suematsu (1973) outlined common self-control factors which are featured in yoga, zen, Morita therapy, Naikan, transcendental meditation, and autogenic training. These diverse approaches all involve regular step-by-step practice to promote self-regulatory function. When functional harmony has been attained, the subjective experience is of "great bliss, serenity, unbounded freedom." At the extremes these are called samadhi (agreement) in yoga, or nibbana or satori (enlightenment) in Therevada or Japanese Buddhism. Therapeutic elements are said to include guidance by an experienced person and participation by the trainee in a program that aims to reduce tension. This is achieved by regular mental exercises in prescribed postures and calm surroundings, a decrease of afferent-efferent activity, effortless maintenance of alertness and avoidance of absentmindedness, drowsiness or sleep, emphasis on controlled breathing, training of inwardly oriented concentration, passive acceptance of spontaneous hallucinatory, sensory, motor, and other release phenomena (Makyo, autogenic discharges), confrontation with "artificial and authentic features of oneself," and promotion of a thoroughly clear and calm mental life like a "cloudless blue sky." The authors report that autogenic training increases physiological and emotional tolerance, makes social contact less inhibited and more natural, and reduces test anxiety and anxiety in psychotherapy. Controlled research has barely begun in this area, and the methodological problems involved are great.

Another attempt at integrating diverse psychotherapeutic procedures was made by Noonan and Lewis (1970). They described "reverse-psychology" psychotherapy techniques which attempt to rid a patient of his complaint by superficially encouraging and reinforcing it. Examples of this in the behavioral modality were thought to be negative practice, stimulus satiation, and Haley's therapeutic paradoxes—e.g., a marital couple would be told to go and have a fight. Included in the affective modality were implosion, induced anxiety, and emotional flooding. In the cognitive modality were paradoxical intention and Morita therapy.

K. Modeling

So rapidly is this field developing that since Rachman (1972) reviewed 17 studies of modeling in fear reduction, at least 13 more have come to light (Hall & Hinkle, 1972; Jaffe & Carlson, 1972; Kazdin, 1973, 1974; Lick & Bootzin, 1970; McFall & Twentyman, 1973; Murphy & Bootzin, 1973; O'Connor, 1972; O'Sullivan, Gilner, & Krinski, 1973; Sarason,

1972b, 1973a; Wine, 1971; Young *et al.,* 1973). Although most reports claim a positive effect from modeling, this variable is nearly always combined with vicarious or live exposure. *Pure* modeling has hardly been investigated and has not been shown to reduce anxiety significantly except in conjunction with exposure. Most reports concern the contribution that modeling makes to exposure of various kinds. This has already been discussed with respect to Bandura *et al.* (1969), whose study argues more for the effect of live exposure than for modeling (see page 67). Vicarious and direct desensitization in fantasy were compared by Mann and Rosenthal (1969) in individual and group settings in test-anxious adolescents. Both vicarious and direct desensitization groups improved with no significant differences between them, which does not support the value of pure modeling.

The point is strengthened by a recent series of experiments in the training of assertive students (McFall & Twentyman, 1973). Whereas behavior rehearsal and coaching significantly decreased social inhibitions measured on self-report and behavior, video-taped modeling added little whether models were tactful or abrupt, or were seen and heard or only seen. Behavior rehearsal is a form of exposure and was facilitatory whether it was covert, overt, or both, and improvement generalized from trained to untrained situations and to real-life situations. McFall and Twentyman (1973) commented that "the tendency to regard modeling . . . as a unitary treatment component has only served to obscure matters" and there is a need to map the "effects of specific, operationally defined procedural components used in fixed treatment programs that have been designed for specific target behaviors." Their results echo those of Roper (1975) in obsessive-compulsive patients, in whom modeling of relaxation after the therapist had no therapeutic effect. In contrast, watching a therapist expose herself to contaminating situations had some effect; modeling with live participation conferred the most benefits, as is usual in experiments in this area (e.g., Bandura, 1970; Bandura *et al.,* 1969; Blanchard, 1970; Lick & Bootzin, 1970; Litvak, 1969; Rimm & Medeiros, 1970; Ritter, 1968).

One study (Hall & Hinkle, 1972) found that test-anxious subjects who watched video-taped models relaxing without exposure to phobic scenes or situations improved as much as students who had active desensitization in fantasy without modeling. However, the possibility was not excluded that modeling subjects were practicing covert rehearsal of fear scenes.

An important study of fantasy exposure and modeling was conducted by Kazdin (1973). He investigated 64 snake-fearful students who were not given any therapeutic instructions. Over two 15-minute sessions of fantasy treatment, subjects were asked to imagine snake scenes up a hierarchy, 14 scenes per session, each scene visualized once only for 15 seconds. The manner in which these scenes were visualized differed in the four treated groups: (1) *Covert coping model:* subjects imagined another student resembling themselves anxiously approaching a snake, hesitating, coping with it by deep breathing and eventually obtaining success. (2) *Covert mastery model:* subjects imagined similar student models gradually approaching snakes while feeling confident and smiling. (3) *"No model" scene control:* despite the label given to this group, subjects did imagine a model student, but in the background not interacting with the snake, and the snake merely present somewhere, e.g., sticking its head out of the cage. (4) *Delayed treatment control:* these subjects were not treated until the first three groups were completed and then had *covert modeling* without cues during which they imagined a student like themselves just approaching the snake, any cues attributed to the model being left to their own imagination. Groups 1–3 had a 3-week follow-up. Group 3 differed from the other 3 covert modeling groups on one potentially crucial factor concerning exposure, in that it was the only one in which no interaction with the snake was visualized.

Posttreatment and at follow-up all three covert modeling groups showed significant increase in approach and decrease in fear, but no-treatment and scene controls did not improve on any measure. Coping models were significantly better than mastery ones, which agrees with the findings of Meichenbaum (1971a), Sarason (1972b), and Jaffe and Carlson (1972). It is noteworthy that in the study by Jaffe and Carlson, an anxious model was more potent than a calm, successful, and rewarded one even when he was not coping and failed, with the therapist denigrating his performance and future prospects. An initially puzzling feature about Kazdin's results is the failure of the scene-only condition to improve. However, total treatment time was only 30 minutes, which is much less than in most successful studies of exposure in fantasy (see Table IIIA).

The results are not an argument for the effect of pure modeling, but for that of *interactional* rather than static exposure. The scene-only subjects in fact watched a model who simply stood near a snake but did not interact with it, whereas all covert modeling groups visualized interaction with the snake. This suggests that the operative ingredient might be interaction with the phobic stimulus, with or without modeling. An appropriate test for this would need a 2-factor study in which subjects see either themselves or a model interacting with or passively in the region of the phobic stimulus, without therapeutic instructions being given.

L. Reward

Praise of therapeutic progress is a natural part of most therapies. With phobias this involves praising the subject's approach to the phobic object, so that reward is inevitably compounded with exposure. The question is whether *systematic* reward enhances outcome. For this, a contrast is needed between identical exposure with and without systematic reward. The effects of such reward have not been large. In studies by Oliveau (1969), Young *et al.* (1973), Emmelkamp and Ultee (1974) (praise) and Vodde and Gilner (1971), systematic reward (money) plus exposure had little effect beyond other comparable exposure conditions. Though several reports noted improvement from "reinforced practice," "shaping," or "successive approximation" in comparison with contrasting procedures (Crowe *et al.,* 1972; Everaerd *et al.,* 1973; Leitenberg & Callahan, 1973; Marks *et al.,* 1971c), comparison was with differing exposure conditions apart from absent reinforcement, so that the role of reward cannot be inferred. The available evidence does not suggest a large contribution from systematic reinforcement added to exposure, though commonsense points to the desirability of encouraging clients' efforts as much as possible.

M. Therapist Variation

Variation in the therapists who administer exposure treatment has not been a significant determinant of outcome in most studies which have examined this effect, whether the difference is in experience or in sex-matching of therapist with client (Bandura *et al.,* 1969; Cotler, 1970; Mann & Rosenthal, 1969; Meichenbaum *et al.,* 1971; Paul & Shannon, 1966). In patients, too, different therapists obtained comparable effects (Boudewyns & Wilson, 1972; Gelder *et al.,* 1973).

N. Imagery during Exposure

Vividness of imagery during fantasy exposure has not been found to correlate with anxiety experienced (Rehm, 1973) or with improvement after treatment (Davis, McLemore, & London, 1970; Orenstein, 1972).

Clinical improvement is accompanied by corresponding changes in dream imagery from being anxiety-provoking to more pleasant (Bergin, 1970). Conversely, as anxiety increases in treatment, "runaway" flows of unpleasant imagery can develop which the subject cannot control (Barrett,

1968). Several guided imagery techniques related to implosion are described by Schutz (1967), Wolpin (1969), and Singer (1972).

O. Time-Saving Strategies in Exposure Treatment

1. Omitting the Therapist

Many workers report that automated taped desensitization in fantasy produces significantly more improvement in volunteers than does no treatment (e.g., Baker, Cohen, & Saunders, 1973; Cotler, 1970; Donner, 1970; Linder & McGlynn, 1971). Donner (1970) followed up test-anxious subjects for 5 months after desensitization in fantasy and found that those treated in the presence of the therapist had gained significantly more in grade-point-average than those desensitized by tape. Donner suggested that the therapist increased efficiency because he brought the situation closer to that of a classroom, i.e., to an *in vivo* session. In contrast, in acrophobic volunteers, taped desensitization actually had slightly better results at 8 months follow-up than therapist-administered desensitization, though both groups maintained their improvement (Baker *et al.,* 1973). In phobic patients, P. D. Evans and Kellam (1973) found comparable amounts of improvement at the 6–20-month follow-up after taped or live desensitization.

Automated desensitization can undoubtedly produce significant improvement, but evidence is conflicting about its efficacy relative to therapist-administered desensitization. Paul and Trimble (1970) found taped relaxation instructions produced less effect than "live" instructions, while Stern and Marks (1973a) observed in patients that taped instructions produced few physiological responses to phobic imagery and no significant improvement with flooding in fantasy, unlike similar treatment given by a live therapist (Watson & Marks, 1971). Furthermore, Tables IIIA and IIIB indicated that most unsuccessful studies of flooding in fantasy utilized taped instructions, while most successful ones had a live therapist present. Attentional factors may well be important, and certain subjects might cooperate better with a therapist than with a tape recorder. While a highly motivated person might work harder at directing his own automated desensitization program than he would with a therapist, a less enthusiastic subject might do better with repeated prodding from a warm therapist.

It might also be more important to have a therapist present with rapid forms of exposure such as flooding, where the patient needs much encouragement to remain in the situation, whereas the more comfortable procedure of desensitization requires less effort and thus less therapist persuasion to keep the patient moving up the hierarchy. Ultimately, whether automated or therapist-directed programs are initiated will depend upon the population being treated, the techniques employed, and the relative importance attached to the cost-effectiveness of the exercise.

2. Using Standardized instead of Individualized Hierarchies

There are many reports of significant improvement utilizing standardized hierarchies for particular fears (e.g., Lutker, Taston, & Jorgensen, 1972; McGlynn, 1971; Nawas *et al.,* 1970). The first two found no difference between desensitization based on particular individuals' hierarchy items and that based on standard items. However, Lutker *et al.* found that subjects whose hierarchy items were individualized and read by them from their own printed cards showed significantly more improvement in avoidance. This might make possible the treatment of subjects with different phobias in the same group.

3. Treatment in Groups

This is an obvious potential saver of therapists' time, and numerous studies have found significant improvement with desensitization in fantasy given in groups (e.g., Donner, 1970; Lutker *et al.,* 1972; Mann & Rosenthal, 1969; McManus, 1971; Taylor, 1971). Fantasy exposure in groups can be given with varying amounts of group interaction, e.g., through headphones individually to subjects who do not interact at all, or through loudspeakers to subjects who can observe one another, or with promotion of group interaction. The latter brings in influences of modeling and small-group morale. It is not yet known how differing the phobias can be among members of a particular group. Social skills training has been given successfully in groups where subjects do not necessarily share identical problems, but learn coping skills from watching and criticizing one another (reviewed by Hersen, Eisler, & Miller, 1973). Group exposure *in vivo* in patients has been successful (Hafner & Marks, 1974; Hand *et al.,* 1974) and will be described later.

4. Massing of Sessions

It is usually more convenient to give one long treatment session than several short ones, so that massing of treatment sessions is another potential time-saver. Suinn and Hall (1970) found that 8 hours of desensitization over 24 hours achieved similar results as when given over 2–3 weeks.

In students with mathematics anxiety, Richardson and Suinn (1973) found equal benefit at 4-weeks follow-up, on a test and subjective discomfort, from nine sessions of desensitization in fantasy given either over 3 weeks or in one 3-hour session. Massed desensitization was applied only to the highest three items, whereas the spaced sessions used graded items, which confounded the analysis. However, it is clear that prolonged exposure in fantasy is effective. The same applies to prolonged exposure *in vivo* in phobic patients (Hand *et al.,* 1974; Stern & Marks, 1973a; Watson *et al.,* 1971) (see page 118).

III. STUDIES IN PATIENTS

Although most papers on patients are anecdotal, a growing volume of controlled reports is at last appearing. The latter are more directly relevant to clinicians than are analogue studies, and will be dwelt on in more detail, but pertinent work in volunteers will be mentioned. Various exposure treatments produce significant reduction of fear in patient populations. Statistical significance does not always imply clinical significance, and evaluation must take into account the broader clinical context of management.

A. Slow Exposure (Desensitization)

Since 1970, desensitization in fantasy has produced significant improvement in phobic patients in at least 10 controlled studies (Benjamin *et al.,* 1972; P. D. Evans & Kellam, 1973; Gelder *et al.,* 1973; Gillan & Rachman, 1974; Husain, 1971; Marks *et al.,* 1971a; L. C. Miller, Barrett, Hampe, & Noble, 1972; Obler & Terwilliger, 1970; Solyom, Heseltine, McClure, Ledwidge, & Kenny, 1971; Solyom, Shugar, Bryntwick, & Solyom, 1973). Desensitization also improved a general psychiatric population in one study (Boudewyns & Wilson, 1972) but not in another (McReynolds, 1970).

Taped desensitization had comparable effects to that given by a live therapist (P. D. Evans & Kellam, 1973) in 24 phobics, half of whom were agoraphobics, treated in sixteen half-hour sessions given weekly. Although significant, overall effects were small.

The longest *follow-up* so far after exposure treatment is 4 years (Marks, 1971). Patients were followed up who had been previously treated by desensitization in fantasy (Gelder & Marks, 1966, 1968; Gelder, Marks, & Wolff, 1967; Marks, Gelder, & Edwards, 1968). Sixty-five outpatients with phobic disorders of more than a year's duration were followed up prospectively for 4 years after completion of treatment. Follow-up rate was 92% of all patients who were treated. Phobias which had improved during treatment remained static over the follow-up period for the group as a whole. While 42% of patients were unimproved in their phobias at the end of follow-up, 15% required further treatment for depressive episodes, during which phobias were temporarily aggravated. The group remained one of phobic disorders and did not develop any other kind of neurotic syndrome.

1. SHAPING *in Vivo*

The work of Crowe *et al.* (1972) is described on page 114. Two other studies are available.

a. Practice without Praise ("Self-Observation") (Emmelkamp & Ultee, 1974). This was a balanced crossover study of 16 agoraphobics, mainly patients. They were assigned at random to repeated practice with praise for progress ("successive approximation," shaping) or without praise ("self-observation"). Subjects had six 90-minute sessions given twice weekly of each condition in balanced order.

Practice consisted of a client being encouraged to go out for increasingly long periods and writing the time down in a book, but with no praise given for progress. Shaping simply added contingent praise to this. Subjects in both conditions were instructed to leave the situation if they felt tense. Results showed that both treatments improved clients significantly, with no difference between them. Gains were small. At the end of six sessions patients became able to walk for 24 feet in the street compared to 41 in the study below.

b. Flooding in Fantasy (Everaerd *et al.,* 1973). This crossover comparison was in 14 chronic agoraphobic volunteers from a phobic club. Treatment began in the client's own home and comprised six 90-minute sessions, given twice weekly, of each condition in a balanced order. Flooding sessions began with 45 minutes of fantasy flooding by phobia-relevant cues for 3–8 minutes at a time, followed immediately by 45 minutes' exposure *in vivo.* When a client could not imagine the phobic situation he was asked to say it aloud as a guided fantasy. Shaping *in vivo* was as in the previous study.

Both treatment groups improved significantly and equally on avoidance, clinical phobia scales and a fear survey schedule, and improvement was maintained at the 3-month follow-up. There was little difference between results in the two conditions. The shaping group had twice longer exposure *in vivo* than the flooding condition, but in interrupted fashion, which confounds interpretation.

In summary, repeated brief exposure *in vivo* has an effect in agoraphobics, and systematic reward has not added much to this.

2. Aversion Relief

This method was used by Solyom and colleagues in several studies, none of which reported follow-up. Solyom *et al.* (1971) assigned 20 phobic patients to 50 half-hour sessions of aversion relief or 25 sessions of desensitization in fantasy, sessions occurring once weekly. Cessation of shock was contingent upon the patient's hearing his own taped narrative of his phobic experiences. Both treatment groups improved significantly in phobias after treatment, with no significant differences between them.

In another study (Solyom, McClure, Heseltine, Ledwidge, & Solyom, 1972b), 27 phobic outpatients were assigned to one of three conditions. In all three, patients heard their own taped phobic narratives; 15-second silences interrupted the narratives prior to anxiety material for an aversion relief and for a habituation group, and randomly for a pseudoconditioning group. In the aversion relief and pseudoconditioning procedures, the silence was followed by shock to a finger. Duration of shock was controlled by the subject, who could press a button to terminate it, which simultaneously restarted the taped phobic narrative. The habituation group heard similar taped phobic narratives and silences, but received no shocks. Treatment involved twenty-four half-hour sessions twice weekly. Results showed no significant differences between the three groups. The aversion relief and habituation groups improved significantly on phobias. Sometimes the aversion-relief occurred simultaneously with the taped phobic narrative, which suggests that shock and exposure rather than shock relief may have been important, perhaps through stress immunization. The pseudoconditioning control which had shock after random periods of silence on the tape also improved, but not significantly.

Another aversion-relief comparison was reported by Solyom *et al.* (1973) in 40 airplane phobics. These received either desensitization in fantasy, aversion relief, habituation or "group psychotherapy," only the last having any form of group participation. Desensitized patients had four hour-long sessions in fantasy and four hour-long viewings of flight films, treatment being given twice weekly to a total of 8 hours over 1 month. Aversion relief subjects wrote their own phobic narrative, which was taped, and then had aversion-relief shocks while they heard this narrative for eight half-hours and then while they watched flight films for a further eight half-hours. "Habituation" subjects had the same experience as aversion-relief patients, but without shock. "Group psychotherapy" patients had five 2-hour sessions weekly during which they discussed air travel fears and other experiences. They then met a pilot and discussed air travel at an airport and subsequently had a 15-minute practice flight as a group with the therapist, treatment time being 12 hours. So-called "group psychotherapy" thus included some exposure *in vivo.* Results showed that the first three groups improved significantly but did not differ significantly from one another or from the "group psychotherapy" condition. They indicate that widely varying forms of exposure produce relief with or without shocks, but confounding of conditions precludes further conclusions.

In view of the work of Meichenbaum and Cameron (1974b), it would be interesting to know whether shocks or other "stress immunizers" can help to generalize improvement after exposure. Data on this point are not yet available in patients.

3. Desensitization in Fantasy with and without Muscular Relaxation

As in volunteers, controlled work in patients has found desensitization in fantasy equally effective with and without muscular relaxation. Systematic comparison of these two conditions was made by Benjamin *et al.* (1972). In a crossover design, 8 phobic outpatients were treated by six sessions of desensitization followed by exposure, or vice versa. In each of the two conditions, treatment was by visualization of phobic images up a hierarchy for 20 seconds at a time, but during desensitization patients were relaxed before and after each phobic image, while during exposure they looked at a neutral slide between phobic fantasies. Before treatment all patients had a single session of 15 minutes of relaxation training and were requested to practice relaxation twice daily for 15 minutes at home until treatment began. Treatment sessions lasted 50 minutes and were given twice weekly. Phobic fantasies lasted 20 seconds and were presented in series of five for each hierarchy item. Within treatment sessions, skin conductance activity became significantly lower during relaxation than during observation of a neutral slide. Progress during treatment was at a similar rate in both treatment conditions for subjective anxiety, skin conductance, and heart rate during phobic imagery. Three days after the last treatment session, patients, therapists, and an independent blind assessor rated the main phobia as significantly improved for both treatments together. However, each of the two treatments contributed similarly to improvement during and also after treatment sessions on measures of the main phobia, and of subjective anxiety and heart rate during phobic fantasies. Both relaxation and relaxation training were thus redundant to the desensitization procedure. Furthermore, no support was found for the idea of Lader and Mathews (1967) that habituation proceeds more rapidly at lower levels of arousal. The few significant correlations between prestimulus arousal and response decrement were in the opposite direction to that predicted, i.e., positive instead of negative.

A second study of this issue is by Gillan and Rachman (1974), who compared desensitization in fantasy without relaxation ("hierarchies") and with relaxation. A mixture of 32 agoraphobic and specific phobic outpatients were treated over thirty 45-minute sessions twice weekly, scenes being imagined for 10 seconds at a time. Desensitization in fantasy was equally effective whether relaxation was present or absent. Results in this study and by Solyom *et al.* (1971) were very comparable to those obtained with desensitization in fantasy by Gelder *et al.* (1967).

B. Desensitization versus Flooding

The confounding nature of these comparisons was discussed on page 85 in volunteers and applies in patients as well.

1. In Mixed Psychiatric Inpatients

Fantasy, implosion, and desensitization were contrasted (Boudewyns & Wilson, 1972) in male inpatients who had high *D* or *Pt* scores on the Minnesota Multiphasic Personality Inventory (MMPI). Implosion lasted about 30 minutes during 50-minute sessions. Either treatment was given up to twelve sessions phased over about 40 days. These were contrasted with a nonrandomly selected group which simply continued in routine psychiatric treatment. There were no significant differences in outcome between implosion and desensitization, while both were significantly better than milieu treatment at 6 months but not at the one-year follow-up. Subjective anxiety during sessions was not predictive of outcome. As patients in this study were rather heterogeneous and the control group was not selected randomly, firm conclusions are precluded.

2. In Phobic Patients

a. Fantasy Desensitization versus Fantasy Flooding without in Vivo Exposure

i. With thiopental or saline. Husain (1971) treated 40 patients with agoraphobia or social phobias in a crossover design by desensitization or flooding in fantasy over six 45-minute sessions given twice weekly. Half the subjects had intravenous thiopental during the sessions, and half had saline. Phobias improved markedly with thiopental flooding but only slightly with saline flooding and moderately with thiopental or saline desensitization. The thiopental flooding group improved most. No follow-up was reported.

ii. Desensitization in fantasy versus flooding in fantasy versus shaping in vivo. In a crossover study (Crowe *et al.,* 1972) 14 phobic outpatients each received three treatments in a balanced design. Every patient had three preparatory interviews and then twelve treatment sessions made up of four successive sessions of each technique. Flooding in fantasy employed only relevant phobic cues. Operant shaping was the method of reinforced practice used by Leitenberg and Callahan (1973). Results on an avoidance test showed that shaping was significantly superior to desensitization, with flooding in between and differing significantly from neither. On clinical scales, shaping improved patients less than did flooding or desensitization. Both flooding and desensitization improved untreated as well as treated phobias, whereas shaping had a more specific effect on treated phobias alone. Therapeutic changes were smaller than in previous trials, perhaps because no single treatment had time to build up much effect before a new one was started. The four sessions per condition were fewer than in previous controlled trials of this kind. Unfortunately both flooding and desensitization were in fantasy only, while shaping was given in practice. This factor might explain the behavioral superiority of shaping. Further work on shaping *in vivo* was described on page 110.

b. Desensitization in Fantasy and in Vivo versus Flooding in Fantasy and in Vivo

i. Maudsley study (Boulougouris, Marks, & Marset, 1971; Marks *et al.,* 1971a). This investigation compared flooding and desensitization given first in fantasy and then *in vivo.* Interest at that time focused on short-term effects, so a crossover design was employed in 16 inpatients and outpatients with severe chronic agoraphobia and other phobias. Patients were randomly allocated either to six 50-minute sessions of desensitization in fantasy followed by six sessions of flooding in fantasy or vice versa. The fifth and sixth sessions of either treatment were followed immediately by 70 minutes of either desensitization or flooding in practice. Treatment was given 3 times weekly over about 5 weeks. All 16 patients received both treatments, 8 in one order and 8 in the other, equal therapeutic time being spent in both. All patients were accompanied by their therapist during practice sessions, except three who specifically asked to do their flooding alone. All were asked to practice outside treatment the relaxation or flooding they had received during treatment. Results showed that flooding produced significantly more improvement on phobia ratings and on heart rate and skin conductance measures during phobic imagery. This difference was present before and after crossover. Anxiety during treatment sessions did not correlate with outcome, a finding that was later repeated by Watson and Marks (1971) and Mathews *et al.* (1974). Patients maintained their improvement to one-year follow-up. Outcome with this study was better than in previous reports of desensitization in fantasy (Marks, 1971). This might have been because of the two *in vivo* sessions that immediately followed the 5th & 6th fantasy sessions in each treatment condition.

ii. Oxford study (Gelder *et al.,* 1973; Mathews *et al.,* 1974). A different balanced but parallel design was employed here. Thirty-six mixed agoraphobic and other chronic phobic patients were assigned randomly to one of three treatments and one of three therapists. Half of each group was given an induction interview during which a glowing picture of treatment potency was given to increase patient expectations. Treatment was over 15 weekly outpatient sessions, the first three of which were history taking, the next eight fantasy treatment, and the last four *in vivo* treatment. Throughout treatment all patients were asked to keep a diary of phobic experiences and counterphobic behavior and were set a weekly goal to be achieved in overcoming phobic avoidance. The three treatment conditions were mainly differentiated on the basis of the eight fantasy sessions. (1) "Nonspecific control" patients were asked to use their phobic imagery as a basis for free-associative psychotherapy. (2) Desensitization subjects had muscular relaxation plus hierarchy images. (3) Flooding in fantasy used relevant cues without dynamic content, usually given by the therapist and occasionally taped, sometimes guided by the patient.

The four sessions of practice were patterned on the form of the three imaginal treatments, although "differences in procedure were found more difficult to maintain. The patient was always given strong encouragement to enter the phobic situation, but little attempt was made to apply specific desensitization or flooding measures while practice was going on, so that the main divergence between treatments was due to hierarchy levels used and the degree of anxiety tolerated." Thus, during the important *in vivo* phase there was much overlap among treatment conditions. Sessions lasted 1–1½ hours, with imaginal procedures lasting 45–60 minutes and practice sessions sometimes continuing to 2 hours. After discharge, patients were followed up for 6 months.

The attempt to increase patient expectations of improvement by an induction interview was not significantly effective, and there was no significant correlation between expectations and outcome. Outcome was also similar across each of the three therapists. Most crucial, there were no important significant differences between desensitization and flooding, though both were significantly more effective than the control procedure.

Improvement was of the same order as that obtained in previous studies of desensitization in fantasy (Gelder *et al.*, 1967) and less than that obtained by Marks *et al.* (1971a). Desensitization did not differ significantly from the control group on clinical ratings and a behavioral test; the only significant differences on phobic measures were on agoraphobia and social anxiety scales of a fear survey schedule, and on patients' estimates of anxiety and symptoms in a phobic situation. Flooding differed significantly from the control group on the latter two measures and also on the "blind" psychiatric rating of the main phobia, the patient's rating of improvement and of anxiety when imagining the phobic situation, behavior avoidance test and the apprehension factor of the 16 PF. At the end of treatment, on phobic measures the control group had improved significantly less than desensitization on 4 and less than flooding on 7 variables.

Further details of this study are reported by Mathews *et al.* (1974). On the scale, "How you would feel when *actually* in phobic situation 'X,' " significant improvement had not appeared by the end of the eight fantasy sessions, but became significant after the first practice session. Nearly all the improvement from desensitization and flooding occurred on this scale during the last four practice sessions (see their Fig. 6). In contrast, on the scale, "How you would feel when *thinking* about phobic situation 'X,' " improvement began early in the fantasy phase and continued through the *in vivo* period. Thus, treatment by thinking about a phobic situation led to improvement in such thoughts, while treatment by actually going out made people feel better about that as well as the thoughts. However, not all the results can be explained by the *in vivo* phase, since control subjects who also had it improved less. Perhaps imagining repeated phobic approach prepares subjects for subsequent overt entry into the phobic situation.

The study strongly suggests that *fantasy* desensitization and flooding have comparable effects. The findings cannot illuminate the question whether *in vivo* exposure is more effective when given rapidly or slowly, as this was not clearly controlled. Mathews *et al.* found no relationship between anxiety level before or during treatment and outcome to either desensitization or flooding. It is possible that the *in vivo* phase washed out any relationship there might have been between pretreatment anxiety and outcome to fantasy treatment alone. Patients who did best at follow-up were more socially outgoing, which had also been found by Marks *et al.* (1971a) and Gelder *et al.* (1967).

iii. Comparison between Maudsley and Oxford studies. The overall improvement in phobia scales after twelve sessions was greater in the Maudsley than in the Oxford study for reasons that are not clear. Two important differences between the two investigations confound interpretation. First, Gelder *et al.* (1973) did not have sharply contrasting conditions across the three groups during exposure *in vivo,* whereas that of Marks *et al.* (1971a) was firmly forceful during flooding but relaxed during desensitization. Much of the superiority of flooding over desensitization which was obtained by Marks *et al.* might thus be attributable to their manipulation of exposure conditions *in vivo* rather than in fantasy. The second difference between the two studies is that Gelder *et al.* gave fantasy and *in vivo* sessions on separate weeks, whereas Marks *et al.* gave exposure *in vivo* immediately after fantasy treatment. It is possible that shortly after fantasy treatment, patients are briefly refractory to anxiety, during which phase exposure *in vivo* might be potentiated.

C. Aspects of Rapid Exposure (Flooding)

1. Relevant versus Irrelevant Fear Imagery (Watson & Marks, 1971)

Improvement during fantasy exposure could conceivably be produced by any frightening material, even if irrelevant, or perhaps by imagery that is not frightening but concerned with other intense emotions, e.g., anger or sexual arousal. Sixteen patients with severe phobias were treated in a balanced crossover design which compared relevant with irrelevant fear imagery. Eight patients had eight sessions of imaginal flooding concerned with their phobias, followed by eight imaginal sessions concerned with normal fear situations, while another eight patients had the same treatment in reverse order. The order of treatment was allocated at random and delay in crossing over from one treatment to the other was 4–8 days. Each session lasted 50 minutes, and treatment was given two to three times weekly.

Relevant flooding included frightening phobia-relevant cues about psychodynamic material, while irrelevant fear cues included themes like being caught, mangled, and eaten by a tiger, being burned to death, and drowning. Three to four themes were used in each session. Themes had to be varied on each repetition because patients habituated rapidly when identical words were repeated and the aim was to elicit maximum fear for as long as possible.

Results showed that the combined effect of relevant and irrelevant fear was a significant reduction of all clinical phobia ratings, of negative attitudes to phobic concepts, and of tachycardia and subjective anxiety during phobic imagery. Physiologic responses to a control fear scene or to neutral imagery did not change. Throughout the trial, attitudes remained consistently negative to the control fear and consistently positive to a control pleasant concept. Each of the two treatments alone produced significant improvement in clinical phobia scales. None of the clinical, attitudinal, or physiologic measures were differently affected by the two procedures except for subjective anxiety during phobic imagery, which was reduced more by irrelevant than by relevant fear.

Anxiety in each treatment session was usually at its peak by 20 minutes and remained at that peak until the end of the session at about 50 minutes. As soon as the session ended, anxiety usually dropped abruptly. Later sessions usually provoked less anxiety than earlier ones, especially with irrelevant fear. When given as first treatment, relevant and irrelevant fear generated similar amounts of anxiety during the session. However, in the second treatment block, after crossover, relevant flooding was more anxiety-provoking than irrelevant fear. Therefore, it was more anxiety-provoking as first than as second treatment. Relevant flooding thus seemed to protect patients from anxiety during subsequent frightening experiences, but irrelevant fear did not.

Despite contrary expectancy by the therapist, relevant and irrelevant fear produced similar therapeutic effect, but had different prognostic correlates. As in the study by Marks *et al.* (1971a), flooding produced greater improvement in those patients who had shown more physiologic anxiety before treatment began. In contrast, irrelevant fear produced less improvement in patients who showed more subjective anxiety at initial assessment; i.e., the more anxious a patient became during imagery at initial assessment, the more likely he was to improve with relevant fear and the less likely with irrelevant fear. Another difference between the two treatments was that, as also found by Marks *et al.* (1971a) and Gelder *et al.* (1973), outcome to relevant flooding did not correlate with the amount of anxiety experienced during treatment. In contrast, outcome to irrelevant fear was better in those patients who showed much anxiety *during* treatment sessions. This suggests that abreaction may be an operative element in irrelevant fear but not in relevant flooding.

Patients maintained greater improvement over 6 months' follow-up than in previous studies of desensitization (Gelder *et al.,* 1967), but less than that obtained by Marks *et al.* (1971a). The overall effect was thought to be reduced by the absence of flooding *in vivo.*

2. Prolonged Exposure in Vivo (Watson et al., 1971; Watson, Gaind, & Marks, 1972)

In this uncontrolled study 10 patients with severe specific phobias (e.g., dogs, spiders, balloons) were attached to a polygraph while in contact with the phobic object for 2–3 hours at a time. Five patients had previously received relevant flooding in fantasy. The patient was encouraged to approach the feared object as closely and as quickly as he could and to remain in contact with it until his anxiety diminished. Avoidance, including averting the head or eyes or drawing the hand away, was discouraged. Attempts to deliberately provoke anxiety were gradually abandoned as these seemed counterproductive, and in later patients sessions were conducted in as free and pleasant a way as possible with minimal praise for progress and modeling where necessary.

All 10 patients showed marked improvement in clinical scales and in heart rate by the end of treatment, maintaining this improvement over 3 months' follow-up. Thus, 2–3 afternoons of treatment *in vivo* over an average of 6 hours in all improved these specific phobics more rapidly than did previous trials over 15 hours of desensitization in fantasy or 8 hours of flooding in fantasy. This work suggested the value of long *in vivo* exposure. A controlled study to examine the short-term effects of duration was then conducted.

3. Brief and Prolonged Flooding in Fantasy and in Vivo (Stern & Marks, 1973a)

In a Latin square crossover design, 16 chronically agoraphobic outpatients were exposed to four sessions (over 2 weeks) of long or short flooding in fantasy and in practice. Each session consisted of exposure in fantasy in the morning and exposure in practice on the afternoon of the same day. Fantasy flooding was given by tape recorder for 80 continuous minutes (long) or in eight 10-minute bursts separated by 5-minute periods of neutral material (short). Long *in vivo* exposure lasted 2 continuous hours, while short *in vivo* exposure was over 4 half-hours separated by 30-minute rest periods. Outcome of exposure *in vivo* was measured 3–4 days after the session.

Neither long nor short taped flooding in fantasy produced autonomic arousal or much improvement. By contrast, 2 hours of flooding in practice reduced phobias significantly more than did 4 half-hour periods of the same procedure in one afternoon, although both conditions led to increased heart rate. During long flooding in practice, heart rate and subjective anxiety decreased more over the second than the first hour of exposure to the real phobic situation; although treatment was directed toward top hierarchy items, bottom items improved more. Improvement was maintained at follow-up. Patients' expectation of improvement at the start of treatment did not correlate with outcome. Good outcome was predicted by high physiological arousal during phobic imagery before treatment (skin conductance deflections and heart rate). As with Marks *et al.* (1971a), Watson and Marks (1971), and Gelder *et al.* (1973), symptoms such as depression, panic, and anxiety did not increase at the end of treatment. For the group as a whole, symptoms were less marked than at the beginning of treatment.

These results with patients fit those with animals and with volunteers which show that longer exposure is usually more therapeutic. The reason for this is unclear. Perhaps the duration of exposure is less important than that of intervals between exposure, and this requires further study. Incubation or cognitive rehearsal between periods of exposure might be responsible. Alternatively, prolonging sessions might increase the chances of some critical but unknown process occurring that facilitates improvement; this idea lies behind past emphases on reaching the point of emotional exhaustion during abreaction of war neuroses (Sargant, 1957).

Implications for clinical practice are that exposure *in vivo* should proceed to the stage of prolonged exposure in real life as quickly as possible. The period of 2 hours might be a guideline for severe chronic patients. For phobias of recent onset, shorter periods of exposure might still be effective. It is not known whether sessions even longer than 2 hours might not be even better. Perhaps better results might be obtained when the duration of flooding is individually tailored to each patient, but the optimum criterion for termination is unknown. Perhaps this occurs when all components of phobic response have subsided, i.e. subjective anxiety, attitude, avoidance, and physiology. The optimum moment might vary from one patient to another. It may be more important to end a session on a "good note" of improvement than to simply have a prolonged session as such.

An invariant fantasy-practice order of treatment had been adopted because at the time it was feared that many patients might refuse *in vivo* exposure unless this was preceded by improvement during preceding fantasy treatment. Later trials showed this fear to be groundless (Hafner & Marks, 1975; Hand *et al.,* 1974). Notwithstanding this design problem, the magnitude of improvement after treatment in practice suggests that this is more powerful than treatment in fantasy whether in long or short bursts. Fantasy treatment can be used in those patients who need preparation before they can endure real-life exposure, or where *in vivo* exposure is impracticable in the session, e.g., with phobias of thunderstorms or of sex.

The absence of physiological arousal during phobic imagery at assessment and during fantasy treatment might be due to the fact that instructions were tape-recorded. In previous studies which obtained significant arousal during phobic imagery, instructions were delivered by therapists facing the patient and speaking to him in a normal voice (Marks & Huson, 1973; Marks *et al.,* 1971b). Patients might pay more attention to the normal voice of a nearby therapist than to a tape-recorded instruction using the same words. The immediate effect of relaxation instructions has been greater when given personally rather than taped (Paul & Trimble, 1970).

4. Cohesive versus Unstructured Group Exposure in Vivo (Hand et al., 1974)

The next step was to examine whether prolonged exposure *in vivo* could be given successfully in groups to save time, and possibly be enhanced in potency, through social cohesion. Two balanced conditions were examined with varying degrees of social cohesion. Twenty-five outpatients with chronic agoraphobia were treated in six groups of 4 or 5 patients each, the first four groups by two therapists, the last two groups by one. Over 1 week each patient had three 4-hour sessions of group exposure *in vivo.* There was one session per day lasting 4 continuous hours interrupted midday for a half-hour lunch break.

Instructions for anxiety management (coping) were the same in all patients during treatment and follow-up. During exposure, *in vivo* patients were trained to deal with phobic and free floating anxiety by accepting that anxiety would occur, attending to the cues that denoted its presence, rating the signs without exaggeration, watching how long it took for them to subside, attending to events to master the situation. The aim was not so much to extinguish anxiety as to manage it so that it did not govern one's actions. The actual method of regulation was not crucial.

Group panic did not appear during any treatment sessions. However, several patients had horror reactions or depression during the nights or free day between treatment sessions. These happened particularly after patients had progressed rapidly during sessions and experienced little anxiety in peak phobic situations. Reactions were remedied by immediate reexposure and motivating group discussion. The mornings before exposure began, patients often complained of depression which lifted during treatment.

An impressive coping device used often by the groups, especially structured ones, was joking and light-hearted humor. Humor is rare during individual flooding sessions.

On behavioral tests and clinical scales, outcome for all groups was at least as good as in previous trials with individual patients. Behavioral avoidance tests were poor measures of clinical performance (see page

76). Both treatment conditions produced so much improvement in avoidance that there was little chance for differences between them. Patients from structured groups felt less overall improvement during the treatment week itself, but all groups had improved similarly on phobic scales 3 days after treatment. Owing to continuing improvement, structured groups became significantly better than nonstructured ones at the 3- and 6-month follow-up on phobia and on global improvement scales. The better results of patients from cohesive groups seemed to be due to their higher motivation for treatment exercises in sessions and at follow-up. Structured groups yielded only 1 of the 4 dropouts, 1 of the 4 total relapses, and 4 of the 12 patients who needed extra treatment during follow-up. Many trial patients showed marital and personality problems before treatment, several with acute exacerbations of these during follow-up. Nevertheless, patients as a whole improved significantly in work, leisure, and social adjustment.

Another value of group exposure was its unplanned contribution to social skills and assertive training. This social "spin-off" presumably resulted from the rehearsal of social behavior which occurred naturally during group treatment. Several patients got used to contacting strangers when anxious in the phobic situation and obtained relief by talking to them about their anxiety. An elevator phobic was on her third run up and down when the operator asked her why she was doing this. Feeling ashamed, she told him the problem. He sympathized and immediately told her about his flying phobia. The patient was so impressed by this experience that she repeated such behavior in other situations.

Another patient with social phobia panicked in a shop while waiting for the salesgirl to give her change. The salesgirl told her to see a psychiatrist. The patient left the shop shaking, ashamed, and angry with the therapist. She was persuaded to return to the shop immediately and tell the same salesgirl that she had just seen a psychiatrist who had told her to go back to her. The patient did so and returned 20 minutes later having had a long talk with the salesgirl, who admitted she disliked customers trying small talk with her as she felt so inhibited. The salesgirl invited the patient to come as often as possible, as she might learn with her to chat to customers. The same patient thereafter completed many more exposure exercises with the same sense of humor.

In summary, Hand *et al.* (1974) found that prolonged group exposure *in vivo* was effective in agoraphobics, especially when group cohesion was fostered.

Yet another study (Hafner & Marks, 1975) found that group exposure was effective in agoraphobics. In that study patients were assigned at random to group or individual exposure *in vivo* for comparable lengths of time. Group exposure showed a consistent trend to produce greater improvement on measures of phobias including those concerning social anxiety. An uncontrolled report by Watson, Mullett, and Pillay (1973) also found significant improvement from group exposure, both in fantasy and in practice.

5. Drugs and Exposure Treatments

This topic is reviewed by Liberman and Davis in this volume and by Marks (1974b). In brief, ORAL *benzodiazepines* (diazepam) (Johnston & Gath, 1973; Marks *et al.,* 1972), *beta-blockers* (alprenolol) (Ullrich, Ullrich, Granbach, & Peikert, 1972), *monoamine oxidase inhibitors* (phenelzine) (Solyom *et al.,* 1973; Tyrer, Candy, & Kelly, 1973) and (iproniazid) (Lipsedge, Hijioff, Huggins, Napier, Pearce, Pike, & Rich, 1973), and *tricyclics* (imipramine) (Gittelman-Klein and Klein, 1971; Klein, 1964) were found in controlled designs to have some value in phobic disorders. Their role in combination with exposure needs much more exploration. The routine use of INTRAVENOUS drugs, such as methohexitone or clomipramine, with behavioral methods is unjustified until more appropriate controlled studies have been completed.

6. Other Aids to Exposure

If contact with the phobic object is usually the chief therapeutic principle in treatment, then any ploy to maintain such contact might be helpful. The utility of humor during group exposure was mentioned by Hand *et al.* (1974), and humor for the reduction of anger was noted by Smith (1973). "Respiratory relief" is another such device (Orwin, 1972, 1973), with or without inhalations of carbon dioxide. The patient pinches his nose and closes his mouth to arrest his breathing voluntarily until he simply must inspire, at which point of relief he is exposed to the phobic stimulus. Running, in agoraphobics, has also been said to be helpful (Orwin, 1973). "Mechanical facilitation" during exposure *in vivo* was described in a man with a phobia of firearms (Naud, Boisvert, & Lamontagne, 1974). The patient was exposed to noises of and real firearms while he had to manually transfer bolts and rings from one set of holes to another. A similar method was used by Poser (cited in Naud *et al.,* 1974). That such techniques enhance the value of exposure has not been established, though they may be helpful aids at difficult moments during treatment.

D. Special Treatment Problems

1. Phobias in Children

Controlled studies on this topic are rare indeed. Obler and Terwilliger (1970) examined desensitization *in vivo* and in fantasy of neurologically impaired children with phobias. Thirty children with severe monophobias of using a bus or of dogs had either no treatment or five hour-long sessions once weekly. The procedure was graded exposure in fantasy and *in vivo* with reward for progress, but no relaxation or hierarchy construction. After treatment, 8 of the 15 treated and none of the untreated patients were rated much improved.

A detailed review of the behavioral treatment of school phobia was reported by Hersen (1971), who reported many single case studies and found no controlled group studies at that time. Since then one has appeared in a mixed school and other phobic population (L. C. Miller *et al.,* 1972) with a one-year follow-up report (Barrett, 1972). This investigation compared desensitization in fantasy, play therapy and a waiting-list control. From a total of 148 children initially screened, 67 phobics age 6–15 were treated. Of these, 46 had school phobia, 14 including separation anxiety. Several had phobias of brief duration. Treatment was given in 24 sessions over 8 weeks. The waiting-list time was 3 months.

Results showed that younger children aged 6–10 did well in all three conditions, although the waiting-list children had a non-significant trend to do less well on the parents' rating of the main phobia and a behavior check list. Children aged 13 or more did the least well; those who did best were aged 11 or less or had parents with high motivation. One year follow-up results were the same as at the end of treatment.

Therapist expectations that desensitization would be the most effective were not confirmed. Although both desensitization and play therapy did equally well, the waiting-list control also showed much improvement. The differential trend in favor of treated groups was not significant. Such a result is always a hazard in a population with a high tendency to spontaneous remission, e.g., children with acute fears, like some in this sample. More important is the failure to obtain even a trend toward different outcomes from play or desensitization therapy. Perhaps phobias in children are responsive to more influences than in adults.

2. Social Skills Deficits

Social skills (assertive) training can help socially anxious subjects by a variety of techniques that expose them to social situations. Numerous clinical researchers are developing methods that help subjects decrease their social fears and, where necessary, develop new interpersonal skills in being pleasant, assertive, or otherwise as the occasion demands. Wide exploration of this field proceeds under labels like behavior or role rehearsal, encounter groups in their manifold forms, and psychodrama. Although results are often gratifying, they can also be time-consuming and disappointing. The technology of changing interpersonal behavior is still primitive, but it does seem to involve a dimension different from that required in nonpersonal fears.

Most work in this area is in volunteers rather than in patients. The literature has been well reviewed by Hersen *et al.* (1973), to which the interested reader is referred. Subsequent studies are by Kazdin (1974), who found in unassertive students the same results as in the snake phobia work reviewed on page 104–5; and by McFall and Twentyman (1973), which was noted on page 104. There is one unpublished study of socially inhibited patients by Ullrich de Muynck and Ullrich (1972), who found that patients improved after thirty sessions of group social skills training, including active role rehearsal between sessions, compared with individual treatments, such as desensitization.

3. Test Anxiety

Although these fears do not appear to be particularly different from other phobias, the problem has been the focus of many experiments, nearly all in volunteers. In an extensive review, Allen (1972) concluded that a mixture of desensitization and "study counseling" yields more improvement than either alone. Study counseling included self-regulatory instructions of the kind described earlier by Wine (1971) and Sarason (1973b).

4. Anger

Undesirable emotions apart from anxiety can be managed by exposure treatments. Two workers experimented with the desensitization of anger in volunteers. Anger while driving was desensitized in 30 subjects, who improved more up to 2 weeks follow-up than subjects who had placebo or no treatment (Rimm, De Groot, Hoord, Heiman, & Dillow, 1971). The anger of race prejudice was studied in 32 students by O'Donnell and Worell (1973). Desensitization in fantasy led to more "improvement" than did no treatment.

Reports with patients are mostly anecdotal. A woman whose temper outbursts with her family were unmanageable improved after nine sessions of imagining anger-inducing scenes plus ludicrous elements suggested by the therapist which made the patient laugh (Smith, 1973). Humor was regarded as a "counter-conditioner." Anger utilized as a therapeutic ingredient was described by Serber, Goldstein, Piaget, and Kort (1969) in "implosive-expressive therapy," and by Ikemi (1972) in aggressive patients; patients improved after they were successfully encouraged to act out their hostility by pillow pounding and throwing of glasses, etc.

5. Sexual Fears

The behavioral management of sexual dysfunction was recently reviewed in detail by Marks (1974a). Suffice to say that only one controlled study has appeared in patients (Kockott, Nussel, & Dittmar, 1974), though others are in progress. Desensitization in fantasy alone conferred no significant advantage over routine treatment, but better results were obtained when subjects were subsequently crossed over to a Masters and Johnson approach. Several controlled studies on the subject are now in progress in various centers.

6. Urination Phobias

Patients commonly complain of inability to urinate in toilets outside their home, although defecation and sexual performance may present no problems. Two patients like these were treated with partial success in sessions conducted after they had consumed excessive fluids. Patients were asked to remain in the hospital toilet (the phobic situation) until they managed to urinate at least a few drops (Lamontagne & Marks, 1973). Initially this took up to 2 hours. Once urination was possible the phobic situation was made progressively more difficult by having people stand outside the lavatory door. Exercises were also prescribed in toilets outside the hospital. Patients rapidly became able to void urine increasingly completely in successive sessions, and improvement generalized, though residual difficulties remained.

The foregoing study employed the principle of prolonged exposure *in vivo* to the inhibiting situation until at least some urination occurred. A modification was described by Wilson (1973) in a man who was unable to urinate or defecate in toilets outside his home. Desensitization in fantasy produced no real-life improvement. The subject was then asked to urinate in "safe" conditions alone, but just at the moment when urination became inevitable to imagine someone walking in. He then had to fade this scene in progressively earlier, and after 2 weeks was able to imagine himself urinating next to another man, after which he was required to do this in real life. Although urination improved he remained unable to defecate in a public toilet. This independence of urination and defecation was also noted in both subjects of Lamontagne and Marks (1973), who had no problems in defecation or sexual function despite severe social inhibitions to urination.

7. Blood and Injury Phobias

Although fainting at the sight of blood is part of our folklore, only recently has it been observed that fainting *in phobics* occurs significantly more during exposure to blood/injury phobia situations than to other phobic stimuli (Connolly, Hallam, & Marks, 1975). On exposure to phobic situations, most phobics show tachycardia whereas blood injury phobics are markedly bradycardic. Whatever the contributions of phylogenesis and learning to this association of fainting with blood/injury situations, this stimulus-specific phobic response can still be extinguished by graded exposure *in vivo,* heart rate rising to normal after treatment. Exposure to other phobic situations produces tachycardia which eventually subsides to normal levels during exposure *in vivo* (Marks & Huson, 1973; Marks *et al.,* 1971b; Mathews, 1971).

8. Flying Phobias

The study by Solyom *et al.* (1973) was noted on page 111. In uncontrolled work Aitken, Daly, Lister, and O'Connor (1971) had encouraging results in 17 aircrew with flying phobias who were treated by a mixture of support, psychotherapy, and desensitization in fantasy and *in vivo.* A similar study in 6 aviators was described by Goorney (1970), 5 of whom returned to full flying duties and were all right at 3-year follow-up.

9. Food Allergies

Such allergies were desensitized by Ikemi, Sugano, Nakagawa, Uewishi, and Sugita (1969). Of 63 allergic subjects who had negative skin tests, desensitization in fantasy alone was effective in 59. In 5 similar subjects who had positive skin tests, desensitization both in fantasy and *in vivo* was needed for improvement to occur.

10. Depression

A common complication of phobias and obsessions (Kendell & Discipio, 1970; Marks, 1969, 1971), depression can retard progress with exposure techniques, and is usually treated by tricyclic drugs. When these fail, the question arises whether flooding can help depression. A few anecdotal reports of fantasy flooding of depression are encouraging (Boulougouris & Tsahtsiris, 1973; Ramsay, 1972), but much more study is needed.

E. Obsessive-Compulsive Disorders

1. Compulsive Rituals

Major advances have developed recently in the treatment of compulsive rituals. Desensitization *in fantasy* has usually been unsuccessful (e.g., Furst & Cooper, 1970; Marks, Crowe, Drewe, Young, & Dewhurst, 1969), though rarely improvement was reported (McGlynn & Linder, 1971; Wisocki, 1970). Methods of exposure *in vivo* have been more encouraging. Sometimes these involve aversion (Kenny, Solyom, & Solyom, 1973; Rubin & Merbaum, 1971). Usually, however, exposure *in vivo* does not involve shock, but may include modeling and response prevention. Numerous uncontrolled reports have appeared of successful treatment by varieties of exposure *in vivo* (Boulougouris & Bassiakos, 1973; Feather & Rhoads, 1972; Gentry, 1970; Mather, 1970; Rainey, 1972; Ramsay & Sikkel, 1971; Solyom *et al.,* 1972a). The longest series in uncontrolled reports is by Meyer and Levy (1970) and Levy and Meyer (1971). They brought patients into contact with situations which triggered compulsive rituals, and interrupted the rituals which ensued, usually helped by nursing supervision 24 hours daily. Nine of their 10 patients showed a great decrease in obsessive-compulsive behavior, which was maintained during two years of follow-up, except for slight relapse in two cases. Anxiety and depression improved concurrently.

Controlled trials in 20 patients by Rachman, Hodgson, and Marks (Hodgson *et al.,* 1972; Marks, 1973a; Rachman *et al.,* 1971, 1973) also found that exposure *in vivo* with response prevention with or without modeling was indeed helpful for compulsive rituals. Exposure *in vivo* describes prolonged contact of the patient in real life with those stimuli that occasion his discomfort or rituals; this might involve wearing of unwashed clothing, touching sticky food, or looking at objects resting out of place on his desk, etc. Response prevention refers to prevention of rituals by asking patients to desist from them for increasing periods of time with or without supervision by a therapist. Modeling implies the therapist demonstrating the required behavior to the patient first and asking the patient to do the same thereafter.

In the controlled studies, the effects were compared of (1) relaxation without modeling, (2) exposure *in vivo* at the top of the hierarchy without modeling, (3) exposure *in vivo* from the bottom of the hierarchy with modeling, (4) exposure *in vivo* at the top with modeling. Each treatment was given on an inpatient basis for 1 hour daily 5 days a week over 3 weeks, to a total of 15 hour-long sessions. After exposure, patients were asked to refrain from carrying out rituals, but there was no nursing supervision to enforce this. Twenty patients were selected who had chronic obsessive-compulsive disorders and whose rituals were triggered by identifiable stimuli in their environment. With or without modeling, treatment by exposure *in vivo* led to more significant improvement in compulsions than did relaxation. Modeling did not significantly enhance the effect of exposure. Improvement was maintained over a 24-month follow-up. Of the 20 chronic patients treated by exposure within the controlled trial, 14 responded very well, 1 moderately well, and 5 only slightly or not at all. The 15 patients who had first received 3 weeks of relaxation treatment did not improve after it on measures of obsessive-compulsive phenomena, even though relaxation produced a significant improvement in self-ratings of depression, anxiety and depersonalization. Patients enjoyed relaxation treatment, but it did their compulsions no good. Although exposure *in vivo* was effective in reducing compulsive rituals, both clinically and on objective tests, some improved patients still experienced problems in resisting rituals and dealing with obsessive thoughts. However, 6 patients were symptom free.

A case illustration might clarify the extent of improvement experienced by patients who were almost symptom-free but still had occasional difficulties. One woman always avoided areas in and around London and the nearby town of Basingstoke, where she had felt contaminated. Before treatment, the mere mention of the word Basingstoke evoked washing rituals, and a visit to the town could not be contemplated. Prior to treatment she washed her hands at least 50 times per day and used 7 giant packets of soapflakes and many bars of soap each week. She moved five times in the 3 years prior to admission in order to escape contamination and threw away much "contaminated" clothing (especially boots), even though she could ill afford to replace them. To prevent contamination she had to clean the whole house every day, including curtains, carpets, floors, and shelves. Treatment involved the complete "contamination" of her hospital environment and of her husband and child when they visited. Some sessions were devoted to shopping expeditions in areas that she avoided; most of these evoked intense anxiety and occasional tearful outbursts. A trip to Basingstoke was undertaken with her permission and resulted in total contamination, severe depression, and a threat to discharge herself.

Her depression lifted after 24 hours. Throughout treatment she managed to resist excessive washing even though she was not supervised. She was simply told that performance of her rituals would interfere with treatment. At the end of treatment and again at 6-month follow-up there was no evidence of excessive washing/cleaning rituals, but she still had some thoughts about contamination. She traveled to Basingstoke a few months after treatment, and although she felt contaminated for 8 hours she managed to resist the urge to wash. Similar feelings occurred from time to time but were always resisted. One week after the 6-month follow-up she became depressed and referred herself to the Emergency Clinic. There had been no return of her washing rituals and after talking to the Duty Doctor she felt better. She now goes out to work every day and is not crippled by obsessive thoughts of compulsive rituals. She is not as socially skilled as she would like to be and occasionally feels contaminated but believes that she will never resume her washing rituals.

This patient's experience is similar to that of 7 patients in the much improved group. She managed to resist the recurrence of time-consuming and frustrating rituals even though she experienced occasional feelings of contamination and depression. During the two-year follow-up, if anything, there was evidence of further improvement rather than deterioration.

No prognostic indices were found by Rachman *et al.* (1973), though the most difficult patients seemed to be those with repetitive, pervasive checking rituals, involving hundreds of checks every day in many situations. Perhaps continuous supervision of such patients along the lines of Meyer and Levy (1970) may facilitate improvement. Motivation is important for outcome, as it allows the cooperation necessary in treatment for improvement to occur. Patients who do not want treatment simply cannot be treated. The best prognosis seemed to be in patients with contamination fears and washing rituals focused upon a restricted number of stimulus situations.

The therapeutic efforts required to improve rituals vary greatly (Marks, 1973a). Sometimes when the principles of exposure *in vivo* with response prevention are explained to relatives or patients, they apply these successfully without the need for further treatment by a therapist (Marks, Connolly, & Hallam, 1973). Rarely do compulsive rituals disappear after one or two afternoons of flooding with response prevention by a therapist. More commonly, several weeks of concerted effort by therapist and patient are required for significant improvement. In a few cases many months of work are needed. Treatment at home or as an inpatient is not always essential, but occasionally rapid results can be obtained by simple outpatient advice. Although many compulsive patients respond gratifyingly to exposure and response prevention, with or without modeling, there are occasional dramatic failures for reasons that are obscure. Some patients may not respond while they are depressed. In these, tricyclic drugs can be helpful. In certain patients the rituals are so fleeting, infrequent, or difficult to prevent, that current methods are not applicable and other strategies need to be devised.

Limited Value of Modeling. The addition of modeling by Rachman *et al.* (1973) did not materially enhance the value of exposure *in vivo*. Some patients reported benefit from modeling procedures, whereas others were emphatic that it did not help. One man kept an image of the therapist with a trash can lid balanced on his head as a coping response which he thought reduced his avoidance of "dirty" objects and situations. In contrast, another patient stated, "I *know* other people don't have trouble with this, therefore watching it doesn't help at all." It is still unclear in which patients modeling is of particular benefit.

From the same group of workers (Roper, 1975) stems controlled evidence in another 10 patients that modeling without exposure is not therapeutic. Ten patients with chronic obsessive-compulsive rituals were treated over 15 sessions either by (1) watching the therapist perform active muscular relaxation exercises and then relaxing themselves in the same way, or (2) watching the therapist model exposure *in vivo* to contaminating situations with response prevention. The patient was not instructed to do the same after the session, and was not actually contaminated within the session. After 15 sessions of either treatment (1) or (2), all patients then crossed over to 15 sessions of (3) watching the therapist model exposure *in vivo* with response prevention and then carrying out the same exposure action themselves *within* the session. As in each of the three conditions, the patient watched a live therapist carrying out the required procedure. Modeling was constant across all three conditions. The comparison conditions were thus essentially (1) relaxation versus (2) vicarious live exposure without participation versus (3) participant live exposure. Results showed that the modeling of relaxation had no significant effect and was significantly inferior to modeling with vicarious exposure. The greatest effect was obtained by modeling of live exposure with subsequent active participation. This fits with other studies in phobics that live exposure rather than modeling is the most powerful condition.

Another study compared response prevention with and without modeling in 24 patients with compulsive rituals (Heyse, 1972). After treatment the two groups improved similarly, though results were not as encouraging as in the studies by Rachman and colleagues or by Levy and Meyer.

2. Direct versus Indirect Treatment of Compulsions

Sometimes exposure approaches make no impact on compulsive rituals, yet subsequent different tactics result in rapid amelioration. No rules can be given when to use a direct and when an oblique approach, but two patients exemplify the issue.

a. Modeling of Maternal Behavior (Marks *et al.,* 1973). A 27-year-old married woman had compulsive picking of scabs on her 18-month-old son's face and body. This necessitated her son being removed from home for long periods until the scabs or scratches had healed. In addition, she often beat her children, was frigid, had marital problems and hypochondriacal ruminations. Extensive previous treatment made no impact despite prolonged exposure in fantasy and *in vivo,* with response prevention and abreaction with intravenous drugs.

The therapeutic strategy was then changed. In the ward it was noticed that the patient showed no maternal behavior toward her son. A female nurse-therapist then modeled maternal behavior for the patient in the hope that this would diminish her tension and thus reduce the scab-picking. Treatment sessions consisted of the therapist playing with the son and cuddling him with the mother present. The mother was encouraged gradually to participate and was praised liberally when she did so. Improvement in the scab-picking rapidly followed. Artificial scabs were now painted onto the child's face and the patient was asked to practice handling her son with these on for increasingly longer periods, first supervised and then unsupervised. The therapist then included threatening situations in the treatment sessions; e.g., the boy stood on tables and chairs and jumped into the therapist's arms and later into the mother's arms. He was encouraged to play in a garden, to run over gravel paths, and to roll on grass, actions which the patient had previously forbidden lest he should fall and scratch himself. The patient was encouraged to undertake everyday tasks in which she would see the artificial scabs—e.g., dressing and undressing the child, bathing and washing his head—activities during which she had formerly been likely to pick scabs and to beat the children. Sessions began with mother as onlooker and gradually she took over under supervision. Home visits were arranged to allow modeling of exposure in other situations and to involve the second child. During the journey by bus and train to home the therapist modeled further maternal behavior. Additional treatment was given for the marital and sexual problems. After forty-five sessions of treatment the patient became able to tolerate the scabs on her son's face without picking them, the relationship with her husband improved to include less mutual criticism, and she related better with her own parents. For the first time she bathed her children and allowed them to roam and play freely around the home and garden. This partial improvement was maintained to 9-months follow-up, though some other problems remained.

Thus, a direct program of exposure to the son's scabs had little effect, but when the treatment focused instead on developing mothering behavior, the scab-picking diminished, upon which exposure *in vivo* with response prevention could be applied more successfully.

b. Contract Marital Therapy. A second example comes from Stern and Marks (1973a). A 31-year-old housewife and mother had a 19-year history of compulsive ritualistic checking. Four months of group psychotherapy and 6 weeks of exposure in fantasy and *in vivo* with response prevention made little impact on the rituals. The focus of treatment was now shifted onto the severe marital discord. Contract marital therapy was given twice weekly to a total of 10 hour-long sessions. Each partner was asked to list positive behaviors desired from the spouse. The husband wanted his wife to allow more frequent coitus and to do more housework. The patient wanted her husband to converse seriously with her and to complete household jobs she had requested. By the second session the marital relationship had improved with the resumption of coitus for the first time in a year. The husband was performing the requisite chores and, most intriguing, the compulsive rituals had diminished. Over the next month this improvement continued and nearly all the rituals were lost, although obsessive ruminations remained. Nine months after discharge the husband began an affair with another woman, and 3 months later he left the patient. She coped well with this crisis, and the rituals did not return. Thus intensive exposure *in vivo* hardly helped the compulsive rituals, yet they disappeared with contract marital therapy and did not return even after the marriage broke up.

These two patients illustrate the complex interplay between interpersonal problems and obsessive-compulsive behavior. It is still too early to formulate rules about the treatment of obsessive-compulsive patients who also have severe interpersonal problems. It is clear that if response prevention with exposure *in vivo* fails, it is well worth trying to deal with any interpersonal problems that may be present. However, only research will tell which psychopathological feature should be treated first. In some patients resolution of the obsessive problem alone is sufficient, while in others, obsessive behavior may not remit until interpersonal troubles have been dealt with. In complex cases like these we need to explore which fulcrum maintains which pathology in order to provide a basis for rational therapeutic strategies.

3. Compulsive Slowness: "Time and Motion Treatment"

Some obsessive-compulsive patients suffer from extremely disabling slowness in carrying out everyday actions, like dressing or crossing a road (Rachman, 1974). These are usually accompanied by endless checking, but are not necessarily linked to fears of contamination and the like, which makes exposure treatment rather inappropriate. A skills-training approach is more relevant, and patients of this kind can respond to "time and motion treatment." Their slow actions are analyzed and timed in detail, and step by step small tasks are set the patient which he is required to complete less and less slowly until after weeks or months of hard practice more efficient behavior can be attained. The author treated one man like this who initially took 7 hours to bathe, several hours to shave or to get dressed, and so on. This led to his unemployment for 3½ years before admission. Treatment consisted of his being asked to try to dress in the mornings first within 1½ hours, then within 1¼ hours, 1 hour, etc. Eventually breakfast was made contingent on his being washed, shaved, and dressed within 40 minutes. At each stage a nurse-therapist supervised his actions, hurried him along, showed him which checks to omit, and, as he speeded up, would fade herself from the situation until the patient could manage on his own. After 7 months and 130 sessions of inpatient treatment, partial improvement occurred in hospital which had not yet generalized much to the home. A few patients have been treated like this by the author and colleagues, with some success (Lindley *et al.,* 1975). The therapeutic effort needed varies greatly—some patients respond lastingly within a couple of months, but others need hundreds of hours of treatment time for worthwhile results to appear. Therapy can sometimes be on an outpatient basis, but at other times requires a supervised inpatient setting with a trained nursing staff, preferably round the clock. There are no controlled reports using this approach of prompting and pacing, and other more efficient procedures do not seem to be available.

4. Obsessive Thoughts without Rituals

Several procedures have been used for these, including the device of thought-stopping (Stern, 1970; Kumar & Wilkinson, 1971; Yamagami, 1971). In this procedure the patient is relaxed and asked to think of his obsessive thought. The therapist shouts, "Stop," and makes a sudden noise at the same time. The patient is then taught to shout, "Stop," himself to dispel the thought, then to whisper, and eventually to employ a subvocal command. Instead of saying, "Stop," to these obsessive thoughts, the patient can stop them by shocking himself from a portable shock box. As yet another alternative he can wear an elastic band on his wrist and snap it onto his skin to disrupt the thoughts (Mahoney, 1971). These methods all interrupt the undesirable behavior. Whether this interruption, relaxation, or an aversive component is essential to thought-stopping is debatable.

Thought-stopping could be construed as a form of self-regulation and coping which the patient learns to employ in controlling his own thoughts. In a controlled trial (Stern, Lipsedge, & Marks, 1973) 4 patients improved as much by learning to stop neutral thoughts as by stopping obsessive thoughts. This argues for the acquisition of a coping set rather than specific extinction of the obsessive ideas.

Another way to treat obsessive thoughts is by flooding in fantasy, but no controlled data are available. Research is needed to contrast this with thought-stopping, with aversion, and with self-regulation. It is also important to examine the possibilities of combining psychological methods with antidepressant drugs, among others, in the treatment of both obsessive thoughts and rituals.

F. General Issues in Management

1. Prognosis (Marks, 1974b)

a. Pervasive Variables

i. In patients. Motivation is obviously important since patients who will not carry out treatment instructions cannot be expected to benefit from them. Motivation is linked to acceptibility of a particular treatment method. A patient may be willing to change by the simple expedient of taking a pill, but not by going through intense anxiety experiences during exposure *in vivo*. The more a patient's involvement is needed in treatment, the higher his motivation needs to be.

Motivation appears to act through the way in which it leads to cooperation of the patient in treatment. It ensures that he will carry out treatment procedures appropriately, increase the number of practice trials, and so enhance his probability of improving with *potent* techniques. Motivation is of little value if it makes the patient practice an ineffective technique like relaxation diligently all day long (Rachman *et al.,* 1973). But the prognosis becomes brighter if the patient is motivated to refrain from carrying out his rituals for long periods so that he learns to tolerate the discomfort engendered by such abstention. Motivation is not a mystic factor that acts merely by being present. It acts by firing the patient to carry out those particular activities necessary for his recovery. A major thrust of research is required in guiding patients and families who are poorly motivated toward cooperation in treatment.

The patient's *warmth* can also play a part by making the therapist more inclined to exert his energies in treatment. Patients with good *self-esteem* and other *positive personality* attributes seem to do better with most treatments.

In general, the more *chronic* the disorder and the more *complex* its ramifications in the patient's life, the more difficult it will be to treat. More short-lived and acute problems are usually easier to help. Nevertheless, duration and complexity need not always be of overriding importance. Specific phobias and even complex obsessions of 20 years' duration can respond to treatment by exposure *in vivo* in two to three afternoons (Marks, 1973a; Watson *et al.,* 1971). Conversely, focal problems can be resistant to some techniques though not necessarily to others.

ii. In techniques. Most "therapist variables" come in here. The therapist's *empathy* and *warmth* will facilitate the patient's motivation, expectancy, and cooperation in any treatment procedure, and thus improve results. The contribution of a pervasive variable to outcome may be statistically significant, but not especially interesting if it accounts for only a small fraction of the variance in a given problem and technique. It may make but a small contribution which is necessary but not sufficient by itself for improvement to occur. In compulsive rituals, empathy and warmth may simply be the vehicle by which the patient is persuaded to expose himself to the noxious situation so that extinction can occur. That tape-recorded fantasy desensitization of phobias in volunteers has some success is evidence that desensitization can work with minimal empathy and warmth. As we have seen, taped fantasy flooding is less successful in phobic volunteers and patients, but this may argue less for empathy than for attentional influences in patients, who may listen more carefully to a live therapist than to a taped voice. The therapist's empathy can improve prognosis by allowing better communication between patient and therapist, and better definition of the problem to be treated. This in turn increases the patient's motivation to work harder toward recovery—a patient will expose himself to the phobic situation more readily, a compulsive is more likely to desist from his rituals.

High therapist *motivation* helps a therapist to attend to the often tiresome detail of complex treatment and to support the patient through difficult periods. Other skills required by a therapist are good powers of observation, knowledge of how to maintain a reasonable distance between himself and the client, and how to satisfy the needs of the patient rather than of himself. Therapist variables are thus not global attributes of personality, but particular skills that can be trained for inclusion in treatment transactions. This naturally assumes basic professional and personal competence, as a silk purse cannot be made out of a sow's ear in any profession.

b. Focal Variables

i. In patients. These are more specific features of psychopathology which influence results; e.g., compulsive neurosis may respond to modeling with exposure *in vivo,* but not to relaxation or desensitization in fantasy; severe depression makes phobics and compulsives refractory to exposure treatment. Focal problems are more amenable to treatment than those where there are no clearly identifiable difficulties. In a given patient the question always arises how different psychopathological differences are interlinked and where to apply the therapeutic lever to effect change.

ii. In techniques. The right technique needs to be applied to the right problem. It can make a great difference whether exposure is given *in vivo* or in fantasy, what its duration is, whether response prevention is added, and so on. Failure to respond to shaping procedures might result from poor contingency management or inability to break down the desired new behavior into sufficiently easy steps for the patient. Potent techniques imply a right and a wrong way to give them, though what is "correct" is often not known. Failure of treatment is sometimes blamed on the therapist's lack of experience. While skill obviously helps, the utility of a technique is proportional to the ease with which it can be administered. Methods that can be used by "novices" are more likely to become widely useful than those that require many years of training. The more explicit the therapeutic steps are for given problems, and the less dependent they are on arcane professional skills, the larger the neurotic population they can reach.

2. Social Context of Treatment

The social context of management is vital to consider. Many patients can be treated without any disequilibrium resulting in their family or social functions. Occasionally, however, improving function in one area may create problems in a patient's relationship with significant others. This can happen just as much after improvement in uncomplicated physical handicap. In a discordant marital couple, the problem with one member may provide an excuse for failure to confront one another with their main dissatisfactions. Before embarking on treatment it is thus essential to review all problems which a patient has and to discuss freely what the potential consequences of change in any one area might be. This is, of course, no more than good clinical management.

There is another point that is related to social repercussions of improvement. Treatment of obsessive-compulsive problems often has to be carried out in the patient's home setting. First, this is because the ramifications of the problem may not be obvious until one sees the patient in his normal environment. Second, improvement in hospital may fail to generalize outside until treatment is carried into the home. Before treatment begins it often seems essential that patients agree to therapists carrying out at least part of the treatment at home, and to the relatives being involved as well, or therapeutic efforts are doomed to failure. This treatment approach involves some radical relearning of roles for traditional therapists, who are used to carrying out treatment of neurosis only in an office or hospital setting. It is a role that therapists are carrying out increasingly in many centers.

As patients stop their rituals, time becomes available for alternative, more rewarding activities, and they need encouragement to develop a normal social life. Obsessive-compulsive behavior can have major social repercussions, which may have to be dealt with by home supervision and support of the family. Relatives have to be taught to avoid involvement in patients' rituals and how to respond to patients' demands on them. The author now runs an obsessive family group which several sets of patients and key relatives attend together (up to 14 people). They are encouraged to discuss mutually useful strategies and role rehearse them in a group setting. The group meets once in 6 weeks and appears to make management easier by increasing motivation and clarifying issues. Much more pilot work is required into the ways in which the families of compulsive patients can be constructively involved in treatment.

3. Widening Sources of Therapists

The perennial scarcity of resources for delivery of services has recently stimulated the development of therapists from outside the traditional ranks of psychiatrists and psychologists. In Britain, current research has shown that psychiatric nurses can carry out a broad range of treatments of phobias and obsessions with limited supervision. These nurse-therapists have treated patients as successfully as psychiatrists and psychologists using similar treatments in comparable psychiatric populations (Marks *et al.*, 1973). Nurse-therapists find their work rewarding, and results suggest that the use of selected psychiatric nurses as skilled therapists can ease the current critical shortage of treatment personnel for phobic and obsessive-compulsive problems.

IV. OVERVIEW AND FUTURE TRENDS

An interim unifying theory of fear reduction is suggested from review of the many forms of exposure treatments and their terminology. Most treatments of fear involve exposure of the subject to the phobic situation, either in fantasy or *in vivo*. Exposure can occur slowly or rapidly, with or without relaxation, anxiety evocation, modeling, reward, shock, or other procedures. The most efficient form of exposure so far seems to be prolonged exposure *in vivo,* though a few patients do not respond even to this. That stress immunization techniques help even when exposure is to stress that is irrelevant to the phobia suggests that extinction is not necessarily specific to the phobia alone, but it can be part of a more general process of learning to cope with noxious situations. Better operational definitions of "coping" as opposed to noncoping responses are needed for further advances. It is unknown why exposure to stressful stimuli sometimes sensitizes and at other times habituates the subject. The role of avoidance is still debatable.

TREATMENT COMPONENTS have mainly been studied in volunteers. Such analogue studies usually involve students who are unrepresentative of the general population and differ from patient populations in being less phobic and having fewer other problems which complicate management. Results from volunteer studies cannot be applied automatically to patients. Experimental designs are easier to interpret when they employ several measures of fear in different dimensions, as avoidance tests alone are too fickle. Follow-up is often nonexistent and necessary in many more studies.

Most controlled studies of exposure in volunteers were in fantasy rather than *in vivo.* Compared to unsuccessful studies those which produced significant improvement had longer total duration of exposure across sessions and rather longer sessions, but comparable durations of phobic scenes within sessions. Most negative experiments utilized taped instructions, while most effective ones used a live therapist. The duration of exposure necessary to reduce fear might be increased when treatment is in fantasy rather than in real life, by tape recorder rather than by a therapist, and intermittent rather than continuous. Some durations of exposure might actually increase fear. Phobic images of 30 seconds are more effective than shorter ones. Interstimulus intervals need more study.

Comparisons of flooding with desensitization have had variable results. They confound several factors, each of which requires separate assessment, viz: anxiety level during phobic approach, hierarchy level at which approach begins, gradation of approach, and spacing or massing of approach trials. Training of muscular relaxation is usually redundant and contributes little to the outcome of desensitization in fantasy. It can reduce general tension temporarily, but this does not help to reduce phobias. Wolpe's model of counterconditioning (reciprocal inhibition) and Lader and Mathews' model of maximal habituation have not been supported in most recent experiments. Equally, evocation of tension during exposure in fantasy does not enhance improvement, which negates Stampfl's model originally used for implosion. Anxiety during treatment does not correlate with better outcome to relevant flooding in fantasy, although it may with outcome to irrelevant stress imagery. Anxiety may be an unfortunate and unhelpful by-product of exposure rather than the chief therapeutic ingredient. Its role in stress immunization remains to be studied.

The few comparisons of live with fantasy exposure which have kept other conditions of exposure constant strongly suggest that *in vivo* treatment is more powerful. Several studies of "modeling," in fact, argue more for *in vivo* over fantasy exposure than for modeling per se, and for interactional rather than static exposure. Pure modeling without exposure is not therapeutic. Similarly, systematic reinforcement adds little to the effect of exposure. It is unclear whether preceding exposure in fantasy can potentiate subsequent exposure *in vivo,* either immediately afterward or after a delay, and whether there is a refractory period after fantasy treatment which might facilitate subsequent real life exposure. No data are yet available on the optimum speed of approach during exposure *in vivo*.

The large literature on expectancy and instruction effects is inconclusive, perhaps because of the great variability across experiments in the timing and frequency of manipulations and the differing ways in which those manipulations might have been perceived by experimental subjects. Further progress here depends upon clearer operational definitions of expectancy in client and therapist during therapy. False feedback of heart rate has also yielded conflicting results, though overall effects seem weak. True feedback of heart rate significantly reduces heart rate during exposure *in vivo* of specific phobic patients, but this does not enhance improvement of GSR or of subjective anxiety in the short term studied so far.

Self-regulatory cognitive processes are subject to increasing experimentation. Self-control is enhanced by greater commitment to future action, more stringent contracts, reward, and being able to use controlling responses with more accurate expectations of what will happen and what needs then to be done. Self-regulatory treatments include covert reinforcement, relaxation, rational-emotive therapy, anxiety management training, self-instructional attentional training, and stress immunization procedures. Coping models in general seem better than masterful ones during exposure. Backward aversion-relief works as well as forward aversion-relief, which argues for a coping-training mechanism rather than conditioning. Stress immunization might lead to greater generalization of effects than simple exposure treatment. Circular definitions of coping and self-regulatory responses need to be avoided in future research. Affinities with oriental psychotherapies like meditation require exploration.

Therapist time can be saved in several ways. Desensitization can be effective in fantasy when taped, but flooding less so. Standardized have been as good as individualized hierarchies in volunteers. Group treatment is effective, and group exposure *in vivo* is enhanced when a group spirit is fostered. Massing of treatment sessions has not impaired results.

IN PATIENTS, useful but limited effects are obtained with slow forms of exposure, like shaping *in vivo,* aversion relief, and desensitization in fantasy. Rapid fantasy flooding is not much more beneficial than slow fantasy desensitization.

Systematic comparison is still required between rapid and slow forms of exposure *in vivo.* Rapid prolonged exposure *in vivo* seems to be the most potent treatment of phobic patients, 2-hour sessions being better than four half-hour sessions the same afternoon. Even chronic specific phobics can respond within 3 afternoons of prolonged exposure *in vivo,* while severe agoraphobics improve less completely and may require 3–25 sessions for marked gains. Results seem quicker, the faster the exposure and the more diligently the patient practices exposure between sessions, but this requires further proof. Prolonged group exposure *in vivo* is effective and can save therapist time and increase improvement, especially if group cohesion is fostered. For reasons that are obscure, a few patients do not habituate to prolonged exposure *in vivo* despite good motivation and no avoidance.

Although several classes of oral drugs have useful if small effects, it is still moot how they should best be combined with exposure treatments. Fluctuating depression commonly coexists with phobias and obsessions and can be helped by oral tricyclic drugs. There is no controlled evidence justifying the use of intravenous rather than oral drugs with exposure.

Social anxieties can respond to social skills training, but therapeutic technology here is sufficiently different for it to require separate consideration from other forms of phobia treatment. Anger as well as anxiety can be treated by exposure treatments.

Blood and injury phobics frequently faint and show slow heart rates in the presence of the phobic stimulus, unlike other phobics, who get tachycardia and rarely faint in the phobic situation.

Obsessive-compulsive rituals usually respond well to exposure *in vivo* with response prevention; adding modeling to exposure *in vivo* only helps certain patients. Relaxation is not beneficial for reduction of rituals. Improvement is often slower than in phobics, and may require from (rarely) one afternoon to (more commonly) many weeks or months of intensive treatment. Extension of treatment to the home setting can be essential, as is involvement of the family in management. Task-oriented groups of several families together appear to facilitate treatment and follow-up. Infrequently, cooperative patients may fail to respond to direct exposure *in vivo,* but lose their compulsions when interpersonal problems are dealt with instead. Obsessive slowness without contamination fears can improve with "time and motion" treatment. This approach can be fairly simple or extremely laborious. Obsessive thoughts may respond to flooding in fantasy or thought interruption by various means which can be construed as forms of self-regulation, but the effect is uncertain and much more controlled study is required.

Phobic and obsessive problems have to be dealt with as part of general clinical management, with aims clearly defined within the social context of treatment. Potential social repercussions of improvement have to be borne in mind. Patients have to be cooperative, or treatment cannot begin. Unmotivated patients or frustrating family milieus can greatly impair outcome.

FUTURE TRENDS are likely to depart from those of the past decade. Repeated experiments have found that anxiety reduction does not depend upon Wolpe's idea of reciprocal inhibition, nor on Stampfl's notion of anxiety arousal. Neither modeling nor positive reinforcement particularly enhances exposure. Not even prevention of avoidance seems vital for outcome. Patients improve whether they are relaxed, neutral, or anxious during exposure. Although further work may yet show that the affective state during exposure can make some difference, it does not appear crucial for improvement to occur. What is crucial is still largely a mystery. The exposure hypothesis should be modified to accommodate at least two awkward facts. First, exposure can sometimes sensitize rather than habituate. Second, phobias can improve with irrelevant fear or stress immunization without any direct exposure to the phobic situation or scenes. If the concept of exposure is broadened into a wider coping theory (people get better when they learn to manage or deal with unpleasant experiences), we will require operational definitions of "manage, cope, deal with," free of the circular reasoning which currently bedevils the area. It is not enough to say coping is that which reduces anxiety, because practically anything can alleviate anxiety, given certain conditions, and it is the latter which have to be unraveled. Progress depends upon our becoming able to describe the parameters that predict whether a particular noxious stimulus will be perceived as noxious at all. It is obvious that multiple conditions are involved which interact with one another, so a satisfactory model cannot be simple.

Several observations seem fatal for pure exposure or coping hypotheses. Occasional patients improve not only without exposure, but also without obvious training in coping. Depressed phobics lose their phobias simply after swallowing antidepressant pills. Marital therapy rarely leads to dramatic resolution of obsessions. The varying interrelations among phobias, obsessions, depression, marital, sexual, and other problems need more systematic description. Fortunately, effective behavioral treatments change some behaviors but not others, so that the interrelationships can be explored. Such techniques are tools of experimental psychopathology which are analogous to ablation experiments in neurophysiology.

Despite the theoretical problems, in practice many more phobics and obsessives can be helped than heretofore, even when they have chronic, severe, and extensive handicaps. For these disorders, trained psychiatric nurses are as effective therapists as psychiatrists and psychologists. Most phobics and compulsive ritualizers without other major problems improve after exposure treatments lasting from a few hours to a few months. However, unexpected failures do occur, rarely mysteriously, more often apparently because of motivational or interpersonal complications. This is an area of great ignorance. Progress depends upon better explication of "cognitive" influences, on self control, the perception of trauma, motivation, and cooperation in treatment. We have few ways of increasing the motivation of patients and their relatives to undergo the tedious chores of treatment. Contingencies can be manipulated, rewards offered, families seen together, and patients treated in groups to bolster morale. All these are useful, but a minority of patients who are referred and seem treatable refuse help. Furthermore, an unknown number of disturbed people in the community who might benefit never seek aid at all. Perhaps this is fortunate, because shortage of treatment personnel is acute, despite the widening sources from which they are being drawn, and the skill which psychiatric nurse-therapists have demonstrated in this area. The cost-effectiveness of treatment is likely to be a growing determinant of future patterns of health care.

REFERENCES

Agras, W. S., Leitenberg, H., Barlow, D. H., Curtis, N., Edwards, J., & Wright, D. The role of relaxation in systematic desensitization therapy. *Archives of General Psychiatry,* 1971, **25,** 511–514.

Aitken, R. C. B., Daly, R. J., Lister, J. A., & O'Connor, P. J. Treatment of flying phobia in aircrew. *American Journal of Psychotherapy,* 1971, **25,** 530–542.

Allen, G. J. The behavioral treatment of test anxiety: Recent research and future trends. *Behavior Therapy,* 1972, **3,** 253–262.

Allen, G. J. Treatment of test anxiety by group-administered and self-administered relaxation. *Behavior Therapy,* 1973, **4,** 349–360.

Anthony, R. M., & Duerfeldt, P. H. The effect of tension level and contingent reinforcement on fear reduction. *Behavior Therapy,* 1970, **1,** 445–464.

Ascough, J. C. Quantitative differences in patients responding to induced anxiety: A reply to Noonan. *Psychotherapy: Theory, Research and Practice,* 1972, **9,** 22–24.

Averill, J. R., Opton, E. M., & Lazarus, R. S. Cross-cultural studies of psychophysiological responses during stress and emotion. *International Journal of Psychology,* 1969, **4,** 83–102.

Baker, B. L., Cohen, D. C., & Saunders, J. T. Self-directed desensitization of acrophobia. *Behaviour Research and Therapy,* 1973, **11,** 79–89.

Bandura, A. Psychotherapy based upon modeling principles. In A. E. Bergin & S. L. Garfield (Eds.), *Handbook of psychotherapy.* New York: Wiley, 1970.

Bandura, A., Blanchard, E. B., & Ritter, B. The relative efficacy of desensitization and modeling approaches for inducing behavioral, affective, and attitudinal changes. *Journal of Personality and Social Psychology,* 1969, **13,** 173–199.

Barrett, C. L. "Runaway imagery" in systematic desensitization therapy and implosive therapy. *Psychotherapy: Theory, Research and Practice,* 1968, **7,** 233–235.

Barrett, C. L. Systematic desensitization versus implosive therapy. *Journal of Abnormal Psychology,* 1969, **74,** 587–592.

Barrett, C. L. One year followup of study using behavior therapy, psychotherapy and waiting list control with phobic children. Paper presented at the meeting of the Society for Psychotherapy Research, Nashville, June 1972.

Baum, M. Extinction of avoidance responding through response prevention (flooding). *Psychological Bulletin,* 1970, **74,** 276–284.

Bellack, A. Reciprocal inhibition of a laboratory conditioned fear. *Behaviour Research and Therapy,* 1973, **11,** 11–18.

Benjamin, S., Marks, I. M., & Huson, J. Active muscular relaxation in desensitization of phobic patients. *Psychological Medicine,* 1972, **2,** 381–390.

Bergin, A. E. A note on dream changes following desensitization. *Behavior Therapy,* 1970, **1,** 546–549.

Blanchard, E. B. The generalization of vicarious extinction effects. *Behaviour Research and Therapy,* 1970, **8,** 323–330.

Blanchard, E. B., & Draper, D. O. Treatment of a rodent phobia by covert reinforcement: A single subject experiment. *Behavior Therapy,* 1973, **4,** 559–564.

Borkovec, T. D. The effects of instructional suggestion and physiological cues on analogue fear. *Behavior Therapy,* 1973, **4,** 185–192. (a)

Borkovec, T. D. The role of expectancy and physiological feedback in fear research: A review with special reference to subject characteristics. *Behavior Therapy,* 1973, **4,** 491–505. (b)

Borkovec, T. D., & Glasgow, R. E. Boundary conditions of false heart-rate feedback effects on avoidance behavior: A resolution of discrepant results. *Behaviour Research and Therapy,* 1973, **11,** 171–177.

Boudewyns, P. A., & Wilson, A. E. Implosive therapy and desensitization therapy using free association in the treatment of inpatients. *Journal of Abnormal Psychology,* 1972, **79,** 259–268.

Boudreau, L. Transcendental meditation and yoga as reciprocal inhibitors. *Journal of Behavior Therapy and Experimental Psychiatry,* 1972, **3,** 97–98.

Boulougouris, J. C., & Bassiakos, L. Prolonged flooding in obsessive-compulsive neurosis. *Behaviour Research and Therapy,* 1973, **11,** 227–231.

Boulougouris, J. C., Marks, I. M., & Marset, P. Superiority of flooding to desensitization as a fear reducer. *Behaviour Research and Therapy,* 1971, **9,** 7–16.

Boulougouris, J. C., & Tsahtsiris, F. Flooding in depression. Paper presented at the 3rd annual conference of the European Association of Behaviour Therapy, Amsterdam, July 1973.

Burns, J. M., & Ascough, J. C. A psychophysiological comparison of two approaches to relaxation and anxiety induction. *Behavior Therapy,* 1971, **2,** 170–176.

Butollo, W. H. Differential effects of "Flooding" and "Sensitization" in the conditioning of autonomic responses. Paper presented at the Conference on Behavior Therapy, Munich, July 1971.

Calef, R. A., & MacLean, G. D. A comparison of reciprocal inhibition and reactive inhibition therapies in the treatment of speech anxiety. *Behavior Therapy,* 1970, **1,** 51–53.

Cohen, R. The effects of group interaction and progressive hierarchy presentation on desensitization of test anxiety. *Behaviour Research and Therapy,* 1966, **4,** 17–24.

Cohen, R., & Dean, S. J. Group desensitization of test anxiety. *Proceedings of the 76th Annual Convention of the American Psychological Association,* 1968, **3,** 615–616.

Connolly, J., Hallam, R. S., & Marks, I. M. Selective association of fainting with blood-injury phobias. *Behavior Therapy,* 1975, in press.

Cooper, A., Furst, J. B., & Bridger, W. H. A brief commentary on the usefulness of studying fears of snakes. *Journal of Abnormal Psychology,* 1969, **74,** 413–414.

Cotler, S. Sex differences and generalization of anxiety reduction with automated desensitization. *Behaviour Research and Therapy,* 1970, **8,** 273–285.

Craighead, W. E. The role of muscular relaxation in systematic desensitization. Paper presented at the meeting of the Association for Advancement of Behavior Therapy, Washington, D.C., September 1971.

Crowder, J. E., & Thornton, D. W. Effects of systematic desensitization, programmed fantasy and bibliotherapy on a specific fear. *Behaviour Research and Therapy,* 1970, **8,** 35–41.

Crowe, M. J., Marks, I. M., Agras, W. S., & Leitenberg, H. Time-limited desensitization, implosion and shaping for phobic patients: A crossover study. *Behaviour Research and Therapy,* 1972, **10,** 319–328.

Davidson, P. O., & Hiebert, S. F. Relaxation training, relaxation instruction, and repeated exposure. *Journal of Abnormal Psychology,* 1971, **78,** 154–159.

Davis, D., McLemore, C. W., & London, P. The role of visual imagery in desensitization. *Behaviour Research and Therapy,* 1970, **8,** 11–13.

Dawley, H. H., & Wenrich, W. W. Group implosive therapy in the treatment of test anxiety: a brief report. *Behavior Therapy,* 1973, **4,** 261–263.

de Moor, W. Systematic desensitization versus prolonged high intensity stimulation (flooding). *Journal of Behavior Therapy and Experimental Psychiatry,* 1970, **1,** 45–52.

Diloreto, A. O. *Comparative psychotherapy: An experimental analysis.* Chicago: Aldine-Atherton, 1971. Cited by R. P. Liberman, *Behavior Therapy,* 1972, **3,** 647–648.

Donaldson, D. W. Positive imagery technique and implosive therapy. Unpublished doctoral dissertation, Fuller Theological Seminary, 1969.

Donner, L. Automated group desensitization—A follow-up report. *Behaviour Research and Therapy,* 1970, **8,** 241–274.

D'Zurilla, T. J., Wilson, G. T., & Nelson, R. A preliminary study of effectiveness of graduated prolonged exposure in the treatment of irrational fear. *Behavior Therapy,* 1973, **4,** 672–685.

Edelman, R. I. Desensitization and physiological arousal. *Journal of Personality and Social Psychology,* 1971, **17,** 259–266.

Emmelkamp, P. M. G. Effects of expectancy on systematic desensitization and flooding. *European Journal of Behaviour Analysis and Modification,* 1974, in press.

Emmelkamp, P. M. G., & Ultee, K. A. A comparison of "successive approximation" and "self-observation" in the treatment of agoraphobia. *Behavior Therapy,* 1974, **5,** 606–613.

Epstein, S., & Fenz, W. D. Habituation to a loud sound as a function of manifest anxiety. *Journal of Abnormal Psychology,* 1970, **75,** 189–194.

Evans, P. D., & Kellam, A. M. P. Semi-automated desensitization: A controlled clinical trial. *Behaviour Research and Therapy,* 1973, **11,** 641–646.

Evans, U. O. The effectiveness of visual imagery on phobic behavior when accompanied by electric shock. Unpublished doctoral dissertation, Fuller Theological Seminary, 1968.

Everaerd, W. T., Rijken, H. M., & Emmelkamp, P. M. A comparison of "flooding" and successive approximation in the treatment of agoraphobia. *Behaviour Research and Therapy,* 1973, **11,** 105–117.

Farmer, R. G., & Wright, J. M. C. Muscle reactivity and systematic desensitization. *Behavior Therapy,* 1971, **2,** 1–10.

Fazio, A. F. Treatment components in implosive therapy. *Journal of Abnormal Psychology,* 1970, **76,** 211–219.

Fazio, A. F. Implosive therapy with semiclinical phobias. *Journal of Abnormal Psychology,* 1972, **80,** 183–188.

Feather, B. W., & Rhoads, J. M. Psychodynamic behavior therapy. *Archives of General Psychiatry,* 1972, **26,** 496–511.

Feldman, M. P. Abnormal sexual behavior in males. In H. J. Eysenck (Ed.), *Handbook of abnormal psychology.* (2nd ed.) London: Pitman, 1973.

Ferstl, R. Desensitization versus anxiety management in stage fright. Paper presented at the Conference on Behavior Therapy, Munich, July 1972.

Foxman, J. Effect of cognitive rehearsal in rat phobic behavior. *Journal of Abnormal Psychology,* 1972, **79,** 39–46.

Frankl, V. E. Paradoxical intention and dereflection. In S. Arieti (Ed.), *World biennial of psychiatry and psychotherapy,* New York: Basic Books, 1974.

Friedman, D. E., & Lipsedge, M. S. Treatment of phobic anxiety and psychogenic impotence by systematic desensitization employing methohexitone-induced relaxation. *British Journal of Psychiatry,* 1971, **118,** 87–90.

Furst, J. B., & Cooper, A. Failure of systematic desensitization in two cases of obsessive-compulsive neurosis marked by fears of insecticide. *Behaviour Research and Therapy,* 1970, **8,** 203–206.

Gaupp, L. A., Stern, R. M., & Galbraith, C. G. False heart-rate feedback and reciprocal inhibition by aversion relief in the treatment of snake avoidance behavior. *Behavior Therapy,* 1972, **3,** 7–20.

Geer, J. H., Davison, G. C., & Gatchel, R. I. Reduction of stress in humans through non-veridical perceived control of aversive stimulation. *Journal of Personality and Social Psychology,* 1970, **16,** 731–738.

Gelder, M. G., Bancroft, J. H. J., Gath, D. H., Johnston, D. W., Mathews, A. M., & Shaw, P. M. Specific and non-specific factors in behavior therapy. *British Journal of Psychiatry,* 1973, **123,** 445–462.

Gelder, M. G., & Marks, I. M. Severe agoraphobia: A controlled prospective therapeutic trial. *British Journal of Psychiatry,* 1966, **112,** 309–319.

Gelder, M. G., & Marks, I. M. Desensitization and phobias: A cross-over study. *British Journal of Psychiatry,* 1968, **114,** 323–328.

Gelder, M. G., Marks, I. M., & Wolff, H. Desensitization and psychotherapy in phobic states: A controlled enquiry. *British Journal of Psychiatry,* 1967, **113,** 53–73.

Gentry, W. D. *In vivo* desensitization of an obsessive breast cancer fear. *Journal of Behavior Therapy and Experimental Psychiatry,* 1970, **1,** 315–318.

Gillan, P., & Rachman, S. An experimental investigation of behavior therapy in phobic patients. *British Journal of Psychiatry,* 1974. **124,** 392–401.

Gittelman-Klein, R., & Klein, D. F. Controlled imipramine treatment of school phobia. *Archives of General Psychiatry,* 1971, **25,** 204–207.

Glass, D., & Singer, J. E. *Stress and adaptation: Experimental studies of behavioral effects of exposure to aversive events.* New York: Academic Press, 1972.

Goldfried, M. R., & Merbaum, M. *Behavior change through self-control.* New York: Holt, 1973.

Goorney, A. B. Treatment of aviation phobias by behavior therapy. *British Journal of Psychiatry,* 1970, **117,** 535–544.

Grim, P. F. Anxiety change produced by self-induced muscle tension and by relaxation with respiration feedback. *Behavior Therapy,* 1971, **2,** 11–17.

Guilani, B. The role of competing response and manner of presentation of the aversive stimulus in modification of avoidance behavior. Unpublished doctoral dissertation, University of California, 1972.

Hafner, J., & Marks, I. M. Role of diazepam and of anxiety level during exposure *in vivo* of agoraphobics. Unpublished manuscript, 1974.

Hall, R. A., & Hinkle, J. E. Vicarious desensitization of test anxiety. *Behaviour Research and Therapy,* 1972, **10,** 407–410.

Hand, I., Lamontagne, Y., & Marks, I. M. Group exposure (flooding) in vivo for agoraphobics. *British Journal of Psychiatry,* 1974, **124,** 588–602.

Hart, J. D. Fear reduction as a function of the assumption and success of a therapeutic role. Unpublished master's thesis, University of Wisconsin, 1966.

Hersen, M. The behavioral treatment of school phobia. *Journal of Nervous and Mental Disease,* 1971, **153,** 99–107.

Hersen, M., Eisler, R. M., & Miller, P. M. Development of assertive responses: Clinical, measurement, and research considerations. *Behaviour Research and Therapy,* 1973, **11,** 505–522.

Heyse, H. Response prevention and modeling in the treatment of obsessive-compulsive neurosis. Paper presented at the 2nd annual conference of the European Association of Behaviour Therapy, Wexford, Eire, September 1972.

Hodgson, R. J., & Rachman, S. An experimental investigation of the implosion technique. *Behaviour Research and Therapy,* 1970, **8,** 21–27.

Hodgson, R. J., Hallam, R., Miller, S., & Rachman, S. An experimental investigation of 'implosion': Replication. Unpublished manuscript, 1971.

Hodgson, R., Rachman, S., & Marks, I. M. The treatment of obsessive-compulsive neurosis: Follow-up and further findings. *Behaviour Research and Therapy,* 1972, **10,** 181–189.

Hogan, R. A., & Kirchner, J. H. Preliminary report of the extinction of learned fears via short-term implosive therapy. *Journal of Abnormal Psychology,* 1967, **72,** 106–109.

Hogan, R. A., & Kirchner, J. H. Implosive, eclectic, verbal and bibliotherapy in the treatment of fears of snakes. *Behaviour Research and Therapy,* 1968, **6,** 167–171.

Horowitz, S. Strategies within hypnosis for reducing phobic behavior. *Journal of Abnormal Psychology,* 1970, **75,** 104–112.

Husain, M. Z. Desensitization and flooding (implosion) in treatment of phobias. *American Journal of Psychiatry,* 1971, **127,** 1509–1514.

Ikemi, Y. A psychosomatic approach to aggressive patients. *Psychosomatics,* 1972, **13,** 155–157.

Ikemi, Y., Luthe, W., Akishige, Y., Ohno, Y., Ishikawa, H., & Suematsu, H. The biologic wisdom of self-regulatory mechanism of normalization in autogenic and oriental approaches to psychotherapy. Paper presented at the 9th International Congress of Psychotherapy, Oslo, June 1973.

Ikemi, Y., Sugano, H., Nakagawa, S., Uewishi, S., & Sugita, M. The significance of anxiety in psychosomatic disorders. *Australian and New Zealand Journal of Psychiatry,* 1969, **3,** 310–314.

Jacobs, A., Edelman, M., & Wolpin, M. Effects of differential anxiety level and the repression-sensitization dimension in desensitization therapy. Paper presented at the American Psychological Association Convention, Washington, D.C., September 1971.

Jacobs, A., & Wolpin, M. A second look at systematic desensitization. In A. Jacobs & L. B. Sachs (Eds.), *Psychology of private events.* New York: Academic Press, 1971.

Jaffe, P. G., & Carlson, P. M. Modeling therapy for test anxiety and the role of model affect and consequences. *Behaviour Research and Therapy,* 1972, **10,** 329–339.

Johnston, D., & Gath, D. Arousal levels and attribution effects in diazepam-assisted flooding. *British Journal of Psychiatry,* 1973, **122,** 463–466.

Jordan, C. S., & Sipprelle, C. N. Physiological correlates of induced anxiety with normal subject. *Psychotherapy: Theory, Research and Practice,* 1972, **9,** 18–21.

Kanfer, F. H., Cox, L. E., Greiner, J. M., & Karoly, P. Contracts, demand characteristics, and self-control. *Journal of Personality and Social Psychology,* 1975, in press.

Kanfer, F. H., & Seidner, M. L. Self-control: Factors enhancing tolerance of noxious stimulation. *Journal of Personality and Social Psychology,* 1973, **25,** 381–389.

Karst, T. O., & Trexler, L. D. An initial study using fixed-role and rational emotive therapy in treating public speaking anxiety. *Journal of Consulting and Clinical Psychology,* 1970, **34,** 360–366.

Kazdin, A. E. Covert modeling and the reduction of avoidance behavior. *Journal of Abnormal Psychology,* 1973, **81,** 87–95.

Kazdin, A. E. Effects of covert modeling and model reinforcement on assertive behavior. *Journal of Abnormal Psychology,* 1974, **83,** 240–252.

Kelly, D. H. W. Measurement of anxiety by forearm blood flow. *British Journal of Psychiatry,* 1966, **112,** 789–798.

Kendell, R. E., & Discipio, W. J. Obsessional symptoms and obsessional personality traits in patients with depressive illnesses. *Psychological Medicine,* 1970, **1,** 65–72.

Kenny, F. T., Solyom, L., & Solyom, C. Faradic disruption of obsessive ideation in the treatment of obsessive neurosis. *Behavior Therapy,* 1973, **4,** 448–457.

Kent, R. N., Wilson, G. T., & Nelson, R. Effect of false heart-rate feedback on avoidance behavior: An investigation of "cognitive desensitization." *Behavior Therapy,* 1972, **3,** 1–6.

Kirchner, J. H., & Hogan, R. A. The therapist variable in the implosion of phobias. *Psychotherapy: Theory, Research and Practice,* 1966, **3,** 102–104.

Klein, D. F. Delineation of two drug-responsive anxiety syndromes. *Psychopharmacologia,* 1964, **5,** 397–408.

Kockott, G., Nussel, T. L., & Dittmar, F. The treatment of erectile impotence by systematic desensitization. *Archives of Sexual Behavior,* 1974, in press.

Koenig, K. P. False emotional feedback and the modification of anxiety. *Behavior Therapy,* 1973, **4,** 193–202.

Kora, T. A method of instruction of psychotherapy. *Jikeikai Medical Journal,* 1968, **15,** 315–325.

Krapfl, J. E., & Nawas, M. M. Differential orderings of stimulus presentation in systematic desensitization. *Journal of Abnormal Psychology,* 1970, **75,** 333–337.

Kumar, K., & Wilkinson, J. C. M. Thought stopping: a useful treatment in phobias of 'internal stimuli.' *British Journal of Psychiatry,* 1971, **119,** 305–307.

Lader, M. H. Predictive value of autonomic measures in patients with phobic states. Unpublished doctoral dissertation, University of London, 1966.

Lader, M. H., & Marks, I. M. *Clinical anxiety.* New York: Grune & Stratton, 1972.

Lader, M. H., & Mathews, A. M. A physiological model of phobic anxiety and desensitization. *Behaviour Research and Therapy,* 1968, **6,** 411–418.

Lader, M. H., & Mathews, A. M. Comparison of methods of relaxation using physiological measures. *Behaviour Research & Therapy,* 1970, **8,** 331–337.

Lader, M. H., Gelder, M. G., & Marks, I. M. Palmar skin conductance measures as predictors of response to desensitization. *Journal of Psychosomatic Research,* 1967, **11,** 283–290.

Lamontagne, Y., & Marks, I. M. Psychogenic urinary retention: Treatment by prolonged exposure. *Behavior Therapy,* 1973, **4,** 581–585.

Lang, P. J. Stimulus control, response control, and the desensitization of fear. In D. J. Levis (Ed.), *Learning approaches to therapeutic behavior change.* Chicago: Aldine, 1970.

Layne, C. C. The effect of suggestion in implosive therapy for fear of rats. Ph.D. dissertation, Southern Illinois University, 1970.

Lehrer, P. M. Physiological effects of relaxation in a double-blind analog of desensitization. *Behavior Therapy,* 1972, **3,** 193–208.

Leitenberg, H., Agras, S., Edwards, J. A., Thomson, L. E., & Wincze, J. P. Practice as a psychotherapeutic variable: An experimental analysis within single cases. *Journal of Psychiatric Research,* 1970, **7,** 215–225.

Leitenberg, H., & Callahan, E. J. Reinforced practice and reduction of different kinds of fears in adults and children. *Behaviour Research and Therapy,* 1973, **11,** 19–30.

Leventhal, H. The emotions: A basic problem for social psychology. Unpublished manuscript, University of Wisconsin, 1973.

Levy, R., & Meyer, V. Ritual prevention in obsessional patients. *Proceedings of the Royal Society of Medicine,* 1971, **64,** 1115–1118.

Lick, J. R., & Bootzin, R. R. Expectancy, demand characteristics, and contact desensitization in behavior change. *Behavior Therapy,* 1970, **1,** 176–183.

Linder, L. H., & McGlynn, F. D. Experimental desensitization of mouse-avoidance following two schedules of semi-automated relaxation training. *Behaviour Research and Therapy,* 1971, **9,** 131–136.

Lindley, P., Marks, I. M., & Snowden, J. Behavioral treatment of obsessive-compulsive neurosis with history of childhood autism. *British Journal of Psychiatry,* 1975, in press.

Lipsedge, M. S. Therapeutic approaches to compulsive neurosis. Unpublished M.Phil. dissertation, University of London, 1974.

Lipsedge, M. S., Hijioff, J., Huggins, P., Napier, L., Pearce, J., Pike, D. J., & Rich, M. The management of severe agoraphobia: A comparison of iproniazid and systematic desensitization. *Psychopharmacologia,* 1973, **32,** 67–80.

Litvak, S. B. A comparison of two brief group behavior therapy techniques on the reduction of avoidance behavior. *Psychological Record,* 1969, **19,** 329–334.

Lopiccolo, J. Effective components of systematic desensitization. Unpublished doctoral dissertation, Yale University, 1969.

Lott, D. R., & Carrera, R. N. The effect of group implosive therapy on snake phobias. Unpublished manuscript, 1971.

Lutker, E. R., Tasto, D. L., & Jorgensen, G. A brief note on multi-hierarchy desensitization. *Behavior Therapy,* 1972, **3,** 619–621.

McFall, R. M., & Twentyman, C. T. Four experiments on the relative contributions of rehearsal, modeling, and coaching to assertion training. *Journal of Abnormal Psychology,* 1973, **81,** 199–218.

McGlynn, F. D. Individual versus standardized hierarchies in the systematic desensitization of snake avoidance. *Behaviour Research and Therapy,* 1971, **9,** 1–5.

McGlynn, F. D., & Linder, L. H. The clinical application of analogue desensitization: A case study. *Behavior Therapy,* 1971, **2,** 385–388.

McGlynn, F. D., Williamson, L. M., & Davis, D. J. Semi-automated desensitization as a treatment for genuinely fearful subjects. *Behaviour Research and Therapy,* 1973, **11,** 313–315.

McManus, M. Group desensitization of test anxiety. *Behaviour Research and Therapy,* 1971, **9,** 51–56.

McReynolds, W. T. Treatment of anxiety in psychiatric inpatients, with behavior therapy and psychotherapy. Paper presented at the annual convention of the Midwestern Psychological Association, Cincinnati, May 1970.

Mahoney, M. J. The self-management of covert behavior: A case study. *Behavior Therapy,* 1971, **2,** 575–578.

Mann, J., & Rosenthal, T. L. Vicarious and direct counterconditioning of test anxiety through individual and group desensitization. *Behaviour Research and Therapy,* 1969, **7,** 359–367.

Marks, I. M. *Fears and phobias.* London: Heinemann Medical, 1969.

Marks, I. M. Phobic disorders four years after treatment: A prospective followup. *British Journal of Psychiatry,* 1971, **118,** 683–686.

Marks, I. M. Flooding (implosion) and related treatments. In W. S. Agras (Ed.), *Behavior modification: Principles and clinical applications.* Boston: Little, Brown, 1972.

Marks, I. M. New approaches to the treatment of obsessive-compulsive disorders. *Journal of Nervous and Mental Disorders,* 1973, **156,** 420–426. (a)

Marks, I. M. The reduction of fear: Towards a unifying theory. *Canadian Psychiatric Association Journal,* 1973, **18,** 9–12. (b)

Marks, I. M. Management of sexual disorders. In H. Leitenberg (Ed.), *Handbook of behavior modification.* New York: Prentice-Hall, 1975, in press. (a)

Marks, I. M. Psycholopharmacology: The combined use of drug and psychological treatments. Paper presented at the meeting of the American Psychopathological Association, Boston, March 1974. (b) To be published in Proceedings.

Marks, I. M. Research in neurosis: II. Treatment. *Psychological Medicine,* 1974, **4,** 89–109. (c)

Marks, I. M., Boulougouris, J., & Marset, P. Flooding versus desensitization in phobic disorders. *British Journal of Psychiatry,* 1971, **119,** 353–375. (a)

Marks, I. M., Boulougouris, J. C., Marset, P., & Huson, J. Physiological accompaniments of neutral and phobic imagery. *Psychological Medicine,* 1971, **1,** 299–307. (b)

Marks, I. M., Cameron, P., & Silberfeld, M. Operant therapy for an abnormal personality. *British Medical Journal,* 1971, **1,** 647–648. (c)

Marks, I. M., Connolly, J., & Hallam, R. S. The psychiatric nurse as therapist. *British Medical Journal,* 1973, **ii,** 156–160.

Marks, I. M., Crowe, M., Drewe, E., Young, J., & Dewhurst, W. Obsessive-compulsive neurosis in identical twins. *British Journal of Psychiatry,* 1969, **115,** 991–998.

Marks, I. M., Gelder, M. G., & Edwards, J. G. A controlled trial of hypnosis and desensitization for phobias. *British Journal of Psychiatry,* 1968, **114,** 323–328.

Marks, I. M., & Huson, J. Physiological aspects of neutral and phobic imagery: Further findings. *British Journal of Psychiatry,* 1973, **122,** 567–572.

Marks, I. M., Viswanathan, R., & Lipsedge, M. S. Enhanced extinction of fear by flooding during waning diazepam effect. *British Journal of Psychiatry,* 1972, **121,** 493–505.

Marshall, W. L., Strawbridge, H., & Keltner, A. The role of mental relaxation in experimental desensitization. *Behaviour Research and Therapy,* 1972, **10,** 355–366.

Marshitz, M. H., Almarza, M. T., Barra, E., & Medina, A. M. Massed and spaced practice in systematic desensitization of test anxiety. Paper presented at the 3rd annual conference of the European Association of Behaviour Therapy, Amsterdam, July 1973.

Martin, I., Marks, I. M., & Gelder, M. G. Conditioned eyelid responses in phobic patients. *Behaviour Research and Therapy,* 1969, **7,** 115–124.

Mather, M. D. The treatment of an obsessive-compulsive patient by discrimination learning and reinforcement of decision-making. *Behaviour Research and Therapy,* 1970, **8,** 315–318.

Mathews, A. M. Psychophysiological approaches to the investigation of desensitization and allied procedures. *Psychological Bulletin,* 1971, **76,** 73–91.

Mathews, A. M., & Gelder, M. G. Psychophysiological investigations of brief relaxation training. *Journal of Psychosomatic Research,* 1969, **13,** 1–18.

Mathews, A. M., Johnston, D. W., Shaw, P. M., & Gelder, M. G. Process variables and the prediction of outcome in behaviour therapy. *British Journal of Psychiatry,* 1974, **125,** 256–264.

Mathews, A. M., & Shaw, P. M. Continuous exposure and emotional arousal in flooding. *Behaviour Research and Therapy,* 1973, **11,** 587–598.

Mawson, A. B. Methohexitone-assisted desensitization in the treatment of phobias. *Lancet,* 1970, **I,** 1084–1086.

Mealiea, W. L., & Nawas, M. M. The comparative effectiveness of systematic desensitization and implosive therapy in the treatment of snake phobia. *Journal of Behavior Therapy and Experimental Psychiatry,* 1971, **2,** 85–94.

Meichenbaum, D. H. Cognitive factors in behavior modification: Modifying what clients say to themselves. Paper presented at the meeting of the Association for Advancement of Behavior Therapy, Washington, D.C., September 1971. (a)

Meichenbaum, D. H. Examination of model characteristics in reducing avoidance behavior. *Journal of Personality and Social Psychology,* 1971, **17,** 298–307. (b)

Meichenbaum, D. Cognitive modification of test anxious college students. *Journal of Consulting and Clinical Psychology,* 1972, **39,** 370–380. (c)

Meichenbaum, D., & Cameron, R. An examination of cognitive and contingency variables in anxiety relief procedures. Unpublished manuscript, 1974. (a)

Meichenbaum, D., & Cameron, R. Stress inoculation. A skills training approach to anxiety management. Unpublished manuscript, 1974. (b)

Meichenbaum, D. H., Gilmore, J. B., & Fedoravicius, A. Group insight versus group desensitization in treatment of speech anxiety. *Journal of Consulting and Clinical Psychology,* 1971, **36,** 410–421.

Melamed, B. G. The habituation of psychophysiological response to tones, and to filmed fear stimuli under varying conditions of instructional set. Unpublished doctoral dissertation, University of Wisconsin, 1969.

Meyer, V., & Levy, R. Behavioral treatment of a homosexual with compulsive rituals. *British Journal of Medical Psychology,* 1970, **43,** 63–68.

Miller, B. V., & Bernstein, D. A. Instructional demand in a behavioral avoidance test for claustrophobic fears. *Journal of Abnormal Psychology,* 1972, **80,** 206–210.

Miller, B. V., & Levis, D. J. The effects of varying short visual exposure times to a phobic test stimulus on subsequent avoidance behavior. *Behaviour Research and Therapy,* 1971, **9,** 17–21.

Miller, H. R., & Nawas, M. M. Control of aversive stimulus termination in systematic desensitization. *Behaviour Research and Therapy,* 1970, **8,** 57–61.

Miller, L. C., Barrett, C. L., Hampe, E., & Noble, H. Comparison of reciprocal inhibition, psychotherapy and waiting list control for phobic children. *Journal of Abnormal Psychology,* 1972, **79,** 269–279.

Murphy, C. M., & Bootzin, R. R. Active and passive participation in the contact desensitization of snake fear in children. *Behavior Therapy,* 1973, **4,** 203–211.

Myerhoff, H. L. Tension and anxiety in deconditioning. Unpublished doctoral dissertation, University of Southern California, 1967.

Mylar, J. L., & Clement, P. W. Prediction and comparison of outcome in systematic desensitization and implosion. *Behaviour Research and Therapy,* 1972, **10,** 235–246.

Naud, J., Boisvert, T. M., & Lamontagne, Y. Treatment of fire-arm (and associated stimuli) phobia by flooding in vivo with mechanical facilitation: A case report. *Journal of Behavior Therapy and Experimental Psychiatry,* 1974, **4,** 407–409.

Nawas, M. M., Fishman, S. T., & Pucel, J. C. A standardized desensitization program applicable to group and individual treatments. *Behaviour Research and Therapy,* 1970, **8,** 49–56.

Nawas, M. M., Mealiea, W. L., & Fishman, S. T. Systematic desensitization as counterconditioning: A retest with adequate controls. *Behaviour Research and Therapy,* 1971, **2,** 345–356.

Noonan, J. R. An obsessive-compulsive reaction treated by induced anxiety. *American Journal of Psychotherapy,* 1971, **25,** 293–299.

Noonan, J. R., & Lewis, P. M. Reverse psychology psychotherapy techniques: A review and evaluation. Paper presented at the meeting of the Southeastern Psychological Association, Louisville, April 1970.

Nunes, J., & Marks, I. M. Heart rate feedback during exposure in vivo. Unpublished manuscript, 1975.

Obler, M., & Terwilliger, R. Pilot study on the effectiveness of systematic desensitization with neurologically impaired children with phobic disorders. *Journal of Consulting and Clinical Psychology,* 1970, **34,** 314–318.

O'Connor, R. D. Relative efficacy of modeling, shaping, and the combined procedures for modification of social withdrawal. *Journal of Abnormal Psychology,* 1972, **79,** 327–334.

O'Donnell, C. R., & Worell, L. Motor and cognitive relaxation in the desensitization of anger. *Behaviour Research and Therapy,* 1973, **11,** 473–482.

Oliveau, D. C. Systematic desensitization in an experimental setting: A followup study. *Behaviour Research and Therapy,* 1969, **7,** 377–380.

Ollendick, J. H., & Gruen, G. E. Treatment of a bodily injury phobia with implosive therapy. *Journal of Consulting and Clinical Psychology,* 1972, **38,** 389–393.

Olley, M., & McAllister, H. Some psychometric reflections on the status of phobic illness. *Psychological Medicine,* 1975, in press.

Orenstein, H. Unpublished master's thesis, University of Wisconsin, 1972.

Orwin, A. Respiratory relief: A new and rapid method for the treatment of phobic states. *British Journal of Psychiatry,* 1972, **119,** 635–637.

Orwin, A. Augmented respiratory relief. *British Journal of Psychiatry,* 1973, **122,** 171–173.

O'Sullivan, M., Gilner, F. H., & Krinski, R. The influence of sex of experimenter on modeling in the reduction of fear. *Behavior Therapy,* 1973, **4,** 535–542.

Paul, G. L. Inhibition of physiological response to stressful imagery by relaxation training and hypnotically suggested relaxation. *Behaviour Research and Therapy,* 1969, **7,** 249–256.

Paul, G. L., & Shannon, D. T. Treatment of anxiety through systematic desensitization in therapy groups. *Journal of Abnormal Psychology,* 1966, **71,** 124–135.

Paul, G. L., & Trimble, R. W. Recorded vs. "live" relaxation training and hypnotic suggestion: Comparative effectiveness for reducing physiological arousal and inhibiting stress response. *Behavior Therapy,* 1970, **1,** 285–302.

Perloff, B. Influence of muscular relaxation and positive imagery on extinction of avoidance behavior through systematic desensitization. Unpublished doctoral dissertation, Stanford University, 1970.

Persely, C., & Leventhal, D. B. The effects of therapeutically oriented instructions and of the pairing of anxiety imagery and relaxation in systematic desensitization. *Behavior Therapy,* 1972, **3,** 417–424.

Powell, G. E., & Watts, F. N. Determinants of expectation in imaginal desensitization. *Perceptual and Motor Skills,* 1973, **37,** 246.

Prochaska, J. O. Symptomatic and dynamic cues in the implosive treatment of test anxiety. *Journal of Abnormal Psychology,* 1971, **77,** 133–142.

Rachman, S. Studies in desensitization: II. Flooding. *Behaviour Research and Therapy,* 1966, **4,** 1–15.

Rachman, S. Treatment by prolonged exposure to high intensity stimulation. *Behaviour Research and Therapy,* 1969, **7,** 295–302.

Rachman, S. Clinical application of observational learning, imitation, and modeling. *Behavior Therapy,* 1972, **3,** 379–397.

Rachman, S. Primary obsessional slowness. *Behaviour Research and Therapy,* 1974, **12,** 9–18.

Rachman, S., Marks, I. M., & Hodgson, R. The treatment of obsessive-compulsive neuroses. *Behaviour Research and Therapy,* 1971, **9,** 237–247.

Rachman, S., Marks, I. M., & Hodgson, R. The treatment of obsessive-compulsive neurotics by modeling and flooding in vivo. *Behaviour Research and Therapy,* 1973, **11,** 463–471.

Rainey, A. An obsessive-compulsive neurosis treated by flooding in vivo. *Journal of Behavior Therapy and Experimental Psychiatry,* 1972, **3,** 117–121.

Ramsay, R. W. Behavior therapy and bereavement. Paper presented at the 2nd annual conference of the European Association of Behaviour Therapy, Wexford, Eire, September 1972.

Ramsay, R. W., & Sikkel, R. J. Behavior therapy and obsessive-compulsive neurosis. Paper presented at the meeting of the European Association of Behaviour Therapy and Modification, Munich, July 1971.

Rehm, L. P. Relationships among measures of visual imagery. *Behaviour Research and Therapy,* 1973, **11,** 265–270.

Rehm, L. P., & Marston, A. R. Reduction of social anxiety through modification of self-reinforcement. *Journal of Consulting and Clinical Psychology,* 1968, **32,** 565–574.

Richardson, F. C., & Suinn, R. M. A comparison of traditional systematic desensitization, accelerated massed desensitization, and anxiety management training in the treatment of mathematics anxiety. *Behavior Therapy,* 1973, **4,** 212–218.

Riddick, C., & Meyer, R. G. The effect of automated relaxation training with response contingent feedback. *Behavior Therapy,* 1973, **4,** 331–337.

Rimm, D. C., De Groot, J. C., Hoord, P., Heiman, J., & Dillow, P. V. Systematic desensitization of an anger response. *Behaviour Research and Therapy,* 1971, **9,** 273–280.

Rimm, D. C., & Mahoney, M. J. The application of reinforcement and participant modeling procedures in the treatment of snake-phobic behavior. *Behaviour Research and Therapy,* 1969, **7,** 369–376.

Rimm, D. C., & Medeiros, D. C. The role of muscle relaxation in participant modeling. *Behaviour Research and Therapy,* 1970, **8,** 127–132.

Ritter, B. The group desensitization of childrens' snake phobias using vicarious and contact desensitization procedures. *Behaviour Research and Therapy,* 1968, **6,** 1–6.

Rohrbaugh, M., & Riccio, D. C. Paradoxical enhancement of learned fear. *Journal of Abnormal Psychology,* 1970, **75,** 210–216.

Rohrbaugh, M., Riccio, D. C., & Arthur, A. Paradoxical enhancement of conditioned suppression. *Behaviour Research and Therapy,* 1972, **10,** 125–130.

Roper, G. Unpublished manuscript, 1975.

Rosen, G. M., Rosen, E., & Reid, J. B. Cognitive desensitization and avoidance behavior. *Journal of Abnormal Psychology,* 1972, **80,** 176–182.

Ross, S. M., & Proctor, S. Frequency and duration of hierarchy item exposure in a systematic desensitization analogue. *Behaviour Research and Therapy,* 1973, **11,** 303–312.

Rubin, R. D., & Merbaum, M. Self-imposed punishment versus desensitization. In R. D. Rubin, H. Fensterheim, A. A. Lazarus, & C. M. Franks (Eds.), *Advances in behavior therapy 1969*. New York: Academic Press, 1971.

Rudolf, G. Deconditioning and time therapy. *Journal of Mental Science,* 1961, **107,** 1097–1101.

Rutner, I. T. The effects of feedback and instructions on phobic behavior. *Behavior Therapy,* 1973, **4,** 338–348.

Sarason, I. G. Verbal learning, modeling, and juvenile delinquency. *American Psychologist,* 1968, **23,** 254–266.

Sarason, I. G. Modeling: An approach to the rehabilitation of juvenile offenders. Report to DHEW for Grant No. 15-p-55303, 1971.

Sarason, I. G. Experimental approaches to test anxiety: Attention and the uses of information. In C. D. Spielberger (Ed.), *Anxiety: Current trends in theory and research.* New York: Academic Press, 1972. (a)

Sarason, I. G. Test anxiety and the model who fails. *Journal of Personality and Social Psychology,* 1972, **22,** 410–413. (b)

Sarason, I. G. Test anxiety and social influence. *Journal of Personality,* 1973, **41,** 261–271. (a)

Sarason, I. G. Test anxiety, attention, and the general problem of anxiety. Paper presented at the NATO Advanced Study Institute on Anxiety and Stress in Modern Life, 1973. (b)

Sargant, W. *Battle for the mind.* London: Heinemann, 1957.

Saul, L. J., Rome, H., & Leuser, E. Desensitization of combat fatigue patients. *American Journal of Psychiatry,* 1946, **102,** 476–478.

Schroeder, H. E., & Hatzenbuehler, L. C. Primary negative reinforcement in implosive therapy. Unpublished manuscript, 1973.

Schutz, W. C. *Joy.* New York: Grove Press, 1967.

Serber, M., Goldstein, A., Piaget, G., & Kort, F. The use of implosive-expressive therapy in anxiety reaction. In R. D. Rubin & C. M. Franks (Eds.), *Advances in behavior therapy 1968.* New York: Academic Press, 1969.

Sherman, A. R. Real life exposure as a primary therapeutic factor in desensitization treatment of fear. *Journal of Abnormal Psychology,* 1972, **79,** 19–28.

Sherman, A. R., & Plummer, I. L. Training in relaxation as a behavioral self-management skill: An exploratory investigation. *Behavior Therapy,* 1973, **4,** 543–550.

Singer, J. L. Imagery and daydream technique employed in psychotherapy. In C. D. Spielberger (Ed.), *Current topics in clinical and community psychology.* New York: Academic Press, 1972.

Sipprelle, C. N. Induced anxiety. *Psychotherapy: Theory, Research and Practice,* 1967, **4,** 36–40.

Smith, R. E. The use of humour in the counterconditioning of anger responses: A case study. *Behavior Therapy,* 1973, **4,** 576–580.

Smith, R. E., & Sharpe, T. M. Treatment of a school phobia with implosive therapy. *Journal of Consulting and Clinical Psychology,* 1970, **35,** 239–243.

Solyom, L., Garze-Perez, J., Ledwidge, B. L., & Solyom, C. Paradoxical intention in the treatment of obsessive thoughts: A pilot study. *Comprehensive Psychiatry,* 1972, **13,** 291–297. (a)

Solyom, L., Heseltine, G. F. D., McClure, D. J., Ledwidge, B., & Kenny, F. Comparative study of aversion relief and systematic desensitization in the treatment of phobias. *British Journal of Psychiatry,* 1971, **119,** 299–303.

Solyom, L., McClure, D. J., Heseltine, G. F. D., Ledwidge, B., & Solyom, C. Variables in the aversion relief therapy of phobics. *Behavior Therapy,* 1972, **3,** 21–28. (b)

Solyom, L., Shugar, R., Bryntwick, S., & Solyom, C. Treatment of fear of flying. *American Journal of Psychiatry,* 1973, **4,** 423–427.

Stadter, M. In vivo facilitation as a variable in the effectiveness of taped flooding. *Behaviour Research and Therapy,* 1973, **11,** 239–241.

Stampfl, T. G. Implosive therapy: The theory, the subhuman analogue, the strategy, and the technique: Part 1. The theory. In S. G. Armitage (Ed.), *Behavior modification techniques in the treatment of emotional disorders.* Battle Creek, Mich.: V.A. Publication, 1967. Pp. 22–37.

Stern, R. S. Treatment of a case of obsessional neurosis using thoughtstopping technique. *British Journal of Psychiatry,* 1970, **117,** 441–442.

Stern, R. S., Lipsedge, M. S., & Marks, I. M. Thought-stopping of neutral and obsessive thoughts: A controlled trial. *Behaviour Research and Therapy,* 1973, **11,** 659–662.

Stern, R. S., & Marks, I. M. Brief and prolonged flooding: A comparison in agoraphobic patients. *Archives of General Psychiatry,* 1973, **28,** 270–276. (a)

Stern, R. S., & Marks, I. M. Contract therapy in obsessive-compulsive neurosis with marital discord. *British Journal of Psychiatry,* 1973, **123,** 681–684. (b)

Strahley, D. F. Systematic desensitization and counterphobic treatment of an irrational fear of snakes. Unpublished doctoral dissertation, University of Tennessee, 1965.

Sue, D. The role of relaxation in systematic desensitization. *Behaviour Research and Therapy,* 1972, **10,** 153–158.

Suinn, R. M. Removing emotional obstacles to learning and performance by visuomotor behavior rehearsal. *Behavior Therapy,* 1972, **3,** 308–310.

Suinn, R. M. Anxiety management training for general anxiety. In R. M. Suinn & R. G. Weigel (Eds.), *The innovative therapies: Critical and creative contributions.* New York: Harper & Row, 1974.

Suinn, R. M., Edie, C. A., & Spinelli, P. R. Accelerated massed desensitization: Innovation in short-term treatment. *Behavior Therapy,* 1970, **1,** 303–311.

Suinn, R. M., & Hall, R. Marathon desensitization groups: An innovative technique. *Behaviour Research and Therapy,* 1970, **8,** 97–98.

Suinn, R. M., & Richardson, F. Anxiety management training: A non-specific behavior therapy program for anxiety control. *Behavior Therapy,* 1971, **2,** 498–510.

Sushinsky, L. W., & Bootzin, R. R. Cognitive desensitization as a model of systematic desensitization. *Behaviour Research and Therapy,* 1970, **8,** 29–33.

Taylor, D. W. A comparison of group desensitization with two control procedures in the treatment of test anxiety. *Behaviour Research and Therapy,* 1971, **9,** 281–284.

Trexler, L. D., & Karst, T. O. Rational-emotive therapy, placebo, and no treatment effects on public-speaking anxiety. *Journal of Abnormal Psychology,* 1972, **79,** 60–67.

Tyrer, P. J., Candy, J., & Kelly, D. H. W. Phenelzine in phobic anxiety: A controlled trial. *Psychological Medicine,* 1973, **3,** 120–124.

Ullrich, R., Grambach, G., & Peikert, V. Three flooding procedures in the treatment of agoraphobics. Paper presented at the 2nd annual conference of the European Association of Behaviour Therapy, Wexford, Eire, September 1972.

Ullrich de Muynck, R., & Ullrich, R. The effectiveness of a standardized assertive-training program. Paper presented at the 2nd annual conference of the European Association of Behaviour Therapy, Wexford, Eire, September 1972.

Valins, S., & Ray, A. A. Effects of cognitive desensitization on avoidance behavior. *Journal of Personality and Social Psychology,* 1967, **7,** 345–350.

Van Egeren, L. F. Psychophysiological aspects of systematic desensitization: Some outstanding issues. *Behaviour Research and Therapy,* 1971, **9**, 65–77.

Vodde, T. W., & Gilner, F. H. The effects of exposure to fear stimuli on fear reduction. *Behaviour Research and Therapy,* 1971, **9,** 169–175.

Waters, W. F., McDonald, D. G., & Koresko, R. L. Psychophysiological responses during analogue desensitization and non-relaxation control procedures. *Behaviour Research and Therapy,* 1972, **10,** 381–393.

Watkins, R. E., & Davidson, P. O. Stress reactions of psychiatric patients to a stressor film: An attempt at experimental reduction of threat. *Behaviour Research and Therapy,* 1970, **8,** 175–178.

Watson, J. P., Gaind, R., & Marks, I. M. Prolonged exposure: A rapid treatment for phobias. *British Medical Journal,* 1971, **I,** 13–15.

Watson, J. P., Gaind, R., & Marks, I. M. Physiological habituation to continuous phobic stimulation. *Behaviour Research and Therapy,* 1972, **10,** 269–278.

Watson, J. P., & Marks, I. M. Relevant and irrelevant fear in flooding—A crossover study of phobic patients. *Behavior Therapy,* 1971, **2,** 275–293.

Watson, J. P., Mullett, G. E., & Pillay, H. The effects of prolonged exposure to phobic situations upon agoraphobic patients treated in groups. *Behaviour Research and Therapy,* 1973, **11,** 531–546.

Watts, F. N. Desensitization as an habituation phenomenon: I. Stimulus intensity as determinant of the effects of stimulus lengths. *Behaviour Research and Therapy,* 1971, **9,** 209–217.

Watts, F. N. Desensitization as an habituation phenomenon: II. Studies of interstimulus interval length. *Psychological Reports,* 1973, **33,** 715–718.

Watts, F. N. The control of spontaneous recovery of anxiety in imaginal desensitization. *Behaviour Research and Therapy,* 1974, **12,** 57–59.

Welch, H. J., & Krapfl, J. E. Order of stimulus presentation in desensitization. Paper presented at the annual convention of the Midwestern Psychological Association, Cincinnati, May 1970.

Willis, R. W. A study of the comparative effectiveness of systematic desensitization and implosive therapy. Unpublished doctoral dissertation, University of Tennessee, 1968.

Willis, R. W., & Edwards, J. A. A study of the comparative effectiveness of systematic desensitization and implosive therapy. *Behaviour Research and Therapy,* 1969, **7,** 387–395.

Wilson, G. T. Innovations in the modification of phobic behaviors in two clinical cases. *Behavior Therapy,* 1973, **4,** 426–430.

Wilson, G. T., & Thomas, M. G. W. Self versus drug-produced relaxation and the effects of instructional set in standardized desensitization. *Behaviour Research and Therapy,* 1973, **11,** 279–288.

Wine, J. An attentional approach to the treatment of test anxiety. Counselling Services Report, No. 2. Feb. University of Waterloo, 1971.

Wisocki, P. A. Treatment of obsessive-compulsive behavior by covert sensitization and covert reinforcement: a case report. *Journal of Behavior Therapy and Experimental Psychiatry,* 1970, **1,** 233–239.

Wisocki, P. A. A covert reinforcement program for the treatment of test anxiety: brief report. *Behavior Therapy,* 1973, **4,** 264–266.

Wolpe, J. *Psychotherapy by reciprocal inhibition.* Stanford: Stanford University Press, 1958.

Wolpin, M. Guided imagining to reduce avoidance behaviour. *Psychotherapy: theory, research & practice,* 1969, **6,** 122–124.

Wolpin, M., & Raines, J. Visual imagery, expected roles and extinction as possible factors in reducing fear and avoidance behaviour. *Behaviour Research and Therapy,* 1966, **4,** 25–37.

Yamagami, T. The treatment of an obsession by thought-stopping. *Journal of Behavior Therapy and Experimental Psychiatry,* 1971, **2,** 233–239.

Young, E. R., Rimm, D. E., & Kennedy, T. D. An experimental investigation of modelling and verbal reinforcement in the modification of assertive behaviour. *Behaviour Research & Therapy,* 1973, **11,** 317–319.

Zane, M. Fighting fear by group confrontation. *World News,* Pp. 76–80, February 1972.

ETHICAL AND LEGAL ISSUES OF BEHAVIOR MODIFICATION

D. A. BEGELMAN
Division of Social Sciences
Kirkland College
Clinton, New York

I. INTRODUCTION

Despite the rapidly accumulating literature on the body of therapeutic practices broadly dubbed "behavior modification," it is unlikely that terms such as "behavior modification" and "behavior therapy" will shed their continued ambiguity. The principal reason for this is that such terms are employed in distinguishable and often contradictory ways by diverse groups. In order to confront significant ethical and legal issues arising from the practice of "behavior modification," an examination of implicit definitions subscribed to in various quarters is required.

On February 20, 1974, the *New York Times* carried a feature article entitled "Behavior Control Issue Unsolved." Essentially, it dealt with a recent governmental decision to ban further use of anticrime funds by the Law Enforcement Assistance Administration (L.E.A.A.) for behavior modification programs in Federal criminal institutions across the nation. The decision was undertaken as the result of a lawsuit by inmates of a penal program in Missouri funded by L.E.A.A., claiming that certain aversive practices in the program (e.g., lengthy periods of isolation) constituted "cruel and unusual punishment." Echoing these sentiments, the Children's Defense Fund and the Senate Subcommittee on Constitutional Rights likewise brought pressure to bear against the funding of L.E.A.A. projects. Both groups, however, avoided an outright denunciation of behavior modification practices, ostensibly because they felt that "some type of such treatment can be beneficially used." It seems clear that governmental or interest-group opposition to behavior modification implicitly rests on the following definition (1): *behavior modification is a set of specialized techniques historically classified as behavioristic, and administered by professionals who have identified themselves as behavior therapists.* Agras (1973) has attempted to outline the various procedures such a definition would ordinarily encompass. They include: systematic desensitization, positive reinforcement, aversive control, including escape and avoidance procedures, classical and covert techniques like sensitization, reinforcement and coverant control, implosion, modeling, negative practice, assertive training, behavioral contracting, etc.

Agras' list, however, reveals a perhaps hitherto unnoticed difficulty, especially with respect to ethical and legal commentary on behavior-therapeutic techniques. It is, in fact, only a partial list of actual techniques practiced by behavior therapists. This can readily be seen by contrasting, for example, systematic desensitization or covert sensitization with positive reinforcement and aversive control. The former two can be considered to be behavioral treatment techniques, because of their relatively unambiguous procedural features, whereas the latter two cannot. Positive reinforcement and aversive control are not particular techniques; they are the psychological principles which, while illustrated in many types of behavioral intervention, are nevertheless not particularly descriptive of them. In this regard, the clinician who administers systematic desensitization to a phobic patient would qualify as a behavior modifier under definition (1). But the clinician who makes use of positive reinforcement or aversive control can in fact be a clinician of any persuasion whatsoever. If his interventions are successful, "positive reinforcement" and "aversive control" become the concepts or principles broadly accounting for behavior change, according to an explanatory paradigm (Kuhn, 1962).

The confusion which has been overlooked is in identifying "positive reinforcement" or "aversive control" as *names* of particular behavioral techniques, rather than explanatory concepts or processes illustrated in numerous therapeutic procedures. The significance of clarifying the confusion is that there is no meaningful ethical or legal argument against the use of "positive reinforcement" or "aversive control," but only against the specific way in which techniques based on such principles may from time to time be employed. Similarly, ethical objections to "operant conditioning" (Krutch, 1953; Matson, 1971) have a near ritualistic place in what Skinner (1971) has termed the "literature of freedom and dignity." Such criticisms notwithstanding, the alleged ethical dangers to individual liberty inherent in the use of operant control have been inadequately articulated, precisely because the negative reaction to a specific misuse of a therapeutic procedure is generalized to "operant conditioning" as if the latter were a unique feature of the behaviorist's clinical armamentarium, but no one else's.

Because of the opposition to *drastic* methods of behavior change on the part of civil libertarian groups such as the A.C.L.U. or Children's Defense Fund, behavior modification has sometimes been defined (definition 2) as *the administration of therapeutic techniques producing major behavior change, usually in relatively brief periods of time.* As can be noted in legal or popular literature, such a definition encompasses modalities such as electroconvulsive treatment (ECT), chemotherapy and psychosurgery, normally understood to be aspects of traditional psychiatric practice, although falling outside of techniques covered by definition (1). In this regard, ethical and legal criticisms of or opposition to behavior modification have probably altered the frequency of certain time-honored psychiatric procedures, as well as those classified as behavior modification according to definition (1). However, a distinct disadvantage of this popularized definition of behavior modification is that, as behavior therapists develop newer and more innovative approaches to treatment, their clinical activities may become subject to legal curtailments not imposed on more traditionally oriented programs which are nevertheless inferior from the standpoint of ethical safeguard.

Despite recent admonitions (Carrera & Adams, 1970) that behavior modification programs necessitate continual vigilance to guard against potential jeopardy to the ethical rights and interests of patients, a more rational outlook in the face of conflicting definitions of the field would be to construe ethical principles as applicable to *all* treatment approaches, irrespective of the methodologies or theoretical outlooks involved. Such a proposal would serve to encourage the recognition that the ethical administration of a treatment technique is independent of whether it is employed by "psychoanalysts," "humanists," "behaviorists," or "psychiatrists," and more related to whether or not it meets significant ethical criteria, however the latter are propounded. The proposal would also facilitate abandonment of the tendency to legitimize a therapeutic procedure because it compares favorably to those that have a historic place in the practice of a recognized professional group. Obviously, there may be many traditionally employed techniques that have not been subjected to the ethical scrutiny that they undoubtedly deserve. In line with this, Ullmann and Krasner (1965) would appear to be begging the question in arguing for the ethical legitimacy of behavioral techniques on the basis that they are no less respectable than a range of popular psychiatric modalities, such as ECT and psychosurgery. If the latter are suspect, they can hardly serve as standards against which the ethical adequacy of newer methods are to be compared or assessed.

A definition (3) of "behavior modification" often favored by behaviorists themselves (Ullmann & Krasner, 1965; Wolpe, 1973) is: *applied learning theory.* While several authors (Franks & Wilson, 1973; Lazarus, 1971) have construed behavior modification to refer to clinical practice involving techniques derived from experimental psychology in general, rather than from learning theory alone, "applied learning theory" and "applied experimental psychology" remain problematic concepts, especially if they are taken to exclude what is typically understood to be alternatives to behavior modification. Thus, is the psychoanalyst or humanistic therapist who produces positive behavior change *not* "applying experimental psychology," if he does so inadvertently? If "experimental psychology" in the broadest sense is that body of principles governing or accounting for most of the behavior change that is the proper purview of the behaviorally oriented clinician, the essential difference between, for example, behavior modification and client-centered therapy cannot be the one between a case of "applying experimental psychology" and a case of "applying something else." In this connection, the psychodynamic clinician who on occasion promotes positive behavior change may indeed be applying experimental psychological principles of which he is unaware (Truax, 1966). Since he differs from his behavioristic counterpart in terms of the theoretical system by which he conceptualizes behavior change, perhaps a more propitious recasting of definition (3) would be definition (4): *the development of techniques of behavior change whose effectiveness can be explained in terms of learning theory or experimentally derived psychological principles.*

Such a definition of behavior modification distinguishes it from alternative therapeutic efforts in terms of its methodological and explanatory approach to problem-behaviors, rather than on the basis of criteria outlined in definitions (1)–(3). As such, it is more clearly in line with definitions already formulated by Bijou (1970) and Yates (1970), emphasizing the application of experimental methods to the treatment of problem-behaviors. Additionally, it possesses the advantage of discouraging the view that established or future developments in the behavior-therapeutic approach to treatment *necessarily* consist in the evolution of techniques that have a recognizable parochiality about them, as suggested by definition (1). Definition (4), in emphasizing the systematic and experimental approach to deviancy which is the heart of behavior modification, does not prohibit the development of techniques similar to those utilized by therapists of diverse alternative persuasions. The crucial difference consists of the empirical validation of a technique as therapeutically effective, based upon operationalized procedures for defining target behaviors, modes of intervention, and the dependent variable. Far from necessitating the creation of techniques conspicuously different from those utilized in, say, humanistic psychotherapy, behavior modification under definition (4) pertains to systematic habits of inquiry, research, and follow-up.

In a similar vein, Day (1971) has attempted to rebut ethical criticisms of behaviorism on the part of humanists like Matson (1971). The latter has maintained that behavioral treatment methods must not only take a different form than humanistic procedures, but are additionally guided by opposed moral goals. Day has challenged Matson's contention that behaviorists, in virtue of their model of Man, tend to renounce interest in interpersonal transactions characterized by mutual interest, love, and respect, that are the immediate focus of humanistic psychology. Day has pointed out that if such interactions can be *demonstrated* to facilitate humanistic goals, the behavior therapist would want to examine them in detail, in order to isolate the relevant independent variables in humanistic methods. Moreover, Day is convinced that only the systematic nature of the behavioral approach could ensure further strengthening of the means whereby humanistic values could be achieved in therapy with a minimum of wasted effort.

II. LEGAL ISSUES

Subscribing to definition (4) may have significant legal implications. In a recent article on behavior modification and the law, Wexler (1973) has pointed out how such landmark judicial precedents as *Wyatt* v. *Stickney*[1] has broadened the category of human rights to which involuntarily hospitalized mental patients are constitutionally entitled. Among these are included the right of privacy, visitations from friends and relatives, mail and telephone communications access, personal possessions, minimum wage standards, and others. Wexler asserts that *Wyatt* v. *Stickney* poses a problem for behavior modifiers in that it enjoins them to guarantee to inmates of state institutions access to reinforcers that are currently available to them solely on a response-contingent basis in many token economy programs. If empirical evidence indicates that certain classes of chronic mental patients fail to improve unless the contingent availability of basic

[1] *Wyatt* v. *Stickney,* 344 F. Supp. 373 (M.D. Ala. 1972) (Bryce and Searcy Hospitals).

reinforcers is established as an aspect of treatment, Wexler feels that a legal reevaluation of *Wyatt* may be in order. He adds, however, that this possibility may be offset by a consideration of treatment programs such as Fairweather's (1964) community adjustment project. Fairweather's program consisted of a system of group achievement coupled with less drastic deprivations than those included in token economy programs, although it apparently led to equally impressive results. Accordingly, Wexler indicates that challenges to *Wyatt* on the basis of results in behavior modification programs utilizing deprivations could well be struck down by the court in citing alternative programs that compare favorably to token economies, but which include less drastic deprivations.

Wexler's article seems to waver over the classification of Fairweather's approach. Speaking of Fairweather, Wexler notes that while he relies on concepts derived from social psychology and small group theory rather than from behaviorism and learning theory, he nevertheless also employs principles of behavior modification. Apparently, however, the fact that Fairweather's investigations were founded on the belief that chronic mental patients must acquire problem-solving and decision-making skills in order to survive in the community has convinced Wexler that Fairweather's community project stands in contrast to behavior modification. Perhaps according to definition (1) it does, but not according to definition (4). Indeed, recent excursions into the area of developing problem-solving abilities (D'Zurilla & Goldfried, 1971) by specialists calling themselves behavior modifiers is a matter of record. Distinguishing between the behavioral goals of token economies and Fairweather's project seems to be —insofar as it can be substantiated—a confusion on Wexler's part between the historically adopted goals of *some* token economies and the intrinsic capabilities of these systems. Moreover, there is no fundamental distinction to be made between Fairweather's project and behavior modification under defintion (4), *providing* Fairweather's approach to clinical problems bears the stamp of the experimental approach to treatment. If this is so, the proper distinction to be drawn is between Fairweather's program and token economy, not behavior modification. The latter distinction can be drawn from an implicit reliance on definition (1).

The problem of contrasting definitions of "behavior modification" is of pressing legal importance in the context of numerous proposals (Carrera & Adams, 1970; Lucero, Vail, & Scherber, 1968; Martin, 1972; Spece, 1972) to place stringent controls on behavior modification. Such proposals can have little meaning under definition (4), especially as they serve to distinguish behavior modification from procedures differing more in terms of the theoretical outlooks or approaches taken than on substantive ethical grounds.

It was previously mentioned that the possibility of legal review of precedents such as *Wyatt* v. *Stickney* presents itself when guarantees of basic rights to mental patients are shown to conflict with other significant values. Thus, constitutional guarantees of visitation rights may be empirically demonstrated to offset the gains produced by programs in which these rights are made contingent upon behavioral improvement. In such cases, and as Wexler (1973) has noted, reexamination of the law is prompted by the conflict of cherished principles: ultimate rehabilitation *versus* the right to see anyone an individual pleases. It is important, however, to stress the fact that reexamination of law by test cases affords the court the opportunity to engage in a judicial assessment of what legal principle should hold sway or receive priority. This is a legal matter, not an experimental issue, although scientific findings should rightfully be considered by the court in rendering decisions. Conceivably, the court might strike down challenges to precedents like *Wyatt,* not because it is derelict in gathering empirical information relevant to the issue it is considering, but because it holds that the inalienability of certain "rights" transcends the importance of behavioral improvement resulting from making them secondary to ultimate treatment goals.

In establishing the contingent availability of religious services for patients in the token economy program at Anna State Hospital, Ayllon and Azrin (1968) appeared to have implicitly challenged the intent of later "right to treatment" rulings, such as *Wyatt.* In effect, they were operating on the assumption that even rights guaranteed under the First Amendment ought to be subordinated to broader rehabilitative aims. While Spece (1972) has indicated the paucity of legal decisions dealing with the issue of whether institutionalized patients have the right to *refuse* treatment, a handful of precedents such as *Winters* v. *Miller*[2] and *Peek* v. *Ciccone*[3] appears to have upheld the Ayllon and Azrin position. Ironically, in *Winters* v. *Miller,* the plaintiff sought damages on religious grounds. Her lawyer argued that since psychiatrists at Bellevue State Hospital coerced her into receiving chemotherapy in violation of her religious convictions as a Christian Scientist, they had in effect violated a right guaranteed to her under the First and Fourteenth Amendments. The court, however, rejected the plaintiff's claim. In *Peek* v. *Ciccone,* the court likewise rejected petitioner's claim that as a federal prisoner, enforced administration to him of tranquilizing medication was unlawful on the grounds of constituting cruel and unusual punishment. Decisions like *Winters* v.

[2] *Winters* v. *Miller,* 306 F. Supp. 1158 (E.D. N.Y. 1969). The case has since been reversed in *Winters* v. *Miller,* 446 F.2d 65 (2d Cir. 1971).

[3] *Peek* v. *Ciccone,* 288 F. Supp. 329 (W.D. No. 1968).

Miller and *Peek* v. *Ciccone* uphold the position of many behavior therapists that rights guaranteed to ordinary citizens become secondary within programs in which their temporary abridgment leads to speedier rehabilitation and subsequent community adjustment. Thus, Miron (1968) urges that the "primary ethical consideration" is the maximum therapeutic benefit to patients, which in many cases may involve the use of contingent punishment.

Along the same lines, Cahoon (1968) argues that it may be unethical "not to apply aversion therapy to severe self-destructive behavior . . . because the technique has been shown to be effective with such problems [Cahoon, 1968, p. 52]." Bragg and Wagner (1968), in propounding the ultimacy of the value of rehabilitating the patient, assert that the use of any techniques—be they conventional or behavioral in scope—"must be justified in terms of results [Bragg & Wagner, 1968, p. 53]." Ball (1968), in defending the "no token, no meal" policy of the token economy program at Pacific State Hospital, reveals an inconsistency between the provisions of later rulings such as *Wyatt* and the techniques employed in a program which nonetheless had "forced many patients out of comfortable and well-established ruts of infantile dependency [Ball, 1968, p. 56]." Schaefer (1968), in a special plea for the therapeutic use of deprivation, believes that ethical and legal criticisms of behavioral deprivation fundamentally spring from confusions in the lay person's mind between the ordinary connotations of the term "deprivation" and its technical use in scientific quarters. Schaefer is convinced that the widespread objections to the judicious use of deprivation in behavioral programs is founded upon ignorance about how such modalities of treatment can be used to benefit, rather than disadvantage, the patient. There is, of course, another side to these controversies.

The fundamental issue responsible for the sometime conflict between behavior therapists and civil libertarians centers around disagreements as to the nature of the proper balance to be struck between the ethical obligation or duty to treat and the legal rights of patients to resist treatment. Several behavior therapists construe the concept of "legal rights to resist treatment" as rights to be protected against unethical treatment practices where the force of the expression "unethical" is closely linked to the notion of an ineffective, but coerced, treatment procedure. That is, many behavior therapists hold that with respect to an involuntary, or captive population of patients, the right to be protected against enforced but ineffective treatment procedures is largely how the legal right to resist treatment *ought* to be defined. Alternatively, civil libertarians tend to take the position that the right to resist treatment must be guaranteed in connection with both effective and ineffective treatment procedures (Begelman, 1971b).

Several behavior therapists, in justifying the ethical character of particular forms of behavioral treatment, frequently refer to the sordid plights that are the lot of certain patients without the administration of, say, aversion therapy. Additionally, they are careful to attest to the minimally damaging or painful properties of the UCS employed, relative to the brutality of such modalities of treatment as ECT or psychosurgery. Miron (1968) for one, documents how aversion therapy "decreased self-destructive behavior in an 11-year-old girl who had spent three years tied hand and foot to prevent her from violently banging her head and severely mutilating her face by digging at skin grafts with her fingernails [Miron, 1968, p. 50]." The author goes on to indicate how the UCS is usually of low amperage and not much more painful than some injections.

Miron's reassurances are redundant if, as Cahoon (1968) and Bragg and Wagner (1968) have insisted, efficacy of treatment technique is the fundamental ethical criterion for administering it. Moreover, if the primary consideration is to rehabilitate, of what conceivable relevance is it to document minimization of discomfort undergone by patients to whom aversive methods are administered? Even in cases in which patients are scarcely foredoomed to negative plights without aversion therapy, or where its administration hypothetically involves prolonged extreme pain and discomfort, why should these facts become relevant if ultimate rehabilitation is the primary criterion for the ethical justification of enforced treatment?

The aforementioned line of reasoning appeared to provide the rationale for the program conducted by Cotter (1970) in a Vietnamese mental hospital. Cotter established a program in which chronic patients who refused to work were submitted to massive exposures of unmodified ECT administered on a three-times-a-week schedule. On the first day of the program one hundred and twenty electroconvulsive treatments were administered, *irrespective of diagnosis.* Cotter's program resulted in an increased number of patients who became motivated to work. He attributed this partially to the fear of ECT, and partially to the alleviation of schizophrenic and depressive symptomatology by electroconvulsive methods. It seems apparent that the refusal to work on the part of a chronic patient is not an extreme plight per se. Additionally, Cotter was not explicit about the nature of work his patients were performing. Whether the work details themselves were tailored to individual needs of his Vietnamese patients is a question which by now must strike the reader as morally insignificant in comparison to the methods utilized by Cotter. Nonetheless, he reported later in his article that the work assignments arranged for patients took the form of "ten-man agricultural teams" which were sent to garrisons in enemy territory. Presumably, the A-teams were responsible for growing crops at the garrisons, in order that the American military force deployed there be supplied with a "better diet," and the cost of the air transport of food be reduced. Apparently, these behavioral goals were established by Cotter after a casual conversation with the commander of a Special Forces group in Vietnam. The latter had complained to Cotter that recruitment for A-teams among Viet Cong prisoners had met with disappointing results. Cotter's article was originally published in the *American Journal of Psychiatry* and subsequently in the second volume of an important collection of papers on behavior modification.

When we compare the pretherapeutic plight of one of Cotter's (1970) patients to that of Miron's (1968) self-mutilating patient, it becomes clear that much more enters into the ethical justification of a given treatment approach than merely the nature of the technique involved or the empirical question of whether the methods employed will be effective in realizing preplanned behavioral goals. Both cases involved aversive contingencies that were instrumental in producing stated behavioral aims, although it is possible to argue that Cotter's program was ethically mismanaged, whereas Miron's was not. Of special importance is the suspect nature of Cotter's entire approach, including the ostensible attempt to define "treatment" in terms of value-neutral concepts such as "back-ward behavior" or "reinforced work patterns" without due respect to the comprehensive sociocultural context in terms of which his program was from the outset heavily *politicized.* The ethical propriety of Cotter's program is no more guaranteed to spring from his professed allegiance to results and operant theory than is the whipping of black slaves by plantation owners justified by empirical evidence that such methods are in the demonstrable service of increasing work productivity.

A growing body of literature (Begelman, 1971b; Ennis, 1970; Katz, 1969; Kittrie, 1971; Szasz, 1961, 1963) has addressed itself to the issue of an arguable constitutional right to refuse treatment. Conceivably, and as Spece (1972) has pointed out, test cases challenging the spirit of rulings such as *Winters* v. *Miller* and *Peek* v. *Ciccone* may in the future lead to reversals on the basis of sustaining a constitutional right to "privacy, autonomy, or freedom of the mind," implicit in such decisions as *Stanley* v. *Georgia,*[4] under which criminal sanctions imposed for the mere possession of pornographic material were adjudged by the court to be in violation of due process, since the state has no business controlling a person's private thoughts, however socially unacceptable. The argument of some behaviorists that recognition of a basic right to be let alone, from which the right to refuse treatment can be derived, should be suspended in programs for which its abridgment augments broader rehabilitative

[4] *Stanley* v. *Georgia,* 394 U.S. 557.

values, is simply the expression of another legal position. Although the position is an ethically motivated one, it would be unfair to assume that its legal opponents propound their own position solely out of ignorance of what strides behavior therapy can make toward returning hospitalized patients to the community.

It is especially noteworthy that the entire issue of subordinating dignitary rights to values inherent in ultimate rehabilitative goals is one arising in connection with involuntarily hospitalized patients or criminals. This fact is of extraordinary importance. Specifically, if the state is enjoined to guarantee certain constitutional rights to ordinary citizens, on what basis are they abridged for mental patients? The argument that is ethically necessary to abridge them in the service of ultimate rehabilitative goals can be legally challenged if it is not extended to the case of the ordinary citizen. In other words, if therapists acknowledge the constitutional right of the ordinary citizen to conduct his affairs in ways that are demonstrably damaging to his self-interests or psychological integrity, by what logic is the principle suddenly controverted when it comes to the institutionalized mental patient? Why should a hospitalized mental patient who refuses treatment be compelled to submit to it on the basis of ethical mandates universally regarded as inapplicable to ordinary citizens pursuing equally disastrous behavioral courses?

Ullmann and Krasner (1965) have attempted to supply an answer to this question. They maintained that the professional staff of institutions caring for involuntary patients are usually paid public servants, obligated to society to treat and return to it as speedily as possible the individuals entrusted to them. In line with this charge, Ullmann and Krasner assert flatly that patients do not have a right to be "sick" (Ullmann & Krasner, 1965, p. 42). The argument emphasizes the ethical obligations of therapists to society, on the basis of their being its salaried servants. A noticeable danger in this focus arises over the assignment of ethical priorities, in the event the interests of the patient and society are in conflict. Attempts to obscure the possibility of such a conflict may be the consequence of an insensitivity to the adversary character of legal proceedings in cases for which the deprivation of liberty, through conferral of the involuntary status, becomes a prominent issue. Moreover, whether patients do or do not have a right to be "sick" is logically prior to determining the nature of obligations attaching to a professional-therapeutic status in being salaried by the state. Obviously, if patients are in the future declared to have a legally constituted right to refuse treatment, the duties of professional persons would be correspondingly modified to provide for the exercise of these rights.

On the personal side, the reader should be informed of a recent communication to the author by a skilled behaviorist on the West Coast. The communicant had taken exception to many of the points in the present author's treatment of the ethics of behavior modification (Begelman, 1971b). Apparently unaware of the fact that the latter is an avowed behaviorist, the communicant endeavored to disabuse him of the myth that behavior therapists are inclined to run amok in the streets, implanting electrodes in the brains of unwilling victims. It had not occurred to the communicant that if rehabilitation by means of whatever treatment modalities could achieve it were the overriding criterion of ethical intervention, the "treatment" of unwilling ordinary citizens ceases to be such an absurd notion. Yet the only difference between the ordinary citizen and the hospitalized mental patient is the involuntary position of the latter, a conferred status apparently crucial for discriminating between a population of persons for whom enforced treatment is sometimes considered an ethical mandate, and a population for whom it is an ethical absurdity!

A possible future dilemma for the law in the event the constitutional right to refuse treatment is established through precedent, is the inevitable conflict that would arise between decisions like Judge Bazelon's in *Rouse* v. *Cameron,*[5] guaranteeing a statutory right to treatment for the involuntary committed patient, or *Wyatt* v. *Stickney,* ensuring a constitutional right to treatment, and "right to refuse treatment" precedents. Thus, an involuntary patient who refuses treatment is automatically also a patient who can seek damages or release from the hospital to which he has been committed on grounds that the institution, in failing to provide adequate treatment, has acted in violation of *Rouse* v. *Cameron* or *Wyatt* v. *Stickney* by not providing the *quid pro quo* treatment program the law demands when involuntary status is conferred. In effect, "right to refuse treatment" precedents provide the future involuntary patient with a legal basis for discharge under the provisions of *Rouse* and *Wyatt*. One way around the dilemma, as Katz (1969) has indicated, is to define "right" as synonymous with "opportunity" in contrast to "duty" or "obligation." On the former definition of "right," a patient has a right to treatment in the sense that the institution is obligated to treat him, contingent upon his wish to accede. Consequently, he has an opportunity to be treated, but not a legal duty to be treated. However, the legal position of the institution under *Rouse* and *Wyatt* is problematic for patients who refuse treatment. A more elegant solution would be to legally minimize or abolish involuntary hospitalization, a theme popular in the radical forensic proposals of the Szaszians.

Up to this point in legal history, precedents like *Wyatt* and *Rouse*

[5] *Rouse* v. *Cameron,* 373 F.2d 451 (D.C. Cir. 1966).

guaranteeing the right to be treated, or the right to resist treatment, have presupposed a fairly unambiguous definition of "treatment." However, if the significance of the legal concept of "treatment" derives predominantly from the notion of *producing behavior change as a result of doing something to a patient,* it is clear that behavior theory can contribute substantially to any future phase of legal reexamination of the concept "treatment." In line with this, it is perhaps an implicit assumption of the law that the guaranteed right to be treated or the right to resist treatment are essentially the right to become a changed organism or to resist being changed. In the light of a considerable body of psychological knowledge accumulated about behavior, the assumption that radical behavior change is a consequence of "treatment" in a narrow sense (i.e., the administration of professionally supervised techniques or programs) is a gratuitous one. Placement in a custodial environment for long periods of time, and without the benefit of professional attention, can no longer be viewed as a static plight or condition. On the contrary, it is the plight of an organism whose behavior is radically altered by a series of accidental contingencies. On the other hand, it would appear that the thrust of *Wyatt* and *Rouse* as well as all right to refuse treatment precedents is predicated on the assumptions that: (a) in not providing "treatment" as conventionally defined, an agency provides nothing in the way of facilitating significant behavior-change, and (b) in guaranteeing the right to refuse "treatment" as conventionally defined, the law protects mental patients against attempts to alter their behavior radically and unwillingly. Obviously, these assumptions are false. Furthermore, the ethical emphasis placed by behavior therapists on rehabilitative procedures and goals (to the exclusion of the exercise of certain rights, according to civil libertarians) might perhaps be better understood in the following light. Behavior therapists believe that if "treatment" is withheld from institutionalized patients, they will nevertheless undergo "treatment" by an accidental series of contingencies in a drastic, and most probably, retrograde manner. Up to this point the law has been silent on whether withholding "treatment" in the conventional sense maintains preexisting patterns of behavior, or promotes retrograde behaviors, developed as a result of custodial environments. It is the reality of the latter process which necessitates a reexamination of the legal concept of "treatment," since it is scientifically naive to assume that continued exposure to institutionalized environments without the benefit of "treatment" in the current legal sense of the term has few, if any, effects on behavior with which the law has been traditionally concerned. A future complexity for legal thought can therefore be summed up by the question: Is an involuntarily committed mental patient who is guaranteed the right to refuse "treatment" in the current legal sense of the term nevertheless being "treated" in an adverse way in a wider sense when he exercises such a right? If so, is the legal position of the involuntary patient who refuses "treatment" untenable, if the law seeks to ensure his welfare?

It is clear from the foregoing remarks that behavioral science can make significant contributions to changing the law. In the previous example, for instance, psychological knowledge concerning the adverse effects on behavior of custodial environments might well prompt reexamination of the legal concept of "treatment." The law itself is a continually evolving body of principles whose direction is determined essentially by the basic values it strives to uphold on particular rulings. Challenges to present laws in the form of test cases likewise spring from the considered need to alter it so that it can be made to honor principles it is currently deemed to neglect or overlook. Legal discourse thus seeks to determine those junctures where "neglect outweighs care [Katz, 1969, p. 783]." Such determinations are continual tasks "which cannot be petrified by final solutions [Katz, 1969, p. 783]." It must be borne in mind, however, that "neglect" and "care" are legal, not behavioral, concepts; their meaning will shift to the degree that the justification for revising how they *ought* to be construed becomes compelling. The upshot of this is that behavioral findings cannot *define* what the law should be; they merely represent another category of significant information that courts rely on in rendering decisions. All too frequently—and perhaps unfortunately—professional therapists regard the law as a kind of benighted brain-child of judges and lawyers, uninformed on that repository of empirical wisdom to which only the scientifically elect are privy. Such attitudes are largely responsible for the resistance of groups like the American Psychiatric Association to the "right to treatment laws" like *Wyatt* and *Rouse,* guaranteeing what courts have construed as the rights of inmates in coerced settings (Bazelon, 1969a, 1969b; Birnbaum, 1971, 1972; Katz, 1969; Robitscher, 1972). Oddly, imagined judicial intrusions into the prerogatives of professional circles frequently appear to exercise the mental health establishment, while the courts are models of forbearance when the process goes in the reverse direction. A case in point is the erosion of the concept of criminal responsibility from its formerly *legal* to currently *psychiatric* status. Specifically, this trend has affected the judicial fate of the concept of insanity, previously held to be legal in status, but currently defined in terms of whatever court-appointed psychiatrists (not juries!) elect it to mean (Gendin, 1973; Leifer, 1964). This turn of events has been initiated over the years by both professional persons seeking to psychiatricize the law, and courts which, at the special pleading of the former, have surrendered their proper authority. Indeed, no other explanation is possible for the steady erosion of principles embodied in the *M'Naghten*[6] rules to those governing Judge Bazelon's decision in *Durham* v. *United States.*[7] The reasoning behind these changes is that the special plea of insanity cannot be based on whether a defendant "can distinguish right from wrong," so that *M'Naghten* requires revision in line with modern scientific thinking. The logic is specious, since the *M'Naghten* rules do not propound criteria of mental disorder (Gendin, 1973). They cannot therefore be faulted for being scientifically narrow. Gendin remarked: "The role of the psychiatrist, under the M-rules, is to state uncontroversial medical facts which the jury may find of some use in making its determination [Gendin, 1973, p. 105]." Nothing in the *M'Naghten* rules themselves require that expert witnesses be queried as to whether the defendant knew the difference between right and wrong. It is therefore gratuitous to argue that such rulings as *Durham* must replace *M'Naghten,* simply because psychiatrists protest that they are incapable of answering questions courts have no business asking them in the first place. Legal problems incurred by the intrinsically unique status of the insanity defense will, however, keep cropping up as long as the defense is retained. A stunning example of a legal proposal balancing the value of due process with requirements of public safety is the one arguing for the abolition of the insanity defense (Katz & Goldstein, 1964). In a telling criticism of justifiable legal bases for the insanity defense, Katz and Goldstein argue that its retention conflicts with fundamental principles of due process. Specifically, a successful plea means that the accused is not guilty by virtue of insanity, and acquitted. His subsequent legal predicament is unique since, in being remanded to the custody of a state mental institution, he is thereby deprived of liberty for a "crime" he has not legally committed.

As has been noted, courts of law seek to determine the most propitious balance to be struck in the preservation of certain values when two or more of them are placed in opposition. For example, the contemporary appeal of the question, "Should a person be allowed to take his own life?" (Begelman, 1971b) derives from the tension between the value of preserving free decisions about one's fate and the value of life. Courts are therefore responsible for assessment procedures the resolution of which cannot be settled by an appeal to empirical or scientific information alone. The current tendency for professionals to redefine the law in their own terms (Leifer, 1964) is a consequence of the failure to appreciate the fact that legal and ethical discourse and principles cannot be reduced to scientific or empirical issues (Begelman, 1971b; Margolis, 1966). A dis-

[6] *M'Naghten Case,* 10 Cl. & F. 200, 8 Eng. Rep. 718 (H.L.) 1843.
[7] *Durham* v. *United States,* 214 F.2d 852 (D.C. Cir. 1954).

agreement over an ethical or legal problem is frequently not a disagreement over the facts, nor is its resolution guaranteed by access to the most complete scientific information.

While it is by now a near platitude to grant that applied science is inescapably wedded to values and ethical issues (London, 1964; Lowe, 1959; Margolis, 1966; Marmor, 1961; May, 1953; Rogers & Skinner, 1956), the philosophical positions taken on the status of ethical principles, be they the kind understood to govern therapeutic practice or otherwise, will understandably have implications for the manner in which behavioral scientists hope to contribute to their study. Behaviorally oriented psychologists have sometimes held that values not only lend themselves to scientific study but are indeed a special area of such inquiry. Krasner (1964), in reviewing the resurgence of interest in values on the part of behavioral scientists, feels that experimenters are in a preferential position to approach moral and value issues on "an objective basis" (Krasner, 1964, p. 203). The emphasis on objectivity in the study of values is a popular theme in behavioristic literature, and may well be motivated by the felt necessity for approaching value-laden issues on something other than a "subjective" basis. In this connection, Krasner's position seems to be strikingly similar to Skinner's, in the latter's debate with Rogers (Rogers & Skinner, 1956). In response to Rogers' assertion that any pure or applied scientific endeavor requires a "prior subjective choice of values," Skinner had indicated that all such expressions imply the abandonment of rigorous methods of science in dealing with our own behavior. He is convinced that an experimental analysis of behavior requires precisely the same standards of inquiry in studying "values" as it does in conjunction with other behaviors. Accordingly, Skinner insists that values are "reinforcers—conditioned or otherwise [Rogers & Skinner, 1956, p. 1064]."

The widely shared conviction among psychologists that moral and ethical issues can readily be construed as experimental ones (once the assumption that value is a psychological concept has been made) compels Skinner to believe that "a prior *subjective* choice of values" refers to a private psychological process, defying inquiry. In fact, Rogers' point is not that value judgments require a mysterious psychological process, but simply that the values inherent in establishing particular behavioral goals are always *logically prior* to—and therefore beyond—the scope of experimental inquiry. In short, ultimate goals established as worth pursuing or achieving are adumbrated in moral positions affirming their importance, not extracted from experimental findings. At best, the latter may be used to determine the most efficient ways to realize such goals; they cannot determine their nature. The present author is convinced that the central issue of values and, *a fortiori,* ethical problems arising from therapeutic efforts is not a psychological or scientific one at all, and can therefore only be misleadingly described as either a "subjective" or "objective" issue. Briefly, it is the problem of which ethical principles *ought* to prevail, a rubric hardly scratched by Skinner's thesis that "a list of values is a list of reinforcers." At best, reinforcers are things persons happen to value. Nonetheless, what ends are pursued or what reinforcers govern behavior is an empirical issue the determination of which is unrelated to what ends ought to be pursued or how persons ought to be reinforced. The ethical significance of preserving international peace is in no way established or affected by the frequency with which nations declare war.

In considering how such larger controversies about values relate to the immediate scope of this paper, it might be fruitful to focus on Lazarus' (1973) comments concerning the limitations of a traditional S-R approach to behavior therapy. Lazarus has undertaken a criticism of the strict S-R approach on the basis of his conviction that it is ill-suited to equip the practicing behavior therapist with the skills necessary for dealing with "moral issues involving divorce, sexual practices, business ventures, and other such daily or indeed *hourly* therapeutic topics [Lazarus, 1973, p. 15]." Franks and Wilson (1973) have paraphrased Lazarus' position by indicating he feels ". . . that S-R learning theory principles are logically independent of ethics and social value systems [Franks & Wilson, 1973, p. 4]."

Lazarus is certainly correct about the limitations of a strict S-R approach, although his argument cannot be used to dramatize the advantage of the "broad-spectrum" approach since, as an applied scientific endeavor, it is similarly limited with respect to the resolution of ethical conflicts or dilemmas. The therapist who confronts such issues with his patients may be performing a valuable human service, although what he thereby accomplishes can only be misleadingly characterized as confirmed by scientific knowledge or findings. Specifically, if a devout Catholic client is referred to a behavior therapist for incapacitating guilt and remorse over masturbation, what strictly "scientific" information or principles can be relied on to guide the therapist's treatment approach? The issue here does not involve the importance of a therapist's awareness of his own values, or his striving not to impose them on clients (Grossman, 1968). It relates to the fact that any course of therapeutic action taken in such a case, be it directed toward the extinction of anxiety, masturbation, or Catholicism, is not dictated by purely "scientific" considerations, but also by decisions in the value realm.

With respect to ethical issues arising in behavior modification practices, the therapist, while guided by broad principles of the type to be discussed presently, operates much like a court of law: frequently he will find himself at junctures whereby a chosen course of therapeutic action will be the result of the need to proceed by subordinating some important value to another when the two are in clear opposition. At such junctures, empirical information concerning the probable effects of instituting this or that therapeutic procedure will of course be relevant to decision making. However, in many cases such information can never be sufficient enough to totally remove the ambiguities introduced into decision making by ethical issues, problems, or dilemmas.

In the main, several broad principles of ethical conduct in the regulation of behavior-therapeutic practice have been suggested by writers on the topic (Bandura, 1969; Franks & Wilson, 1973; Krasner, 1969; Wilson & Davison, 1974; Yates, 1970). They include: (a) informed and voluntary consent to treatment, (b) the client as decision maker in the value realm, (c) the administration of effective modalities of treatment, and (d) the modification of undesirable target behaviors. It is important to emphasize the limited applicability of the foregoing four criteria of ethical therapeutic intervention. By no means can they be construed as invariant principles of ethical practice, for several reasons. First, there are contexts in which they are obviously inapplicable. For example, the principle of informed and voluntary consent to treatment is irrelevant in cases of nonverbal, severely retarded, or psychotic patients who are incapable of being informed, much less consenting to or refusing treatment. Even in cases where the principle can be made to apply, it may not be unethical to proceed with a treatment program in spite of the refusal of the patient to be helped. These are cases where the behavior disorder is so severe that abandonment of a therapeutic program is tantamount to a life and death issue. Indeed, if in general medical practice the informed and voluntary consent of children to receive inoculations can be agreed on to constitute an inappropriate ethical principle, it would likewise appear to be so for self-mutilating or self-destructive children.

Second, there are contexts in which ethical practice actually consists in going against one of the foregoing principles. Bandura (1969) has suggested that decisions as to the direction of behavior change are rightfully the client's, whereas the choice of appropriate techniques best utilized to produce changes in that direction are reserved for the therapist. However, such a guideline admits of enough permissible exceptions to render it of wide, but limited, applicability. Thus, a therapist may be illustrating the highest ethical standards when he refuses to produce behavior change if the request in question is assessed as an inappropriate or damaging one for the client. It is a not uncommon occurrence for a youngster to request change along lines endorsed by domineering parents. Such "generation gap" phenomena must be evaluated from the standpoint of determining whose "problem" is actually being referred.

Third, attention must be drawn to the open texture (Waismann, 1963) of prescriptive rules. Behavior therapists who have suggested ethical guidelines for therapeutic practice appear to believe that such principles lend themselves to unambiguous formulations as to the particular character of ethical interventions or their violations across the widest range of treatment contexts. This is not true, any more than an early handful of legal precedents serving to define "due process" is sufficient to allow a court to rule on its violation in an infinite number of possible future cases. In a previous publication (Begelman, 1973) the present author attempted to draw attention to the open texture of ethical principles by describing a case in which the presence or absence of "informed consent" to treatment can only be determined by a quasi-legal or stipulative operation, not merely by obtaining further information or data. Briefly, the context is that of a claustrophobic client being treated by a flooding method (Polin, 1959; Rachman, 1966; Stampfl, 1966) involving exposure to a confined environment until extinction of the CR (anxiety) is complete. She is fully informed about the rationale for the treatment and insists the therapist keep her in the confined environment until he is assured that extinction has occurred. After the patient is placed in a locked room, she panics and pleads with the therapist to release her.

Whether or not the patient is "withdrawing consent" originally obtained by the therapist would appear to depend on a stipulation as to whether her subsequent behavior can appropriately be classified as "withdrawing consent" in contrast to being a "natural and expected consequence of high anxiety." This is precisely the kind of conundrum a court of law convenes to adjudicate in the legal sphere. The open texture of prescriptive rules or ethical principles is associated with their inherent *vagueness*. That is, while an ethical criterion such as informed consent to treatment broadly governs ethical practice, frequent decisions concerning whether the criterion has in fact been upheld will tend to be a rather commonplace occurrence. An overlooked problem in behavioristic commentary on ethical issues is precisely this feature of prescriptive principles. In other words, even if general agreement among professionals is obtained for the relevance of certain ethical rules or guidelines, there still remains the recurring problem of stipulating what constitutes governance by or violation of consensually validated principles in sundry contexts.

A somewhat related problem arises in connection with the ethical mandate to treat only undesirable target behaviors, referred to in the behavioral literature as "maladaptive behaviors" or "problem behaviors." There is little disagreement as to the importance of this principle; nevertheless, the specification of what patterns constitute "problem behaviors" is an issue of momentous significance and controversy. The concept of "problem behavior" is itself problematic; it presupposes a moral evaluation of events to which it is held to apply. Designating a pattern of conduct as a behavioral "problem" is, *inter alia,* engaging in a negative assessment of it in terms of implicit, albeit often unrecognized, norms, themselves vulnerable to revision in the wake of external trends in ideology or social policy. Because of this, it would be a mistake to assume that the relationship between the expression "problem behavior" and the pattern of conduct it typically or historically designated has a stamp of eternality. A "problem behavior" is not simply one that causes personal unhappiness or social disapproval. It is essentially one judged to be undesirable according to tacit moral rules embedded in human traditions. An interesting confluence of issues of this type can readily be discerned in recent discussions on the so-called "problem" of homosexuality.

III. HOMOSEXUALITY

In mid-December of 1973, a majority of trustees of the American Psychiatric Association approved a decision to remove homosexuality from its list of "mental disorders" as contained in the APA's *Diagnostic and Statistical Manual of Mental Disorders, Second Edition.* The trustees acted favorably on the recommendation to undertake the change by the APA task force on nomenclature and statistics. Dr. R. L. Spitzer, a spokesman for the task force, indicated that pressure from Gay Liberation groups had indeed prompted the decision, although it was psychiatrically sound. The decision additionally involved the substitution of the diagnostic category "homosexuality" with a newer one: "sexual orientation disturbance," which is used to cover individuals whose sexual interests are directed primarily toward people of the same sex and who are either disturbed by, in conflict with, or wish to change their sexual orientation.

It would appear that the APA decision on nomenclature is more in line with current behavioristic conceptions (Bandura, 1969; Ullmann & Krasner, 1969; Wilson & Davison, 1974), which have largely abandoned the notion of homosexuality as a "mental illness." In spite of this, the present author is convinced that what remains to be clarified about the concept of "problem behavior," and its essentially *moral* underpinnings, renders the APA decision a trivial one indeed. The reader will note that the newer concept of "sexual orientation disturbance" covers individuals who are "disturbed" only when their sexual interests are directed toward persons of the *same* sex. The fascinating omission, of course, is the category of persons who are "disturbed" when their sexual interests are directed toward persons of the *opposite* sex.

Franks and Wilson (1973), in calling for what they term "the most searching and unrelenting tests of methodological adequacy [Franks & Wilson, 1973, p. 5]" in order to offset the rhetoric of battling theoretical factions within behaviorism, urge the necessity of more well controlled studies of ". . . such major problems as homosexual behavior . . . phobic reaction . . . obesity . . . smoking [Franks & Wilson, 1973, p. 5]." The conspicuous omission from the authors' inventory of the major problem of *heterosexuality* is noteworthy if, indeed, their implicit criteria for "problems" are target behaviors generating personal grief, unhappiness or social disapproval. The paradox is more than easily dispelled, however, once it is realized that Franks and Wilson have omitted nothing: there is no such thing as "the problem of heterosexuality" in the psychiatric or behavioral lexicon. The category is typically parsed as "the problem of marital discord," or "the problem of aggressive behaviors," or "the problem of impotence," or "the problem of frigidity," and so forth. This is scarcely a terminological accident or quirk; it is actually the consequence of a moral double standard for heterosexuals and homosexuals. The double standard is an ingrained feature of a tacitly acknowledged value system, the hard edge of which legislates what life-styles must be relegated to the limbo of deviancy and negative evaluation, and the soft edge of which finds expression in dicta remaining ostensible mysteries as to their origin. One such specimen is the following: "When a heterosexual has a problem, it is because he is impotent; when a homosexual has a problem, it is because he is a homosexual." Another specimen may be distinguished by its clever ellipsis: "Homosexuals are homosexual because of anxieties concerning heterosexual relationships" (Bieber *et al.,* 1962; Feldman & MacCulloch, 1971). The formulation is only partially complete, since it invites the *quid pro quo:* "Heterosexuals are heterosexual because of anxieties concerning homosexual relationships." Is it such a far cry from the moralizing propensities of spokesmen for the disease model who, like Bergler (1956), argue that "Homosexuality is not the 'way of life' these sick people gratuitously assume it to be, but a neurotic distortion of the total personality [Bergler, 1956, p. 9]."

In discussing the behavioral approach to homosexuality, Wilson and Davison (1974) have indicated their agreement with Bandura's (1969) emphasis on the choice of behavioral goals being the *client's.* They insist that this ethical tenet is in opposition to the traditional psychiatric view of homosexuals as *ipso facto* being "sick" and in need of treatment, as well as in opposition to Gay Liberation persons who wish to "deny the right of the homosexual individual to seek treatment aimed at heterosexual reorientation [Wilson & Davison, 1974, p. 24]." In the authors' view, the treatment of homosexuals in behavior therapy, coupled with the paucity of programs aimed at enabling homosexuals to adjust to a more satisfactory homosexual life-style, have been used by Gay Liberation and other groups to "perpetuate the erroneous public impression about behavior therapy being bent on eradicating homosexual behavior [Wilson & Davison, 1974, p. 25]." The authors feel that the voluntary nature of behavior-therapeutic practice contradicts such charges. Unfortunately, the issue is more complex than the analysis offered by Wilson and Davison.

To begin with, Wilson and Davison charge that members of Gay Liberation wish to deny the right of homosexuals to receive treatment aimed at sexual identity change. In fact, Gay Liberation—to the best of the present author's knowledge—has only demanded that behavior therapists discontinue changing homosexuals into heterosexuals. The distinction here is of some significance, since "denying homosexuals their right to be treated" suggests active interference with a voluntary decision or resolution on the part of a homosexual person. On the other hand, insisting that behavior therapists stop reorienting homosexual patterns involves the demand that behaviorists halt practices *which by their very existence constitute a significant causal element in reinforcing the social doctrine that homosexuality is bad*. Indeed, the point of the activist protest is that behavior therapists contribute significantly to preventing the exercise of any *real* option in decision-making about sexual identity, by further strengthening the prejudice that homosexuality is a "problem behavior," since treatment may be offered for it. As a consequence of this therapeutic stance, as well as a wider system of social and attitudinal pressures, homosexuals tend to seek treatment *for being homosexuals*. Heterosexuals, on the other hand, can scarcely be expected to seek voluntary treatment for being "heterosexual," especially since all the social forces arrayed—including the unavailability of behavior therapy for heterosexuality—attest to the acknowledgment of the idea that whatever "problems" heterosexuals experience are not due to their sexual orientation. The upshot of this is that contrary to the disclaimer that behavioral therapy is ". . . not a system of ethics [Bandura, 1969, p. 87]," the very act of providing therapeutic services for homosexual "problems" indicates otherwise.

The endorsement by Wilson and Davison (1974) of Bandura's principle of patient determination of behavioral goals is of further interest in this connection. As was mentioned earlier, if it is sometimes sound ethical practice to challenge a client's choice of goal—as in cases of self-destructive or parentally imposed goals—why do Wilson and Davison urge acceptance of Bandura's tenet in cases of homosexuals who request sexual reorientation, unless there were an implicit recognition of heterosexuality as a "proper" behavioral goal, independently of client choice?

If the notion of "problem behavior" could be analyzed as "a potentially modifiable pattern of socially unacceptable behavior causing personal distress or unhappiness," there is no compelling reason why behavior therapists should refuse to shape racial bigotry in a client who voluntarily requested such change because his liberal politics were responsible for much of his grief in a predominantly segregated community. But a refusal to implement such self-elected goals would suggest that far from undertaking the treatment of homosexuality because it is a "problem" for homosexual clients, behaviorists initiate it because, like "bigotry," it is to be negatively assessed. Consequently, it is ethically permissible to replace it with something which, like liberal politics, can be positively assessed: heterosexuality.

In spite of the recognition of the influential role of social reinforcement in the behavioral literature (Bandura, 1969; Rotter, 1954), the present author is unaware of any mention in it that the so-called "problem of homosexuality" is a sheer sociological creation. That is, while behaviorists for the most part conceptualize homosexuality as a learned pattern of behavior, there is a concomitant lack of sensitivity in the literature to the moral significance of the distinction between "homosexual problem-behaviors" and "problem behaviors of homosexual persons"—the two are far from synonymous. The former implies that a pattern of conduct is a problem explicitly because it is not a heterosexual pattern; whereas the latter implies that sexual behaviors may be problems for homosexual, heterosexual, bisexual, transsexual, or asexual persons. Interestingly enough, moral partiality is historically extended to asexuals, not merely heterosexuals. Temptations of the flesh on the part of Catholic priests are never categorized as "the problems of asexuals" or "asexual problems"; they are merely listed as the sexual problems priests experience.

The foregoing analysis challenges the widespread belief held by behavior therapists that their approach to problem behaviors is based *solely* on scientific considerations and consistently applied ethical criteria. The terms "disorder" and "problem behavior" are as value impregnated as is the expression "mental illness." Proposals for new diagnostic or behavioral coding systems (Cautela, 1973), aside from their obvious virtues in developing finer discriminations out of entities traditionally conceived as "syndromes" or "reactions," appear to represent little more than linguistic revisions of twice-told tales (e.g., DSM I and DSM II). The most significant and influential legacy of the medical model is not its disease-based metaphysics, but those aspects of it which are least scrutinized: its tacit canons of moral assessment governing which events are to be declared "desirable" or not. It is difficult, but important, to see the influence of the model when the behavioral treatment of a liberal for anxiety takes the form of enabling the client to develop social skills requisite to combat the effects of an unenlightened social environment, while the treatment of a homosexual person for a similar behavioral condition often takes the form of changing him into a heterosexual. If no other implied moral dictates were operating, logic demands that the behavior therapist: (a) change liberals into bigots upon request, *or* (b) equip homosexual clients with skills necessary to reduce the oppressions perpetrated on them by a larger social environment for which intolerance of diversity seems to be the order of the day. In this regard, it should be noted that the most enlightened recommendation concerning the "problem" of homosexuality was put forth by Wilson and Davison (1974) at the end of their paper. They urged that behavior therapists support the attempt to repeal laws legislating against "certain sexual activities among consenting adults and against the right to assemble publicly [Wilson & Davison, 1974, p. 25]."

Extending the argument, it is possible to view the behavioral reorientation of homosexual persons as an example of the individual system model approach to behavior disorder criticized by the sociologist Scheff (1966). Scheff's critique is of therapeutic endeavors focusing on the modification of individual behaviors, rather than on the social system which defines them as "problems." The emphasis here is a *moral* one, and stands in contrast to the well known behavioristic emphasis on restructuring environments in order to produce individual change. That is, Scheff's sociological analysis, similar to the trend found in the writings of commentators like Szasz (1960), Goffman (1961), Laing (1966), and the radical therapists (Agel, 1971), examines issues centering around the justification of codes reflecting traditional social values.

Behavior therapists should give due consideration to abandoning the treatment of homosexuals when the behavioral objective is sexual identity change or reorientation. If there is little evidence to suggest that whatever "problems" homosexuals experience about their sexual identity are not those perpetuated by oppressive social structures, continued behavioral services to such clients merely reinforce the value system originally responsible for self-referrals. Behaviorists should make strides in the resolution of the real "problem": the public derogation of diverse life styles.

Apparently, implicit criteria for "problem behaviors" employed by members of Gay Liberation who have lobbied for a more enlightened treatment of the homosexual person are, ironically, sometimes also deficient. For example, a homosexual psychologist, Charles Silverstein, has argued before the Nomenclature Committee of the American Psychiatric Association that homosexuality cannot be viewed as a "disorder" since there is no evidence to suggest that homosexuals are any the more emotionally disturbed than heterosexuals. What Silverstein overlooks is that evidence of emotional disturbance in homosexuals is *irrelevant* as a criterion of whether this sexual orientation is a "disorder." There are two reasons for this.

First, if there is evidence of relatively greater emotional disturbance among homosexuals, such a finding may simply be an indirect consequence of the social belief system about their essential "abnormality." But there is a second point to be made, which has deeper *logical* implications. If what qualifies as "disorder" were linked to independent psychological measures of emotional disturbance, there should be no reason to preclude heterosexuality as a "disorder" in the event data on comparisons between heterosexual and homosexual populations went in the unexpected direction. What is being overlooked in Silverstein's argument is that criteria for the "normalcy" of heterosexuality and "abnormality" of "homosexuality" have nothing whatsoever to do with independent empirical measures of adjustment. Criteria for "sexual disorder" are nothing more than the extent of departure from morally acceptable standards of conduct. Such standards are *logically* exempt from qualifying as disorder, just as the standard-meter rod in the Parisian Bureau is exempt from qualifying (i.e., being measured) as longer or shorter than a meter. Because of this, the question, "Is heterosexuality a disorder?" is actually a *senseless* question, not an empirical one.

A similar confusion appears to plague most research on the etiology of homosexuality. Studies finding differences between heterosexuals and homosexuals in developmental or familial patterns (Bieber *et al.,* 1962; Evans, 1969) or hormonal patterns (Loraine, Adamopoulos, Kirkham, Ismail, & Dove, 1971) do not attest to the *pathogenic* determination of homosexuality, but simply to a difference between experimental populations. The concept of "pathology" is strictly applicable only to the causal determinants of behaviors already socially evaluated as "undesirable" (Begelman, 1971a).

IV. AVERSIVE PROCEDURES

Aversive techniques have perhaps been the most frequent focus of ethical criticism. The wildest fears about "conditioning therapies" appear to be activated in the popular imagination by such fictional treatments of the subject as *The Manchurian Candidate* and *Clockwork Orange*. The recent decision by the government to abandon behavior modification programs funded by the L.E.A.A. was directly related to opposition on the part of interest groups to the use of aversive methods in Federal programs like the one in Missouri. Inclusion of aversive techniques in behavior modification programs in Minnesota were likewise largely responsible for that state's decision to greatly restrict them (Lucero *et al.,* 1968). Behavior modification has had a high price to pay for the development of this relatively limited aspect of its technological armamentarium. Discussion of its use from the ethical perspective is therefore timely.

Behavior therapists in general (Bandura, 1969; Begelman, 1971b; Franks & Wilson, 1973; Rachman & Teasdale, 1969) have insisted that the administration of aversive procedures, except in rare cases of nonverbal or self-mutilative individuals, ethically requires the voluntary and informed consent to treatment on the part of the client. On reflection, the requirement may strike one as a bit *odd,* inasmuch as the recommendation that it become an essential feature of aversive procedures would appear to suggest it is *not* a similar requirement for nonaversive forms of treatment. A possible explanation of the emphasis, however, might be the following. Since the imagined threat to human dignity or rights inherent in behavior modification practices is greatest in relation to aversion therapy, behavior therapists themselves tend to lean over backward in reassuring the public that the approach taken is characterized by exemplary ethical standards (Ball, 1968; Bragg & Wagner, 1968; Cahoon, 1968; Rachman & Teasdale, 1969). It is not difficult to understand why the defense of aversive techniques on the part of several behaviorists reacting to the curtailment of their use in Minnesota, as well as the defense of that curtailment (Lucero *et al.,* 1968) was little more than an exercise in abstract homilies. Both sides of this famous controversy had in effect discussed the ethics of a particular behavioral technique, failing to distinguish this from the ethics of its administration in various treatment contexts (Begelman, 1971b).

The argument that aversive procedures per se are unethical because they involve pain or discomfort to clients or patients is totally without validity. Indeed, if the absence of pain were a necessary condition of any treatment procedure, we all would have succumbed to one or another of a variety of infectious conditions we have been immunized from by a *painful* inoculation. Rachman and Teasdale (1969) have indicated they are not impressed with arguments aimed at establishing the ethical respectability of aversive techniques on the basis of analogies to procedures in medicine invariably accompanied by pain. In line with this, they have pointed out that unlike aversion therapy, medical procedures are only incidentally accompanied by pain (Rachman & Teasdale, 1969, p. 94). The present author is at a loss to know what to make of this distinction. Obviously, the conscientious administration of an aversive procedure is hardly undertaken with the sole aim of inflicting pain on clients. It is undertaken with the ultimate goal of ameliorating a behavioral problem, and in this sense, the pain involved is incidental. The relevant point is that no treatment procedure involving pain as a direct or indirect consequence of the methods employed can be declared unethical on this abstract basis alone.

It is still a far cry from pointing out the invalidity of arguments against the ethical propriety of aversive techniques per se, and condoning their use in whatever treatment context behavior therapists choose to employ them. In line with this, the arguments of Ball (1968), Bragg and Wagner (1968), Cahoon (1968), Miron (1968), and Schaefer (1968) defend the use of aversive techniques when characterized by high ethical standards. These arguments are clearly irrelevant except in relation to abstract criticisms aimed at rejecting such methods out of hand. The crucial point is not whether these techniques are ethically permissible when used judiciously, but what particular clinical undertakings can be characterized as a judicious use of them. We can already document ethical mismanagement of such techniques in the outrageous program conducted by Cotter (1970). If *that* is a widespread paradigmatic use of aversive techniques, the present author would feel little compunction about favoring the total abandonment of *all* aversion techniques administered to captive populations, for fear that programs like Cotter's would serve as inappropriate models for clinicians entering the field. The fact that Cotter's paper was published in a classic text on behavior modification is further cause for alarm. Apparently, promoting the cause of applied science took precedence in the minds of its editors over yet another assault on the Vietnamese people.

Administrative decisions to abandon the use of aversive techniques do not presuppose that the ethics of a particular treatment method is suspect, but perhaps only the way in which or reasons for which it is administered in this or that context. As was indicated earlier, inmates of the L.E.A.A.-funded program in Missouri have filed a petition charging that aversive procedures used in the program are unconstitutional since they represent "cruel and unusual punishment." If the courts uphold the plaintiffs' claim, the program at Missouri will constitute a violation of constitutional rights in the eyes of the law. Even if the courts strike down the claim, the Association for Advancement of Behavior Therapy would do well to take the bull by the horns and develop vehicles through which forensic psychological issues can be studied and acted upon with dispatch. It is time that behavioral clinicians recognized that development of well-researched modalities of treatment is but a part of what it is to be an applied scientist. We cannot remain impervious to the fact that above all things we are part of a moral order, a scheme we may occasionally glimpse when we ask ourselves the unscientific question: "What I have done is socially (professionally, scientifically) approved, but is it right?" Thereby, said the kangaroo sitting on the edge of a precipice, hangs a tale.

REFERENCES

Agel, J. *The radical therapist.* New York: Ballantine Books, 1971.

Agras, W. S. Toward the certification of behavior therapists? *Journal of Applied Behavior Analysis,* 1973, **6,** 167–173.

Ayllon, T., & Azrin, N. *The token economy: A motivational system for therapy and rehabilitation.* New York: Appleton, 1968.

Ball, T. S. The re-establishment of social behavior. *Hospital and Community Psychiatry,* 1968, **19,** 230–232.

Bandura, A. *Principles of behavior modification.* New York: Holt, 1969.

Bazelon, D. L. The right to treatment: The court's role. *Hospital and Community Psychiatry,* 1969, **20,** 129–135. (a)

Bazelon, D. L. Implementing the right to treatment. *University of Chicago Law Review,* 1969, **36,** 742–754. (b)

Begelman, D. A. Misnaming, metaphors, the medical model, and some muddles. *Psychiatry,* 1971, **34,** 38–58. (a)

Begelman, D. A. The ethics of behavioral control and a new mythology. *Psychotherapy: Theory, Research and Practice,* 1971, **8,** 165–169. (b)

Begelman, D. A. Ethical issues in behavioral control. *Journal of Nervous and Mental Disease,* 1973, **156,** 412–419.

Bergler, E. *Homosexuality: Disease or way of life?* New York: Hill & Wang, 1956.

Bieber, I., Dain, H. H., Dince, P. R., Drellich, M. G., Grand, H. C., Gundlach, R. H., Kremer, M. W., Rifkin, A. H., Wilbur, C. B., & Bieber, T. B. *Homosexuality: A psychoanalytical study.* New York: Random House, 1962.

Bijou, S. W. What psychology has to offer education now. *Journal of Applied Behavior Analysis,* 1970, **3,** 65–71.

Birnbaum, M. Some remarks on "the right to treatment." *Alabama Law Review,* 1971, **23,** 623–639.

Birnbaum, M. The right to treatment—some comments on implementation. *Duquesne Law Review,* 1972, **10,** 579–608.

Bragg, R. A., & Wagner, M. K. Can deprivation be justified? *Hospital and Community Psychiatry,* 1968, **19,** 229–230.

Cahoon, D. D. Balancing procedures against outcomes. *Hospital and Community Psychiatry,* 1968, **19,** 228–229.

Carrera, F., & Adams, P. L. An ethical perspective on operant conditioning. *Journal of the American Academy of Child Psychiatrists,* 1970, **9,** 607–623.

Cautela, J. A behavioral coding system. Presidential address to the seventh annual meeting of the Association for Advancement of Behavior Therapy, Miami, December 1973.

Cotter, L. H. Operant conditioning in a Vietnamese mental hospital. In R. Ulrich, T. Stachnik, & J. Mabry (Eds.), *Control of human behavior.* Vol. 2. *From cure to prevention.* Glenview, Ill.: Scott, Foresman & Co., 1970. Pp. 100–105.

Day, W. F. Humanistic psychology and contemporary behaviorism. *Humanist,* 1971, **31,** 13–16.

D'Zurilla, T. J., & Goldfried, M. Problem solving and behavior modification. *Journal of Abnormal Psychology,* 1971, **78,** 107–126.

Ennis, B. J. Civil liberties and mental illness. *Criminal Law Bulletin,* 1970, **7,** 101–127.

Evans, R. B. Childhood parental relationships of homosexual men. *Journal of Consulting and Clinical Psychology,* 1969, **33,** 129–135.

Fairweather, G. W. *Social psychology in treating mental illness; An experimental approach.* New York: Wiley, 1964.

Feldman, M. P., & MacCulloch, M. J. *Homosexual behavior: Therapy and assessment.* Oxford: Pergamon, 1971.

Franks, C. M., & Wilson, G. T. (Eds.), *Annual review of behavior therapy: Theory and practice.* New York: Brunner/Mazel, 1973.

Gendin, S. Insanity and criminal responsibility. *American Philosophical Quarterly,* 1973, **10,** 99–110.

Goffman, E. *Asylums.* Garden City, N.Y.: Doubleday, 1961.

Grossman, D. Of whose unscientific methods and unaware values? *Psychotherapy: Theory, Research and Practice,* 1968, **5,** 53–54.

Katz, J. The right to treatment—an enchanting legal fiction? *University of Chicago Law Review,* 1969, **36,** 755–783.

Katz, J., & Goldstein, J. Abolish the insanity defense—why not? *Journal of Nervous and Mental Disease,* 1964, **138,** 57–69.

Kittrie, N. N. *The right to be different: Deviance and enforced therapy.* Baltimore, Md.: Johns Hopkins Press, 1971.

Krasner, L. Behavior control and social responsibility. *American Psychologist,* 1964, **17,** 199–204.

Krasner, L. Behavior modification—values and training: The perspective of a psychologist. In C. M. Franks (Ed.), *Behavior therapy: Appraisal and status.* New York: McGraw-Hill, 1969. Pp. 537–566.

Krutch, J. W. *The measure of man.* Indianapolis: Bobbs-Merrill, 1953.

Kuhn, T. S. *The structure of scientific revolutions.* Chicago: University of Chicago Press, 1962.

Laing, R. D. *The divided self.* London: Penguin Books, 1966.

Lazarus, A. A. *Behavior therapy and beyond.* New York: McGraw-Hill, 1971.

Lazarus, A. A. Behavior therapy and clinical probelms: A critical overview. In C. M. Franks & G. T. Wilson (Eds.), *Annual review of behavior therapy: Theory and practice.* New York: Brunner/Mazel, 1973. Pp. 9–36.

Leifer, R. The psychiatrist and tests of criminal responsibility. *American Psychologist,* 1964, **19,** 825–830.

London, P. *The modes and morals of psychotherapy.* New York: Holt, 1964.

Loraine, J. A., Adamopoulos, D. A., Kirkham, E. E., Ismail, A. A. A., & Dove, G. A. Patterns of hormonal excretion in male and female homosexuals. *Nature,* 1971, **234,** 552–555.

Lowe, C. M. Value orientations: An ethical dilemma. *American Psychologist,* 1959, **14,** 687–693.

Lucero, R. J., Vail, D. J., & Scherber, J. Regulating operant-conditioning programs. *Hospital and Community Psychiatry,* 1968, **19,** 53–54.

Margolis, J. *Psychotherapy and morality: A study of two concepts.* New York: Random House, 1966.

Marmor, J. Psychoanalytic therapy as an educational process: Common denominators in the therapeutic approaches of different psychoanalytic "schools." Paper read at the Academy of Psychoanalysis, Chicago, May 1961.

Martin, M. Behavior modification in the mental hospital. *Hospital and Community Psychiatry,* 1972, **23,** 287–289.

Matson, F. W. Humanistic theory: The third revolution in psychology. *Humanist,* 1971, **31,** 7–11.

May, R. Historical and philosophical presuppositions for understanding therapy. In O. H. Mowrer (Ed.), *Psychotherapy theory and research.* New York: Ronald Press, 1953.

Miron, N. B. The primary ethical consideration. *Hospital and Community Psychiatry,* 1968, **19,** 226–228.

Polin, A. The effect of flooding and physical suppression as extinction techniques on an anxiety-motivated avoidance locomotor response. *Journal of Psychology,* 1959, **47,** 253–255.

Rachman, S. Studies in desensitization. II. Flooding. *Behaviour Research and Therapy,* 1966, **4,** 1–6.

Rachman, S., & Teasdale, J. *Aversion therapy and behavior disorders: An analysis.* Miami: University of Miami Press, 1969.

Robitscher, J. Courts, state hospitals, and the right to treatment. *American Journal of Psychiatry,* 1972, **129,** 298–304.

Rogers, C. R., & Skinner, B. F. Some issues concerning the control of human behavior: A symposium. *Science,* 1956, **124,** 1057–1066.

Rotter, J. B. *Social learning and clinical psychology.* Englewood Cliffs, N.J.: Prentice-Hall, 1954.

Schaefer, H. H. The ethics of deprivation. In R. D. Rubin & C. M. Franks (Eds.), *Advances in behavior therapy 1968.* New York: Academic Press, 1968. Pp. 83–92.

Scheff, T. J. *Being mentally ill: A sociological theory.* Chicago: Aldine, 1966.

Skinner, B. F. *Beyond freedom and dignity.* New York: Knopf, 1971.

Spece, R. G. Conditioning and other technologies used to "treat?" "rehabilitate?" "demolish?" prisoners and mental patients. *Southern California Law Review,* 1972, **45,** 616–684.

Stampfl, T. G. Implosive therapy: The theory, the subhuman analogue, the strategy, and the technique. In S. G. Armitage (Ed.), *Behavior modification techniques in the treatment of emotional disorders.* Battle Creek, Mich.: V.A. Publication, 1966. Pp. 12–21.

Szasz, T. S. The myth of mental illness. *American Psychologist,* 1960, **15,** 113–118.

Szasz, T. S. *The myth of mental illness: Foundations of a theory of personal conduct.* New York: Harper (Hoeber), 1961.

Szasz, T. S. *Law, liberty and psychiatry.* New York: Macmillan, 1963.

Truax, C. B. Reinforcement and nonreinforcement in Rogerian psychotherapy. *Journal of Abnormal Psychology,* 1966, **71,** 1–9.

Ullmann, L. P., & Krasner, L. *Case studies in behavior modification.* New York: Holt, 1965.

Ullmann, L. P., & Krasner, L. *A psychological approach to abnormal behavior.* Englewood Cliffs, N.J.: Prentice-Hall, 1969.

Waismann, F. Verifiability. In A. G. N. Flew (Ed.), *Logic and language.* 1st Ser. Oxford: Blackwell, 1963. Pp. 117–144.

Wexler, D. B. Token and taboo: Behavior modification, token economies, and the law. *Behaviorism: A Forum for Critical Discussion,* 1973, **1,** 1–24.

Wilson, G. T., & Davison, G. C. Behavior therapy and homosexuality: A critical perspective. *Behavior Therapy,* 1974, **5,** 16–28.

Wolpe, J. The compass of behavior therapy. In C. M. Franks & G. T. Wilson (Eds.), *Annual review of behavior therapy: Theory and practice.* New York: Brunner/Mazel, 1973. Pp. 37–39.

Yates, A. J. *Behavior therapy.* New York: Wiley, 1970.

BEHAVIOR MODIFICATION WITH DELINQUENTS[1]

Curtis J. Braukmann and Dean L. Fixsen
Department of Human Development and Bureau of Child Research
University of Kansas
Lawrence, Kansas

I. INTRODUCTION

The development of the juvenile court system in the United States has been accompanied by idealistic goals and high hopes for preventing criminal careers. However, recently a major reexamination of the juvenile court system has taken place (President's Commission on Law Enforcement and Administration of Justice, 1967). The impetus for this reexamination derives from a growing awareness that the system is not effective in protecting society and treating youthful offenders. For example, it is

[1] The preparation of this manuscript was supported by grants MH-20030 and MH-13644 from the National Institute of Mental Health (Center for Studies of Crime and Delinquency) to the Bureau of Child Research and Department of Human Development at the University of Kansas, Lawrence, Kansas. The authors would like to thank Montrose Wolf and Elery Phillips for their many helpful suggestions, and Rosemary McLaughlin, Vicki Martin, and Joan Fixsen for expert assistance in locating references and typing the manuscript.

estimated that one in every nine youths will have contact with the juvenile court during adolescence (Conger, 1973). However, the discretionary behavior of police officers and court intake officers makes it likely that only a few detected law violations will result in court action (Erickson & Empey, 1963; Lerman, 1970).

The importance of developing effective prevention and treatment programs for youths who engage in illegal and antisocial behavior has been underscored by Robins' (1966) classic 30-year follow-up of over 400 offenders who had been referred to a child guidance clinic for antisocial behavior. Most of the antisocial youths subsequently had histories of illegal juvenile behavior, with 80% appearing before the juvenile court; of these 50% were sent to correctional institutions. Most of these youths became antisocial adults characterized by: (a) multiple arrests leading to prison terms, (b) poor work histories, (c) financial dependence, (d) marital problems, (e) excessive drinking, and (f) social isolation. Robins also found that antisocial adults, more often than "normal" adults, had children who were antisocial, thus suggesting that the "chain" might be broken if effective treatment programs could be devised to socialize these youths during adolescence.

In the last decade a number of new treatment programs have been developed to socialize delinquent youths. Although these programs are still in the process of being evaluated, the early results of many are promising.

II. PROGRAM EVALUATION

While there is a critical need to assess the effectiveness of the various juvenile treatment and delinquency prevention programs (Shah, 1968, 1970), traditionally very little emphasis has been given and few funds have been allotted for systematic program evaluation (Keller & Alper, 1970; President's Commission on Law Enforcement and Administration of Justice, 1967). Evaluations that have been conducted (see reviews by Logan, 1972; Slaikeu, 1973) generally fall short of meeting the criteria of scientific research (Sarri & Selo, 1974).

There are numerous problems in conducting rigorous scientific evaluations of juvenile treatment programs. Although control groups with pre- and postmeasures are required (Lerman, 1968), it is often not feasible to assign youths to experimental and control groups on a random or matched basis. For example, juvenile judges are frequently unwilling to allow such assignment (Keller & Alper, 1970). Some studies have used *ex post facto* designs (Campbell & Stanley, 1966) to accomplish pretreatment equation of groups by a process of matching on relevant variables. The difficulty in interpreting such *post hoc* comparisons stems from the fact that *all* relevant matching variables must be included. Nevertheless, this paradigm seems to be superior to designs that do not use a comparison group or that use a static-group comparison (Campbell & Stanley, 1966).

Most program evaluations rely on a recidivism measure (i.e., a measure of whether released youths are reinstitutionalized after release). Recidivism does not provide a sensitive measure of new law-violating behavior. To the contrary, it is a better measure of the court's behavior than of the youth's. It is also an all-or-nothing measure that provides no differential qualitative feedback on youthful behavior after treatment (Costello, 1972; Shah, 1968).

A more sensitive index of juvenile posttreatment behavior is provided by police and court contact measures. Police and court contact measures are made even more sensitive by assessment of the seriousness of the offense that resulted in such contact (Shah, 1968). Scales for quantitatively weighing the degree of severity of offenses have been developed and employed by Sellin and Wolfgang (1964) and Wolfgang, Figlio, and Sellin (1972).

Police and court contact measures and recidivism rates are better indices of failure than of success (Fixsen, Phillips, Harper, Mesigh, Timbers, & Wolf, 1972; Lerman, 1968). More "positive" measures have been suggested in regard to educational, vocational, employment, social, and interpersonal adjustment following treatment. Several studies with juveniles utilized school records to obtain data on attendance, suspensions, disciplinary action, and grades (Berleman, Seaberg, & Steinburn, 1972; Fixsen *et al.,* 1972). Projects aimed at remediating the academic retardation of adjudicated youths have relied on achievement and IQ test data (Cohen, Filipczak, Bis, Cohen, & Larkin, 1970b). Social adjustment and functioning have been evaluated with rating scales that are completed by the youths' teachers, parents, peers, and other community members (Fischer, 1973; Jessor, Graves, Hanson, & Jessor, 1968). Measures of employment and vocational functioning (e.g., promptness, absences, salary, ratings of job performance, and occupational records) could be used in the follow-up evaluation of youths who are or have been employed (Shah, 1970). While attitude and personality measures are often employed in program evaluation, these measures are difficult to interpret owing to their questionable relationship to overt behavior (Mischel, 1968; Sowles & Gill, 1970).

In evaluating their success, some programs have considered only youths who "graduate" instead of all individuals initially accepted into the program. Since "in-program" failure rates are often as high as 30%, programs should report follow-up data on all youths who are accepted for treatment (Lerman, 1968). Other programs have reported follow-up measures only for youths who have completed an "after-care" regime that may extend for several years subsequent to release (Lerman, 1968). This practice has obvious shortcomings because it is during the first two post-release years that youths appear to be most likely to evidence recidivism (Weeks, 1958).

A. Behavioral Approach

The disappointing results of traditional treatment approaches with juvenile offenders is in part responsible for the increased emphasis on procedures derived from learning principles (Schwitzgebel, 1972). These treatment procedures are based on both respondent and operant conditioning principles (Stumphauzer, 1973). Skinner's (1953) *Science and Human Behavior* has been cited as a major source for operant treatment and Wolpe's (1958) *Psychotherapy by Reciprocal Inhibition* as a major source for respondent therapy (Stuart, 1970; Tharp & Wetzel, 1970). While there has been some application of respondent therapy with juvenile offenders, especially with alcohol, drug, and sexual problems (Cautela, 1967; MacCulloch, Williams, & Birtles, 1971), most applications to juvenile problems have been based on operant principles. Underlying operant treatment procedures is the view that behavior (including deviant behavior) is learned through reciprocal interaction between an individual and his environment (Bandura, 1969). This has been termed an "educational" model for deviant development as opposed to the traditional "medical" model in which deviant behavior is perceived as a symptom of underlying pathology (Shah, 1966). The educational model suggests that the deviant youth has a "behavioral deficiency" (Wolf, Phillips, & Fixsen, 1972) in that he has not learned socially appropriate behaviors that will allow him to successfully interact with others in an acceptable fashion (Sarason, 1968; Shah, 1966, 1968, 1970).

Behavioral treatment typically involves the effective implementation of differential reinforcement of desired prosocial behavior. Bandura (1969) has identified three sets of variables involved in effective implementation of reinforcement principles. First, it is essential to devise an incentive system that is capable of maintaining a high level of responsiveness over long periods. Second, reinforcing events must be made contingent upon occurrences of desired behavior. Third, methods must be used that are powerful enough to teach or elicit target behaviors with sufficient frequency for them to be strongly established through positive reinforcement.

The first condition for the effective implementation of reinforcement principles is an incentive system. Two types of incentive systems are used in the consequation of behavior in most behavioral treatment programs for delinquent and predelinquent youths: the token economy and the behavioral contract. Token economies utilize tokens (i.e., "generalized conditioned reinforcers"—plastic chips, checks on a card, points, etc.) that are exchanged for various "backup" privileges and tangible reinforcers according to a particular schedule (e.g., daily, weekly, etc.). Token systems have been used with a variety of populations including chronic hospitalized patients (Ayllon & Azrin, 1968; Krasner, 1968), retardates (Birnbrauer, Wolf, Kidder, & Tague, 1965; Girardeau & Spradlin, 1964), school-age children (see review by O'Leary & Drabman, 1971), adult felons (McKee, 1973), and with predelinquent and delinquent youths in institutional settings (Cohen, Filipczak, & Bis, 1968), community-based residential settings (Phillips, 1968), community-based day-treatment settings (Davidson, 1970), and classroom settings (Meichenbaum, Bowers, & Ross, 1968).

Kazdin and Bootzin (1972) delineate the following advantages of a token economy: (a) it allows the consequation of any response at any time, (b) it bridges the delay between target responses and backup reinforcers, (c) it can maintain performance over extended periods of time when the backup reinforcers cannot be administered, (d) it allows sequences of responses to be reinforced without interruption, (e) the reinforcing effects of tokens are relatively independent of deprivation states and less subject to satiation effects, and (f) it allows the use of the same reinforcer for subjects with preferences for different backup reinforcers. A token system can be "flexible" or "fixed" (Phillips, Phillips, Fixsen, & Wolf, 1971). In a fixed economy, a specified number of tokens are available for certain target behaviors each day, and a specified number of tokens are required to purchase privileges. In a flexible economy there are many opportunities to earn tokens required to purchase the desired privileges. In a flexible economy, the loss of tokens does not mean the loss of privileges, but rather that additional token-earning behavior is required to purchase privileges.

The behavioral (contingency) contract is based on specification of various consequences that will be provided contingently upon occurrence of defined target behaviors. These contracts are usually negotiated agreements between the youth and someone in authority (e.g., his parents, treatment personnel, etc.). Stuart (1971) stated that good behavioral contracts contain five components: (a) a detailed list of privileges, (b) a detailed list of responsibilities essential to secure each privilege, (c) a system of sanctions for failure to meet the responsibilities, (d) a bonus clause specifying positive reinforcement for compliance with contract terms, and (e) a means of recording rates and consequences of behaviors.

The second set of requirements needed for effective implementation of reinforcement principles is to provide reinforcement contingent upon the occurrence of the desired behavior. This involves monitoring the youth's behavior by a contingency manager who is responsible for the systematic consequation of that behavior. Monitoring can be of two types: direct observation and remote monitoring. In the latter case, behaviors that occur in settings that are not easily observed by the contingency manager can be monitored by others in those settings. Observations are then reported (by phone, checks on a card, etc.) to the contingency manager, who subsequently provides appropriate consequences. This procedure has been used both in behavioral contracting and in token economies (Bailey, Wolf, & Phillips, 1970; Cohen, Keyworth, Kleiner, & Brown, in press; Stuart, Tripodi, & Jayaratne, in press; Tharp & Wetzel, 1970; Thorne, Tharp, & Wetzel, 1967).

The consequences for occurrence or nonoccurrence of each target behavior are specified in contingency contracts. In token systems, on the other hand, such consequences are not always prespecified. A token economy can be "standardized" or "individualized" (Kazdin & Bootzin, 1972). In an individualized economy, the same behavior by two different subjects might result in different token consequences depending on the subjects' particular problems and histories. This flexibility has obvious advantages since each youth has different behavioral deficits that are the result of different learning experiences.

The last of the three sets of variables that Bandura (1969) identified as being involved in the effective implementation of reinforcement principles is the use of techniques sufficiently powerful to elicit desired behaviors at a high enough rate to allow for positive consequation. When the desired behaviors do not already exist in a youth's repertoire, the teaching of more adaptive and socially acceptable behaviors is necessary to remediate his deficits. Contingency management is a motivational tool but does not teach new behaviors. One method to develop the desired behaviors is to shape those behaviors through selective reinforcement of successively closer approximations to the desired behaviors. However, Bandura (1969) suggests that "in most cases complex responses can be more rapidly created by the provision of performance guides in the form of appropriate verbal or behavioral modeling clues [p. 283]." Such teaching involves breaking down complex behaviors into their component behaviors, describing the component behaviors to the youth, and giving him feedback on his performance (Kaufman & Wagner, 1972; Phillips, Phillips, Fixsen, & Wolf, 1972; Rose, Flanagan, & Brierton, 1971; Sarason, 1968; Sarason & Ganzer, in press). Bandura (1969) described still another method of inducing desired modes of responses when they are already available but rarely exhibited. This method depends upon initially prompting the desired behavior and then fading out the prompts as the behavior becomes more frequent.

Of primary concern is the fact that generalization of behavioral changes from a treatment environment to the natural environment needs to be programmed (Baer, Wolf, & Risley, 1968; Kazdin & Bootzin, 1972). Generalization of behavioral changes is facilitated if the behaviors modified are likely to meet with reinforcement in the natural environment (Ayllon & Azrin, 1968). It also has been suggested that the probability of generalization is enhanced the closer the treatment setting approximates the youth's posttreatment environment (Bandura, 1969). Therefore, community-based treatment settings would seem to be preferable to institutional settings, family-style group homes preferable to half-way houses, and so forth.

Another method of programming generalization is through the gradual fading of the youth's environment from one involving extrinsic incentives such as tokens to one involving natural consequences such as verbal feedback. Token economy programs sometimes utilize a system in which a youth can earn his way through various levels. At each level his responsibilities as well as his privileges increase. The final level usually involves the removal of the token system to approximate more natural conditions and reduce the dependency of behaviors on immediate consequences. Fading out of tokens can be accomplished by increasing the delay between (a) the occurrence of a target behavior and token reinforcement, or (b) the delivery of the token and the purchase of backups. In addition, youths can be faded out of treatment by spending increasing periods of time in their natural environments (Kazdin & Bootzin, 1972).

B. Early Behavioral Programs

The earliest reported treatment programs that were based on behavioral principles could be classified with respect to degree of structure. On the one hand, there were several nonresidential "street-corner" programs in which delinquent youths were hired to participate for 1 hour two or three days per week (Schwitzgebel, 1964; Schwitzgebel & Kolb, 1964; Slack, 1960, 1964). On the other hand, there were highly structured treatment programs for youths in closed institutions, e.g., the CASE II project which began in 1965 (Cohen, Filipczak, & Bis, 1970a) and the Intensive Training Unit program at North Carolina's Murdoch Center (Burchard, 1967). Schwitzgebel (1964) and Schwitzgebel and Kolb (1964) described a Boston area street-corner research project. Twenty 15- to 21-year-old delinquents, each with multiple arrests and court appearances, were recruited from the streets and were paid an hourly wage to participate in taped interviews. Hourly interviews took place several times per week for an average of 9 months. In a three-year follow-up these youths were compared to a control group of youths who were matched *post hoc* on variables of background and prior contact with the juvenile justice system. Treated youths had significantly fewer arrests and number of months incarcerated than controls. While not statistically significant, the recidivism rate of the experimentals (35%) was lower than that of the controls (45%).

In 1965, Harold Cohen, James Filipczak, and their colleagues instituted the two-year CASE II project (Contingencies Applicable for Special Education) at the former National Training School for Boys in Washington, D.C. (Cohen & Filipczak, 1971). They established a token economy program in a four-story hall on the grounds, and 25 boys at a time participated in the project. Each of 41 youths (age range = 13 to 19), with offenses ranging from auto theft to homicide, spent an average of 8 months in this program. The project emphasized training in social, vocational, self-help, and academic skills. The youths spent 6 hours a day working on programmed instructional material. Points were received (token reinforcement) for completing the material at 90% accuracy. The points allowed them to purchase such backup reinforcers as store items, the use of a lounge containing a television and jukebox, the use of a private room, and the use of a private office (Cohen *et al.,* 1968; Cohen *et al.,* 1970a, 1970b; Cohen, Goldiamond, & Filipczak, 1973).

Effectiveness of CASE II as a learning environment was evaluated in terms of the youths' performance over time on standardized achievement and IQ tests. Cohen and Filipczak (1971) report that on two different achievement tests the youths averaged 1.5 and 2.0 grade level increases per year, respectively. Most of the youths located in a three-year follow-up had maintained or increased their achievement test scores. The authors also report an average IQ gain of 12.5 points for 24 subjects who were retested approximately 7 months after their initial evaluation. However, this finding should be interpreted with caution as points were contingent on the second, but not on the first, test. Increases in IQ scores based only on motivational change have been reported elsewhere (Zigler, 1970).

Thirty-one of the 41 youths who participated in the program were located in a three-year follow-up of the project. Twenty-seven of the located youths had been in the project at least 90 days. Eleven of these 27 were released directly from CASE II, and the remaining 16 were released from other penal programs between one month and two and one-half years later. Four (36%) of the 11 youths released directly from CASE II and 11 (69%) of the 16 youths released from other penal programs required reinstitutionalization. Thus, 15 (56%) of the 27 youths recidivated over the three-year period. Thirteen of these youths (48%) had been reinstitutionalized by the end of the first year. Cohen and Filipczak (1971) reported that previous National Training School data indicate that 76% of similar juveniles recidivate during the first year. Unfortunately, no control group comparisons were conducted. Costello (1972) suggested that the CASE II program might have benefited from less emphasis on academic target behaviors and more emphasis on programming the transfer of social behaviors from the teaching environment into the subject's natural environment.

Based on earlier work at the former Fort Worden Treatment Center in Port Townsend, Washington (Burchard & Tyler, 1965), Burchard (1967) developed a token program in the Intensive Training Unit at Murdoch Center in North Carolina from 1966 to 1971. At the time of the 1967 article there were twelve 12- to 20-year-old mildly retarded youths with histories of violent antisocial behavior in the Unit. Tokens earned in the program were backed up with meals, commissary items, clothes, and recreational activities. Timeout and seclusion procedures were used to consequate fighting, lying, stealing, cheating, assault, tantrums, and property damage. When offenses were minor they resulted in a 3–5-minute timeout period (sitting in a chair) and a four-token fine. More serious infractions resulted in 30 minutes of seclusion and a fine of 15 tokens. While no program evaluation data were presented, procedural evaluations were carried out (Burchard, 1967; Burchard & Barrera, 1972). These will be discussed in a later section. No provisions for fading youths out of the program were in effect, but Burchard (1967) described how a system in which movement from an Intensive Training Unit through a quarterway and halfway house community placement could be implemented.

C. Residential Behavioral Programs

The early institutional programs described above were conducted with relatively small groups of youths. These programs provided a model for the adoption of institution-wide token economies. However, "point" and "level" systems apparently were being used in juvenile reformatories as early as 1876 (Keller & Alper, 1970). In this section, residential behavioral programs at the institutional, group-center and group-home level will be described. Where available, follow-up program effectiveness data will be presented.

Token systems are currently in use in a number of juvenile institutions including Kennedy Youth Center (Karacki & Levinson, 1970), Hawaii Youth Correction Facility (Kubo, unpublished), Hudson School for Girls in New York (Kalsmith, 1972), Nevada Youth Training Center (C. T. Barkshire, personal communication), and two California Youth Authority institutions: Karl Holton School for Boys (Jesness & De Risi, 1973) and Fred Nelles School for Boys (Cannon, Sloane, Agosto, De Risi, Donovan, Ralph, & Della-Piana, 1972). These institutions are usually composed of four to ten cottages with capacities of up to 50 youths each. Full-time school programs are also available. Usually the economy is institution-wide but may include subeconomies in the institutional school (e.g., Jesness & De Risi, 1973) or cottages (e.g., Karacki, unpublished).

Points are earned in accordance with specific criteria or on the basis of staff ratings. Economies in these programs are fixed rather than flexible in that there is a maximum number of points that may be earned in each of three or four categories. Typical categories are social behavior, academic behavior, and "convenience" behavior. Behaviors included in the latter category are those deemed necessary for the smooth functioning of the program (such as being prompt and orderly). Additionally, points are earned by the youths for improvements in their individual behavior problems. These behaviors are often specified in a contract between the youth and his counselor (Cannon *et al.,* 1972; Jesness & De Risi, 1973; Kubo, unpublished).

Institutional programs of this nature usually have three or four levels. The privileges available to a youth and their cost vary from one level to the next. Typical backup privileges include use of the telephone and television, going outside and off-grounds, recreational activities, rental of a private room, and goods in a store. Being considered for parole often has as a requirement the earning of a predetermined number of points. Sanctions for relatively minor inappropriate behavior involve fines. More serious misbehavior may result in increases in the number of points needed by the youth for parole or in unfavorable reports that will affect the youth's chances for parole. There are occasionally other backup sanctions such as timeout and "temporary lockup."

Evaluation of the effectiveness of a number of these institutional programs (employing token economic principles) has been conducted. In one evaluation (Jesness, De Risi, McCormick, & Wedge, 1972), youths were randomly assigned to either the Karl Holton School for Boys or the adjacent O. H. Close School for Boys, where the treatment program was based on transactional analysis. Follow-up data indicated that, after a 12-month parole exposure period, 31% of the Close subjects and 32% of the Holton subjects had been removed from parole. These figures were lower than the preexperimental violation rates for the two institutions (44% and 42%) and lower than the violation rates from two other California Youth Authority institutions (46%). Cannon *et al.* (1972) reported a recidivism rate of 58% at Nelles School for Boys. No comparison group was employed. Costello (1972) described a follow-up study by Karacki, Schmidt, and Cavior (1972) of 171 students who successfully completed the token economy program at Kennedy Youth Center. Recidivism was defined as "any commitment to a correctional facility except for non-felony commitments of less than two months." At the end of one year, the recidivism rate was 27% compared to a recidivism rate of 33% for a random sample of comparative youths released from other federal penitentiaries. A two-year follow-up of 27 youths who had successfully completed the program at Kennedy Youth Center yielded a recidivism rate of 44%. Apparently, these data were based only on program graduates and did not take into account in-program failures.

It will be recalled that Bandura suggested three essential components in the application of reinforcement principles in a treatment setting: an incentive system, contingent consequences, and a means of establishing appropriate behavior. The institutional programs described above clearly include the first of these components. However, remediation of behavioral deficiencies by modeling or teaching appropriate behavior and providing consistent contingent consequences appears to be difficult in institutional settings. Staff in behaviorally oriented institutional programs have the major responsibility for determining the specific behaviors that are reinforced, extinguished, shaped, punished, etc. However, such staff often lack the skills necessary for teaching appropriate social behaviors to the inmates (Cannon *et al.,* 1972; Karacki & Levinson, 1970; Kazdin & Bootzin, 1972; Lackenmeyer, 1969; Tyler & Brown, 1967). Also, institutional staff tend to respond inconsistently to inmates' misbehaviors (Buehler, Patterson, & Furniss, 1966; Feldman, Wodarski, Flax, & Goodman, 1972; Sanford, 1973). The problem of consistent staff response is further compounded by shift work and staff turnover (Costello, 1972; Hall & Baker, 1973; Lackenmeyer, 1969). As a result of these problems the incentive systems in institutions often become tools for management and control rather than teaching (Costello, 1972; Karacki & Levinson, 1970). The final result is all too often the inadvertent reinforcement of deviance and dependence (Hall & Baker, 1973; Kazdin & Bootzin, 1972).

There is a need for effective and practical training programs to teach institutional staff the skills involved in effectively using consequences and teaching procedures (Cannon *et al.,* 1972; Hall & Baker, 1973). Modeling, guided trainee practice to criterion, and differential feedback appear to be effective in teaching staff requisite skills (Gardner, 1972, 1973; Martin & Pear, 1970). The maintenance of skills learned in such training also involves monitoring the trainees' behavior and providing them with differential feedback and consequation (Ayllon & Azrin, 1968; Kazdin & Bootzin, 1972; Panyon, Boozer, & Morris, 1970).

A primary consideration in any residential treatment concerns the generalization of behavioral changes to the natural environment (Shah, 1966). Since institutional programs are markedly different from the natural social environment, appropriate behavior changes initiated in the treatment setting are unlikely to transfer automatically to the natural environment (J. D. Burchard, personal communication, 1973; Costello, 1972; Feldman *et al.,* 1972).

Another problem with most institutional programs concerns the minimal participation youths are permitted in developing rules and regulations for their particular environments. Even when formal mechanisms are established whereby grievances and suggestions for change are presented, these mechanisms are often exceedingly complicated and slow (Sloane & Ralph, in press). Rather than peers being actively involved in the treatment process through self-government procedures, they are often actively shaping antisocial behavior (Buehler *et al.,* 1966; Feldman *et al.,* 1972).

As demonstrated by the Valley View program in Illinois, it is possible for an institutional program to avoid many of the problems described above (Rose *et al.,* 1971; Valley View Program, J. R. Platt, personal communication, 1973). The program utilizes a token and level system. Actual point transactions occur at weekly "court," at which time each youth can collect his point earnings in addition to presenting his case to a staff clinician in relation to any fines he has received. If the youth feels that a decision is unfair he can appeal it. At Valley View, youth counselors conduct skills-learning groups aimed at teaching appropriate interaction behaviors through modeling, practice, and feedback procedures. These sessions are similar to those described by Sarason (1968). The youths also are able to maintain contact with and interact in their natural home environment by earning furloughs. About 60 out of 160 youths in the program were reported to be on furlough at any one time. Youths on furlough have behavioral assignments that are monitored by their parents, allowing their behavior to be consequated when they return to Valley View. No follow-up data on the effectiveness of this program were available.

Several group center residential programs utilize behavioral programs. The PACE (Program for Adolescent and Community Education) program at the Adolf Meyer Center serves 18 Illinois counties and consists of a residential unit for 20 boys and one for 20 girls (Wagner & Breitmeyer, in press). The 13- to 18-year-old youths admitted to the program have histories of truancy, aggressive behaviors, promiscuity, drug abuse, running away, and personality problems. The center utilizes both a level system and a token system. As in the Valley View program, role-playing sessions are aimed at teaching a variety of community-oriented social interaction skills. There are also planned home visits during which time the parents are asked to monitor the youth's behavior using a checklist. Both of these procedures help ensure the occurrence of appropriate behaviors and promote their generalization to the natural environment. Parent-training sessions, in which behavioral management skills are taught, are also held to promote generalization into the natural environment. In a follow-up of 100 youths who received services (38% of whom never completed the program), the recidivism rate was found to be 46%. However, no comparison group was used and some of the youths had only been discharged from the program for a short time.

The number of behavior modification group homes for predelinquent and delinquent youths is growing. Many of these programs (Mahoney & Mahoney, 1973; Tsosie & Giles, unpublished; Wasik, 1972; Williams & Harris, unpublished) are based in part on the Teaching-Family model group-home treatment program developed at Achievement Place, a community-based, community-controlled group-home for 12- to 16-year-old boys in Lawrence, Kansas (Phillips *et al.,* 1972; Phillips, Phillips, Wolf & Fixsen, 1973). The treatment program developed at Achievement Place is centered around teaching-parents, a couple responsible both for directing and carrying out the treatment program. The program is conducted in a small (6 to 8 youths) family-style setting which is usually an older renovated home in the community. This setting allows the teaching-parents to provide individualized attention and treatment for each of the youths in their program. It also permits the youths to participate in the direction and operation of the program through self-government mechanisms of the manager system and the family conference. In the manager system the youths exercise self-government through the democratic election of a manager who oversees and teaches routine social and self-help skills (Phillips *et al.,* 1973). In the daily family conference, youths participate in the establishment of rules and in decisions regarding alleged violations (Fixsen, Phillips, & Wolf, 1973).

The most important role of teaching-parents is educational. They teach youths a variety of social, academic, vocational, and self-help skills to equip them with alternative, more adaptive behaviors, thereby increasing their chances of survival and success in the community. The teaching-parents utilize a series of motivational steps to enhance their effectiveness as educators. When a youth first enters the program he typically participates in a daily point system in which he earns points to buy privileges (e.g., television, snacks, allowance, phone) for the next day. Points are earned for learning and engaging in appropriate, adaptive behaviors and lost for engaging in inappropriate, maladaptive behaviors. The youth then progresses to a system in which he earns his privileges for one week at a time. The youth subsequently earns his way to the merit system in which points are no longer required for privileges. Nevertheless, the youth is expected to maintain appropriate behaviors he has learned while on the point system. Through this progression the youth gradually moves from a structured program to a more natural feedback system (i.e., the merit system). Success on the merit system advances the youth to the homeward-bound system, during which time he interacts progressively longer in his natural or foster family setting before being released from the program.

Operating a community-based program allows the teaching-parents to work directly with a youth in natural settings, such as his home (to which he typically returns on weekends) and the public school (which he continues to attend). This increases the probability that appropriate behaviors developed in these settings will be maintained once he leaves the program. Being community-based also allows the teaching-parents to monitor and, if necessary, to provide additional treatment for the youth after he graduates from the program.

The role of procedural evaluation in the development and refinement of the Achievement Place model has been extensive. For example, procedural evaluations have been conducted on three primary treatment components of the model: the motivation system (Phillips, 1968; Phillips *et al.,* 1971), the self-government systems (Fixsen *et al.,* 1973; Phillips *et al.,* 1973), and teaching procedures (Ford, Christopherson, Fixsen, Phillips, & Wolf, unpublished; Timbers, Timbers, Fixsen, Phillips, & Wolf, 1973). A preliminary evaluation of the Achievement Place model has also been carried out at the program level (Fixsen *et al.,* 1972). Pre- and post-treatment comparisons were made *post hoc* between the first 16 youths treated at Achievement Place and 28 other youths who, in the opinion of the probation officer, could have been candidates for Achievement Place. Of these, 13 youths had been placed on probation and 15 had been placed in the state industrial school. It should be noted that these data are only suggestive since these youths were not randomly assigned to the two groups. The preliminary follow-up results indicated that youths who participated in the Achievement Place program were progressing better than comparable youths who were placed on probation or sent to the state training school. For example, only 20% of the Achievement Place youths required further treatment within one year after their release as compared to 58% of the training school youths and 36% of the probation youths. In addition, one year after their release from treatment, 78% of the Achievement Place youths continued to attend public school as compared to only 44% of the training school youths and 55% of the probation youths.

A model has been developed for training teaching-parents to operate treatment programs based on the Achievement Place program (Fixsen, Phillips, Phillips, & Wolf, in press; Kirigin, Ayala, Braukmann, Brown, Fixsen, Phillips, & Wolf, in press). The training model is a one-year program which provides couples with extensive, in-home, practical experience in operating a Teaching-Family treatment milieu. Initial and follow-up training workshops are concentrated on teaching and refining the basic skills critical to operating the model. Feedback on how well the trainees are performing their teaching-parent functions is obtained through periodic consumer and professional evaluations. These evaluations allow training staff to determine problem areas and provide corrective feedback to the trainee couples. A successful first annual consumer and professional evaluation results in certification of the couple as professional teaching-parents.

D. Nonresidential Behavioral Programs

There are a variety of nonresidential behavioral treatment and prevention programs for delinquent and predelinquent youths. In some of these programs a youth participates in a token-economy group-treatment setting during the day (Cohen, 1973; Cohen *et al.,* in press; Davidson, 1970). In others, the youths participate in individualized programs through behavioral contracts with parents, teachers, and probation officers (Stuart, 1971). Other programs involve the use of a variety of behavioral procedures to modify the behavior of youths with serious social problems in their schools and homes (Nagoshi, 1973; Rose, Sundee, DeLarge, Corwin, & Palumbo, 1970; Tharp & Wetzel, 1970). One program for younger boys (5 to 13 years old), with aggressive-disruptive behavior problems, involves training their parents in operant child management procedures (Patterson, Cobb, & Ray, 1972).

Youths who participate in the Kentfields Rehabilitation Program (Davidson, 1970) attend a programmed instruction classroom in the morning and work for the road commission, park department, drain commission, and other projects of local governments that fund this Grand Rapids, Michigan program. The mean length of stay in 1972 was 8 weeks and the costs were under $400 per boy (DeHaan & Robinson, unpublished). The 75 boys who participated in the first year were 14 to 16 years of age and generally close to being institutionalized. An evaluation of the program at the end of the first year of operation indicated that 37% of the boys had further court referrals for law violations after being accepted for treatment.

A number of school programs have been employed for students who are not court adjudicated but who have a wide range of serious academic and social problems. Several of these programs have provided a learning environment outside of the public school system for adolescent youths who have been expelled from classes (Cohen, unpublished; Martin, Burkholder, Rosenthal, Tharp, & Thorne, 1968). At the Anne Arundel Learning Center (Cohen, unpublished) individuals earned access to a Student Activity Center for appropriate classroom behavior. By completing programmed instructional materials, the youths earned points toward grades and rewards at home as part of their contingency contracts with their parents. S. I. Cohen (personal communication, 1973) reported that 72% of the students who met the criteria for return to regular schools were succeeding with an average grade of 1.9 on a 4.0 scale. The percentage of youths who returned to the regular schools was not specified.

The PICA (Programming Interpersonal Curricula for Adolescents) program (Cohen, 1972, 1973) was a half-day out of school program for 12 predelinquent youths per year who were on the verge of being expelled from school. Points were earned for completing self-instructional material designed to teach academic, vocational, and interpersonal skills. An extension of the PICA program into community schools is called the PREP (Preparation through Responsive Educational Programs) program. The evaluation of the PREP program in one junior high school revealed that PREP youths were performing significantly better than a control group on measures of achievement test performance, grades, and discipline referrals (Filipczak, 1973).

Thorne *et al.* (1967) and Ray and Kilburn (1970) suggested the use of behavioral techniques by probation officers. These techniques often involve the use of behavioral contracts in which the juveniles earn a reduction in probation time (Fitzgerald, 1972). Similar contracts have been used with adults (Polakow & Doctor, 1973). T. S. Allison (personal communication, 1974) reported that a large-scale attempt was underway to facilitate the use of behavior modification procedures by probation officers in the California Youth Authority's Cooperative Behavior Demonstration Project.

Perhaps the program making the most extensive use of contracting is the Family and School Consultation Project (Jayaratne, Stuart, & Tripodi, 1974; Stuart & Lott, 1972; Stuart & Tripodi, 1973). In this program therapists work with the families of 13- to 14-year-old males referred for severe social disruption in school. Pre- and posttest measures are taken on the youths' school performance (e.g., grades, attendance, and suspension), social behavior at home and in the community (e.g., parent evaluation forms and court contacts), and attitude.

In two studies (Stuart & Tripodi, 1973; Stuart *et al.,* in press) pre- and posttest comparison group designs were used to evaluate the relative effect of differing amounts of therapist contact on outcome measures for 165 youths. No differences in outcome were found between groups in a one-year follow-up evaluation. In addition, there was no systematic overall improvement in the behavior of the youths as assessed by the outcome measures employed (Jayaratne *et al.,* 1974). However, lack of improvement cannot be taken as a demonstration of no effect (e.g., intervention might have prevented deterioration, Fischer, 1973). This possibility received some support in the significant deterioration seen in a quasi-control group of 15 referrals to the project who refused treatment. The authors noted that these youths (quasi-control) may not have been comparable to those treated. A third study comparing youths who receive contracting services to youths who participate in a weekly "activity-discussion" group meeting is currently in progress (Jayaratne *et al.,* 1974; Stuart *et al.,* in press).

A number of nonresidential programs have been implemented through parents and teachers of the youths. This approach uses a triadic model of intervention first described by Tharp and Wetzel (1970). In the triadic (consultant-mediator-target) model, a consultant familiar with behavior change technology assists a mediator (anyone in the environment who controls reinforcers for the youth) in modifying the behavior of the youth (target). In Tharp and Wetzel's Behavior Research Project, consultants worked with mediators on 163 social, academic, and home-chore behavior problems of seventy-seven 6- to 16-year-old youths referred by local schools in the Tucson area. The consultants assisted the mediators in the rearrangement of environmental contingencies (e.g., the establishment of point systems and behavioral contracts) and taught them to use shaping, prompting, and modeling procedures to develop new behavior.

Mediators were asked to obtain measures of target behaviors during baseline and treatment phases. Of 163 behaviors assessed, measures on 135 provided sufficient data to allow evaluation. Treatment levels of 120 of 135 behaviors showed substantial improvements over baseline levels. Unfortunately, absence of assessments of the reliability of mediator observation makes these data difficult to interpret (Yule, 1971).

Another program that offers treatment for youths through a triadic intervention model is conducted at the Oregon Research Institute. The program's therapists work with parents of 5- to 13-year-old boys referred for their aggressive and disruptive behavior problems by the juvenile court, local schools, and the mental hygiene clinic. Treatment procedures used with these families evolved through case studies (Patterson & Brodsky, 1966; Patterson, McNeal, Hawkins, & Phelps, 1967) and a pilot project with five boys (Patterson, Ray, & Shaw, 1968). The resultant treatment procedures require parents to read a programmed textbook describing operant child management procedures (Patterson & Gullion, 1968). In addition, parents attend sessions in which they learn to carefully define, pinpoint, track, and record rates of deviant and prosocial behaviors. The therapists then help parents construct and implement modification programs in their homes (Patterson & Reid, 1973).

Patterson and his colleagues have reported the use of these procedures with the families of 27 aggressive boys (Patterson, in press; Patterson *et al.,* 1972; Patterson & Reid, 1973). Effectiveness of the treatment procedures with each of these cases has been evaluated primarily through the use of home observation sessions that were conducted before treatment, during treatment, and periodically for one year following treatment. In these sessions trained observers scored occurrences of deviant and prosocial behaviors using a 29-category observation code. It is possible that the observers' presence might have affected the youths' behavior (Patterson & Cobb, in press; White, unpublished), but the nature of such effects has not been determined (Patterson & Reid, 1973). Data from home observations revealed that about three-fourths of the youths demonstrated reductions in overall deviant behavior by 30% or more (Reid & Patterson, unpublished). Furthermore, there was a 60% average reduction on those deviant behaviors that parents specifically targeted and included in their management programs. Reductions in deviant behavior were generally maintained during the one-year follow-up period. In accordance with decreases in problem behavior as measured by home observational measures, parents generally reported fewer instances of referral problem behaviors during intervention and follow-up phases than during the baseline phase (Patterson, in press).

Most boys treated in the Oregon Research Institute program also required special classroom intervention due to their aggressive and disruptive behavior in the schools (Patterson, in press). Intervention procedures, developed in a pilot study by Patterson, Shaw, and Ebner (1969), involved the target youth's earning points toward extra recess time for the entire class. Timeout and behavioral contracts used in the home were often based on the youth's classroom behavior (Patterson, Cobb, & Ray, 1973). An evaluation of the effect of these intervention procedures on 11 consecutive cases revealed substantial increases in appropriate behavior for 10 of the

11 as measured during class observation periods. These increases were maintained during a 3-month follow-up.

The initial steps in developing a unique behavioral program that utilizes contracting in the natural environment is described by Burchard, Harig, Miller, and Amour (in press). Unlike most programs that have involuntary clients, this program is centered on a biweekly voluntary youth-center program at a local junior high school. The youth center contains a variety of activity areas including a lounge, coffee house, gymnasium, arts and crafts area, and library. In the first year of operation, an average of fifty-five 12- to 15-year-old male and female youths participated each night the center was open. An attempt was made to attract youths with school and community adjustment problems. One-third of the youths recruited for the program had police records.

While at the center, the youths earned points for engaging in activities for the first hour and one-half and spent them to participate in the activities available the last hour and one-half. The authors stated that the next step would be to contract with the problem youths to provide points for participation at the center contingent on their classroom behavior as assessed by the youth's teachers. In a personal communication, J. D. Burchard (1973) indicated that this phase of the research is underway.

III. PROCEDURE EVALUATION

The overall evaluation of programs in terms of their long-term effects on the lives of delinquent youths is extremely important. However, long-term evaluations require complex experimental designs (e.g., a factorial design) to determine which parts of a program are most effective. Such complex designs are almost impossible to implement in applied settings, especially when a treatment program continues to be refined and changed. Thus, another type of evaluation, procedure evaluation, is often carried out to provide more immediate feedback to program administrators concerning the immediate effectiveness of particular aspects of a program.

Procedure evaluations are especially useful when a program is being developed or modified in some aspect. Alternative treatment procedures can be empirically tested to determine which one produces the most beneficial effects on a youth's behavior. For example, one goal of a program might be to improve the school grades and attendance of the youths. To accomplish this goal, objective measures of the youths' school grades and attendance would first be developed. Then various procedures could be implemented to ascertain the one that produces the greatest effects.

A. Measurement and Design

To carry out procedural research, the applied researcher must be able to objectively measure the target behaviors. This usually requires the development of clear definitions of the youths' behavior and *reliable observation procedures* (Baer *et al.,* 1968; Hall, 1972; Romanczyk, Kent, Diament, & O'Leary, 1973; Wolf & Risley, 1971). The "objectivity" of definitions and recording procedures is measured by having two observers simultaneously but independently record the youths' behavior. If the two observers substantially agree (80% or better) as to occurrence of the target behavior(s), then the measurement procedure is said to be reliable and objective. Agreement between observers is frequently improved by clarifying definitions of target behaviors or by simplifying recording procedures.

Once objective measurement procedures are developed they can be used to collect data on the behavior of interest. Procedure evaluations begin by measuring the youths' behavior (prior to implementing the procedure) to determine baseline levels. After several days of baseline measurements the new treatment procedure can be implemented while concurrent behavioral changes are monitored. If behavior changes in the desired direction, then the procedure *may have been* the responsible agent. At this point the applied researcher still cannot be certain whether the procedure caused the effect or whether the change in behavior was due to some other correlated variable (e.g., practice, expectancy, maturation). To determine whether the new procedure effected the change in behavior, the researcher sequentially withdraws and reintroduces the procedure for several days. If the behavior returns to baseline levels when the procedure is withdrawn and again changes in the desired direction when the procedure is reintroduced, then the applied researcher has evidence that the procedure *caused* the change in the youths' behavior. This type of experimental strategy is known as an A-B-A-B "withdrawal design."

Sometimes the withdrawal design is undesirable or impossible to use when the behavior is dangerous or when the improved behavior immediately comes under the control of the natural environment. In these cases a "multiple-baseline design" can be used to demonstrate that a procedure causes a change in behavior. To use a multiple-baseline design, two or more baselines are recorded simultaneously. These could be baselines on two or more behaviors of a single youth, the same behavior of two or more youths, or the behavior of one youth in two or more settings (see Hall, Cristler, Cranston, & Tucker, 1970). After the initial baselines are established, treatment is then applied to each baseline under "time-lagged" conditions. If each baseline improves only after treatment is applied to it, then the researcher has evidence that the procedure *caused* the change in behavior (Wolf & Risley, 1971).

Both the withdrawal and multiple-baseline designs are within-subject or within-group strategies. Each subject in the procedure evaluation serves as his/her own control since the critical comparison is between the youth's baseline (untreated) level of behavior and the same youth's level of behavior under conditions of the new procedure.

B. Social Validity

Most of the applied research with delinquents is concerned with socially important behaviors such as reducing police and court contacts, improving school grades and attendance, reducing aggressive behavior, etc. These behaviors have obvious social relevance since they are often in violation of the law and are the reasons for incarcerating youths. Other behaviors are not so obviously important. For example, eye contact, table manners, personal hygiene, negotiation skills, and conversational skills may or may not be considered by the authorities as socially important behaviors. However, it would appear that development of the aforementioned skills would enable delinquents to adapt better to their nondelinquent peer groups.

One way to determine the social impact of certain behaviors is to ask relevant judges (e.g., laymen, juvenile judges, parents, potential employers, other youths) to rate pre- and posttreatment target responses of youths (the behaviors may be "live" or on audio- or videotape). For example, the experiment may be concerned with improving conversational skills of a delinquent youth (Minkin, Braukmann, Minkin, Timbers, Timbers, Fixsen, Phillips, & Wolf, 1973). Judges could be asked to view videotapes of the youth's pre- and posttreatment conversational behavior and to rate each conversation on a seven-point scale. Judges also could be asked to rate the importance of good conversational skills in interacting successfully with others. If judges discriminate posttreatment from pretreatment conversations by consistently rating them higher, and if they give a high rating to the importance of good conversational skills, then that behavior is considered socially desirable. Although measures of social relevance have only recently been used systematically, such measures should become a standard part of all applied research.

C. A Review of Procedure Evaluations

Many of the classic behavior modification investigations with delinquents were case studies that dealt with antisocial behavior (Buchard &

Tyler, 1965; Schwitzgebel, 1964). These case studies prompted a great deal of interest in the field, and later investigators produced experimental evaluations of many of the procedures initially described. This portion of the review will focus on studies that describe treatment procedures that were experimentally evaluated using measurement and design techniques discussed in the previous section. These experimental studies cover a broad range of behavior but can be roughly divided into five areas: social behavior, self-government behavior, academic behavior, self-help behavior, and vocational behavior.

1. Social Behavior

Aggressiveness is an often cited characteristic of many delinquent youths, and it was this form of antisocial behavior that was the concern of some of the early experimenters in the area. Using a withdrawal design, Tyler and Brown (1967) analyzed a "timeout" procedure for reducing rates of throwing objects, hitting, scuffling, and arguing that often occurred among youths who were playing pool in an institutional setting. After each instance of undesirable behavior a youth was placed in 4 × 8 foot "timeout" room for 15 minutes. This procedure resulted in a very low rate of undesirable behavior around the pool table. In the second phase of the experiment the staff gave verbal reprimands (e.g., "Now cut it out," "I'm warning you") following each undesirable behavior, but no timeout was used. This procedure resulted in a greatly increased number of undesirable behaviors among the youths. In the final phase, the staff again used the timeout procedure resulting in a low rate of undesirable behavior. Thus, the 15-minute timeout procedure produced marked reductions in the incidence of undesirable aggressive behavior. Burchard (1967) used a 30-minute timeout procedure combined with token-loss to reduce incidence of fighting, property damage, physical and verbal assault, stealing, and lying. This experiment involved retarded delinquents who were institutionalized. Using a withdrawal design similar to Tyler and Brown's, Burchard found only a small change in the behavior of the youths that was attributable to the use of the timeout procedure. In a more recent study with a similar population, Burchard and Barrera (1972) found a substantial reduction in undesirable behavior when either a 30-minute timeout or a loss of 30 tokens was contingent on the behavior. These conditions were compared with a 5-minute timeout or a loss of 5 tokens in a counterbalanced design. The 30-minute timeout condition and the 30-token loss condition were essentially equal in effectiveness, while the 5-minute timeout condition and the 5-token loss condition were not effective in reducing the youths' inappropriate behavior. However, Burchard and Barrera did not analyze their data for an order effect. Data collected by White, Nielson, and Johnson (1972) indicated that timeout of 1 minute was effective in reducing aggression, tantrums, and self-destructive behavior in retarded youths provided that they had not previously experienced the 15- or 30-minute timeout conditions. When the 1 minute timeout *followed* the longer timeout conditions, there was generally an increase in undesirable behavior above baseline levels.

The results of these studies indicate that timeout should be used cautiously and evaluated carefully to determine its effectiveness. Also, Burchard and Barrera (1972) and White *et al.* (1972) pointed out that timeout procedures were not effective for all of the youths and in some cases even increased levels of inappropriate behaviors.

In other experiments concerned with aggression, Phillips (1968; Experiment I) found that delinquent youths in a group home setting had a high level of aggressive statements (e.g., "I'll kill you"). Using a withdrawal design, Phillips found that the level of aggressive statements was reduced to zero when each aggressive statement resulted in a loss of tokens for the youth. Horton (1970) set up a card game situation where the winner of each play had the option of slapping the hand of the loser (an aggressive response) or having the loser forfeit one poker chip (the poker chips had no value other than potentially keeping track of the score). Using a withdrawal design, Horton found a near-zero level of hand-slapping during baseline, but this level was greatly increased when a small amount of money was made contingent on hand-slapping. Furthermore, Horton found that the aggressive behavior of the youths generalized to another game situation where there were no contingencies in effect but where aggressive behavior was measured. Also, staff informally noted that amount of other more serious aggressive behavior among youths in the cottage increased when hand slaps were reinforced during the game situation.

In the preceding studies, aggressive or inappropriate behaviors were reduced using timeout or token-loss procedures. These are mild punishment procedures that are designed to eliminate, or at least substantially reduce, the level of inappropriate behavior. However, it is suggested that timeout, token-loss, and other punishment procedures should be implemented only in the context of reinforcing other more appropriate behavior. Gittelman (1965) and Kaufman and Wagner (1972) suggested "behavioral rehearsal" or "roleplaying" as a technique for actively teaching delinquent youths the appropriate behaviors they need to display in place of their aggressive or inappropriate behavior. A study by Timbers *et al.* (1973) combined these elements to teach delinquent girls in a group home how to accept criticism or negative feedback without engaging in arguing, pouting, or verbally aggressive behavior. During a baseline period, Timbers *et al.* found that the girls' responses to negative feedback were appropriate only 7% of the time. Using a multiple-baseline design, Timbers *et al.* then taught each girl how to respond to negative feedback: she should establish eye contact, acknowledge the feedback by saying "OK," and not engage in any inappropriate behavior, such as frowning, pouting, throwing objects, stamping her feet. Each girl was taught by first instructing her in the appropriate behaviors and then having her roleplay in practice sessions. Subsequently, points (tokens) and praise for appropriate responses to negative feedback were administered while a response cost procedure for inappropriate behavior was instituted. Following training the behavior of each girl improved dramatically, and the girls' responses to negative feedback were appropriate 83% of the time.

A similar procedure was used by Phillips, Phillips, Fixsen, and Wolf (unpublished) to teach a youth instruction-following skills. During the baseline period, Phillips *et al.* found that the youth followed only about 20% of the simple instructions that were given to him in a group home setting. Instead of following instructions the youth made negative verbal comments, pouted, or pounded on nearby objects. These were behaviors the public school teachers had reported as reasons for suspending the youth from school. The youth was then taught how to follow routine instructions; he was first instructed to listen to the instruction and then asked to carry it out without engaging in inappropriate behavior. During this condition the youth earned points for following instructions and lost points for not complying. His instruction-following behavior improved to 100% for all sessions. When baseline conditions were reinstituted the instruction-following behavior declined substantially and then increased to 100% once again when the treatment condition was reinstated. In a second study, Phillips *et al.* used a similar teaching and point consequence procedure to teach a youth introduction skills (i.e., appropriate behavior while being introduced to a stranger). Using a multiple-baseline design, they found that each introduction behavior increased to 100% when the skill was taught and point consequences were made available for engaging in the behavior.

In the studies by Timbers *et al.* and by Phillips *et al.* a combination of teaching (instructions and roleplaying practice) and motivational (points or tokens) procedures were used to help youths acquire appropriate behaviors. A study by Ford *et al.* (unpublished) was designed to evaluate the relative contributions of the teaching and motivational components. Using a multiple-baseline design across a number of social and household maintenance behaviors, Ford *et al.* first established a baseline for each behavior and then provided points to the youths for engaging in each behavior. In the third phase of the experiment, the youths were taught how to engage in each behavior and were also given points contingently. The authors found that the motivation system alone increased the behaviors from a baseline level of about 25% to about 50%. However, after the teaching component was added to the motivational component, the level of behavior increased to nearly 100%. In a second experiment with different youths, Ford *et al.* reversed the order of conditions by first carrying out the teaching procedure (without points) and then adding the motivational component in the third phase of the experiment. Essentially the same results were obtained, indicating that both the teaching and motivational components are necessary to help delinquent youths develop appropriate behaviors.

Similar teaching and motivational procedures have been used to improve other social behaviors of delinquent youths. Maloney, Harper, Braukmann, Fixsen, Phillips, and Wolf (1972) found that information-volunteering and posture of delinquent girls during a conversation could be improved. Using a multiple-baseline design, Maloney *et al.* found that the girls' information-volunteering increased from about 30% to nearly 100% while their posture improved from about 70% appropriate to nearly 100%. Similarly, Minkin *et al.* (1973) observed the conversational behavior of delinquent girls and found that a combination of teaching and motivation procedures improved the girls' behavior. Measures taken were of "conversational questions" (i.e., questions that asked for information from the other conversant) and "positive feedback" (i.e., approval statements or statements of agreement). Using a multiple-baseline design, Minkin *et al.* found that these behaviors improved substantially after the girls were taught each behavior and were offered a small amount of money for engaging in the behavior.

The above-noted studies are especially interesting because they included a social validity measure. Maloney *et al.* (1972) requested five judges (i.e., a social worker, a teacher, a student, a probation officer, a counselor) to score a randomly selected baseline session and posttreatment session for each girl. Judges scored the girls' behavior on the dimensions of politeness and cooperation, and were nearly unanimous in their opinions that their behavior was more polite and cooperative post- than pretraining. Minkin *et al.* (1973) obtained a different social validity measure. They videotaped five female college students and five female junior high school students while they conversed with previously unknown adults. The "conversational ability" of each girl was then evaluated by a group of adult judges who viewed each tape and rated each conversant from "poor" to "excellent" on a seven-point rating scale. The average rating of each girl by the judges correlated highly ($r = .85$) with the behavioral measures of "conversational questions" and "positive feedback." To avoid the pitfalls of a "fold-back design" (Blumenfeld, 1972), Minkin *et al.* replicated the procedure with a new group of female college and junior high school students and obtained an equally high correlation between judges' ratings and behavioral measures. These data suggest that the behavioral measures were essentially tapping the same skills that people judge as important in maintaining good conversation. Minkin *et al.* also asked judges to rate pre- and posttraining conversational skills of the delinquent girls. The results indicated that posttreatment ratings (mean = 4.2) were higher than pretreatment ratings (mean = 2.9). The posttreatment mean rating of the delinquent girls (4.2) was between the average rating of the junior high girls (3.4) and the college girls (5.2), while the delinquent girls averaged lower ratings (2.9) than their junior high peers prior to training.

In addition, research has been carried out to evaluate procedures to teach other social skills. Phillips (1968, Experiment V) showed that point consequences and a correction procedure that consisted of suggesting an appropriate alternative were effective in eliminating "ain't" from one youth's behavior. In another study, Bailey, Timbers, Phillips, and Wolf (1971) modified the articulation errors of two of the boys by using the boys' peers in the home as trainers. In Experiment I, using a multiple-baseline experimental design, error words involving the /l/, /r/, /th/, and /ting/ sounds were successfully modified by both a group of peers and by individual peers. Generalization occurred to words that were not trained. The speech correction procedure used by the peers involved a number of variables including modeling, peer approval, contingent points, and feedback. It was demonstrated that peers could function as speech therapists without instructions, feedback, or the presence of an adult. It was also found that payment of points to peers for detecting correct articulations produced closer agreements with the experimenter than when they were paid points for finding incorrect articulations. The results were replicated in a second experiment with another subject who had similar articulation errors. In addition, the second experiment showed that peer speech correction procedures resulted in some generalization to the correct use of target words in sentences and significant improvements on standard tests of articulation. In other research, promptness in returning from errands (Phillips, 1968, Experiment II) and promptness at meal time (Phillips *et al.,* 1971, Experiment I) were improved in a group home by making a small point loss contingent on each minute the youths were late.

2. Self-Government Behavior

The strong influence of a peer group on individual behavior has been discussed for some time (e.g., Cohn, 1955; McCorkle & Korn, 1970; Thrasher, 1939), and a few self-government systems have been described (e.g., Empey, 1966; Makarenko, 1953; Neill, 1960; Phillips *et al.,* 1972). However, these descriptions usually lack the detail that would permit others to replicate self-government procedures. Moreover, few experimental evaluations have been conducted.

One set of experiments was reported by Phillips, *et al.* (1973). These investigators evaluated several procedures for involving the youths in the administration of routine household tasks in a group home. Each procedure was evaluated in terms of: (1) its effectiveness in accomplishing the tasks, and (2) the preference of the youths. The results indicated that the procedure that met the criteria for effectiveness and youth preference involved a democratically elected peer "manager" who had the authority both to administer and remove points for his peers' performances. The "manager" could also earn or lose points depending upon how well the tasks had been accomplished. A measure of the youths' preferences was an important part of these studies since there were several procedures that met the effectiveness criterion. The authors stated that, "In . . . voluntary programs, the clients maintain some (at least implicit) consequences for staff behavior that makes them unhappy. However, in treatment settings where the client is not a voluntary participant, the staff must develop other means of evaluating the clients' preferences because the clients cannot simply drop out of the program or vigorously register their dissatisfaction with the treatment procedures [Phillips, *et al.,* 1973, p. 560]."

Fixsen *et al.* (1973) developed a *self-government* system that was designed to teach youths many of the social skills involved in democratic decision making and problem solving. The youths were taught to establish democratically many of their own rules, to determine an accused youth's guilt or innocence, and to determine consequences for a youth who violated a rule. These discussions occurred during daily "family conferences." The role of the youths' participation in the self-government system was examined in two experiments. Experiment I demonstrated that more boys participated in the discussion of consequences for a rule violation when they had complete responsibility for setting the consequences during family conferences than when staff set the consequences for each rule violation before the family conference. An analysis of rule violations in this experiment indicated that the boys reported more rule violations than were reported by the teaching-parents, school personnel, or natural parents. Boys reported rule violations that occurred in the community and at school as well as at Achievement Place, including most of the serious rule violations that came to the attention of the teaching-parents. In Experiment II the results indicated that more family conferences were held when the teaching-parents rather than the youths were responsible for asking for discussions of violations reported by peers. When youths earned points for requesting discussions of rule violations the average number of such discussions increased, but more trivial rule violations were considered during the family conferences.

The results suggest that aspects of the democratic decision-making process in a small group of youths can be examined, and variables that affect participation can be identified. However, more work is warranted in this area to discover self-government procedures that are effective in encouraging peer group influence for pro-social behavior and that are preferred by the youths. This area will also acquire added importance as legal decisions are made regarding the rights of incarcerated youths.

3. Academic Behavior

An important area of research is concerned with the social and academic behavior of delinquent youths in school settings. Since the school has rules to obey, instructions to follow, authorities to get along with, and tasks that must be accomplished, it is often seen as a microcosm of society. The schools are also a major source of juvenile court referrals. Thus, as the President's Commission on Law Enforcement and Administration of Justice (1967) has pointed out, an important social goal is to find procedures that will help delinquent youths be successful in the public school classroom.

Meichenbaum *et al.* (1968), working in a classroom in an institution for delinquent girls, developed a set of in-class contingencies for appropriate behavior. Using a multiple-baseline design across two class periods (morning and afternoon), the authors found that instructing the girls in appropriate classroom behavior and providing frequent feedback and monetary consequences during class improved the girls' appropriate classroom behavior from about 50% to about 90%. In another classroom, Meichenbaum *et al.* tested the social validity of their behavioral measure by correlating the measure with ratings made by the teacher. They found a strong positive relationship between the behavioral measure and the teacher's ratings.

The *immediate reinforcement* procedures developed by Meichenbaum *et al.* for improving in-class behavior were very effective but required the presence of classroom personnel who scored the appropriateness of the girls' behavior and provided feedback and consequences every 10 minutes. Bailey *et al.* (1970) developed a *remote reinforcement* procedure that did not require additional classroom personnel. The remote reinforcement procedure consisted of having a delinquent boy in a group home carry a "daily report card" checked by the teacher. The card listed several categories of behavior that were suggested by the teacher; for example, acceptable use of class time, following classroom rules, assignment completed on time, a grade of ____ on an assignment or a quiz (a grade the youth could attain was inserted in the blank), and overall classroom behavior. At the end of class the youth turned in the "daily report card" to the teacher who simply checked each category ("yes" or "no") to indicate how well the youth behaved in class that day. The youth then gave his completed card to the group home staff after school and he could earn or lose privileges or points based on the teacher's judgment of his class performance. Using a withdrawal design, Bailey *et al.* found that the youths' appropriate classroom behavior improved from about 40% to about 90% when the daily report card was used in the public schools. The remote reinforcement procedure was replicated by Kirigin, Bailey, Phillips, Fixsen, and Wolf (unpublished), and they found similar effects on the youths' social behavior in a remedial classroom. Whereas Kirigin *et al.* (unpublished) found no improvement in the youths' academic output (assignments completed), Kirigin, Phillips, Fixsen, and Wolf (1972) found that the remote reinforcement procedure had a substantial effect on the percentage of assignments handed in and the weekly grades of youths in the public school classrooms.

Harris, Finfrock, Giles, Hart, and Tsosie (in press) used a similar remote reinforcement procedure with older delinquent youths in a group home. In this study, however, the youths were engaging in serious misbehavior in the classroom (e.g., swearing, physical aggression). Using a multiple-baseline design, Harris *et al.* found that the remote reinforcement procedure backed-up with loss of privileges in the group home eliminated inappropriate behavior for each youth. In another study, Harris *et al.* (1973) showed that the remote reinforcement procedure was effective in increasing the percentage of assignments the youths completed at school from about 40% to about 75%. They also noted that there was a correlated increase in the youths' grades in school.

Cohen *et al.* (in press) have extended the remote reinforcement procedure to include a variety of feedback mechanisms. They used behavioral contracts between teachers and natural parents, phone calls from the teachers to the natural parents, and daily school notes. They found that behavioral contracts and daily school notes sent to the parents improved the class performance of the youths whereas the phone calls to parents did not. They also found that, of the three procedures, the daily school note procedure was the easiest to implement.

These studies indicate that the class behavior of delinquent youths can be improved substantially using either immediate reinforcement procedures or remote reinforcement procedures. Similar remote reinforcement procedures have also been used in group homes to improve the youths' behavior in their natural homes (e.g., Turnbough, Brown, Fixsen, Phillips, & Wolf, unpublished).

Phillips (1968) used a withdrawal design and found that points contingent on homework completion in a group home increased the youths' behavior from about 0% completion to nearly 100%. Bednar, Zelhart, Greathouse, and Weinberg (1970) employed a group design and found that monetary consequences for attention and reading achievement increased the reading proficiency of delinquent boys. Bednar *et al.* also tested the social validity of their findings by having teachers rate on a seven-point scale the youths' persistence, attention, liking school, sociability, and cooperation. On each dimension the experimental youths were rated significantly higher than the control youths. Kirigin, Timbers, Ayala, Fixsen, Phillips, and Wolf (1973) evaluated several strategies to improve the independent reading behavior of delinquent girls. These were point consequences for reading, point consequences plus tutoring, and finally a "tutor-avoidance" condition where the youths could avoid the tutoring session through independent study. The only condition that produced an effect was the "tutor-avoidance" condition, suggesting that for some individuals tutoring is an aversive event that can be used as an avoidance contingency. Tyler and Brown (1968) used a group design and found that giving youths tokens for their scores on a current events quiz based on the evening news produced a small but significant increase in their scores. A replication of that study by Phillips *et al.* (1971, Experiment IV) showed a somewhat greater improvement in scores when points were contingent. Also, a substantial increase in the percent of youths in the group home who watched the news was noted.

4. Vocational Behavior

This area is closely related to the academic behavior area because of the potential long-term effects that education and vocation both have on the lives of members of our society. However, there has been very little research on vocationally related behaviors.

Braukmann, Maloney, Fixsen, Phillips, and Wolf (1974) developed an "instructional package" to teach job interview skills to delinquent boys in a group home. The "instructional package" contained a detailed description of appropriate interview behaviors and a detailed description of a training procedure consisting of instructions, demonstrations of appropriate behaviors, and differential feedback to the youth on his performance while rehearsing these behaviors during training. Braukmann *et al.* carried out three experiments and found that the "instructional package" was effective in teaching each youth appropriate interview behaviors. In one experiment the "trainers" were people who had no previous experience in vocational education or the behavioral sciences. However, they were able to follow the instructions provided in the "package" and trained the youths in appropriate interview behavior.

Ayala, Minkin, Phillips, Fixsen, and Wolf (1973) developed a set of training and feedback procedures that were effective in improving the youths' performance on a part-time job. Training consisted of instructing the youths in how to carry out tasks, demonstrating appropriate behavior, and having them practice the appropriate behavior. Feedback was provided during training and each day on the job. The results indicated that training and feedback were effective in producing substantial improvements in the youths' behavior at work. Ayala *et al.* also found that with continued training the improved behavior generalized to other work settings.

5. Self-Care Behavior

Many treatment programs are designed to prepare youths for independent or semi-independent living in the community. With this goal it is important to teach the youths self-management to enable them to take care of their own clothes, budget their money, keep up an apartment, cook for themselves, etc. Phillips *et al.* (1971, Experiment III) evaluated a procedure to encourage the youths to save money. They found that the youths saved money only when points were made contingent upon deposits in their savings. However, when no points were available very little money was saved even though each youth had a specific item he wanted to purchase. In another experiment, Phillips *et al.* (1971, Experiment II) found that giving points for appropriate room cleaning and taking away points for rooms that were not cleaned produced nearly perfect room cleaning behavior. The results of this study also indicated that point consequences could be faded so that they occurred approximately once in 12 days, with little loss of effectiveness. Phillips (1968) used a similar procedure but had a peer "manager" who supervised cleaning the bathrooms and delivering point consequences. The bathrooms were about 25% clean under baseline conditions and about 75% clean under the "manager" conditions. Sanford (1973) employed a multiple-baseline design to evaluate a token procedure for encouraging the youths to pick up their clothes. He found that giving points produced a high level of the desired behavior as long as the points could be used to purchase entry to a weekly movie. When the points could no longer be used to purchase items, the youths' performance dropped sharply.

IV. CONCLUSION

We were impressed with several dimensions of the programs and experiments that are discussed in this review. First, a wide range of behaviors has been effectively modified. It seems that a large number of well-described, practical procedures that have been experimentally developed and evaluated are now available for use with a variety of behaviors in the field of delinquency. Second, many of these procedures have been organized into full-scale treatment programs in settings that include state institutions, residential community-based programs, and nonresidential community programs. These settings include nearly all of those routinely used by most juvenile courts. Third, the emphasis of the programs and experiments seems to be changing from control of unwanted behavior to teaching desirable behavior by means of instructions, practice, and feedback. This is a very important trend that eventually may have broad implications for rehabilitation efforts. However, an emphasis on teaching new behaviors may also lead to more difficult questions concerning identification of specific behaviors that require shaping. A reliance on social validity measures may help answer some of these questions. Fourth, as the emphasis changes from control to teaching, many authors are stressing the need for better-trained staff to effectively carry out the more complex teaching procedures while maintaining pleasant relationships with the youths. Staff training would seem to be especially important for the replication of effective treatment procedures in other treatment settings.

There are also two very recent developments that undoubtedly will have far-reaching effects on the field. One of these developments involves the recent court rulings on the "right to treatment" of juveniles (Renn, 1973). Although the full implications of these court decisions will not be known for some time, it is likely that the treatment techniques, and especially the evaluation procedures described in this review, will be more widely used in the future to document compliance with the law. This development would seem to indicate a more rapid expansion of behavior modification in corrections and other social service fields. On the other hand, a second recent legal development concerns "informed consent" (Federal

Register, 1973), where the individual has the right to be fully informed about the treatment program and any possible alternatives that are available to him. The participant maintains the right at any time to refuse to be involved in any aspect of the treatment program. Essentially, the participant must agree to volunteer.

Thus, the "right to treatment" issue demands that effective treatment procedures be made available to adjudicated youths, but the "informed consent" issue allows any youth to refuse to participate in the treatment. Although these critical issues are obviously not yet fully resolved, it appears that the field of behavior modification possesses the technology to develop treatment programs that are at once effective and preferred by the youths.

REFERENCES

Ayala, H. E., Minkin, N., Phillips, E. L., Fixsen, D. L., & Wolf, M. M. Achievement Place: The training and analysis of vocational behaviors. Paper read at the American Psychological Association, Montreal, Canada, 1973.

Ayllon, T., & Azrin, N. *The token economy*. New York: Appleton, 1968.

Baer, D. M., Wolf, M. M., & Risley, T. R. Some current dimensions of applied behavior analysis. *Journal of Applied Behavior Analysis,* 1968, **1,** 91–97.

Bailey, J. S., Timbers, G. D., Phillips, E. L., & Wolf, M. M. Modification of articulation errors of pre-delinquents by their peers. *Journal of Applied Behavior Analysis,* 1971, **4,** 265–281.

Bailey, J. S., Wolf, M. M., & Phillips, E. L. Home-based reinforcement and the modification of pre-delinquents' classroom behavior. *Journal of Applied Behavior Analysis,* 1970, **3,** 223–233.

Bandura, A. *Principles of behavior modification*. New York: Holt, 1969.

Bednar, R. L., Zelhart, P. F., Greathouse, L., & Weinberg, S. Operant conditioning principles in the treatment of learning and behavior problems with delinquent boys. *Journal of Counseling Psychology,* 1970, **17,** 492–497.

Berleman, W. C., Seaberg, J. R., & Steinburn, T. W. The delinquency prevention experiment of the Seattle Atlantic Street Center: A final examination. *Social Service Review,* 1972, **46,** 323–346.

Birnbrauer, J., Wolf, M., Kidder, J., & Tague, C. Classroom behavior of retarded pupils with token reinforcement. *Journal of Experimental Child Psychology,* 1965, **2,** 119–135.

Blumenfeld, W. S. I am never startled by a fish. *APA Monitor,* 1972, **3,** 3.

Braukmann, C. J., Maloney, D. M., Fixsen, D. L., Phillips, E. L., & Wolf, M. M. Analysis of a selection interview training package. *Criminal Justice and Behavior,* 1974, **1,** 30–42.

Buehler, R. E., Patterson, G. R., & Furniss, J. M. The reinforcement of behavior in institutional settings. *Behaviour Research and Therapy,* 1966, **4,** 157–167.

Burchard, J. D. Systematic socialization: A programmed environment for the habilitation of antisocial retardates. *Psychological Record,* 1967, **11,** 461–476.

Burchard, J. D. Personal communication, 1973.

Burchard, J. D., & Barrera, F. An analysis of timeout and response cost in a programmed environment. *Journal of Applied Behavior Analysis,* 1972, **5,** 271–282.

Burchard, J. D., Harig, P. T., Miller, R. B., & Amour, J. New strategies in community-based intervention. In E. L. Ribes-Inesta (Ed.), *The experimental analysis of delinquency and social aggression.* New York: Academic Press, in press.

Burchard, J. D., & Tyler, V. O. The modification of delinquent behavior through operant conditioning. *Behaviour Research and Therapy,* 1965, **2,** 245–250.

Campbell, D. T., & Stanley, J. C. *Experimental and quasi-experimental designs for research.* Chicago: Rand McNally, 1966.

Cannon, D., Sloane, H., Agosto, R., De Risi, W., Donovan, J., Ralph, J., & Della-Piana, G. The Fred C. Nelles School for Boys rehabilitation system. Salt Lake City: Bureau of Educational Research, University of Utah, 1972.

Cautela, J. R. Covert sensitization. *Psychological Reports,* 1967, **20,** 459–468.

Cohen, H. L. Programming alternatives to punishment: The design of competence through consequences. In S. W. Bijou & E. L. Ribes-Inesta (Eds.), *Behavior modification.* New York: Academic Press, 1972. Pp. 63–84.

Cohen, H. L. Behavior modification in education. In C. E. Thoreson (Ed.), *The seventy-second yearbook of the national society for the study of education.* Chicago: University of Chicago Press, 1973.

Cohen, H. L., & Filipczak, J. A. *A new learning environment.* San Francisco: Jossey-Bass, 1971.

Cohen, H. L., Filipczak, J. A., & Bis, J. S. CASE project. In J. Schlien (Ed.), *Research in psychotherapy.* Vol. 3. Washington, D.C.: American Psychological Association, 1968. Pp. 34–41.

Cohen, H. L., Filipczak, J. A., & Bis, J. S. A study of contingencies applicable to special education: CASE I. In R. Ulrich, T. Stachnik, & J. Mabry (Eds.), *Control of human behavior.* Vol. II. Glenview, Ill.: Scott-Foresman, & Co., 1970. Pp. 51–69. (a)

Cohen, H. L., Filipczak, J. A., Bis, J. S., Cohen, J., & Larkin, P. Establishing motivationally oriented educational environments for institutionalized adolescents. In *The psychopathology of adolescents.* New York: Grune & Stratton, 1970. Pp. 57–73. (b)

Cohen, H. L., Goldiamond, I., & Filipczak, J. Maintaining increased education for teen-agers in a controlled environment. In A. R. Roberts (Ed.), *Readings in prison education.* Springfield, Ill.: Thomas, 1973.

Cohen, S. I. A contingency management design for behavioral change in educational settings. Unpublished manuscript, Anne Arundel Learning Center, 1972.

Cohen, S. I., Keyworth, J. M., Kleiner, R. I., & Brown, W. L. Effective behavior change at the Anne Arundel Learning Center through three different minimum contact interventions. In R. Ulrich, T. Stachnik, & J. Mabry (Eds.), *Control of human behavior.* Vol. III. Glenview, Ill.: Scott, Foresman, in press.

Cohn, A. *Delinquent boys: The culture of the gang.* Glencoe, Ill.: Free Press, 1955.

Conger, J. J. *Adolescence and youth.* New York: Harper, 1973.

Costello, J. Behavior modification and corrections. Washington, D.C.: The Law Enforcement Assistance Administration (National Technical Information Service #PB-223-629/AS), 1972.

Davidson, W. Kentfields rehabilitation program: An alternative to institutionalization. Unpublished manuscript, Grand Rapids, Michigan: Kent County Juvenile Court, 1970.

DeHaan, M., & Robinson, M. Kentfields rehabilitation program: Third annual report. Unpublished manuscript, Grand Rapids, Michigan: Kent County Juvenile Court, 1972.

Empey, L. T. *The provo experiment: A brief review.* Los Angeles: Youth Studies Center, University of Southern California, 1966.

Erickson, M. L., & Empey, L. T. Court records, undetected delinquency, and decision-making. *Journal of Criminal Law, Criminology, and Police Science,* 1963, **54,** 456–469.

Federal Register. HEW guidelines on protection of human subjects. *Federal Register,* 1973, **38,** No. 221, Part II.

Feldman, R. A., Wodarski, J. S., Flax, N., & Goodman, M. Treating delinquents in traditional agencies. *Social Work,* 1972, **17,** 71–78.

Filipczak, J. Press and community response to behavior modification in the public schools. Paper read at the American Psychological Association, Montreal, Canada, 1973.

Fischer, J. Is casework effective? A review. *Social Work,* 1973 (Jan.), 5–20.

Fitzgerald, T. J. Contingency contracting: Work projects with male juvenile delinquent probationers. Unpublished manuscript, 1972.

Fixsen, D. L., Phillips, E. L., Harper, T., Mesigh, C., Timbers, G., & Wolf, M. M. The teaching-family model of group home treatment. Paper read at the American Psychological Association, Honolulu, Hawaii, 1972.

Fixsen, D. L., Phillips, E. L., Phillips, E. A., & Wolf, M. M. Training teaching-parents to operate group home treatment programs. In M. D. Bernal (Ed.), *Training in behavior modification.* Monterey, Calif.: Brooks/Cole, in press.

Fixsen, D. L., Phillips, E. L., & Wolf, M. M. Achievement Place: Experiments in self-government with pre-delinquents. *Journal of Applied Behavior Analysis,* 1973, **6,** 31–47.

Ford, D., Christopherson, E., Fixsen, D., Phillips, E., & Wolf, M. Parent-child interaction in a token economy. Unpublished manuscript, University of Kansas, 1973.

Gardner, J. M. Teaching behavior modification to nonprofessionals. *Journal of Applied Behavior Analysis,* 1972, **5,** 517–521.

Gardner, J. M. Training the trainees: A review of research on teaching behavior modification. In R. D. Rubin, J. P. Brady, & J. D. Henderson (Eds.), *Advances in behavior therapy.* New York: Academic Press, 1973.

Girardeau, F. L., & Spradlin, J. E. Token rewards in a cottage program. *Mental Retardation,* 1964, **2,** 345–351.

Gittelman, M. Behavior rehearsal as a technique in child treatment. *Journal of Child Psychology and Psychiatry,* 1965, **6,** 251–255.

Hall, J., & Baker, R. Token economy systems: Breakdown and control. *Behaviour Research and Therapy,* 1973, **11,** 253–264.

Hall, R. V. *Managing behavior.* Lawrence, Kans.: H & H Enterprises, Box 3342, 1972.

Hall, R. V., Cristler, C., Cranston, S. S., & Tucker, B. Teachers and parents as researchers using multiple baseline designs. *Journal of Applied Behavior Analysis,* 1970, **3,** 247–255.

Harris, V. W., Finfrock, S. R., Giles, D. K., Hart, B. M., & Tsosie, P. C. The effects of performance contingencies on the assignment completion behavior of severely delinquent youth. Paper read at Behavior Analysis in Education Conference, Lawrence, Kansas, 1973.

Harris, V. W., Finfrock, S. R., Giles, D. K., Hart, B. M., & Tsosie, P. C. The use of home-based consequences to modify the classroom behavior of institutionalized delinquent youth. *Journal of Applied Behavior Analysis,* in press.

Horton, L. E. Generalization of aggressive behavior in adolescent delinquent boys. *Journal of Applied Behavior Analysis,* 1970, **3,** 205–211.

Jayaratne, S., Stuart, R. B., & Tripodi, T. Methodological issues and problems in evaluating treatment outcomes in the family and school consultation project, 1970–1973. In P. O. Davidson, F. W. Clark, & L. A. Hamerlynck (Eds.), *Evaluation of behavioral programs.* Champaign, Ill.: Research Press, 1974. Pp. 141–174.

Jesness, C. F., & De Risi, W. J. Some variations in techniques of contingency management in a school for delinquents. In J. S. Stumphauzer (Ed.), *Behavior therapy with delinquents.* Springfield, Ill.: Thomas, 1973. Pp. 196–235.

Jesness, C. F., De Risi, W. J., McCormick, P. M., & Wedge, R. F. *The youth center research project.* Sacramento: California Youth Authority, 1972.

Jessor, R., Graves, T. D., Hansen, R. C., & Jessor, S. L. *Society, personality, and deviant behavior.* New York: Holt, 1968.

Kalsmith, L. Behavior modification. Program paper for the New York Division for Youth, 1972.

Karacki, L. Behavior modification techniques and strategies for youthful offenders. Unpublished manuscript, Morgantown, W. Va.: Kennedy Youth Center, 1972.

Karacki, L., & Levinson, R. B. A token economy in a correctional institution for youthful offenders. *Howard Journal of Penology and Crime Prevention,* 1970, **13,** 20–30.

Karacki, L., Schmidt, A., & Cavior, H. E. The 1972 follow-up of Kennedy Youth Center releasees. Morgantown, W. Va.: Kennedy Youth Center, 1972.

Kaufmann, L. M., & Wagner, B. R. Barb: A systematic treatment technology for temper control disorders. *Behavior Therapy,* 1972, **3,** 84–90.

Kazdin, A. E., & Bootzin, R. R. The token economy: An evaluative review. *Journal of Applied Behavior Analysis,* 1972, **5,** 343–372.

Keller, O. J., & Alper, B. S. *Half-way houses: Community-centered correction and treatment.* Lexington, Mass.: Heath, 1970.

Kirigin, K. A., Ayala, H. E., Braukmann, C. J., Brown, W. G., Fixsen, D. L., Phillips, E. L., & Wolf, M. M. Training teaching-parents: An evaluation and analysis of workshop training procedures. In E. Ramp & G. Semb (Eds.), *Behavior analysis: Areas of research and application.* Englewood Cliffs, N.J.: Prentice-Hall, in press.

Kirigin, K. A., Bailey, J. S., Phillips, E. L., Fixsen, D. L., & Wolf, M. M. The effects of home-based reinforcement on the study behavior and academic performance of pre-delinquent boys. Unpublished manuscript, University of Kansas, 1971.

Kirigin, K. A., Phillips, E. L., Fixsen, D. L., & Wolf, M. M. Modification of the homework behavior and academic performance of pre-delinquents with home-based reinforcement. Paper read at the American Psychological Association, Honolulu, Hawaii, 1972.

Kirigin, K. A., Timbers, G. D., Ayala, H. E., Fixsen, D. L., Phillips, E. L., & Wolf, M. M. The negative effects of "positive" tutoring on the independent reading behavior of delinquent adolescents. Unpublished manuscript, University of Kansas, 1973.

Kirigin, K. A., Timbers, G. D., Ayala, H. E., Fixsen, D. L., Phillips, E. L., & Wolf, M. M. Effects of home-based reinforcement on the modification of academic behavior of three delinquent girls. Paper read at the American Psychological Association, Montreal, Canada, 1973.

Krasner, L. Assessment of token economy programs in psychiatric hospitals. Symposium on the role of learning in psychotherapy, London, 1968.

Kubo, R. M. The Hawaii youth correction facility behavior modification program. Unpublished manuscript, The Hawaii Correction Facility, 1973.

Lackenmeyer, C. Systematic socialization: Observations on a programmed environment for the habilitation of antisocial retardates. *Psychological Record,* 1969, **19,** 247–257.

Lerman, P. Evaluative studies of institutions for delinquents: Implications for research and social policy. *Social Work,* 1968, **13,** 55–64.

Lerman, P. *Delinquency and social policy.* New York: Praeger, 1970.

Logan, C. H. Evaluation research in crime and delinquency: A reappraisal. *Journal of Criminal Law, Criminology, and Police Science,* 1972, **63,** 378–387.

McCorkle, L. W., & Korn, R. Resocialization within walls. In N. Johnson, L. Savitz, & M. E. Wolfgang (Eds.), *The sociology of punishment and correction.* New York: Wiley, 1970. Pp. 409–418.

MacCulloch, M. J., Williams, C., & Birtles, C. J. The successful application of aversion therapy to an adolescent exhibitionist. *Journal of Behavior Therapy and Experimental Psychiatry,* 1971, **2,** 61–66.

McKee, J. M. *Experimental manpower laboratory for corrections: Phase III final report.* Montgomery, Ala.: Rehabilitation Research Foundation, P. O. Box 3587, 1973.

Mahoney, M. J., & Mahoney, F. E. A residential program in behavior modification. In R. D. Rubin, J. P. Brady, & J. D. Henderson (Eds.), *Advances in behavior therapy.* New York: Academic Press, 1973. Pp. 93–102.

Makarenko, A. S. *The road to life.* Vols. I, II, & III. Moscow: Foreign Language Publishing House, 1953.

Maloney, D. M., Harper, T. M., Braukmann, C. J., Fixsen, D. L., Phillips, E. L., & Wolf, M. M. Effects of training pre-delinquent girls on conversation and posture behaviors by teaching-parents and juvenile peers. Paper read at the American Psychological Association, Honolulu, Hawaii, September 1972.

Martin, G. L. Teaching operant technology to psychiatric nurses, aides, and attendants. In F. W. Clark, D. R. Evans, & L. A. Hamerlynck (Eds.), *Implementing behavioral programs for schools and clinics.* Champaign, Ill.: Research Press, 1972. Pp. 63–88.

Martin, G. L., & Pear, J. J. Short term participation by 130 undergraduates as operant conditioners in an ongoing project with autistic children. *Psychological Record,* 1970, **20,** 327–336.

Martin, M., Burkholder, R., Rosenthal, T., Tharp, R., & Thorne, G. Programming behavior change and reintegration into school milieux of extreme adolescent deviates. *Behaviour Research and Therapy,* 1968, **6,** 371–384.

Meichenbaum, D. H., Bowers, K. S., & Ross, R. R. Modification of classroom behavior of institutionalized female adolescent offenders. *Behaviour Research and Therapy,* 1968, **6,** 343–353.

Minkin, N., Braukmann, C. J., Minkin, B. L., Timbers, G. D., Timbers, B. J., Fixsen, D. L., Phillips, E. L., & Wolf, M. M. Analysis, validation, and training of conversation skills in pre-delinquent youths. Paper read at the American Psychological Association, Montreal, Canada, 1973.

Mischel, W. *Personality and assessment.* New York: Wiley, 1968.

Nagoshi, J. T. *The buddy system.* Honolulu, Hawaii: Social Welfare Development and Research Center, University of Hawaii, 1973.

Neill, A. S. *Summerhill.* New York: Hart Publishing Co., 1960.

O'Leary, K. D., & Drabman, R. Token reinforcement programs in the classroom: A review. *Psychological Bulletin,* 1971, **75,** 379–398.

Panyan, M., Boozer, H., & Morris, N. Feedback to attendants as a reinforcer for applying operant techniques. *Journal of Applied Behavior Analysis,* 1970, **3,** 1–4.

Patterson, G. R. Follow-up evaluations of a program for parents' retraining their aggressive boys. *Canadian Psychiatric Association Journal,* in press.

Patterson, G. R., & Brodsky, G. A behavior modification program for a child with multiple problem behaviors. *Journal of Child Psychology and Psychiatry,* 1966, **7,** 277–295.

Patterson, G. R., & Cobb, J. A. Stimulus control for classes of noxious behavior. In J. F. Knutson (Ed.), *The control of aggression: Implications from basic research.* Chicago: Aldine, in press.

Patterson, G. R., Cobb, J. A., & Ray, R. S. Direct intervention in the classroom: A set of procedures for the aggressive child. In F. W. Clark, D. R. Evans, & L. A. Hamerlynck (Eds.), *Implementing behavioral programs for schools and clinics.* Champaign, Ill.: Research Press, 1972. Pp. 151–201.

Patterson, G. R., Cobb, J. A., & Ray, R. S. A social engineering technology for retraining the families of aggressive boys. In H. E. Adams & I. P. Unikel (Eds.), *Issues and trends in behavior therapy.* Springfield, Illinois: Thomas, 1973. Pp. 139–224.

Patterson, G. R., & Gullion, M. E. *Living with children: New methods for parents and teachers.* Champaign, Ill.: Research Press, 1968.

Patterson, G. R., McNeal, S., Hawkins, N., & Phelps, R. Reprogramming the social environment. *Journal of Child Psychology and Psychiatry,* 1967, **8,** 181–195.

Patterson, G. R., Ray, R. S., & Shaw, D. A. Direct intervention in families of deviant children. *Oregon Research Institute Bulletin,* 1968, **8** (9).

Patterson, G. R., & Reid, J. B. Intervention for families of aggressive boys: A replication study. *Behaviour Research and Therapy,* 1973, **11,** 1–12.

Patterson, G. R., Shaw, D. A., & Ebner, M. J. Teachers, peers, and parents as agents of change in the classroom. In F. A. M. Benson (Ed.), *Modifying deviant social behaviors in various classroom settings.* Vol. 1. Eugene, Oregon: University of Oregon, 1969. Pp. 13–47.

Phillips, E. A., Phillips, E. L., Fixsen, D. L., & Wolf, M. M. Experimental analysis of the social behavior of a pre-delinquent youth at Achievement Place. Unpublished manuscript, University of Kansas, 1973.

Phillips, E. L. Achievement Place: Token reinforcement procedures in a home-style rehabilitation setting for "pre-delinquent" boys. *Journal of Applied Behavior Analysis,* 1968, **1,** 213–223.

Phillips, E. L., Phillips, E. A., Fixsen, D. L., & Wolf, M. M. Achievement Place: The modification of the behaviors of pre-delinquent boys within a token economy. *Journal of Applied Behavior Analysis,* 1971, **4,** 45–59.

Phillips, E. L., Phillips, E. A., Fixsen, D. L., & Wolf, M. M. *The teaching-family handbook.* Lawrence, Kans.: University of Kansas, Printing Service, 1972.

Phillips, E. L., Phillips, E. A., Wolf, M. M., & Fixsen, D. L. Achievement Place:

Development of the elected manager system. *Journal of Applied Behavior Analysis,* 1973, **6,** 541–561.

Polakow, R. L., & Doctor, R. M. A behavioral modification program for adult probationers. Unpublished manuscript, San Fernando Valley State College, 1973.

President's Commission on Law Enforcement and Administration of Justice. *The challenge of crime in a free society*. Washington, D.C.: U.S. Government Printing Office, 1967.

Ray, E. T., & Kilburn, K. L. Behavior modification techniques applied to community behavior problems. *Criminology,* 1970, **8,** 173–184.

Reid, J. B., & Patterson, G. R. The modification of aggression and stealing behavior of boys in the home setting. Unpublished manuscript, Oregon Research Institute, 1973.

Renn, E. The right to treatment and the juvenile. *Crime and Delinquency,* 1973 (Oct.), 477–484.

Robins, L. N. *Deviant children grown up*. Baltimore: Williams & Wilkins, 1966.

Romanczyk, R. G., Kent, R. N., Diament, C., & O'Leary, K. D. Measuring the reliability of observational data: A reactive process. *Journal of Applied Behavior Analysis,* 1973, **6,** 175–184.

Rose, S. D., Flanagan, J., & Brierton, D. Counseling in a correctional institution: A social learning approach. Authors' Forum National Conference on Social Welfare, Dallas, Texas, 1971.

Rose, S. D., Sundee, M., DeLarge, J., Corwin, L., & Palumbo, A. The Hartwig Project: A behavioral approach to the treatment of juvenile offenders. In R. Ulrich, T. Stachnik, & J. Mabry (Eds.), *Control of human behavior.* Vol. II. Glenview, Ill.: Scott, Foresman, & Co., 1970. Pp. 220–230.

Sanford, D. A. An operant analysis of control procedures in a New Zealand borstal. *British Journal of Criminology,* 1973, 262–268.

Sarason, I. G. Verbal learning, modeling, and juvenile delinquency. *American Psychologist,* 1968, **23,** 254–266.

Sarason, I. G., & Ganzer, V. J. Modeling and group discussion in the rehabilitation of juvenile delinquents. *Journal of Counseling Psychology,* in press.

Sarri, R. C., & Selo, E. Evaluation process and outcome in juvenile corrections: Musings on a grim tale. In P. O. Davidson, F. W. Clark, & L. A. Hamerlynck (Eds.), *Evaluation of behavioral programs.* Champaign, Ill.: Research Press, 1974. Pp. 253–302.

Schwitzgebel, R. K. *Street corner research: An experimental approach to the juvenile delinquent.* Cambridge, Mass.: Harvard University Press, 1964.

Schwitzgebel, R. K. Limitations on the coercive treatment of offenders. *Criminal Law Bulletin,* 1972, **8,** 269–319.

Schwitzgebel, R. L., & Kolb, D. A. Inducing behavior change in adolescent delinquents. *Behaviour Research and Therapy,* 1964, **1,** 297–304.

Sellin, T., & Wolfgang, M. E. *The measurement of delinquency.* New York: Wiley, 1964.

Shah, S. A. A behavioral conceptualization of the development of criminal behavior, therapeutic principles, and applications. A report to the President's Commission on Law Enforcement and the Administration of Justice, 1966.

Shah, S. A. Preparation for release and community follow-up. In H. L. Cohen, I. Goldiamond, J. A. Filipczak, and R. Pooley (Eds.), *Training professionals in procedures for the establishment of educational environments.* Silver Spring, Md.; Institute for Behavioral Research; Educational Facility Press, 1968.

Shah, S. A. A behavioral approach to out-patient treatment of offenders. In H. C. Rickard (Ed.), *Unique programs in behavior readjustment.* Oxford: Pergamon, 1970.

Skinner, B. F. *Science and human behavior.* New York: Free Press, 1953.

Slack, C. W. Experimenter-subject psychotherapy: A new method of introducing intensive office treatment for unreachable cases. *Mental Hygiene,* 1960, **44,** 238–256.

Slack, C. W. Research and development with stigmatized people. A report to the Ford Foundation, 1964.

Slaikeu, K. A. Evaluation studies on group treatment of juvenile and adult offenders in correctional institutions: A review of the literature. *Journal of Research in Crime and Delinquency,* 1973 (Jan.), 87–100.

Sloane, H. N., & Ralph, J. L. The grant dormitory: A case history. *Journal of Offender Therapy,* in press.

Sowles, R. C., & Gill, J. H. Institutional and community adjustment of delinquents following counseling. *Journal of Consulting and Clinical Psychology,* 1970, **34,** 398–402.

Stuart, R. B. Behavioral contracting within the families of delinquents. Paper read at the American Psychological Association, Miami, Florida, 1970.

Stuart, R. B. Behavioral contracting within the families of delinquents. *Journal of Behavior Therapy and Experimental Psychiatry,* 1971, **2,** 1–11.

Stuart, R. B., & Lott, L. A. Behavioral contracting with delinquents: A cautionary note. *Journal of Behavior Therapy and Experimental Psychiatry,* 1972, **3,** 161–169.

Stuart, R. B., & Tripodi, T. Experimental evaluation of three time-constrained behavioral treatments for pre-delinquents and delinquents. In R. D. Rubin, J. P. Brady, & J. D. Henderson (Eds.), *Advances in behavior therapy.* New York: Academic Press, 1973.

Stuart, R. B., Tripodi, T., & Jayaratne, S. The family and school treatment model of services for pre-delinquents. *Journal of Research in Crime and Delinquency,* in press.

Stumphauzer, J. S. *Behavior therapy with delinquents.* Springfield, Ill.: Thomas, 1973.

Tharp, R. G., & Wetzel, R. J. *Behavior modification in the natural environment.* New York: Academic Press, 1970.

Thorne, G. L., Tharp, R. G., & Wetzel, R. J. Behavior modification techniques: New tools for probation officers. *Federal Probation,* 1967, **31,** 21–27.

Thrasher, F. *The gang.* Chicago: University of Chicago Press, 1939.

Timbers, G. D., Timbers, B. J., Fixsen, D. L., Phillips, E. L., & Wolf, M. M. Achievement Place for pre-delinquent girls: Modification of inappropriate emotional behaviors with token reinforcement and instructional procedures. Paper read at the American Psychological Association, Montreal, Canada, 1973.

Tsosie, P., & Giles, D. Intermountain Youth Center program description. Unpublished manuscript, Intermountain Youth Center, 1973.

Turnbough, P. D., Brown, W. G., Fixsen, D. L., Phillips, E. L., & Wolf, M. M. Monitoring youths' and parents' behavior in the natural home. Unpublished manuscript, University of Kansas, 1973.

Tyler, V. O., & Brown, G. D. The use of swift, brief isolation as a group control device for institutionalized delinquents. *Behaviour Research and Therapy,* 1967, **5,** 1–9.

Tyler, V. O., & Brown, G. D. Token reinforcement of academic performance with institutionalized delinquent boys. *Journal of Educational Psychology,* 1968, **59,** 164–168.

Wagner, B. R., & Breitmeyer, R. G. PACE: A residential, community-oriented behavior modification program for adolescents. *Adolescence,* in press.

Wasik, B. H. Janus House for delinquents: An alternative to training schools. Workshop on New Treatment Approaches to Juvenile Delinquency, University of Tennessee, Memphis, 1972.

Weeks, H. A. *Youthful offenders at Highfields.* Ann Arbor: University of Michigan Press, 1958.

White, G. D. The effect of observer presence on mother and child behavior. Unpublished doctoral dissertation, University of Oregon, 1972.

White, G. D., Nielson, G., & Johnson, S. M. Time-out duration and the suppression of deviant behavior in children. *Journal of Applied Behavior Analysis,* 1972, **5,** 111–120.

Williams, M. G., & Harris, V. W. Program description. Unpublished manuscript, Southwest Indian Youth Center, 1973.

Wolf, M. M., Phillips, E. L., & Fixsen, D. L. The teaching-family: A new model for the treatment of deviant child behavior in the community. In S. W. Bijou & E. L. Ribes-Inesta (Eds.), *Behavior modification.* New York: Academic Press, 1972. Pp. 51–62.

Wolf, M. M., & Risley, T. R. Reinforcement: Applied research. In R. Glaser (Ed.), *The nature of reinforcement.* Columbus, Ohio: Merrill, 1971. Pp. 310–325.

Wolfgang, M. E., Figlio, R. M., & Sellin, T. *Delinquency in a birth cohort.* Chicago: University of Chicago Press, 1972.

Wolpe, J. *Psychotherapy by reciprocal inhibition.* Stanford, Calif.: Stanford University Press, 1958.

Yule, W. A book review of behavior modification in the natural environment. *Behaviour Research and Therapy,* 1971, **9,** 304.

Zigler, E. The environmental mystique: Training the intellect versus development of the child. *Childhood Education,* 1970, **46,** 402–412.

RECENT ADVANCES IN TOKEN ECONOMY RESEARCH[1]

ALAN E. KAZDIN
Department of Psychology
The Pennsylvania State University
University Park, Pennsylvania

I. INTRODUCTION

The application of operant techniques has advanced considerably in recent years. The advances can be readily discerned by perusing early studies in the field and tracing briefly the evolution of operant work in applied settings. Early work in the field was characterized by notable features. First, the application of operant principles often was restricted to only one or a few individuals at one time (e.g., Isaacs, Thomas, & Goldiamond, 1960). Second, procedures were often conducted during specific

[1] Preparation of this chapter was facilitated by a grant from the National Institute of Mental Health (MH23399 01A1).

experimental sessions rather than during the ordinary ward routine (e.g., King, Armitage, & Tilton, 1960). Third, only one or a few reinforcers were used (e.g., Azrin & Lindsley, 1956). Fourth, the focus was restricted to one or a few target behaviors at one time (e.g., Wickes, 1958). Fifth, many applications served primarily demonstrational rather than therapeutic purposes per se (e.g., Ferster & DeMyer, 1961). Finally, scrutiny of response characteristics served as a major goal (e.g., Barrett & Lindsley, 1962; Lindsley, 1960). With an appropriately narrow focus, the early work provided careful analyses of procedures which today are taken for granted.

The initial work of Ayllon and his colleagues warrants a place of its own in the recent history of present day applications. Indeed, these studies are of great heuristic value. In a number of reports with institutionalized psychiatric patients, principles were applied to train patients to feed themselves, to behave appropriately in dining facilities, to dress appropriately, and to cease bizarre habits, psychotic talk, and somatic complaints (Ayllon, 1963, 1965; Ayllon & Azrin, 1965; Ayllon & Haughton, 1962, 1964; Ayllon & Michael, 1959). Davison (1969) has reviewed these earlier efforts in some detail.

During the early 1960s other significant advances were made. Ferster and DeMyer (1961, 1962) and Staats and his associates (Staats & Butterfield, 1965; Staats, Minke, Finley, Wolf, & Brooks, 1964; Staats, Staats, Schultz, & Wolf, 1962) were exploring the use of generalized conditioned reinforcers (Kelleher & Gollub, 1962). Staats and his associates trained children to perform various tasks, such as reading for long periods of time. Tokens exchangeable for a variety of backup rewards sustained performance beyond that achieved with nongeneralized reinforcers. The demonstrated potency of token reinforcers has proved to be of substantial significance in group reinforcement programs. Additional studies of historical importance, far too numerous to credit here, contributed greatly to the present form of reinforcement practices in applied settings.

Present day applications of operant procedures, as reflected in token economies, stemmed directly from much of the work outlined above as well as basic animal research (cf. Ayllon & Azrin, 1968; Kelleher & Gollub, 1962). Token economies stand in sharp contrast with early research in the field. As will be elaborated upon below, in token programs, many individuals are often incorporated into the contingencies, the focus is on behavior on the ward, a variety of reinforcers are made available, several behaviors are consequated, and the ends are primarily therapeutic rather than merely demonstrational.

Token economies have been implemented in diverse settings, as discussed in a number of literature reviews (Carlson, Hersen, & Eisler, 1972; Kazdin & Bootzin, 1972; Liberman, 1968; Milby, 1972; O'Leary & Drabman, 1971; Turton & Gathercole, 1972). Because the field has been thoroughly reviewed, the present discussion will concentrate on recent trends, areas where concentrated research might be useful, and future directions. The discussion of token economies will emphasize programs in psychiatric hospitals but will draw upon research in other settings as well. Recent token economies reflect an increasing sophistication as shown by the selection of target behaviors, assessment of concomitant changes which are associated with alteration of specific response targets, comparisons of token programs with other treatments or in combination with other procedures, careful evaluation of punishment, consideration of economic principles to complement operant principles, and the use of peer or self-managed contingencies. Despite the new procedures and issues that arise with more ambitious programs, recurrent themes significant even in early token programs remain. The major issue is response maintenance and transfer of training of patient gains to nontreatment settings. A final topic will be addressed briefly, viz., the use of token economies to ameliorate "social ills," which in many ways transcends applications to problems traditionally considered under the rubric of mental health. Various issues important in token economies such as training staff (Kazdin & Bootzin, 1973), altering the behavior of intractable clients (Kazdin, 1973c), handling practical problems of administering the system (J. Hall & Baker, 1973), and employing experimental desiderata (Kazdin, 1973e) will not be treated in this paper since they have been surveyed elsewhere.

II. COMPLEX AND THERAPEUTICALLY "RELEVANT" BEHAVIORS ("SYMPTOMS")

A large number of studies have focused upon general ward behavior of patients, including self-care skills, grooming, attending and participating in activities, engaging in jobs on and off the ward, and related adaptive behaviors in the hospital setting (Allen & Magaro, 1971; Arann & Horner, 1972; Atthowe & Krasner, 1968; Ayllon & Azrin, 1965; Cohen, Florin, Grusche, Meyer-Osterkamp, & Sell, 1972; Ellsworth, 1969; Hartlage, 1970; Heap, Boblitt, Moore, & Hord, 1970; Hersen, Eisler, Smith, & Agras, 1972; Lawson, Greene, Richardson, McClure, & Padina, 1971; Lloyd & Garlington, 1968; McReynolds & Coleman, 1972; Schaefer & Martin, 1966; Stayer & Jones, 1969; Steffy, Hart, Craw, Torney, & Marlett, 1969; Suchotliff, Greaves, Stecker, & Berke, 1970; Winkler, 1970).

Although extrahospital adjustment is in a social sense the ultimate criterion by which token programs are evaluated, development of skills within the hospital is also relevant to this end. There is justification for focusing on behaviors adaptive to the hospital setting at least as long as there are institutions of the sort that presently exist (Kazdin, 1972a). First, institutionalization often fosters maladaptive and dependent behaviors (cf. Paul, 1969). Reinforcement for assuming responsibility can militate against behavioral deterioration that might otherwise occur. Second, development of adaptive ward behaviors can eliminate bizarre behaviors that might interfere with community adjustment. Bizarre behaviors can be altered by establishing functional behaviors. For example, O'Brien and Azrin (1972) modified the high rate of screaming of a female schizophrenic patient by providing tokens for "functional behaviors" such as social skills, housekeeping, and grooming (which were not necessarily incompatible with screaming). An increase in desirable behaviors was associated with a decrease in screaming. The authors suggested that positive behaviors "functionally displaced" the screaming.

Similarly, Hersen, Eisler, Alford, and Agras (1973) provided tokens to three neurotically depressed males for work, occupational therapy, and personal hygiene. An increase in token-earning behaviors was associated with a reduction in depression as measured by behavioral ratings. In an ABA design, depression systematically varied (inversely) with the performance of desirable behaviors. Other hospital programs have reported a reduction in psychotic "symptomatology" (e.g., psychotic belligerence) and increased self-esteem in patients who were verbally reinforced for personal appearance (DiScipio & Trudeau, 1972). In the above reports, an increase in adaptive behaviors on the ward was associated with changes in bizarre or "symptomatic" behaviors. (See Section III on changes in nontarget behaviors.)

Target "symptoms" have been focused upon directly rather than being displaced by reinforcing other adaptive behaviors alone. Wincze, Leitenberg, and Agras (1972) found that token reinforcement effectively altered delusional talk in therapy sessions with paranoid schizophrenics. Feedback for delusional talk (i.e., "that was incorrect") did not consistently alter verbal behavior. Evaluation of verbal behaviors on the ward showed less dramatic change even though tokens were delivered for nondelusional talk with the staff.

Reisinger (1972) treated "anxiety depression" in an institutionalized patient. Tokens were delivered for smiling and were withdrawn for crying. At the end of treatment, tokens were eliminated and praise alone was delivered for smiling. Smiling was maintained for the four remaining weeks before the patient was discharged.

Kazdin (1971a) suppressed psychotic speech in an adult prepsychotic retardate. Delusional statements were suppressed by contingently withdrawing tokens. The statements decreased dramatically and did not recover over a 6-month follow-up period. Similarly, Bartlett, Ora, Brown, and Butler (1971) reduced psychotic speech in an autistic child. Rational speech was developed using token reinforcement.

A significant response class for psychiatric patients is social behaviors. Of course, a precondition for social interaction may be elimination of certain bizarre behaviors. However, elimination of deviant behaviors alone does not ensure the appearance of social behaviors. An increasing number of investigations have been concerned with shaping social behaviors.

Liberman (1972) trained four withdrawn and verbally inactive psychiatric patients to engage in conversation with a group. Conversation increased substantially under token reinforcement contingencies based either upon individual or group performance. Similarly, Bennett and Maley (1973) reinforced two psychiatric patients for conversing with each other in experimental sessions. Social interaction increased in the sessions and on the ward as well.

Horn and Black (1974) reinforced chronic patients for emitting verbal responses in a group situation. Group participation increased substantially although it is unclear how many of the 38 patients were favorably affected. Regrettably, albeit predictably, when tokens and backup reinforcers (candy and cigarettes) were withdrawn, participation immediately returned to baseline levels.

Leitenberg, Wincze, Butz, Callahan, and Agras (1970) treated a patient who avoided social interaction with staff by providing contingent token reinforcement for conversation. Neither instructions nor noncontingent reinforcement had increased social behavior. The same patient had an additional problem, namely, fear of injury, which was altered by praising contact with feared objects. [Other investigations have shown token reinforcement to be effective in reducing fear, i.e., "rat phobias" in female college students (Vodde & Gilner, 1971).]

Behaviors focused upon in token economies have progressed well beyond grooming and self-care skills. Routine ward behaviors remain exceedingly important, particularly since reinforcement of these behaviors sometimes is associated with generalized effects (Atthowe & Krasner, 1968; Hersen *et al.,* 1973; Maley, Feldman, & Ruskin, 1973). However, development of social skills, and especially countersymptom behaviors is likely to be crucial for community adjustment (Freeman & Simmons, 1963). Altering aberrant behaviors in patients is not new (e.g., Ayllon, 1963; Ayllon & Michael, 1959). However, focusing upon aberrant behaviors ("symptoms"), which ostensibly lead to specific diagnoses, will present invaluable information of the mutability of relatively complex behaviors. The thrust of token programs will be even more apparent if responses traditionally viewed as representing psychopathology are repeatedly shown to be alterable. Alteration of complex responses in general without specific relationships to psychopathology will provide important advances in the field (cf. Ingham & Andrews, 1973; Scott, Peters, Gillespie, Blanchard, Edmunson, & Young, 1973).

III. CHANGES IN NONTARGET BEHAVIORS

The effects of token reinforcement contingencies usually are evaluated on specific target behaviors (i.e., those consequated) without examining other concurrent changes that may result from application of the consequences. Recently, this emphasis has been redirected by looking for broad changes beyond those achieved in the target responses (cf. Kazdin, 1973a, 1973b). Specifically, investigators have sought evidence of response generalization. Anecdotal evidence suggests that changes in the frequency of a response are associated with topographical response changes (Burchard & Tyler, 1965; Hauserman, Zweback, & Plotkin, 1972; Hawkins, Peterson, Schweid, & Bijou, 1966).

Supportive evidence for changes beyond those achieved with target responses has mounted. Shean and Zeidberg (1971) contrasted token reinforcement procedures with traditional ward treatment in developing self-care and role behaviors, and increasing extrahospital visits in psychiatric patients. Token reinforcement led to greater patient cooperativeness on the ward, communication skills, social interaction, participation in hospital activities, time out of the hospital, and a reduction in the use of medication relative to the control ward. The majority of these improvements were not directly shaped with reinforcement. Winkler (1970) used token reinforcement and response cost to alter behaviors of chronic psychiatric patients to develop self-help skills, participation in exercises, and attendance to meals. Violence and noise on the ward, which were initially excluded from the contingencies, decreased while the program was in effect.

Maley *et al.* (1973) compared psychiatric patients reinforced with tokens for a variety of behaviors on the ward with controls who received custodial treatment. Behaviors during a standardized interview and ratings of video-taped behavior served as dependent measures. Patients in the token economy ward were better oriented, more able to perform a discrimination task, and more likely to follow complex commands and to handle money in making business purchases than were control patients. Additionally, behavior ratings revealed that token economy patients showed more appropriate mood states, were more cooperative, and displayed better communication skills than control patients. Importantly, token economy patients were rated in less need of hospitalization and more likable. Since patients were reinforced for specific behaviors on the ward (e.g., grooming), the beneficial effects obtained for behaviors not included in the contingencies represent generalized effects. Similarly, Bennett and Maley (1973) noted changes in mood, communication, and social skills in two psychotic patients who were reinforced for conversing with each other. Reinforced patients showed greater token earnings on the ward and greater participation in activities than did controls. Since the behaviors specifically reinforced in the experimental sessions were restricted verbal interactions, the effect of the contingencies generalized considerably.

Gripp and Magaro (1971) reported a program with psychiatric patients who received tokens for job performance and other "preselected desirable behaviors." After 6 months of the program, patients on the token economy ward showed significant reductions in withdrawal, thought disorder, and depression on the Psychotic Reaction Profile. Nurses rated patients as improved on social competence, neatness, irritability, and manifest psychosis. Improvement in these areas either was markedly less or not apparent on control wards which did not receive token reinforcement. It is difficult to discern whether the broad changes reported are evidence of generalized effects, since the precise behaviors which were reinforced were not made explicit.

In classroom token economies concurrent effects have also been demonstrated. Mulligan, Kaplan, and Reppucci (1973) evaluated the effects of token reinforcement in a special elementary school classroom. Tokens were delivered for appropriate classroom behavior and completion of arithmetic and reading assignments. Aside from changes in the target behaviors, gains were reported in IQ and arithmetic achievement scores. A slight decrease was also noted in anxiety. Kubany, Weiss, and Sloggett (1971) reduced disruptive classroom behavior of a 6-year-old boy with combined token reinforcement and time-out procedures. The child's punctuality to class from recess improved even though this behavior was not included in the contingencies. Similarly, Twardosz and Sajwaj (1972) reported that token reinforcement for in-seat behavior of a hyperactive child increased appropriate social interaction and individual play behaviors. Horton (1970) demonstrated generalization of aggressive responses with delinquent boys in a home for emotionally disturbed children. The effects of token reinforcement for aggressive responses on one task generalized to other forms of aggressive behavior.

The above research provides an increasing body of evidence showing the beneficial effects of reinforcement programs beyond specific response targets. Unfortunately, the mechanism responsible for such change is not well understood. The notion of response generalization is frequently invoked to provide an explanation of broad program effects. This notion is usually misused and at best only describes rather than explains current research findings. Concurrent changes following reinforcement for a response target do not necessarily entail response generalization. In some cases, the occurrence of one response is inadvertently associated with the presence or the absence of another response. Although the investigator has not designed the consequences to follow this other response, the contingency is present nevertheless. Subsequent assessment may reveal behavior change beyond the intended target. Yet these changes may represent the direct operation of the contingency (e.g., Pendergrass, 1972). In addition, alteration of one behavior may place the individual under different reinforcement contingencies in the "natural" environment. New behaviors not originally selected as target responses may be reinforced directly by individuals other than staff who administer the programmed contingencies (cf. Buell, Stoddard, Harris, & Baer, 1968). [See Sajwaj, Twardosz, and Burke (1972) and Schick (1971) for a discussion of pertinent data and conceptual analyses.]

A change in one response does not always result in changes in other responses which might seem to be related. For example, Ferritor, Buckholdt, Hamblin, and Smith (1972) found that token reinforcement of attentive classroom behavior was unrelated to academic performance. Similarly, improvement of academic performance did not increase attentive behaviors. The authors caution against hoping for by-products of reinforcement contingencies. If a particular behavior change is required, the behavior should be included in the contingencies. While these recommendations are well taken, the increasing evidence for concurrent changes across responses within behavior therapy paradigms is generally compelling (e.g., Bandura, Blanchard, & Ritter, 1969; Kazdin, 1973a, 1974a; Meichenbaum, 1969; Meichenbaum & Cameron, 1973; Nordquist, 1971; Paul, 1967). Concurrent behaviors should be assessed to determine whether additional changes are associated with those effected in target response areas.

IV. COMPARATIVE STUDIES AND COMBINED TREATMENTS

The majority of token economy programs have been evaluated with intrasubject replication designs in the absence of comparison groups (Kazdin & Bootzin, 1972). However, many research questions require the use of comparison groups (Kazdin, 1973e) including: the relative efficacy of token programs to traditional procedures and to untreated groups, the magnitude of behavior change attributable to the token program relative to other treatments, and the contribution of specific variables or parametric variations of a given variable in a token economy. Moreover, comparison groups are required to evaluate effects due to sequence of experimental conditions or multiple-treatment interference (Kazdin, 1973e). An increasing number of studies have compared token economy procedures with other treatments including, but not limited to, custodial ward care. Additionally, investigators have combined token reinforcement with other treatment strategies.

Marks, Sonoda, and Schalock (1968) compared reinforcement and relationship (individual) therapy with chronic schizophrenics. Each of two groups received both treatments, but in a counterbalanced order. Reinforcement consisted of tokens delivered by staff (at their discretion) for improvement in individualized problem areas (e.g., personal appearance, expressing feelings). On most measures there were no differences between treatments. The authors mention the operational difficulties in keeping the treatments distinct (e.g., avoiding reinforcement in relationship therapy). Since the reinforcement program was not evaluated on specific target behaviors and reinforcement was not delivered in a consistent fashion for well specified responses, the results are difficult to interpret.

Hartlage (1970) compared traditional therapy (insight) and reinforcement therapy (social reinforcement, privileges, and consumables) for "adaptive" responses. Pre- and posttreatment comparisons showed greater adjustment resulting from reinforcement therapy. However, with respect to self-concept data, treatments were not significantly different. Therapists' ratings of improvement favored reinforcement therapy.

Birky, Chambliss, and Wasden (1971) compared the efficacy of a token economy versus traditional ward care on discharge rates. Although there were no differences in the *number* of patients discharged from the token economy and two control wards (i.e., patients who remained out of hospital for at least 6 months), the patients discharged on a token economy ward had a significantly greater length of previous hospitalization. Thus, the reinforcement procedure had a greater effect in discharging patients who were more chronic.

Gripp and Magaro (1971) compared token reinforcement with routine hospital treatment on a number of dimensions. Schizophrenic patients on a token economy ward made several changes on scales reflecting cognitive and affective concomitants of psychoses, whereas fewer gains (and some regression) were noted for patients on control wards.

Olson and Greenberg (1972) exposed psychiatric patients to one of three treatments for 4 months: milieu therapy, interaction (milieu plus 2 hours of weekly group therapy), and token reinforcement. The reinforcement group earned tokens for making group decisions regarding ward administration and for attendance to activities. The token reinforcement condition led to more patients spending days on town passes, having days out of the program, and attending activities. Although not all measures favored the token system (e.g., ratings of social adjustment), the program tended to be more effective than other procedures.

Heap *et al.* (1970) compared behavior-milieu therapy consisting of token reinforcement, ward government, and other adjunctive procedures, with traditional ward care in developing self-care skills. The reinforcement group showed greater performance of self-care skills and rate of discharge than the control ward. The conclusions of this study have been criticized on the basis of several methodological flaws (Carlson *et al.,* 1972; Hersen & Eisler, 1971; Kazdin, 1973e).

The benefits derived from research comparing token economies with other treatments are unclear at this point in time. Comparative studies of the effectiveness of token programs require extensive methodological effort on the part of investigators. Frequently, the desiderata for adequate experimental design are not easily met. Understandably, methodological problems often delimit the clarity of the results. Although token programs in psychiatric hospitals seem to result in greater therapeutic effects relative to other procedures, they are sometimes confounded with a change of setting (Heap *et al.,* 1970), selection of special staff for the token ward (Gripp & Magaro, 1971), initial differences in patients (Shean & Zeidberg, 1971), and expectation for behavior change (Gripp & Magaro, 1971).

A potential problem in adding token reinforcement to other existing therapy procedures is that the *combination* is rarely scrutinized empirically. It is unclear whether the combined treatment is any better than the component procedures given alone. For example, Hauserman *et al.* (1972) increased initiations of verbal statements of hospitalized adolescents participating in group therapy by using token reinforcement. Although the authors went to great lengths to demonstrate the effect of tokens by using a combined ABAB and multiple-baseline design, the contribution of group therapy to behavior change was not evaluated. Carpenter and Carom (1968) used tokens (S & H Green stamps) to reinforce preadolescent delinquent boys in group meetings. Target behaviors included attendance, talking during discussions, punctuality, improvement in grades, and other behaviors. Additionally, psychodynamic techniques such as catharsis, ego support, and others were used in the group. Since no data were presented, the contribution of the combined procedure to behavior change is unclear. While there may be several advantages in combining token reinforcement with other techniques, it would be useful to determine whether the "other" procedure or the token program alone is less effective than the combination.

V. ROLE OF PUNISHMENT

Token economies rely heavily on the use of positive reinforcement of appropriate behavior, even when the goal is to decrease inappropriate behavior. Despite this emphasis, an increasingly large number of token programs employ some form of aversive control. The role of punishment in token economies has only recently been subjected to careful scrutiny. Usually two forms of punishment are used either alone or in combination, namely, reinforcer withdrawal, in the form of time-out from reinforcement, or response cost (Kazdin, 1972c). The distinction between time-out and response cost is that in time-out there is a period of *time* during which reinforcers are no longer available (Leitenberg, 1965), whereas with response cost, there is no necessary temporal restriction for earning further reinforcers (Kazdin, 1972c). Isolation exemplifies time-out, whereas a fine (loss of tokens) exemplifies response cost. The distinction becomes blurred in some token programs where clients are punished by having to *pay* more *tokens* for back-up reinforcers than the usual cost for a certain period of *time* (Winkler, 1971a). Indeed, some authors have suggested a synthesis in conceptualizing time-out and response cost (e.g., Striefel, 1972). Time-out and response cost have been investigated independently of the token economy (Kazdin, 1972c; Sherman & Baer, 1969).

Sample investigations exemplify the use of punishment in token programs. Burchard and Barrera (1972) evaluated response cost (fines) and time-out (isolation) in a token economy for mildly retarded antisocial boys. Punishment was used to suppress swearing, personal assault, damage to property, and similar acts. Four experimental groups were exposed to different time-out/response cost combinations. Variations were made in the duration of isolation (from 0 to 30 minutes) and amount of the fine (from 0 tokens to 20 tokens). Larger fines and longer time-out periods led to greater response suppression. Unexpectedly, low magnitude time-out durations or fines led to increased instances of deviant acts. [It should be noted that the relationship between time out and response suppression is not merely a function of duration (White, Nielsen, & Johnson, 1972).]

Loss of tokens (i.e., fines) has been used increasingly in token economies. Winkler (1970) showed that fines effectively controlled episodes of violence and noise on a psychiatric ward. These behavior changes were apparently the result of "generalization" effects of contingencies placed on other target behaviors. Yet, levying a cost led to further reductions. When fines were lifted, the disruptive behaviors increased.

Upper (1973) used a "ticket" system to reduce rule violations on a psychiatric ward. Whenever an infraction occurred, a ticket was administered to the patient who was responsible. The tickets were backed-up with token losses at the end of the day. The data suggested the efficacy of the cost procedure, although no reversal phases were included in the design.

Parrino, George, and Daniels (1971) charged patients tokens for taking pills (PRN medication). By the end of a 20-week period there was a substantial reduction in the use of unnecessary PRN medication.

Of course, the "punishment" procedures involving token loss are not always effective. Boren and Colman (1970) found that response cost with hospitalized delinquent soldiers was ineffective in increasing attendance to an activity. Fines levied for staying in bed *increased* absenteeism from a group meeting rather than eliminating the problem. Similarly, time-out when supplementing token reinforcement has been reinforcing in some cases (Steeves, Martin, & Pear, 1970).

Based upon laboratory evidence, Azrin and Holz (1966) concluded that an efficient use of punishment is in combination with reinforcement for alternate responses. Although many programs use reinforcement and punishment, different and seemingly unrelated behaviors may operate under each type of contingency. The beneficial effects of combining each procedure may be maximized by delivering reinforcers for a response which is incompatible with or functionally displaces the response to be suppressed (e.g., Wahler, Winkel, Peterson, & Morrison, 1965). The combined use of punishment and reinforcement is easily implemented when the occurrence of a behavior is punished and other behaviors are reinforced (DRO) along the same reinforcer dimension (e.g., token presentation and withdrawal). For example, in the Kubany *et al.* (1971) program token reinforcement and time-out were combined to control behavior of a disruptive boy. Accumulated time on a clock earned stars and backup reinforcers (shared with peers). Time-out consisted of terminating the running clock when disruptive behavior was performed. As mentioned earlier, Reisinger (1972) combined response cost and reinforcement to alter "anxiety-depression" of an institutionalized patient. Token and social reinforcement for smiling were paired with response cost for crying. Ultimately, smiling was maintained with social reinforcement.

The addition of punishment to a reinforcement program certainly warrants careful scrutiny in applied settings (Kazdin, 1975). Investigations have shown convincingly that token programs can be based upon response cost alone (e.g., Kaufman & O'Leary, 1972; Sulzbacher & Houser, 1968). The client can be given a sum of tokens and only lose them for undesirable behavior (Kazdin, 1973a). With few exceptions (e.g., McLaughlin & Malaby, 1972) response cost is as effective as token reinforcement for desirable behavior (Bailey & Iwata, 1973; Bucher & Hawkins, 1973; Kaufman & O'Leary, 1972). Yet, there may be subtle differences between cost and reward programs. For example, administering tokens (i.e., reinforcing) appears to increase the frequency of staff social approval to the clients, whereas removing tokens (i.e., punishing) does not affect the frequency of approval (Bailey & Iwata, 1973). The use of punishment in applied settings requires the evaluation of various issues such as the presence of any undesirable side effects, the range of effects across administering agents, the permanence of response suppression, and the parameters which contribute to its efficacy (Johnston, 1972; Kazdin, 1973g). As attempts increase to alter more complex behavior, the use of punishment may proliferate (cf. Kazdin & Craighead, 1973).

VI. ROLE OF ECONOMICS

Until a few years ago token economies were explained, at least by behavior modifiers, almost entirely in terms of operant principles or reinforcement theory. Limitations of the procedures were considered primarily in terms of failures in implementation (Kazdin, 1973d). However, the recent work of Winkler and his colleagues (Kagel & Winkler, 1972; Winkler, 1971b, 1972; Winkler & Krasner, 1971) shows that patient performance in a token economy depends upon more than the parameters of reinforcement. Specifically, notions from economic theory can supplement reinforcement theory and make specific predictions regarding patient performance.

First, the notion of *consumption schedule* is relevant to patient behavior in a token economy. This schedule describes the relationship between income and expenditures. Individuals with more income spend more. Generally, spending falls within 10% of income. Individuals who have extremely low incomes spend more, but individuals with high incomes spend far below this percentage. A problem with extrapolating the relationship from national economies to token systems is that certain conditions are not always met in token programs. For example, for a person who earns few tokens to spend more than his earnings requires that he either borrow tokens or use accumulated savings (Fethke, 1972, 1973; Winkler, 1973). Yet, in many token economies borrowing is not permitted because this might constitute "noncontingent reinforcement" if not carefully executed. Also, if accumulated savings are used, performance can be independent of current income altogether. Nevertheless, the general relationship following consumption schedules holds (Winkler, 1971b). At high levels of income, spending attenuates, and presumably, tokens take on less value. Winkler (1972) also has noted that the discrepancy between income and expenditure, or *savings* in token economies may reach a *critical limit.* If savings fall below an individual's critical limit, token earning behaviors should increase;

if savings fall within a critical range, performance should reach an equilibrium (i.e., no change in performance). Of course, the goal of most token economies is to increase performance and not to stabilize performance at low rates.

The implications of consumption schedules for token economies are clear. If token earning behaviors and token income are to increase, one of three solutions is available: (1) prices of backup reinforcers can be increased, (2) the value of tokens can be decreased, thereby altering the value of savings, and (3) the range of goods (backup reinforcers) available can be increased. Any of these solutions can be used to alter the level of earnings. As Winkler (1972) has noted, if reinforcement does not affect consumption schedules or the critical range of savings, levels of performance and earnings will stabilize.

A second relevant principle from economics is referred to as *Engel's law*. Simply stated, as income increases, the proportion of total expenditure spent on urgent needs decreases, whereas expenditure on luxuries increases. Indeed, this relationship was supported in token economy expenditures when meals were considered essential and canteen items were considered luxuries (Winkler, 1917b). One implication is that items which can be considered luxuries should be expanded because they will be in increased demand as incomes increase.

A third principle relates to the responsiveness of consumer demand to price changes. The economic notion of *elasticity of a demand curve* measures this responsiveness and is defined as the percentage change in demand resulting from a 1% change in price. For some items, a price drop leads to a relatively larger percentage of demand than the actual drop (i.e., items with elastic demands). That is, the percentage of sales of the items increases. For other items, a decrease in price will result in an increase in demand that is smaller than the price drop (i.e., items with inelastic demands). Necessities usually are inelastic whereas luxury items are usually elastic. On an applied level, if prices of backup reinforcers are to be increased on a token economy, items with inelastic demands (necessities) should be relatively expensive to stimulate spending. If the price of items with elastic demands (luxuries) is increased, percentage spending may decrease (cf. Hayden, Osborne, Hall, & Hall, 1972). Recent reports have attempted to evaluate reinforcer preferences of backup reinforcers in token economies (Ruskin & Maley, 1972). It may be useful to catalog the relative elasticity or inelasticity of items which can best be used to stimulate spending (Winkler, 1971b), particularly for individuals who respond minimally to the program (Kazdin, 1972b, 1973c).

Operant principles do not always make precise and easily testable predictions about expenditures, earnings, and performance. While a few operant principles are employed, their relation to performance is not precise enough to be easily tested. For example, it is clear that magnitude of token reinforcement can be increased to stimulate performance in token economies (e.g., Wolf, Giles, & Hall, 1968). Satiation is considered to be one limiting condition for unlimited gains derived from increases in magnitude. Yet, economic principles can supplement reinforcement theory in clarifying the relationship between performance and increased token earnings. For example, satiation is likely to occur when token savings begin to surpass the critical range of savings. Since an individual's critical level of savings can be determined (Winkler, 1972), predictions can be advanced as to *when* satiation will begin. More importantly, satiation can be avoided by altering the prices of backup items or the value of tokens, reducing savings, or increasing the range of available backup items. These latter solutions are predicted from economic theory.

VII. USE OF PEERS

Increasingly, peers (fellow patients, clients, residents, and students) are employed in some aspect of the token economy either to serve in a function that is usually reserved for staff (e.g., data collection, token delivery), or to augment the efficacy of the contingencies. A direct attempt is made to replace dependency, apathy, and institutionalization with responsibility and active participation (Atthowe & Krasner, 1968; Schaefer & Martin, 1966). Instead of having treatment imposed upon them, patients are called upon to make decisions about matters related to their own treatment (O'Brien, Azrin, & Henson, 1969; Olson & Greenberg, 1972; Pomerleau, Bobrove, & Harris, 1972).

The decisions are not just "token" acts to convey a quasi-democratic structure of the institution, but require serious planning and decision making on the part of patients. The expanded role is clear in token programs where patients can participate in their own "treatment" (e.g., deciding policy in the program or designing contingencies) and administer "treatment" programs to others (e.g., provide consequences for behavior, collect and summarize program data) (Kazdin, 1972a).

A frequent use of patients on the ward is to develop group peer social structure which supports and actively contributes to the appropriate behavior of individual patients. The contingencies are devised so that each individual's performance dictates the consequences delivered to the group, and the group's performance dictates the consequences delivered to the members. For example, in one psychiatric hospital (Pomerleau *et al.,* 1972) patients were grouped into dyads. The dyads formed larger groups. Consequences in the program (e.g., fines) ordinarily imposed upon a single individual were shared by other members of the dyad or by other dyads. By making patients accountable to others for their behavior and by making the individual accountable to the group, there is the expectation that the group will exert influence on behavior. Such an influence may persist once the program is withdrawn. Olson and Greenberg (1972) also have employed sharing of consequences with peers on a psychiatric ward. To exert group pressure, patients were allowed access to their funds (or coupons negotiable at the local canteen) on the basis of their own performance and the performance of the group to which they belonged. Group performance was evaluated on the basis of attendance to scheduled activities and weekly progress. The contribution of the group contingency to overall program efficacy was not determined.

Group contingencies have frequently been employed in nonpsychiatric settings. For example, Medland and Stachnik (1972) devised a group contingency to control disruptive classroom behavior. The class was divided into two groups. Points were *given* to the group when a member *violated* a class rule. Either or both group(s) earned extra minutes of recess if there were fewer than a certain number of points earned. Disruptive behavior decreased substantially under the group contingency.

In some programs, the performance of one individual is used as the sole basis for providing reinforcing consequences to peers. Wolf, Hanley, King, Lachowicz, and Giles (1970) used token reinforcement in a classroom. The behavior of one child was not controlled by individual punishment (loss of tokens from a daily sum given to the particular child). However, a contingency was developed so that tokens earned (i.e., not lost for inappropriate behavior) were divided among her peers. Behavior improved markedly when the tokens were shared with peers. A number of investigations have show that group contingencies and reinforcer sharing control the behavior of individuals (Axelrod, 1973; Perline & Levinsky, 1968; Schmidt & Ulrich, 1969; Walker & Buckley, 1972). Programs using group contingencies rarely systematically assess the precise peer interaction that purportedly occurs. Some anecdotally report peer encouragement and praise (Patterson, 1965), whereas others note an increase in peer censure and reprimands (Axelrod, 1973; Schmidt & Ulrich, 1969). Certainly, a great deal of systematic research is required to evaluate the specific peer contingencies (both reinforcing and punishing) that contribute to the efficacy of group contingencies and consequence sharing.

Clients in reinforcement programs may be utilized more directly in the execution of the program than sharing consequences delivered to others. For example, psychiatric patients have been used to administer and evaluate the program. Dominguez, Acosta, and Carmona (1972) employed patients as observers on a token economy ward. The "patient-assistants" were reinforced for reliably observing the behavior of fellow patients on the ward. Interestingly, an objective of training patients to collect data on others was to change their own behavior as a result. Aside from observing other patients, patient-assistants were responsible for distribution of tokens, calculation and tabulation of token earnings of others, and drawing graphs. In other programs, patients have been used in a variety of fashions. For example, Heap *et al.* (1970) utilized patients to supervise work assignments of others on the ward. Pomerleau *et al.* (1972) maintained a police force composed of patients to maintain nonviolence on the ward. Ayllon and Azrin (1968) utilized patients to give tours of the token economy ward to visitors.

Perhaps, the most interesting use of peers is in the direct administration of reinforcement programs. Recent research at Achievement Place, a home-style living facility for predelinquents, has utilized peers in several ways. In one report a dramatic utilization of peers in a token economy was described (Bailey, Timbers, Phillips, & Wolf, 1971). Some predelinquent boys served as therapists for others who had speech problems (articulation errors). Peers earned points for identifying words said correctly or incorrectly by the subjects. A subject either earned or lost points on the basis of his own performance. The peers effectively trained correct word pronunciation. These effects were obtained, although the peers had no specific speech training and almost no adult supervision. Only brief instructions were given, and adults remained absent from the sessions. The efficacy of the procedures was robust. In fact, the effects of speech training generalized to words not included in training and were maintained after two months.

Group contingencies are used to involve peers in the program. Yet peer involvement is somewhat indirectly programmed in most group contingency studies. If peers are to change behavior, they should be utilized directly as reinforcing agents (Axelrod, Hall, & Maxwell, 1972; Solomon & Wahler, 1973). Sometimes peers are used to collect data and observe other patients in the hopes that the patients who assume staff functions will change significantly (Dominguez *et al.,* 1972). Presently, there appears to be little empirical support justifying this strategy. However, there may be other advantages to the use of peers (outlined above) than the effect on their own behavior. The use of peers in reinforcement programs may provide less restricted stimulus control over patient performance (which may result from complete reliance upon staff-administered contingencies), more frequent reinforcement (planned and unplanned) for performance of target behaviors (Kazdin, 1973d), and may free staff for supervisory functions making more efficient use of their time (Kazdin, 1972a). Thus, the use of peers in traditional staff functions entails a number of considerations. Reprogramming the environment by developing reinforcing and punishing skills in peers has only begun to be explored as a viable technique in token programs.

VIII. SELF-REINFORCEMENT

Recently, self-reinforcement has been evaluated in token economies. Providing reinforcing consequences to oneself seems to be useful on prima facie grounds, especially since the goal of most hospital programs is to increase individual responsibility. Moreover, self-reinforcement does *not appear* to be a particularly complex procedure. The only conceptual and practical requirement for self-reinforcement is the freedom of a client to reinforce himself at any time whether or not he performs a particular response (Skinner, 1953). The majority of token programs employing self-reinforcement have been conducted in classroom settings.

Applications of self-reinforcement may involve two different procedures. First, the client can determine the response requirements for a given amount of reinforcement (i.e., when to deliver reinforcement and the amount to be delivered). When the individual determines the criteria for reinforcement this is referred to as *self-determined reinforcement* (Glynn, 1970). Second, the individual can dispense reinforcement depending upon achieving a particular performance criterion which may or may not be self-determined. When the individual administers reinforcers to himself, this is referred to as *self-administered reinforcement.* Who administers the reinforcers (oneself or someone else) is not crucial. The crucial elements are determining when to deliver the reinforcer and for what behaviors. Of course, if an individual is not permitted to self-administer reinforcers, there may be constraints which influence actual self-consequation. Thus, self-reinforcement is best achieved when the individual can determine and administer reinforcement.

A number of classroom studies have shown the efficacy of self-reinforcement. Glynn, Thomas, and Shee (1973) required elementary school students to record whether they were paying attention in class whenever a "beep" sounded (at randomly selected intervals) from a tape recorder. Each time a student recorded paying attention, he earned 1 minute of free time. When students recorded their own behavior, and thereby determined their own reinforcement, the rate of paying attention was higher than in baseline. Similar findings have been noted in classroom token programs where students reward themselves with points exchangeable for backup reinforcers (Bolstad & Johnson, 1972; Glynn, 1970; Lovitt & Curtiss, 1969).

An obvious concern with self-reinforcement is that individuals will provide consequences to themselves independently of their actual behavior. There is justification for this concern. In a psychiatric hospital, "emotionally disturbed" children participated in a special classroom project (Santogrossi, O'Leary, Romanczyk, & Kaufman, 1973). The effects of teacher-determined versus self-determined points on disruptive behavior were evaluated. When the teacher administered points, disruptive classroom behavior decreased. However, when the students were given the opportunity to reward themselves, they did so noncontingently and disruptive behavior increased. Self-reinforcement led to administration of rewards for undesirable behavior. Other studies of self-reinforcement have demonstrated that individuals who self-determine reinforcement tend to become increasingly lenient over time (Felixbrod & O'Leary, 1973; McReynolds & Church, 1973). Thus, self-reinforcement may result in "noncontingent reinforcement" a procedure which is not usually associated with target behavior change. Two related solutions to the problem of noncontingent self-reinforcement are reinforcing the clients on the basis of how accurately they assess their own behavior (Bolstad & Johnson, 1972) or reinforcing individuals for reinforcing themselves contingently (Drabman, Spitalnik, & O'Leary, 1973). Although these solutions ameliorate noncontingent self-consequation, they also grossly distort the notions of "self-control" and "self-reinforcement" (cf. Kazdin, 1975; Morgan & Bass, 1973; Stuart, 1972).

A minor point deserves commentary. In many self-reinforcement programs, the clients observe their own behavior and base their self-administered consequences on the extent to which these data meet some criterion. Since self-observation alone can account for behavior change (Kazdin, 1974b), the precise role of self-consequation is sometimes obscured. In clinical contexts, self-reinforcement often requires self-observation, so the separation of these procedures may be specious (cf. Kanfer, 1970).

There is little doubt that self-control procedures will be increasingly incorporated into token economies. In many programs, groups of clients are given major responsibility for making decisions about their own fate and the fate of others (e.g., Fixsen, Phillips, & Wolf, 1973; Olson & Greenberg, 1972). Shifting control of the program from the staff to the clients represents an initial step away from external control of the contingencies. Certainly, a logical extension is to shift control to the individual for his own performance. The procedures used to successfully achieve the transition from external to self-control remain to be perfected.

IX. RESPONSE MAINTENANCE AND TRANSFER OF TRAINING

Since the efficacy of token programs has been firmly demonstrated, the major issue is achieving long-term maintenance of responses following program termination and transfer of these responses to extratreatment settings. Several token programs in hospital settings report improved discharge and/or readmission rates following participation in a token economy (Atthowe & Krasner, 1968; Birky *et al.*, 1971; Ellsworth, 1969; Heap *et al.*, 1970; Henderson & Scoles, 1970; Stayer & Jones, 1969). However, the precise role of the reinforcement contingencies in these measures is not always clear (Kazdin & Bootzin, 1972). There is considerable evidence that responses developed with token reinforcement are not maintained once the contingencies are withdrawn and are not likely to transfer automatically to nontreatment settings. The areas of response maintenance and transfer of training remain the most fertile for research.

Behaviors developed through token reinforcement do not always return to baseline levels after the contingencies are withdrawn (Hewett, Taylor, & Artuso, 1969; Kazdin, 1971a, 1973f; Medland & Stachnik, 1972; Surratt, Ulrich, & Hawkins, 1969; Whitman, Mercurio, & Caponigri, 1970), although these are exceptions (Kazdin & Bootzin, 1972). When behaviors are maintained, the reason is frequently unclear. Three alternate interpretations are usually offered to account for unplanned response maintenance. First, it is possible that behaviors developed through token reinforcement come under control of extraexperimental reinforcers (Baer, Wolf, & Risley, 1968; Bijou, Peterson, Harris, Allen, & Johnston, 1969). Events associated with tokens may acquire conditioned reinforcement value and serve to maintain behaviors following token withdrawal (Medland & Stachnik, 1972). For example, investigators working in a classroom setting have suggested that teachers may more readily function as secondary reinforcers after being associated with a token economy (Chadwick & Day, 1971). A second interpretation of unplanned maintenance is that after tokens are withdrawn reinforcing consequences which are derived directly from the activities themselves maintain behavior. For example, token reinforcement for social interaction may be unnecessary to maintain behavior because of the "natural" reinforcement which follows (see Kazdin & Polster, 1973). A third interpretation is that a token program alters staff behavior in some permanent fashion so that they continue desirable response consequation after tokens are discontinued. Even though tokens are withdrawn, staff are utilizing contingent reinforcement, prompting, and executing other procedures developed in their repertories during the token program. In spite of the reasonable nature of each of these explanations, and partial support which might be provided for each, it is usually a matter of conjecture why a response is maintained without specific programming (Kazdin, 1975).

Typically, programming response maintenance is required because removal of the contingencies frequently results in a decrease in appropriate performance. Some procedures which might be useful in achieving maintenance have been discussed elsewhere (Kazdin & Bootzin, 1972). The procedures, listed below, are not necessarily independent, mutually exclusive, nor exhaustive. [For more detail, see Kazdin (1975).]

1. Systematically substituting social reinforcers. Behavior can be maintained after tokens are no longer delivered by substituting social reinforcers for the tokens. Praise alone has been effective in maintaining behavior changes in token programs (Chadwick & Day, 1971; Reisinger, 1972). In some cases, praise may not be effective initially. However, after being paired consistently with token delivery, praise effectively maintains behavior after tokens are withdrawn (Wahler, 1968).

2. Gradually fading tokens. Tokens can be withdrawn gradually, particularly if the individual has shown consistent and prolonged performance of the target responses (Atthowe & Krasner, 1968; Garlington & Lloyd, 1966; Schaefer & Martin, 1969). Some programs place patients in one of various levels depending upon their performance (Lloyd & Abel, 1970). Initial levels provide immediate reinforcement for relatively small behavioral requirements. Consistent performance permits advancement to higher levels where a wider selection of reinforcers is available. By the time the individual achieves the highest level, tokens may be eliminated entirely. Tokens also can be faded by gradually decreasing their value after high levels of performance have been achieved. Tokens are earned continuously, but their ability to purchase backup reinforcers can be eliminated gradually (cf. Jones & Kazdin, 1975). The ultimate complete withdrawal of tokens is not as abrupt because the value of tokens has diminished over time.

3. Training individuals in the client's environment. Individuals in the client's environment, such as spouses, parents, teachers, and peers, can be trained to continue application of the contingencies. Since target responses often are readily modified in the natural environment, paraprofessionals can be trained to carry out the entire program (see Ayllon & Wright, 1972 for review). When the natural environment is indeed the therapeutic environment, behaviors are more likely to be maintained than when training takes place in a treatment facility. This is expected, of course, because of the failure to form a discrimination between treatment and extratreatment settings (Kazdin, 1971b). When treatment is conducted in a special setting, the long-range success of the program may be determined, in part, by whether the relatives have been trained to continue the procedures after training has terminated (Lovaas, Koegel, Simmons, & Long, 1973).

4. Scheduling intermittent reinforcement. As is widely demonstrated in laboratory studies, resistance to extinction can be increased by using intermittent reinforcement. In some token programs, an extremely thin schedule has been effective in maintaining high levels of performance (Phillips, Phillips, Fixsen, & Wolf, 1971). In other studies, intermittent reinforcement is used to develop resistance to extinction after the tokens are withdrawn entirely (Kazdin & Polster, 1973). Although intermittent reinforcement increases resistance to extinction, it is unclear whether the effects are transient or result in long-term maintenance.

5. Varying the stimulus conditions of training. While a token program is in effect, behavior should be reinforced in a wide range of situations and settings to broaden the stimulus control over behavior. When behavior is established in the presence of varied cues, it may be less likely to revert to baseline or near baseline levels when the program is withdrawn (cf. Goocher & Ebner, 1968; Lovaas & Simmons, 1969). One way to increase the conditions under which behavior is trained is to expose the individual to extra-treatment settings while the program is in effect (Kelley & Henderson, 1971). Presumably, this procedure develops stimulus control of the target responses in the setting where the individual will ultimately function.

6. Self-reinforcement training. If the individual can be trained to monitor and reinforce his own behavior, behavior may be maintained across a variety of settings and situations. As noted earlier, self-reinforcement has been restricted to a limited range of applied settings. It is unclear to what extent initial behavior changes can be achieved with diverse treatment groups, to say nothing of maintenance of these changes. There have been a few evaluations of self-reinforcement on resistance to extinction in classroom settings. The preliminary results suggest the value is dubious in ensuring response maintenance (Bolstad & Johnson, 1972; Johnson, 1970). Obviously, conclusions in this area would be premature.

7. Self-instruction training. Self-instruction training focuses on the antecedent events, i.e., verbal prompts, which the client can use to guide his own behavior. Meichenbaum (1969) noted a serendipitous finding that self-instruction facilitated generalization of trained responses across tasks, time, and situations. Subsequent experiments demonstrated that altering the instructions one gives to oneself exerts control over a variety of nonverbal behaviors (Meichenbaum & Cameron, 1973; Meichenbaum & Goodman, 1971). Moreover, many behaviors altered with self-instruction seem to be maintained. Thus, training clients to "talk to themselves" (Meichenbaum & Cameron, 1973) may reliably maintain responses. As yet, this technique has not been employed as part of a token economy.

8. Manipulating reinforcement delay. Reinforcement can be delayed in two ways, either of which may facilitate resistance to extinction. First, the delay between performance of the target response and token delivery can be increased (Atthowe & Krasner, 1968). Second, the delay between token delivery and the exchange of tokens for backup reinforcers can be increased (Cotler, Applegate, King, & Kristal, 1972). The effect of these procedures on long-term maintenance has not been evaluated in token economies.

9. Simultaneously manipulating several reinforcement parameters. Simultaneously altering a number of aspects of reinforcement delivery (i.e., varied reinforcement), such as magnitude, delay, place, quality, and schedule, may effectively enhance resistance to extinction. Laboratory evidence suggests that the greater the sources of variation, the greater the resistance to extinction (McNamara & Wike, 1958). This technique, or perhaps combination of techniques, has not been reported in the token economy literature.

Although each of these methods might be useful in response maintenance, they have not been extensively evaluated in token economies (Kazdin & Bootzin, 1972). The effects of specific procedures following reinforcement withdrawal have been dealt with in a few studies in which schedules of reinforcement were examined. Phillips *et al.* (1971, Experiment II) provided token reinforcement and fines to control room-cleaning behavior. In a final experimental phase, point consequences were faded using an "adjusting consequence" procedure. The number of days in which room-cleaning was checked was gradually decreased (i.e., increased intermittency). However, on any day that the response was checked, the number of points earned or lost was multiplied by the number of previous days in which behavior had not been checked. This procedure ensured that both the frequency and magnitude of reinforcement were not reduced simultaneously, since the potential number of points remained the same during the fading period. Ultimately, in this report, performance remained high even though checks were made only 8% of the time.

Kazdin and Polster (1973) evaluated token reinforcement on the behavior of two withdrawn adult retardates. Continuous token reinforcement for social interaction led to marked increases in this behavior, but the effects were lost in a reversal phase. Subsequently, one client was given continuous and the other intermittent reinforcement. In a final extinction period, the client who previously had been reinforced intermittently maintained a high rate of social interaction for the 5-week follow-up period. The continuously reinforced subject, however, returned to base levels of social interaction. These findings suggest that schedules may prove useful in delaying extinction. Yet, manipulation of reinforcement schedules is not without its problems such as decrements in behavior as the schedule is thinned (cf. Zifferblatt, 1972).

A great deal of additional work is required to determine what procedures can be used to maintain behavior. One solution is to substitute other behavior modification programs after token reinforcement is withdrawn (e.g., Walker & Buckley, 1972). However, in many settings where programs are not continued in any form, resistance to extinction must be enhanced with little or no aid from a specifically designed and carefully executed program in the new environment.

Generally, the above comments are restricted to building resistance to extinction. Response maintenance often is a prior issue to transfer of behavior to nontreatment settings. A patient's behavior needs to be maintained in the hospital when the program is withdrawn before considering transfer of the behavior to a nonhospital setting. (However, a concern might be whether target behaviors transfer to situations in which the contingencies are not being carried out while the program is in effect in one setting.) Generalization of behavior across situations seems to be the exception (Bennett & Maley, 1973; Kazdin, 1973f; Walker, Mattson, & Buckley, 1971) rather than the rule (see Kazdin & Bootzin, 1972). Some of the procedures outlined above may enhance generalization across situations. In particular, training individuals in the nontreatment environment to administer the contingencies, developing self-reinforcement and self-instructional skills, and providing reinforcement in varied settings during training may facilitate transfer of training.

No doubt there are a variety of procedures which may be useful in building response maintenance and ensuring transfer of training to extratreatment settings. Effective maintenance and transfer strategies need to be isolated so they can be readily incorporated into ongoing programs. The success of token programs will be assessed ultimately by how well behaviors are maintained outside of the training setting rather than the extent of behavior changes in the training setting when the contingencies are in effect.

X. INCREASING COMMUNITY INVOLVEMENT

The main focus of token economies is to alter contingencies within the treatment or educational setting. Relatively few programs have attempted to enmesh the program with community living and noninstitutional influences. It is important to extend token programs into the community so that the transition from one setting (e.g., hospital, school) to another (e.g., home) is facilitated. Initial efforts along these lines seem promising. Henderson (1969) described a facility for psychotic men situated in the community. The residents earned tokens for social, vocational, and countersymptom behaviors. Visitors from the community (volunteers) were incorporated into treatment. Residents were reinforced for socially interacting with the visitors (Henderson & Scoles, 1970). Degrees of social involvement were differentially reinforced including superficial participation, interpersonal transactions indicative of social involvement, and initiation of conversation. Social skills were reinforced during activities in the facility and in the community (e.g., at a YMCA). Additionally, activities of patients, such as securing job interviews or employment, were reinforced. Employers were involved in the program by providing feedback so consequences would be delivered for community performance (Kelley & Henderson, 1971).

Community involvement has included a host of paraprofessionals who contribute greatly to the habilitation of individuals in various treatment facilities (Ayllon & Wright, 1972). Bailey, Wolf, and Phillips (1970) provided token reinforcement for predelinquent boys living in a home-style cottage on the basis of academic performance at school. The teacher made daily reports on cards which determined privileges earned at the home. The teacher also participated in shifting subjects from continuous to intermittent reinforcement by gradually fading the use of the report card. In a school setting, McKenzie, Clark, Wolf, Kothera, and Benson (1968) reinforced academic behaviors in a class of children with learning disabilities. Weekly grades were given as reinforcers. Parents were trained to systematically praise good grades and mildly disapprove of poor grades. Eventually parents gave monetary allowances contingent upon grade performance.

Token programs are increasingly more frequent in the home. Therapists have consulted with parents on an outpatient basis to develop token programs for children. Christopherson, Arnold, Hill, and Quilitch (1972) instructed two sets of parents to implement token programs to modify behavior of their children. In one family, three children were reinforced for making their beds, going to bed on time, and not whining or bickering. Using a multiple-baseline design across behaviors, the effects of token reinforcement and response cost were carefully demonstrated. Other investigators have shown dramatic effects in training parents as experimenters and observers in altering child behaviors (R. V. Hall, Axelrod, Tyler, Grief, Jones, & Robertson, 1972; Herbert & Baer, 1972). In many cases relatively little consulting time (e.g., a few hours plus phone calls) (Christopherson *et al.*, 1972) is required.

Increasingly, relatives, employers, teachers, and peers are called upon to alter behavior of subjects whose behavior has been labeled or singled out as deviant. Treatment programs often can be carried out in the home to avoid institutionalization. If institutionalization has previously taken place or the client is participating in some program (e.g., educational), the efficacy of the procedures can then be enhanced by continuing the use of similar contingencies in the community and home. The implications for the use of nonprofessionals include preventive treatment for individuals who are prospective patients as well as follow-up of patients who are discharged.

XI. SOME NEW DIRECTIONS

The main thrust of token economies has been in treatment, rehabilitation, and educational settings with individuals whose behaviors are viewed as abnormal, maladaptive, or deficient. The majority of applications are directed toward groups including psychiatric patients, the mentally retarded, the emotionally disturbed, and delinquents (Kazdin & Bootzin, 1972).

Preliminary work has extended reinforcement techniques, particularly token reinforcement, to contemporary social concerns (Kazdin, 1975). Extension of reinforcement to social issues embraces behaviors not typically viewed as in the domain of psychological treatment. For example, reinforcement has been applied to racial integration, ecological problems, community organization, and military training. Investigations in these areas by no means purport to resolve important issues. Yet, such work reveals preliminary applications of reinforcement systems to socially significant issues. Future directions in behavior modification will probably emphasize amelioration of social ills as well as continuing the work in mental health, rehabilitation, and education. Samples of research dealing with socially important issues in a somewhat modest but highly promising fashion are illustrated briefly below.

A. Racial Integration

Racial integration represents a multifaceted issue. Certainly no attempt should be made to define a simple response as the sole target behavior for social integration of groups exposed to discrimination. However, it is reasonable to make initial attempts to operationalize aspects of prejudice to effect behavior change. Traditionally, procedures to facilitate racial integration have been aimed at changing attitudes. Unfortunately, changes in racial attitudes do not necessarily result in corresponding changes in behavior (Mann, 1959). Changes in the behaviors which the attitudes putatively dictate must be dealt with more directly.

A recent token program centered on socially integrating five black children in a predominantly white first grade classroom (Hauserman, Walen, & Behling, 1973). All students in the classroom were reinforced for sitting with "new friends" during lunch. "New friends" included interracial combinations of students although this was not specified to the children. Whenever the children were sitting with their "new friends," they received praise and a token. Tokens were redeemable after lunch for a cookie, candy, or another snack. Interracial interactions increased when reinforcers were delivered. Interestingly, interaction generalized to a free-play period during which no token reinforcement had been provided. Unfortunately, when the program was withdrawn, racial integration returned to its baseline levels. No particular procedures were employed to ensure response maintenance or transfer of training. Nevertheless, as a preliminary application of token reinforcement to integration, the results are promising. They suggest that interracial social interaction can be readily programmed in naturalistic settings. Social interaction has been examined in a number of studies (e.g., Bennett & Maley, 1973; Buell *et al.,* 1968; Kale, Kaye, Whelan, & Hopkins, 1968). Yet, racial interaction represents a relatively unexplored area in behavior modification.

B. Littering

Littering in public places represents a problem of increased social concern. Government expenditures to handle litter are vast. Moreover, in recent years the cost has increased (Clark, Burgess, & Hendee, 1972). National campaigns have attempted to reduce littering. Although campaigns may make individuals more sensitive to the problem and change attitudes toward littering, the relationship between antilitter attitudes and littering behavior is not clear. Investigations have shown that merely instructing people not to litter and using campaign materials do not result in consistent changes in littering (Baltes, 1973; Burgess, Clark, & Hendee, 1971; Kohlenberg & Phillips, 1973). Recently, reinforcement has been used to control littering in national campgrounds, parks, movie theaters, and school settings.

In one program (Clark *et al.,* 1972), littering was controlled in a national campground during a summer weekend. The campground (over 100 acres) was divided into separate areas so that litter could be counted on foot. One weekend served as baseline to determine the amount of accumulated litter. Litter (bags, beverage cans, bottles) was planted in the campground to provide a consistent level for the weekends of baseline and the program. During the weekend of the program, seven families were asked whether the children would help. The children were told they could earn any of various items (e.g., a Smokey Bear shoulder patch, comic book, ranger badge, gum, and so on). Children were given a large plastic bag and told they had one day to earn the reinforcer. They were not told where to look for litter or how much had to be collected. The amount of campground litter was markedly reduced during the incentive program, with the children collecting between 150 and 200 pounds of litter. The rewards given to them cost approximately $3.00. To accomplish the clean-up using camp personnel would have cost approximately $50 to $60. These results show that a relatively inexpensive reinforcement incentive system may provide a viable solution to a practical problem of littering.

C. Mass Transportation

Increasingly, major cities are developing mass transit systems in the hopes of decreasing reliance upon automobiles. The number of individuals who drive cars to work is overwhelming. Only recently has it been emphasized that the use of personal transportation is ecologically unsound. The use of mass transit in place of cars would conserve energy (fuel), decrease pollutants in the air, and reduce crowding and noise attributable to traffic. Moreover, the expense of law enforcement required for traffic control would be reduced with mass transit. The issues of energy conservation and pollution are particularly salient.

Recently, token reinforcement has been used to increase bus ridership. To demonstrate this on a relatively small scale, bus ridership on a large university campus was altered (Everett, 1973; Everett, Hayward, & Meyers, 1974). Buses in the university traveled a number of routes within campus. To increase bus ridership, boarders received either $.25 for riding the bus (Everett, 1973) or tokens (slips of paper) (Everett *et al.,* 1974) which could be saved and spent either toward future bus rides or at various stores in town for items such as food, movies, cigarettes, beer, and other rewards. Throughout the program, riders continued to pay the usual $.10 bus fee. However, the $.25 or ticket was delivered to them immediately after boarding a specially marked bus. The program increased ridership during the reinforcement phases as shown in an ABAB design. However, the influence of token reinforcement on bus ridership was especially pronounced with those individuals who walked rather than those who used a car. Of course, the major concern with mass transit is to increase ridership to those who ordinarily use their cars. However, these initial investigations were conducted on a university campus where automobile transportation was already minimal. Nevertheless, the efficacy of the token system in altering bus ridership was demonstrated.

D. Training Self-Help of Welfare Recipients

Welfare recipients have mutual concerns in the community which might be expressed and resolved given united action among community members. However, it is unlikely that such individuals will consistently attend self-help group meetings in which such issues as urban renewal, city government, and education are discussed. Lower socioeconomic status individuals usually participate less than middle class individuals in volunteer organizations (Berelson & Steiner, 1964). Moreover, long-range goals of self-help programs may be too delayed to provide sufficient incentives to attend meetings.

Miller and Miller (1970) increased attendance of welfare recipients at self-help meetings. During the initial phase of the project, a welfare counselor mailed notices to each self-help group member indicating when the next meeting was scheduled. During the reinforcement phase, group members were informed that they could select two free Christmas toys for each of their children if they attended the meeting. Toys were donated by "concerned middle-class citizens." In an ABAB design, the effect of reinforcement on attendance to self-help group meetings was demonstrated. Moreover, while the reinforcement contingency was in effect, new members were attracted to the self-help group. Of course, developing attendance to self-help group meetings is far from resolving the community issues that face welfare recipients. Indeed, attendance alone is unlikely to ensure that the group will actually engage in socially significant activities. Nevertheless, it does suggest that an incentive program might be useful in priming community action. The rewards for community action are usually delayed. A reinforcement program can provide interim incentives to initiate social action.

E. Military Training

Training individuals to function in the military is a task for virtually every government. Typically, initial training is intense and may lead to severe psychological distress. Although basic training is inherently physically demanding, investigators have questioned the necessity of placing recruits under severe psychological stress as part of training (Datel & Legters, 1970). Much of indoctrination into the military and techniques for behavior change are based upon aversive control. Seemingly arbitrary punishments and unnecessary penalties are levied for minor offenses. Moreover, individuals are required to submit and surrender to authority and adhere to demands that may seem unreasonable. Self-devaluation may then result

(Goffman, 1961). Some of the problems of morale may be a function of reliance upon aversive control. An initial attempt to deemphasize aversive control in the military was reported by Datel and Legters (1970). Positive reinforcement for desirable behavior was emphasized rather than punishment for undesirable behavior. The recruits earned tokens for performance at daily inspections, training formations, proficiency in physical combat, marksmanship, written test performance, and work. Performance which surpassed minimal requirements on a task (e.g., drill sergeant's daily evaluation or barracks inspection) achieved extra points. The tokens (punches on a card carried by the trainee) could be spent for a variety of backup reinforcers highly valued by recruits, such as attending a movie, taking an overnight pass off the base, or consideration for promotion. Points were delivered immediately after performance.

Although the purpose of the system was to increase the morale of the recruits and minimize the aversive contingencies usually present, no evidence was provided regarding the success of the program. However, the program represents an initial attempt in only one training camp to modify an institution which has relied heavily on aversive control.

The illustrations of programs applied to social concerns represent the early stages of a technology. Presently, behavior modification is applied primarily to the individuals whose behavior has been identified as problematic. Yet, a technology devoted primarily to amelioration of problems is only in its germinal developmental stage. The analog in medicine would be only *treating* diseases when they occur rather than *preventing* them entirely. When behavioral programs are applied to prevent problems, the technological advances will be more evident. Positive social implications of behavior modification have not yet been realized. Albeit the technology is impressive, extrapolation to social systems will require extensive research beyond that presently available. Additionally, ethical concerns which are aggravated by social applications of therapeutic techniques need to be voiced if not resolved in an interim fashion (cf. Kazdin, 1975; Wheeler, 1973). The feasibility of extrapolations to resolve and prevent social ills is evident. Actual long term advances await further research.

XII. CONCLUDING COMMENTS

Token economy research has progressed substantially since the "early" programs reported in the last decade. The settings in which token economies have been applied have proliferated to include not only psychiatric facilities, institutions for the retarded, educational settings but also the home, correctional facilities, and, indeed, society at large. Further, the complexity and clinical "relevance" of behaviors altered has increased. Severe behaviors which putatively reflect underlying pathology often are included as part of the contingencies. Interestingly, as complex behaviors are altered, it is becoming apparent that the effects of the contingencies are not restricted to those responses initially identified as targets. Response covariation in a number of instances has shown positive changes across a wide range of responses. The number and type of responses altered with token reinforcement either as a result of the direct manipulation of consequent events or as a concomitant effect are impressive.

Research on token economies has advanced in other ways. Experimental designs increasingly reflect a concern with questions that transcend within-subject alternation of baseline and token reinforcement phases. For example, evaluation of the relative effects of different treatment packages including the combined effects of token programs with other therapeutic strategies requires different groups. The increase in between-group program analyses is an addition to, rather than a replacement of, the carefully executed intrasubject functional analyses.

A number of interesting topics are being researched. For example, the relationship of token reinforcement to other operant procedures, such as punishment, and to related disciplines, such as economics, have been explored recently. One fascinating area is the alteration of peer group contingencies to support adaptive target behaviors in select individuals whose behavior is particularly problematic. A related trend in shifting control away from external agents is directed toward behavioral self-control. Although the technology for implementing self-control procedures on a group basis and ensuring that self-consequation is contingent has not been elaborated, preliminary work is promising.

Token economies are beginning to be investigated as a means to ameliorate significant social problems outside of the realm of what has been traditionally included as part of "mental health." Programs are conducted in society at large where control over the clientele and available consequences is substantially less than in closed treatment settings. No doubt the problems encountered in socially relevant research will be enormous. Yet the potential rewards of such work are commensurate with the problems.

Amid the enthusiasm over the progress already made in token economy research and the exciting trends, there remains a major void. There have been relatively few advances in developing a behavioral technology which can be used effectively to maintain behavior and to ensure transfer of training to settings where the contingencies are not rigidly programmed. To many, the long-term maintenance of target behaviors developed through token reinforcement represents an unfulfilled promissory note. The highest priority, in the opinion of the author, is for empirical demonstrations of effective maintenance strategies. A number of techniques, reviewed earlier, are available which provide researchers with some plausible guidelines for maintenance strategies. In many instances, the techniques are based on well established laboratory research. Preliminary results employing only a few of these techniques suggest that response maintenance is by no means an elusive or insurmountable goal. It is surprising, as well as disconcerting, that maintenance of changes is not more thoroughly studied. Of course, it is still important to demonstrate the extent to which token economies can be applied across diverse settings and behaviors. However, the concern in all areas must be with follow-up assessment. In many operant programs follow-up data are gathered. Yet, the follow-up is usually employed to determine whether behavior was accidentally maintained (perhaps through some divine intervention). Follow-up assessment needs to be used to directly test different maintenance strategies. As token economies continue, efforts no doubt will be directed toward this end.

REFERENCES

Allen, D. J., & Magaro, P. A. Measures of change in token-economy programs. *Behaviour Research and Therapy,* 1971, **9,** 311–318.

Arann, L., & Horner, V. M. Contingency management in an open psychiatric ward. *Journal of Behavior Therapy and Experimental Psychiatry,* 1972, **3,** 31–37.

Atthowe, J. M., & Krasner, L. Preliminary report on the application of contingent reinforcement procedures (token economy) on a "chronic" psychiatric ward. *Journal of Abnormal Psychology,* 1968, **73,** 37–43.

Axelrod, S. Comparison of individual and group contingencies in two special classes. *Behavior Therapy,* 1973, **4,** 83–90.

Axelrod, S., Hall, R. V., & Maxwell, A. Use of peer attention to increase study behavior. *Behavior Therapy,* 1972, **3,** 349–351.

Ayllon, T. Intensive treatment of psychotic behaviour by stimulus satiation and food reinforcement. *Behaviour Research and Therapy,* 1963, **1,** 53–62.

Ayllon, T. Some behavioral problems associated with eating in chronic schizophrenic patients. In L. P. Ullmann & L. Krasner (Eds.), *Case studies in behavior modification.* New York: Holt, 1965. Pp. 73–77.

Ayllon, T., & Azrin, N. H. The measurement and reinforcement of behavior of psychotics. *Journal of the Experimental Analysis of Behavior,* 1965, **8,** 357–383.

Ayllon, T., & Azrin, N. H. *The token economy: A motivational system for therapy and rehabilitation.* New York: Appleton, 1968.

Ayllon, T., & Haughton, E. Control of the behavior of schizophrenic patients by food. *Journal of the Experimental Analysis of Behavior,* 1962, **5,** 343–352.

Ayllon, T., & Haughton, E. Modification of symptomatic verbal behavior of mental patients. *Behaviour Research and Therapy,* 1964, **2,** 87–97.

Ayllon, T., & Michael, J. The psychiatric nurse as a behavioral engineer. *Journal of the Experimental Analysis of Behavior,* 1959, **3,** 323–334.

Ayllon, T., & Wright, P. New roles for the paraprofessional. In S. W. Bijou & E. Ribes-Inesta (Eds.), *Behavior modification: Issues and extensions.* New York: Academic Press, 1972. Pp. 115–125.

Azrin, N. H., & Holz, W. C. Punishment. In W. K. Honig (Ed.), *Operant behavior: Areas of research and application.* New York: Appleton, 1966. Pp. 380–447.

Azrin, N. H., & Lindsley, O. R. The reinforcement of cooperation between children. *Journal of Abnormal and Social Psychology,* 1956, **52,** 100–102.

Baer, D. M., Wolf, M. M., & Risley, T. R. Some current dimensions of applied behavior analysis. *Journal of Applied Behavior Analysis,* 1968, **1,** 91–97.

Bailey, J. S., & Iwata, B. A. Reward versus cost token systems: An analysis of effects on students and teacher. *Proceedings of the 81st Annual Convention of the American Psychological Association,* 1973, **8,** 887–888.

Bailey, J. S., Timbers, G. D., Phillips, E. L., & Wolf, M. M. Modification of articulation errors of pre-delinquents by their peers. *Journal of Applied Behavior Analysis,* 1971, **4,** 265–281.

Bailey, J. S., Wolf, M. M., & Phillips, E. L. Home-based reinforcement and the modification of pre-delinquents' classroom behavior. *Journal of Applied Behavior Analysis,* 1970, **3,** 223–233.

Baltes, M. M. Operant principles applied to acquisition and generalization of non-littering behavior in children. *Proceedings of the 81st Annual Convention of the American Psychological Association,* 1973, **8,** 889–890.

Bandura, A., Blanchard, E. B., & Ritter, B. Relative efficacy of desensitization and modeling approaches for inducing behavioral, affective, and attitudinal changes. *Journal of Personality and Social Psychology,* 1969, **13,** 173–199.

Barrett, B. H., & Lindsley, O. R. Deficits in acquisition of operant discrimination and differentiation shown by institutionalized retarded children. *American Journal of Mental Deficiency,* 1962, **67,** 424–436.

Bartlett, D., Ora, J. P., Brown, E., & Butler, J. The effects of reinforcement on psychotic speech in a case of early infantile autism, age 12. *Journal of Behavior Therapy and Experimental Psychiatry,* 1971, **2,** 145–149.

Bennett, P. S., & Maley, R. F. Modification of interactive behaviors in chronic mental patients. *Journal of Applied Behavior Analysis,* 1973, **6,** 609–620.

Berelson, B., & Steiner, G. A. *Human behavior.* New York: Harcourt, 1964.

Bijou, S. W., Peterson, R. F., Harris, F. R., Allen, K. E., & Johnston, M. S. Methodology for experimental studies of young children in natural settings. *Psychological Record,* 1969, **19,** 177–210.

Birky, H. J., Chambliss, J. E., & Wasden, R. A comparison of residents discharged from a token economy and two traditional psychiatric programs. *Behavior Therapy,* 1971, **2,** 46–51.

Bolstad, O. D., & Johnson, S. M. Self-regulation in the modification of disruptive behavior. *Journal of Applied Behavior Analysis,* 1972, **5,** 443–454.

Boren, J. J., & Colman, A. D. Some experiments on reinforcement principles within a psychiatric ward for delinquent soldiers. *Journal of Applied Behavior Analysis,* 1970, **3,** 29–37.

Bucher, B., & Hawkins, J. Comparison of response cost and token reinforcement systems in a class for academic underachievers. In R. D. Rubin, J. P. Brady, &

J. D. Henderson (Eds.), *Advances in behavior therapy*. Vol. 4. New York: Academic Press, 1973. Pp. 271–278.

Buell, J., Stoddard, P., Harris, F., & Baer, D. M. Collateral social development accompanying reinforcement of outdoor play in a preschool child. *Journal of Applied Behavior Analysis,* 1968, **1,** 167–173.

Burchard, J. D., & Barrera, F. An analysis of time-out and response cost in a programmed environment. *Journal of Applied Behavior Analysis,* 1972, **5,** 271–282.

Burchard, J. D., & Tyler, V. O. The modification of delinquent behaviour through operant conditioning. *Behaviour Research and Therapy,* 1965, **2,** 245–250.

Burgess, R. L., Clark, R. N., & Hendee, J. C. An experimental analysis of anti-litter procedures. *Journal of Applied Behavior Analysis,* 1971, **4,** 71–75.

Carlson, C. G., Hersen, M., & Eisler, R. M. Token economy programs in the treatment of hospitalized adult psychiatric patients: Current status and recent trends. *Journal of Nervous and Mental Diseases,* 1972, **155,** 192–204.

Carpenter, P., & Carom, R. Green stamp therapy: Modification of delinquent behavior through food trading stamps. *Proceedings of the 76th Annual Convention, American Psychological Association,* 1968, **3,** 531–532.

Chadwick, B. A., & Day, R. C. Systematic reinforcement: Academic performance of underachieving students. *Journal of Applied Behavior Analysis,* 1971, **4,** 311–319.

Christopherson, E. R., Arnold, C. M., Hill, D. W., & Quilitch, H. R. The home point system: Token reinforcement procedures for application by parents of children with behavior problems. *Journal of Applied Behavior Analysis,* 1972, **5,** 485–497.

Clark, R. N., Burgess, R. L., & Hendee, J. C. The development of antilitter behavior in a forest campground. *Journal of Applied Behavior Analysis,* 1972, **5,** 1–5.

Cohen, R., Florin, I., Grusche, A., Meyer-Osterkamp, S., & Sell, H. The introduction of a token economy in a psychiatric ward with extremely withdrawn chronic schizophrenics. *Behaviour Research and Therapy,* 1972, **10,** 69–74.

Cotler, S. B., Applegate, G., King, L. W., & Kristal, S. Establishing a token economy program in a state hospital classroom: A lesson in training student and teacher. *Behavior Therapy,* 1972, **3,** 209–222.

Datel, W. E., & Legters, L. J. The psychology of the army recruit. Paper presented at the meeting of the American Medical Association, Chicago, June 1970.

Davison, G. C. Appraisal of behavior modification techniques with adults in institutional settings. In C. M. Franks (Ed.), *Behavior therapy: Appraisal and status.* New York: McGraw-Hill, 1969. Pp. 220–278.

DiScipio, W. J., & Trudeau, P. F. Symptom changes and self-esteem as correlates of positive conditioning of grooming in hospitalized psychotics. *Journal of Abnormal Psychology,* 1972, **80,** 244–248.

Dominguez, B., Acosta, T. F., & Carmona, D. Discussion: A new perspective: Chronic patients as assistants in a behavior rehabilitation program in a psychiatric institution. In S. W. Bijou & E. Ribes-Inesta (Eds.), *Behavior modification: Issues and extensions.* New York: Academic Press, 1972. Pp. 127–132.

Drabman, R. S., Spitalnik, R., & O'Leary, K. D. Teaching self-control to disruptive children. *Journal of Abnormal Psychology,* 1973, **82,** 10–16.

Ellsworth, J. R. Reinforcement therapy with chronic patients. *Hospital and Community Psychiatry,* 1969, **20,** 36–38.

Everett, P. B. Use of the reinforcement procedure to increase bus ridership.

Proceedings of the 81st Annual Convention of the American Psychological Association, 1973, **8,** 891–892.

Everett, P. B., Hayward, S. C., & Meyers, A. W. The effects of a token reinforcement procedure on bus ridership, *Journal of Applied Behavior Analysis,* 1974, **7,** 1–9.

Felixbrod, J. J., & O'Leary, K. D. Effects of reinforcement on children's academic behavior as a function of self-determined and externally imposed contingencies. *Journal of Applied Behavior Analysis,* 1973, **6,** 241–250.

Ferritor, D. E., Buckholdt, D., Hamblin, R. L., & Smith, L. The noneffects of contingent reinforcement for attending behavior on work accomplished. *Journal of Applied Behavior Analysis,* 1972, **5,** 7–17.

Ferster, C. B., & DeMyer, M. K. The development of performances in autistic children in an automatically controlled environment. *Journal of Chronic Diseases,* 1961, 13, 312–345.

Ferster, C. B., & DeMyer, M. K. A method for the experimental analysis of the behavior of autistic children. *American Journal of Orthopsychiatry,* 1962, **1,** 87–110.

Fethke, G. C. The relevance of economic theory and technology to token reinforcement systems: A comment. *Behaviour Research and Therapy,* 1972, **10,** 191–192.

Fethke, G. C. Token economies: A further comment. *Behaviour Research and Therapy,* 1973, **11,** 225–226.

Fixsen, D. L., Phillips, E. L., & Wolf, M. M. Achievement Place: Experiments in self-government with predelinquents. *Journal of Applied Behavior Analysis,* 1973, **6,** 31–47.

Freeman, E. H., & Simmons, O. G. *The mental patient comes home.* New York: Wiley, 1963.

Garlington, W. K., & Lloyd, K. E. The establishment of a token economy ward at the State Hospital North in Orofino, Idaho. Paper presented at the research meeting, Fort Steilacoom, Washington, November 1966.

Glynn, E. L. Classroom applications of self-determined reinforcement. *Journal of Applied Behavior Analysis,* 1970, **3,** 123–132.

Glynn, E. L., Thomas, J. D., & Shee, S. M. Behavioral self-control of on-task behavior in an elementary classroom. *Journal of Applied Behavior Analysis,* 1973, **6,** 105–113.

Goffman, E. *Asylums.* Garden City, N.Y.: Anchor Doubleday, 1961.

Goocher, B. E., & Ebner, M. A behavior modification approach utilizing sequential response targets in multiple settings. Paper presented at the meeting of the Midwestern Psychological Association, Chicago, May 1968.

Gripp, R. F., & Magaro, P. A. A token economy program evaluation with untreated control ward comparisons. *Behaviour Research and Therapy,* 1971, **9,** 137–149.

Hall, J., & Baker, R. Token economy systems: Breakdown and control. *Behaviour Research and Therapy,* 1973, **11,** 253–263.

Hall, R. V., Axelrod, S., Tyler, L., Grief, E., Jones, F. C., & Robertson, R. Modification of behavior problems in the home with a parent as observer and experimenter. *Journal of Applied Behavior Analysis,* 1972, **5,** 53–64.

Hartlage, L. C. Subprofessional therapists' use of reinforcement versus traditional psychotherapeutic techniques with schizophrenics. *Journal of Consulting and Clinical Psychology,* 1970, **34,** 181–183.

Hauserman, N., Walen, S. R., & Behling, M. Reinforced racial integration in the first grade: A study in generalization. *Journal of Applied Behavior Analysis,* 1973, **6,** 193–200.

Hauserman, N., Zweback, S., & Plotkin, A. Use of concrete reinforcement to facilitate verbal initiations in adolescent group therapy. *Journal of Consulting and Clinical Psychology,* 1972, **38,** 90–96.

Hawkins, R. P., Peterson, R. F., Schweid, E., & Bijou, S. W. Behavior therapy in the home: Amelioration of problem parent-child relations with the parent in a therapeutic role. *Journal of Experimental Child Psychology,* 1966, **4,** 99–107.

Hayden, T., Osborne, A. E., Hall, S. M., & Hall, R. B. Behavioral effects of price changes in a token economy. *Proceedings of the 80th Annual Convention of the American Psychological Association,* 1972, **7,** 203–204.

Heap, R. F., Boblitt, W. E., Moore, C. H., & Hord, J. E. Behavior-milieu therapy with chronic neuropsychiatric patients. *Journal of Abnormal Psychology,* 1970, **76,** 349–354.

Henderson, J. D. The use of dual reinforcement in an intensive treatment system. In R. D. Rubin & C. M. Franks (Eds.), *Advances in behavior therapy 1968.* New York: Academic Press, 1969. Pp. 201–210.

Henderson, J. D., & Scoles, P. E. A community-based behavioral operant environment for psychotic men. *Behavior Therapy,* 1970, **1,** 245–251.

Herbert, E. W., & Baer, D. M. Training parents as behavior modifiers: Self-recording of contingent attention. *Journal of Applied Behavior Analysis,* 1972, **5,** 139–149.

Hersen, M., & Eisler, R. M. Comments on Heap, Boblitt, Moore, and Hord's "Behavior-milieu therapy with chronic neuropsychiatric patients." *Psychological Reports,* 1971, **29,** 583–586.

Hersen, M., Eisler, R. M., Alford, G. S., & Agras, W. S. Effects of token economy on neurotic depression: An experimental analysis. *Behavior Therapy,* 1973, **4,** 392–397.

Hersen, M., Eisler, R. M., Smith, B. S., & Agras, W. S. A token reinforcement ward for young psychiatric patients. *American Journal of Psychiatry,* 1972, **129,** 142–147.

Hewett, F. M., Taylor, F. D., & Artuso, A. A. The Santa Monica Project: Evaluation of an engineered classroom design with emotionally disturbed children. *Exceptional Children,* 1969, **35,** 523–529.

Horn, J., & Black, W. A. M. The effect of token reinforcement on verbal participation in a social activity with long stay psychiatric patients. *Australian and New Zealand Journal of Psychiatry,* 1974, in press.

Horton, L. E. Generalization of aggressive behavior in adolescent delinquent boys. *Journal of Applied Behavior Analysis,* 1970, **3,** 205–211.

Ingham, R. J., & Andrews, G. An analysis of a token economy in stuttering therapy. *Journal of Applied Behavior Analysis,* 1973, **6,** 219–229.

Isaacs, W., Thomas, J., & Goldiamond, I. Application of operant conditioning to reinstate verbal behavior in psychotics. *Journal of Speech and Hearing Disorders,* 1960, **25,** 8–12.

Johnson, S. M. Self-reinforcement vs. external reinforcement in behavior modification with children. *Developmental Psychology,* 1970, **3,** 147–148.

Johnston, J. M. Punishment of human behavior. *American Psychologist,* 1972, **27,** 1033–1054.

Jones, R., & Kazdin, A. E. Programming response maintenance after withdrawing token reinforcement. *Behavior Therapy,* 1975, in press.

Kagel, J. H., & Winkler, R. C. Behavioral economics: Areas of cooperative research between economies and applied behavior analysis. *Journal of Applied Behavior Analysis,* 1972, **5,** 335–342.

Kale, R. J., Kaye, J. H., Whelan, P. A., & Hopkins, B. L. The effects of reinforcement on the modification, maintenance, and generalization of social responses of mental patients. *Journal of Applied Behavior Analysis,* 1968, **1,** 307–314.

Kanfer, F. H. Self-regulation: Research, issues, and speculations. In C. Neuringer & J. L. Michael (Eds.), *Behavior modification in clinical psychology,* New York: Appleton, 1970. Pp. 178–220.

Kaufman, K. F., & O'Leary, K. D. Reward, cost, and self-evaluation procedures for disruptive adolescents in a psychiatric hospital school. *Journal of Applied Behavior Analysis,* 1972, **5,** 293–309.

Kazdin, A. E. The effect of response cost in suppressing behavior in a pre-psychotic retardate. *Journal of Behavior Therapy and Experimental Psychiatry,* 1971, **2,** 137–140. (a)

Kazdin, A. E. Toward a client administered token reinforcement program. *Education and Training of the Mentally Retarded,* 1971, **6,** 52–55. (b)

Kazdin, A. E. Implementing token programs: The use of staff, patients, and the institution of maximizing change. Paper presented at the sixth annual meeting of the Association for Advancement of Behavior Therapy, New York, October 1972. (a)

Kazdin, A. E. Nonresponsiveness of patients to token economies. *Behaviour Research and Therapy,* 1972, **10,** 417–418. (b)

Kazdin, A. E. Response cost: The removal of conditioned reinforcers for therapeutic change. *Behavior Therapy,* 1972, **3,** 533–546. (c)

Kazdin, A. E. The effect of response cost and aversive stimulation in suppressing punished and nonpunished speech disfluencies. *Behavior Therapy,* 1973, **4,** 73–82. (a)

Kazdin, A. E. The effect of vicarious reinforcement on attentive behavior in the classroom. *Journal of Applied Behavior Analysis,* 1973, **6,** 71–78. (b)

Kazdin, A. E. The failure of some patients to respond to token programs. *Journal of Behavior Therapy and Experimental Psychiatry,* 1973, **4,** 7–14. (c)

Kazdin, A. E. Issues in behavior modification with mentally retarded persons. *American Journal of Mental Deficiency,* 1973, **78,** 134–140. (d)

Kazdin, A. E. Methodological and assessment considerations in evaluating reinforcement programs in applied settings. *Journal of Applied Behavior Analysis,* 1973, **6,** 517–531. (e)

Kazdin, A. E. Role of instructions and reinforcement in behavior changes in token reinforcement programs. *Journal of Educational Psychology,* 1973, **46,** 63–71. (f)

Kazdin, A. E. Time-out for some considerations on punishment. *American Psychologist,* 1973, **28,** 939–941. (g)

Kazdin, A. E. Covert modeling, model similarity, and reduction of avoidance behavior. *Behavior Therapy,* 1974, **5,** 325–340. (a)

Kazdin, A. E. Self-monitoring and behavior change. In M. J. Mahoney & C. E. Thoresen (Eds.), *Self-control: Power to the person.* Belmont, Calif.: Brooks/Cole, 1974. Pp. 218–246. (b)

Kazdin, A. E. *Behavior modification in applied settings.* Homewood, Ill.: Dorsey Press, 1975.

Kazdin, A. E., & Bootzin, R. R. The token economy: An evaluative review. *Journal of Applied Behavior Analysis,* 1972, **5,** 343–372.

Kazdin, A. E., & Bootzin, R. R. The token economy: An examination of issues. In

R. D. Rubin, J. P. Brady, & J. D. Henderson (Eds.), *Advances in behavior therapy*. Vol. 4. New York: Academic Press, 1973. Pp. 159–176.

Kazdin, A. E., & Craighead, W. E. Behavior modification in special education. In L. Mann & D. A. Sabatino (Eds.), *The first review of special education*. Vol. 2. Philadelphia: Buttonwood Farms, 1973. Pp. 51–102.

Kazdin, A. E., & Polster, R. Intermittent token reinforcement and response maintenance in extinction. *Behavior Therapy,* 1973, **4,** 386–391.

Kelleher, R. T., & Golub, L. R. A review of positive conditioned reinforcement. *Journal of the Experimental Analysis of Behavior,* 1962, **5,** 543–597.

Kelley, K. M., & Henderson, J. D. A community-based operant learning environment II: Systems and procedures. In R. D. Rubin, H. Fensterheim, A. A. Lazarus, & C. M. Franks (Eds.), *Advances in behavior therapy 1969*. New York: Academic Press, 1971. Pp. 239–250.

King, G. F., Armitage, S. G., & Tilton, J. R. A therapeutic approach to schizophrenics of extreme pathology: An operant-interpersonal method. *Journal of Abnormal and Social Psychology,* 1960, **61,** 276–286.

Kohlenberg, R., & Phillips, T. Reinforcement and rate of litter depositing. *Journal of Applied Behavior Analysis,* 1973, **6,** 391–396.

Kubany, E. S., Weiss, L. E., & Sloggett, B. B. The good behavior clock: A reinforcement/time out procedure for reducing disruptive classroom behavior. *Journal of Behavior Therapy and Experimental Psychiatry,* 1971, **2,** 173–179.

Lawson, R. B., Greene, R. T., Richardson, J. S., McClure, G., & Padina, R. J. Token economy program in a maximum security correctional hospital. *Journal of Nervous and Mental Diseases,* 1971, **152,** 199–205.

Leitenberg, H. Is time-out from positive reinforcement an aversive event? A review of the experimental evidence. *Psychological Bulletin,* 1965, **64,** 428–441.

Leitenberg, H., Wincze, J., Butz, R., Callahan, E., & Agras, W. Comparison of the effect of instructions and reinforcement in the treatment of a neurotic avoidance response: A single case experiment. *Journal of Behavior Therapy and Experimental Psychiatry,* 1970, **1,** 53–58.

Liberman, R. P. A view of behavior modification projects in California. *Behaviour Research and Therapy,* 1968, **6,** 331–341.

Liberman, R. P. Reinforcement of social interaction in a group of chronic mental patients. In R. D. Rubin, H. Fensterheim, J. D. Henderson, & L. P. Ullmann (Eds.), *Advances in behavior therapy*. New York: Academic Press, 1972. Pp. 151–159.

Lindsley, O. R. Characteristics of the behavior of chronic psychotics as revealed by free-operant conditioning methods. *Diseases of the Nervous System,* 1960, **21** (Monogr. Suppl.), 66–78.

Lloyd, K. E., & Abel, L. Performance on a token economy psychiatric ward: A two year summary. *Behaviour Research and Therapy,* 1970, **8,** 1–9.

Lloyd, K. E., & Garlington, W. K. Weekly variations in performance on a token economy psychiatric ward. *Behaviour Research and Therapy,* 1968, **6,** 407–410.

Lovaas, O. I., Koegel, R., Simmons, J. Q., & Long, J. S. Some generalization and follow-up measures on autistic children in behavior therapy. *Journal of Applied Behavior Analysis,* 1973, **6,** 131–166.

Lovaas, O. I., & Simmons, J. Q. Manipulation of self-destruction in three retarded children. *Journal of Applied Behavior Analysis,* 1969, **2,** 143–157.

Lovitt, T. C., & Curtiss, K. A. Academic response rate as a function of teacher- and self-imposed contingencies. *Journal of Applied Behavior Analysis,* 1969, **2,** 49–53.

McKenzie, H. S., Clark, M., Wolf, M. M., Kothera, R., & Benson, C. Behavior modification of children with learning disabilities using grades as tokens and allowances as back-up reinforcers. *Exceptional Children,* 1968, **34,** 745–752.

McLaughlin, F. T., & Malaby, J. Reducing and measuring inappropriate verbalizations in a token classroom. *Journal of Applied Behavior Analysis,* 1972, **5,** 329–333.

McNamara, H. J., & Wike, E. L. The effects of irregular learning conditions upon the rate and permanence of learning. *Journal of Comparative and Physiological Psychology,* 1958, **51,** 363–366.

McReynolds, W. T., & Church, A. Self-control, study skills development and counseling approaches to the improvement of study behavior. *Behaviour Research and Therapy,* 1973, **11,** 233–235.

McReynolds, W. T., & Coleman, J. Token economy: Patient and staff changes. *Behaviour Research and Therapy,* 1972, **10,** 29–34.

Maley, R. F., Feldman, G. L., & Ruskin, R. S. Evaluation of patient improvement in a token economy treatment program. *Journal of Abnormal Psychology,* 1973, **82,** 141–144.

Mann, J. H. The effect of inter-racial contact on sociometric choices and perceptions. *Journal of Social Psychology,* 1959, **50,** 143–152.

Marks, J., Sonoda, B., & Schalock, R. Reinforcement vs. relationship therapy for schizophrenics. *Journal of Abnormal Psychology,* 1968, **73,** 379–402.

Medland, M. B., & Stachnik, T. J. Good-behavior game: A replication and systematic analysis. *Journal of Applied Behavior Analysis,* 1972, **5,** 45–51.

Meichenbaum, D. H. The effects of instruction and reinforcement on thinking and language behaviour of schizophrenics. *Behaviour Research and Therapy,* 1969, **7,** 101–114.

Meichenbaum, D. H., & Cameron, R. Training schizophrenics to talk to themselves: A means of developing attentional controls. *Behavior Therapy,* 1973, **4,** 515–534.

Meichenbaum, D. H., & Goodman, J. Training impulsive children to talk to themselves: A means of developing self-control. *Journal of Abnormal Psychology,* 1971, **77,** 115–126.

Milby, J. B. A brief review of token economy treatment. Paper presented at the American Psychological Association, Honolulu, September 1972.

Miller, L. K., & Miller, O. L. Reinforcing self-help group activities of welfare recipients. *Journal of Applied Behavior Analysis,* 1970, **3,** 57–64.

Morgan, W. G., & Bass, B. A. Self-control through self-mediated rewards. In R. D. Rubin, J. P. Brady, & J. D. Henderson (Eds.), *Advances in behavior therapy.* Vol. 4. New York: Academic Press, 1973. Pp. 117–126.

Mulligan, W., Kaplan, R. D., & Reppucci, N. D. Changes in cognitive variables among behavior problem elementary school boys treated in a token economy special classroom. In R. D. Rubin, J. P. Brady, & J. D. Henderson (Eds.), *Advances in behavior therapy.* Vol. 4. New York: Academic Press, 1973. Pp. 83–92.

Nordquist, V. M. The modification of a child's enuresis: Some response-response relationships. *Journal of Applied Behavior Analysis,* 1971, **4,** 241–247.

O'Brien, F., & Azrin, N. H. Sympton reduction by functional displacement in a token economy: A case study. *Journal of Behavior Therapy and Experimental Psychiatry,* 1972, **3,** 205–207.

O'Brien, F., Azrin, N. H., & Henson, K. Increased communications of chronic mental patients by reinforcement and response priming. *Journal of Applied Behavior Analysis,* 1969, **2,** 23–29.

O'Leary, K. D., & Drabman, R. Token reinforcement programs in the classroom: A review. *Psychological Bulletin,* 1971, **75,** 379–398.

Olson, R. P., & Greenberg, D. J. Effects of contingency contracting and decision-making groups with chronic mental patients. *Journal of Consulting and Clinical Psychology,* 1972, **38,** 376–383.

Parrino, J. J., George, L., & Daniels, A. C. Token control of pill-taking behavior in a psychiatric ward. *Journal of Behavior Therapy and Experimental Psychiatry,* 1971, **2,** 181–185.

Patterson, G. R. An application of conditioning techniques to the control of a hyperactive child. In L. P. Ullmann & L. Krasner (Eds.), *Case studies in behavior modification.* New York: Holt, 1965. Pp. 370–375.

Paul, G. L. Insight versus desensitization in psychotherapy two years after termination. *Journal of Consulting Psychology,* 1967, **31,** 333–348.

Paul, G. L. Chronic mental patient: Current status—future directions. *Psychological Bulletin,* 1969, **71,** 81–94.

Pendergrass, V. E. Timeout from positive reinforcement following persistent, high-rate behavior in retardates. *Journal of Applied Behavior Analysis,* 1972, **5,** 85–91.

Perline, I., & Levinsky, D. Controlling maladaptive classroom behavior in the severely retarded. *American Journal of Mental Deficiency,* 1968, **73,** 74–78.

Phillips, E. L., Phillips, E. A., Fixsen, D. L., & Wolf, M. M. Achievement Place: Modification of the behaviors of pre-delinquent boys within a token economy. *Journal of Applied Behavior Analysis,* 1971, **4,** 45–59.

Pomerleau, O. F., Bobrove, P. H., & Harris, L. C. Some observations on a controlled social environment for psychiatric patients. *Journal of Behavior Therapy and Experimental Psychiatry,* 1972, **3,** 15–21.

Reisinger, J. J. The treatment of "anxiety-depression" via positive reinforcement and response cost. *Journal of Applied Behavior Analysis,* 1972, **5,** 125–130.

Ruskin, R. S., & Maley, R. F. Item preference in a token economy ward store. *Journal of Applied Behavior Analysis,* 1972, **5,** 373–376.

Sajwaj, T., Twardosz, S., & Burke, M. Side effects of extinction procedures in a remedial preschool. *Journal of Applied Behavior Analysis,* 1972, **5,** 163–175.

Santogrossi, D. A., O'Leary, K. D., Romanczyk, R. G., & Kaufman, K. F. Self-evaluation by adolescents in a psychiatric hospital school token program. *Journal of Applied Behavior Analysis,* 1973, **6,** 277–287.

Schaefer, H. H., & Martin, P. L. *Behavioral therapy.* New York: McGraw-Hill, 1969.

Schick, K. Operants. *Journal of the Experimental Analysis of Behavior,* 1971, **15,** 413–423.

Schmidt, G. W., & Ulrich, R. E. Effects of group contingent events upon classroom noise. *Journal of Applied Behavior Analysis,* 1969, **2,** 171–179.

Scott, R. W., Peters, R. D., Gillespie, W. J., Blanchard, E. B., Edmunson, E. D., & Young, L. D. The use of shaping and reinforcement in the operant acceleration and deceleration of heart rate. *Behaviour Research and Therapy,* 1973, **11,** 179–185.

Shean, J. D., & Zeidberg, Z. Token reinforcement therapy: A comparison of matched groups. *Journal of Behavior Therapy and Experimental Psychiatry,* 1971, **2,** 95–105.

Sherman, J. A., & Baer, D. M. Appraisal of operant therapy techniques with children and adults. In C. M. Franks (Ed.), *Behavior therapy: Appraisal and status.* New York: McGraw-Hill, 1969. Pp. 192–219.

Skinner, B. F. *Science and human behavior.* New York: Macmillan, 1953.

Solomon, R. W., & Wahler, R. G. Peer reinforcement control of classroom problem behavior. *Journal of Applied Behavior Analysis,* 1973, **6,** 49–56.

Staats, A. W., & Butterfield, W. H. Treatment of nonreading in a culturally deprived juvenile delinquent: An application of learning principles. *Child Development,* 1965, **4,** 925–942.

Staats, A. W., Minke, K. A., Finley, J. R., Wolf, M., & Brooks, L. O. A reinforcer system and experimental procedure for the laboratory study of reading acquisition. *Child Development,* 1964, **35,** 209–231.

Staats, A. W., Staats, C. K., Schultz, R. E., & Wolf, M. The conditioning of textual responses using "extrinsic" reinforcers. *Journal of the Experimental Analysis of Behavior,* 1962, **5,** 33–40.

Stayer, S. J., & Jones, F. Ward 108: Behavior modification and the delinquent soldier. Paper presented at the Behavioral Engineering Conference, Walter Reed General Hospital, 1969.

Steeves, J. M., Martin, G. L., & Pear, J. J. Self-imposed time-out by autistic children during an operant training program. *Behavior Therapy,* 1970, **1,** 371–381.

Steffy, R. A., Hart, J., Craw, M., Torney, D., & Marlett, N. Operant behaviour modification techniques applied to severely regressed and aggressive patients. *Canadian Psychiatric Association Journal,* 1969, **14,** 59–67.

Striefel, S. Timeout and concurrent fixed-ratio schedules with human subjects. *Journal of the Experimental Analysis of Behavior,* 1972, **17,** 213–219.

Stuart, R. B. Situational versus self-control. In R. D. Rubin, H. Fensterheim, J. D. Henderson, & L. P. Ullmann (Eds.), *Advances in behavior therapy.* New York: Academic Press, 1972. Pp. 129–146.

Suchotiff, L., Greaves, S., Stecker, H., & Berke, R. Critical variables in the token economy. *Proceedings of the 78th Annual Convention of the American Psychological Association,* 1970, **5,** 517–518.

Sulzbacher, S. I., & Houser, J. E. A tactic to eliminate disruptive behaviors in the classroom: Group contingent consequences. *American Journal of Mental Deficiency,* 1968, **73,** 88–90.

Surratt, P. R., Ulrich, R. E., & Hawkins, R. P. An elementary student as a behavioral engineer. *Journal of Applied Behavior Analysis,* 1969, **2,** 85–92.

Turton, B. K., & Gathercole, C. E. Token economies in the U.K. and Eire. *Bulletin of the British Psychological Society,* 1972, **25,** 83–87.

Twardosz, S., & Sajwaj, T. Multiple effects of a procedure to increase sitting in a hyperactive, retarded boy. *Journal of Applied Behavior Analysis,* 1972, **5,** 73–78.

Upper, D. A "ticket" system for reducing ward rules violations on a token economy program. *Journal of Behavior Therapy and Experimental Psychiatry,* 1973, **4,** 137–140.

Vodde, T. W., & Gilner, F. H. The effects of exposure to fear stimuli on fear reduction. *Behaviour Research and Therapy,* 1971, **9,** 169–175.

Wahler, R. G. Behavior therapy for oppositional children: Love is not enough. Paper read at the Eastern Psychological Association, Washington, D.C., April 1968.

Wahler, R. G., Winkel, G. H., Peterson, R. F., & Morrison, D. C. Mothers as behavior therapists for their own children. *Behaviour Research and Therapy,* 1965, **3,** 113–124.

Walker, H. M., & Buckley, N. K. Programming generalization and maintenance of treatment effects across time and across settings. *Journal of Applied Behavior Analysis,* 1972, **5,** 209–224.

Walker, H. M., Mattson, R. H., & Buckley, N. K. The functional analysis of behavior within an experimental class setting. In W. C. Becker (Ed.), *An empirical basis for change in education.* Chicago: Science Research Associates, 1971. Pp. 236–263.

Wheeler, H. (Ed.), *Beyond the punitive society.* San Francisco: Freeman, 1973.

White, G. D., Nielsen, G., & Johnson, S. M. Timeout duration and the suppression of deviant behavior in children. *Journal of Applied Behavior Analysis,* 1972, **5,** 111–120.

Whitman, T. L., Mercurio, J. R., & Caponigri, V. Development of social responses in two severely retarded children. *Journal of Applied Behavior Analysis,* 1970, **3,** 133–138.

Wickes, I. G. Treatment of persistent enuresis with the electric buzzer. *Archives of Disease in Childhood,* 1958, **33,** 160–164.

Wincze, J. P., Leitenberg, H., & Agras, W. S. The effects of token reinforcement and feedback on the delusional verbal behavior of chronic paranoid schizophrenics. *Journal of Applied Behavior Analysis,* 1972, **5,** 247–262.

Winkler, R. C. Management of chronic psychiatric patients by a token reinforcement system. *Journal of Applied Behavior Analysis,* 1970, **3,** 47–55.

Winkler, R. C. Reinforcement schedules for individual patients in a token economy. *Behavior Therapy,* 1971, **2,** 534–537. (a)

Winkler, R. C. The relevance of economic theory and technology of token reinforcement systems. *Behaviour Research and Therapy,* 1971, **9,** 81–88. (b)

Winkler, R. C. A theory of equilibrium in token economies. *Journal of Abnormal Psychology,* 1972, **79,** 169–173.

Winkler, R. C. A reply to Fethke's comment on "The relevance of economic theory and technology to token reinforcement systems." *Behaviour Research and Therapy,* 1973, **11,** 223–224.

Winkler, R. C., & Krasner, L. The contribution of economics to token economies. Paper presented at the Eastern Psychological Association, New York, April 1971.

Wolf, M. M., Giles, D. K., & Hall, R. V. Experiments with token reinforcement in a remedial classroom. *Behaviour Research and Therapy,* 1968, **6,** 51–64.

Wolf, M. M., Hanley, E. L., King, L. A., Lachowicz, J., & Giles, D. K. The timer-game: A variable interval contingency for the management of out-of-seat behavior. *Exceptional Children,* 1970, **37,** 113–117.

Zifferblatt, S. M. The effectiveness of modes and schedules of reinforcement on work and social behavior in occupational therapy. *Behavior Therapy,* 1972, **3,** 567–578.

THE PROCESS OF INDIVIDUAL BEHAVIOR THERAPY

JOSEPH R. CAUTELA
Department of Psychology
Boston College
Chestnut Hill, Massachusetts
AND
DENNIS UPPER
Brockton Veterans Administration Hospital
Brockton, Massachusetts

I. INTRODUCTION

While a variety of books (Franks, 1969; Lazarus, 1971; Wolpe, 1973) and papers (Beech, 1963; Cahoon, 1968; Cautela, 1965; Davison, 1968; Gelder, 1968; Goldiamond, 1965; Kanfer, 1972; Krasner, 1966; Kushner & Sandler, 1966; Lazarus, 1964; Lomont, 1964; Meyer & Crisp, 1966; Weinberg & Zaslove, 1963) have discussed specific aspects of the individual behavior therapy process, a concise description and analysis of the entire course of behavior therapy with individuals is lacking. The present authors contend that the discipline of behavior therapy has evolved to a point where it is now possible to make a concise and integrated presentation of this treatment orientation. A detailed analysis of the dyadic behavior therapy process is both timely and necessary, in view of the broad expansion in the use of behavioral intervention techniques by individual therapists, increased public awareness of the availability of behaviorally oriented treatment, and the proliferation of clinical training programs which emphasize behavioral approaches (Benassi & Lanson, 1972). The present chapter focuses in detail on the specific phases of the individual treatment process including goals and rationale, behavioral assessment, choice of treatment techniques, problems encountered, the therapist–client interaction, and evaluation of treatment outcome. This chapter is oriented primarily toward the nonbehaviorally oriented clinician and beginning practitioner of behavior modification. This description of the use of behavior modification in individual therapy may also be of value to the sophisticated behavior therapist in that it provides a basis for a comparison with his procedures and viewpoints. Also the experienced therapist and teacher can utilize this overview in the training of graduate students.

II. BEGINNING THE THERAPY RELATIONSHIP

A. Goals

Among the general goals of the individual behavior therapy process are the following: (a) to identify (and for the client and therapist to agree upon) specific client behaviors that need to be altered and that will be the focus of treatment; (b) to apply or to teach the client techniques that will result in the desired behavioral changes, leaving the client with adaptive skills that will be retained after termination of treatment (Cautela, 1969; Goldfried & Merbaum, 1973); and (c) to accomplish this process as efficiently as possible, by continually evaluating the client's progress in achieving the desired behavioral changes and by varying the treatment strategy accordingly.

The behaviors identified as targets for change may be overt or covert, related to each other or discrete, of long standing or recently acquired, and of high or low frequency. The only necessary requirements are that the target behaviors can be specified and that the client and therapist agree that these shall be the focus of treatment. This agreement depends, to a certain extent, upon how well the value systems of therapist and client are matched. It is desirable for the therapist to delineate his own value system as clearly as possible to himself, so that he can use this awareness to correct for his biases when he makes clinical judgments, and to the client, so that he truly may give informed consent for treatment to proceed. For example, a therapist who believes that married couples should stay together at all costs would certainly approach the problem of treating a couple having marital difficulties differently than would a therapist who considers the possibility of treatment leading to separation and divorce. In some cases, the client may have as his goal a therapeutic outcome that is contrary to the therapist's value system (e.g., a person who wishes to reduce his guilt about homosexual behavior while retaining the behavior). Under these circumstances, it is desirable for the therapist to explain the basis for his decision not to work with the client toward achieving this goal, to delineate alternative goals toward which he feels treatment should be directed, and possibly to refer the client to another therapist if this were desirable.

As far as the choice of specific intervention procedures is concerned, it is important to let the client feel, as much as possible, that he is acquiring techniques that will allow him to be his own agent of change. This tends to decrease his dependence upon the therapist, to promote feelings of dignity and self-esteem, and (most important) to increase the probability of successful handling of new problems (or the recurrence of past problems) that may arise. In a sense, then, the process of individual behavior therapy is primarily an educational one, the primary goal of which is increasing the client's adaptive skills and degree of control over his own behavior.

The goal of making the intervention procedures as effective and efficient as possible is one that is central to the individual behavior therapy process. The behavior therapist's approach to the problem of altering the client's maladaptive behaviors is essentially an empirical one, which involves selection of experimentally validated treatment procedures, modification of these procedures in light of individual differences among clients, and evaluating effects of intervention through observable and clearly specified criteria. For example, a behavior therapist probably would define a client's progress in treatment in terms of a decrease in the frequency with which maladaptive behaviors occurred, rather than choosing less operationally defined criteria, such as "increased ego strength" or "greater depth of insight."

It is very useful for the behavior therapist to operationally define treatment goals for the client at the beginning of the therapy process, since these goals dictate the framework within which the client and the therapist will work. Until agreement about these general goals is reached, the formulation and application of specific intervention procedures will be delayed.

B. Expectations and Misconceptions

The client may come to the behavior therapist (as they may do to therapists of other persuasions) with certain preconceptions concerning the goals, techniques, and outcome of treatment. It is useful for the therapist to discuss the client's expectations in these areas, so that any misconceptions can be identified and corrected. Many clients, for example, present themselves for therapy with high expectations of being "cured" in only a few sessions. These clients should be informed that behavior therapy does not offer a rapid, almost miraculous elimination of the client's problems, even though behavioral treatment can be briefer than other types of treatment. It helps if the therapist can provide a general estimate of the probable length of treatment, based upon his experience with similar cases or upon evidence gleaned from the behavior therapy literature. For example, he might say that the successful elimination of a snake phobia generally requires 10–15 sessions.

Related to the misconception that behavior therapy will be very brief is the view that, given a particular problem (e.g., smoking), the behavior therapist applies his techniques immediately and in a standardized, impersonal manner (i.e., almost by rote). In order to prevent the client from becoming impatient while waiting for therapy to "begin," the therapist should inform the client that a careful behavioral analysis is necessary before specific behavioral techniques are applied. Each case (even if it is the 100th smoking-reduction case treated by that particular therapist) requires modifications of the basic strategies based upon individual differences, the client's rate of progress, and problems encountered during therapy.

Clients sometimes expect that treatment techniques will be applied only by the therapist (as in electrical aversion therapy) and that, therefore, less effort will be required on the part of the client than in other types of therapy. The therapist should point out that use of behavioral techniques often requires *more* cooperation and *more* effort on the part of the client than do other kinds of techniques. For example, covert reinforcement (Cautela,

1970b) requires the client's active cooperation in developing, elaborating, and imagining the required scenes, as well as his firm commitment to practicing scenes regularly between sessions.

Finally, the client may have the misconception that behavior therapy is helpful in cases involving simple, overt, and circumscribed behaviors, but that its techniques are insufficient for coping with more complex "emotional" problems. Since this view may lead the client to refrain from discussing information related to problems which he perceives as being outside the domain of behavior therapy, the therapist should indicate to the client (both during the initial behavioral analysis and the course of treatment) his willingness and capability to deal with more generalized problems.

There are a number of expectations that are useful for the therapist to convey to the client during the initial phases of therapy. For example, since the course of therapy rarely runs smoothly, the client should be prepared for possible "bad days." A period of apparent progress may be followed by a relapse, during which the client may feel that he is regressing or that the treatment is not effective. It should be pointed out to the client that sometimes his environment will expose him to stimuli that are strong enough to cancel temporarily the therapeutic gains. For example, if a person who has an intense fear of dogs is chased by a large, playful dog, he may exhibit great panic. This does not indicate that desensitization or covert reinforcement techniques are not effective, but simply that he has not proceeded far enough in the desensitization hierarchy to control his feelings of panic. In another example, if a patient's treatment is directed toward decreasing the frequency of homosexual urges and there have been only a few covert sensitization (Cautela, 1967) or electrical aversion sessions, it is quite possible that the reinforcing properties of a homosexual contact will override the effects of the early stages of treatment, resulting in even a large number of homosexual contacts during this period.

In terms of creating positive expectations, Wolpe (1958) argues that it is also desirable for the behavior therapist to reassure the client that all his reactions are explicable and that there is no virtue in immediately confronting the phobic defect unless the therapist plans to use flooding techniques (Baum, 1970; DeMoor, 1970) or implosive therapy (Stampfl & Levis, 1967). In the former case, clients who periodically experience acute anxiety or high frequency depressive thoughts (whose origins are unclear) often express less apprehension when they are made aware that these problematic behaviors have identifiable antecedents (which are determined by the therapist and client through careful behavioral analysis). In the latter case, the client's apprehensions with respect to "facing up" to the situations that evoke anxiety may decrease his motivation to cooperate with the therapist. When this seems to be the case, it is beneficial to inform the client that graduated and controlled exposure to disturbing stimuli are more likely to be effective, and that therapy will be aimed at *gradually* reducing the anxiety-evoking potential of these stimuli.

C. Social Reinforcement

Although experienced therapists of both behavioral and nonbehavioral persuasions generally display a facility in shaping the client's verbalizations in the desired direction, behavior therapists attempt to accomplish this in a more systematic fashion. The process of behavioral change begins from the moment that the therapist and client first meet. Social reinforcement provided by the therapist is extremely important, since it influences the frequency with which the client emits certain kinds of verbal behaviors, his choice of content areas, and the nature of the rapport (or "transference") between therapist and client. In general, the more effective the therapist is as a social reinforcer to his client, the more effective he will be in changing the client's behavior.

The therapist provides three types of social response following the client's behavior: (a) reinforcement (e.g., expressing verbal agreement, approval, praise, or encouragement, smiling, nodding, paying attention); (b) extinction (remaining silent, looking away, changing the subject); or (c) punishment (expressing disagreement or disapproval, shaking head, showing facial disapproval). In addition to the general procedures of reinforcing the client for appropriate therapeutic verbalizations and extinguishing those that are irrelevant or tangential, the therapist may provide selective attention and reinforcement as an integral part of treatment. For example, in the course of teaching a patient to decrease depressive ideation by using thought-stopping, the therapist might also extinguish or punish verbalizations about depressive thoughts that occur during the course of the therapy sessions. The goal is not only to alter the frequency of the client's overt, verbal behaviors, but to decrease covert maladaptive ones as well (i.e., what the client "says to himself," Meichenbaum, 1971). The appropriate manipulation of reinforcement contingencies by the therapist enhances the effectiveness of the structured behavior therapy techniques being used, as well as the client's motivation to make use of the procedures between sessions.

It is important to note that the client's selective attention and social reinforcement can shape the therapist's behavior as well. Krasner (1963) contends that, "behavioral control is a two-way affair and counter-controls are being asserted by the patients. Yet, part of the training of the therapist is to be able to counter the counter-controls and, to the extent that he can do so, he will be a successful therapist [p. 603]." A specific, session-to-session treatment plan (which he presents to and discusses with the client) serves to impose some structure on therapy sessions and to reduce prolonged discussion by the client of issues which are related only tangentially to the therapy process.

III. BEHAVIORAL ANALYSIS, ASSESSMENT, AND DIAGNOSIS

Central to the process of individual behavior therapy is the behavioral analysis (or assessment)—both formal and informal—that occurs throughout treatment. Cautela (1968) has noted that there is a widespread misunderstanding about the role of assessment in behavior therapy. In general, behavioral assessment procedures have been regarded as simple, almost perfunctory ones. This view probably has developed for the following reasons:

1. The basic principles underlying behavior therapy procedures are relatively specific and well defined, and, because of this, the "cure" may seem relatively "cut-and-dried" (i.e., it appears that all that is necessary is to identify the bad habit and to use a simple conditioning procedure to eliminate it).

2. Published reports describing behavior therapy cases generally do not include many important details that are necessary for a full understanding of the diagnostic and treatment procedures that have been used by the therapist.

Behavioral analysis and assessment usually occur in three overlapping stages. In the first stage, the maladaptive behaviors that will be the focus of therapy (together with their antecedents and consequences) are identified. In the second stage, the therapist develops and applies treatment strategies. This process generally involves three phases—deciding upon specific treatment procedures, evaluating the on-going therapy process, and deciding when to terminate treatment. In the third stage, an evaluation of treatment outcome is undertaken.

Central to the process of behavioral analysis is the operational definition of the client's problems. As opposed to the psychodynamic orientation, which focuses on the characteristics an individual "has," the behavioral view of human functioning emphasizes what a person "does" in various situations (Mischel, 1968). Because the successful implementation of behavior therapy techniques depends directly upon an adequate assessment of the specific behaviors in need of change and those variables maintaining these behaviors, the behavior therapist chooses as the basic unit for his consideration the client's response to specific aspects of his environment. Behavior is seen as being determined not only by the client's social learning history but also by the current environmental antecedents and/or consequences of the behavior in question (Goldfried & Kent, 1972).

Rather than making use of traditional broad-gauge test instruments that purport to reveal essential personality mechanisms, behavior therapists use pretreatment assessment procedures for the following purposes (Kanfer, 1972): (a) to help pinpoint specific target behaviors which, if altered, would alleviate the client's discomforts or inefficiencies, and which are potentially changeable by the means at the therapist's and the client's disposal; (b) to reveal the psychological and biological resources of the client (and of the client's environment) that could be utilized in bringing about behavioral changes; and (c) to offer some clues concerning the appropriateness of different therapeutic techniques for the individual client's set of problems.

A variety of structured assessment instruments have been useful to behavior therapists in their formulation of treatment strategies and evaluation of treatment effectiveness. *Life-history questionnaires,* such as Cautela's Behavioral Analysis History Questionnaire (1970a) and Wolpe's Life History Questionnaire (see Wolpe, 1969), when filled out by the client, provide the therapist with demographic and background data such as current marital and vocational status, family, religious, sexual, health, and educational histories, and specific information concerning the problems for which the client seeks therapy.

Problem checklists, such as the Behavioral Self-Rating Checklist (Upper, Cautela, & Brooke, 1974) (see Table I) ask the client to review a relatively extensive list of problematic behaviors and to indicate those that are causing him particular difficulty. An advantage of using comprehensive checklists of this type is that they require the client to assess the adaptiveness of his functioning in a wide variety of behavioral areas, which may result in his identifying some problems on the checklist which he might not have brought up in general discussion with the therapist (and which might be related to the primary problems he presents).

A variety of *survey schedules* are designed to provide detailed information which the therapist needs in order to make use of a particular therapeutic technique, such as systematic desensitization or covert reinforcement. Among these are (a) the Reinforcement Survey Schedule (Cautela, 1972; Cautela & Kastenbaum, 1967) and Homme's Reinforcement Menu (Homme, Csanyi, Gonzales, & Rechs, 1969), which ask the client to evaluate the reinforcement value of a variety of items and experiences that may be used as reinforcers in overt or covert conditioning programs; (b) the Fear Survey Schedule (Wolpe & Lang, 1964), which asks the client to rate a series of objects and experiences in terms of their fear-evoking potential, usually as a precursor to desensitization or covert sensitization treatment; and (c) the Cues for Tension and Anxiety Survey Schedule (Cautela, 1973b), on which the client indicates the specific ways in which he feels tense or anxious (e.g., rapid heartbeat, tension in neck muscles, tingling sensations in the limbs), information which is used by the therapist in developing an individualized program of relaxation and self-control.

Self-monitoring and behavioral recording charts can be quite useful in giving the therapist and client specific information about the frequency, time, and place of occurrence, and fluctuations over time of the target behaviors of interest. For example, the therapist may ask a client he is treating for obesity to keep records of each item eaten, the quantity eaten (and perhaps its caloric value), when and where the eating occurred, and any other variable of interest. Having the client (or someone else in his environment) keep a regular count of the frequency of the target behaviors being treated provides on-going feedback, from session to session, about the effectiveness of the treatment procedures, just as pretreatment baseline recordings provide the therapist and client with a basis for judging the ultimate success of the intervention procedures. Regular recording also permits the early identification and correction of any problems that may arise during treatment, such as the client's failure to practice or to implement prescribed techniques.

In general, these structured assessment instruments are administered by having the client fill them out between therapy sessions, which does not necessitate taking time during treatment sessions for their administration. Since many of the behavioral treatment techniques require that the client perform "homework" assignments (i.e., practice specific procedures) between sessions, this type of assessment procedure both establishes the expectation that therapy consists of more than what goes on in the therapist's office and provides a behavioral sample that serves to evaluate the client's cooperation. If, for example, the client fails to return the completed instruments at the assigned time or hurriedly fills them out just before entering the therapist's office, it may be necessary for the therapist to stress the importance of completing assignments, particularly to avoid unnecessary prolongation of treatment.

The wide variety of assessment instruments currently in use is a measure of the creativity which has marked the growth of the field. If a therapist finds that he is treating a number of clients with the same general complaint (e.g., high alcoholic intake, frequent thoughts about suicide), he may find it useful to devise his own questionnaire or rating scale, which is designed to elicit information of particular interest. The behavior therapist evaluates each of the assessment instruments in detail with the client, asking him to elaborate upon his responses, to give specific examples of situations in which the problematic behaviors in question occurred, and to indicate any relation-

TABLE I

Behavioral Self-Rating Checklist

Name ______________________________ Date ________________

Directions: The behaviors that a person learns determine to a large extent how well he gets along in life. Below is a list of behaviors that can be learned. Check the ones that *you* think you need to learn in order to function more effectively or to be more comfortable.

I need to learn:

____ 1. to stop drinking too much.
____ 2. to stop smoking too much.
____ 3. to stop eating too much.
____ 4. to control my feelings of attraction to members of my own sex.
____ 5. to control my feelings of attraction to members of the opposite sex.
____ 6. to overcome my feelings of nausea when I'm nervous.
____ 7. to stop thinking about things that depress me.
____ 8. to stop thinking about things that make me anxious.
____ 9. to feel less anxious in crowds.
____10. to feel less anxious in high places.
____11. to stop worrying about my physical condition.
____12. to feel less anxious in airplanes.
____13. to stop stuttering.
____14. to stop washing my hands so often.
____15. to stop cleaning or straightening things up so often.
____16. to stop biting my fingernails.
____17. to take better care of my physical appearance.
____18. to feel less anxious in enclosed places.
____19. to feel less anxious in open places.
____20. to feel less afraid of pain.
____21. to feel less afraid of blood.
____22. to feel less anxious about contamination or germs.
____23. to feel less anxious about being alone.
____24. to feel less afraid of the darkness.
____25. to feel less afraid of certain animals.
____26. to stop thinking the same thoughts over and over.
____27. to stop counting my heartbeats.
____28. to stop hearing voices.
____29. to stop thinking people are against me or out to get me.
____30. to stop seeing strange things.
____31. to stop wetting the bed at night.
____32. to stop taking medicine too much.
____33. to stop taking too many pills.
____34. to stop taking dope.
____35. to stop having headaches.
____36. to control my urge to gamble.
____37. to be able to fall asleep at night.
____38. to control my desire to expose myself.

TABLE I (*Continued*)

____39. to control my desire to put on clothing of the other sex.
____40. to control my feelings of sexual attraction to other people's clothing, or belongings.
____41. to control my sexual feelings toward young children.
____42. to control my desire to hurt other people or be hurt.
____43. to control my desire to steal.
____44. to control my tendency to lie.
____45. to stop daydreaming a lot.
____46. to control my desire to yell at or hit other people when I'm angry.
____47. to manage money better so that I have enough for what I really need.
____48. to stop saying "crazy" things to other people.
____49. how to carry on a conversation with other people.
____50. to feel more comfortable carrying on a conversation with other people.
____51. to stop bugging other people too much.
____52. to be less forgetful.
____53. to stop thinking about committing suicide.
____54. to control my urge to set fires.
____55. to hold down a steady job.
____56. to feel comfortable on my job.
____57. to stop swearing at other people.
____58. how not to be upset when others criticize me.
____59. to speak up when I feel I'm right.
____60. to stop putting off things that need to be done.
____61. to stop thinking so much about things that make me feel guilty.
____62. to feel less anxious when my work is being supervised.
____63. to feel less anxious about sexual thoughts.
____64. to feel less anxious about kissing.
____65. to feel less anxious about petting.
____66. to feel less anxious about sexual intercourse.
____67. to be able to make decisions when I have to.
____68. to feel at ease just being with other people in a group.
____69. to feel at ease talking with other people in a group.
____70. to feel less anxious about ____________________.
____71. to control my desire to ____________________.
____72. to feel less guilty about ____________________.
____73. to change my ____________________.

ships he sees between his problematic behaviors and environmental factors. An important by-product of this detailed analysis of the client's behavior is that the client is the recipient of useful feedback which enables him to initiate behavior changes immediately. Often the mere process of counting the number of times a maladaptive behavior occurs results in a more determined effort on the client's part to change the rate of that behavior. The behavioral assessment process also provides the therapist with an opportunity to give the client new labels for his own behavior. For example, the client who says to himself, "I need to reduce the frequency of my drinking behavior and to control my urges to drink alcoholic beverages" will probably express greater optimism about treatment success and cooperation in treatment than will the client who says, "I'm a hopeless alcoholic."

In general, most behavior therapists find diagnostic labels derived from standard psychiatric nomenclature (e.g., "anxiety neurosis, with depressive features") to be of little value. Aside from the stigmatizing and dehumanizing aspects of such a labeling process (see Laing, 1967), criticisms have been leveled at the traditional system of psychiatric classification on purely practical grounds (Arthur, 1969; Ferster, 1966; Phillips & Draguns, 1971). Among these are: (a) that they are not based on any one consistent classificatory principle, but mix together categories based on behavior, age, severity, etiology, etc.; (b) that they are not based upon meaningful and discernible behaviors; and (c) that they do not address the question of what type of intervention is needed in order to help the person whose behavior disorder is being classified.

In order to meet the need for a standardized system for classifying behavioral disorders based upon clearly defined behaviors and related to therapeutic intervention procedures, Cautela and Upper (1973) recently have devised the Behavioral Coding System (B.C.S.). The B.C.S. includes 283 specific maladaptive behaviors, divided into 21 major behavioral categories (e.g., fears, sex, imagery, vocational adjustment, emotional behavior). It is both a viable alternative to current psychiatric classification systems and a useful adjunct to the problem-oriented record-keeping procedures that have recently come into vogue.

In individual therapy, the therapist and client can discuss the behavioral assessment material and can agree upon the appropriate behavioral diagnosis. The problematic behaviors can be listed in the order in which they will be treated during the course of therapy. Since the behavioral diagnosis is directly related to specific client behaviors, the stigmatizing aspects of psychiatric labeling are absent.

Following the process of behavioral assessment and diagnosis, the specific treatment strategy is formulated: (a) which maladaptive behaviors to treat (and in what order to treat them); (b) which intervention techniques to use; (c) how to begin; (d) how quickly to proceed; and (e) how to evaluate progress. The therapist's decisions about which behaviors to treat first and how quickly to begin often are influenced by the severity of the problem behavior and its consequences. For example, the client may be having frequent and serious thoughts about committing suicide or may be in danger of losing his job. Sometimes there are other less serious kinds of situations that necessitate rapid behavioral change, such as the case of a female client who had a phobia about public speaking but wanted to give a valedictory address at her college commencement ceremonies.

If the client is pessimistic about his ability to change his behaviors (or has been unsuccessful in previous therapy situations), the therapist may select as the first behavior to be modified one that has proved to be relatively easy to change (e.g., mild attacks of anxiety, which can be controlled by using progressive relaxation). If the client has a success experience during the early stages of therapy, he may be much more motivated to deal with those problems that are more complex and require a fair amount of time to modify.

IV. TREATMENT CHOICE

The therapist's choice of the appropriate treatment procedures for changing the client's problematic behaviors depends upon a number of factors, including the nature of the problem, client characteristics, treatment setting, significant others in the client's environment, and therapist variables.

A. Nature of the Problems

As was mentioned above, there are instances when the client's maladaptive behaviors are serious enough (in terms of danger to the client, others, or potential degree of interference with his life) to require immediate intervention. In these cases, a technique that is likely to produce immediate behavioral changes (e.g., contingent electrical stimulation) would be the treatment of choice. In dealing with behaviors that occur at a low rate (e.g., as those subsumed under the rubric "depression"), the use of positive reinforcement procedures might be indicated. On the other hand, thought-stopping might be the treatment of choice when the client is emitting high-frequency behaviors, such as anxiety-evoking thoughts.

The comparative efficacy of different treatment techniques applicable to the same maladaptive behavior should be determined through controlled clinical research. Contraindications to the use of specific techniques with certain clinical problems should also be determined through theoretical speculation, anecdotal observation, and experimental investigation.

B. Client Variables

There are a number of client variables, including age, intellectual level, and physiological problems, that need to be considered in selecting intervention procedures. For example, techniques involving electrical aversion or thought-stopping (i.e., shouting "Stop!") should be avoided when the client is physically incapacitated or elderly. Very young children (three years old or younger) may have difficulty using imagery procedures, and operant behavior-shaping procedures probably would be more appropriate than covert conditioning techniques with persons who function at a low level intellectually. Organic limitations such as blindness may preclude the use of techniques involving imagery (e.g., desensitization) unless the therapeutic procedures are modified accordingly (Monroe & Ahr, 1972). Information taken from structured assessment instruments (e.g., the life-history questionnaires cited above) is extremely useful in tailoring the intervention procedures to the individual client, by taking into account his specific strengths and weaknesses.

C. Treatment Settings and Dealing with Significant Others

In many instances, the treatment procedure is partly determined by an individual's living arrangements vis-à-vis significant others. If a private client is in a hospital ward or living in another institutional setting, a procedure should be chosen that emphasizes self-control and can easily be supplemented by ward staff. In our experience, it is futile to treat a client in an institution without ward cooperation in terms of record-keeping, continuing treatment procedures employed in private sessions, and consequating appropriate and inappropriate behavior in a systematic manner. If this caution is not heeded, the clinician will find that while he is making progress in the 1-hour session, the progress is often being nullified by staff members not under his direct supervision.

There are a number of treatment strategies that require (or at least are enhanced by) the cooperation of significant others in the client's environment. This approach is quite different from that espoused by Freud (1912b), who expressed despair about working cooperatively with relatives. For example, in dealing with sexual incompatibility, it is almost always useful for the therapist to see both members involved. In fact, some therapists will refuse to treat only one member of a couple who are experiencing sexual problems because these therapists feel that their attempts to change the client's sexual behavior without the cooperation of his partner may be destined for failure.

There are a number of methods for helping a client with his problems vis-à-vis another person without the active cooperation of that person. Situations in which the client interacts with another person can be created through the use of imagery. Roleplaying and modeling procedures can be used both to change the client's interpersonal behaviors and to teach him ways of shaping the behavior of significant others. If behavioral analysis indicates that other people in the client's environment are reinforcing maladaptive behavior and if the therapist cannot enlist their cooperation in helping the client to change, covert extinction (Cautela, 1971a) can be used to overcome the reinforcing effect of the other individual's behavior. In this situation, the client is asked to imagine himself performing the maladaptive behavior in the other person's presence without eliciting a reinforcing response from that person. For example, a wife who frequently complains of physical problems in order to prevent her husband from going out in the evening would be asked to imagine situations in which she voices a physical complaint but he leaves nevertheless. It is necessary for the therapist to be ingenious enough to devise therapeutic strategies that can be of help even if the cooperation of significant others is minimal or nonexistent.

D. Therapist Variables

The therapist's selection of certain treatment strategies depends upon a number of factors related to his training, clinical experience, and even (in some cases) aesthetic preferences. Among the specific variables involved in his choice are his degree of familiarity with various procedures, the degree of success he has had in using different techniques, and perhaps even his curiosity and interest in testing a procedure with which he is relatively unfamiliar or which he is devising.

Some therapists do not use aversive techniques (at least overt ones such as electrical or chemical aversion) for aesthetic reasons—they simply do not like to administer pain- or nausea-evoking stimuli. A number of therapists have reported that they have difficulty using covert sensitization (Cautela, 1966, 1967) because it makes *them* nauseous or because they feel uncomfortable about producing feelings of nausea in others. Of course, if the therapist experiences discomfort about applying a particular procedure, this may have an adverse effect on the efficacy of the treatment techniques used. It may be desirable in some cases for the therapist to desensitize himself to using a particular therapeutic procedure or to neutralize the aversive components of the procedure by reinforcing himself (either overtly or covertly) for using it when indicated.

E. Specific Treatment Procedures

A classification of the most commonly used treatment procedures is presented in Table II. The procedures are classified according to two general criteria: (a) whether the procedures are overt or covert, and (b) whether

TABLE II

Classification of Treatment Procedures

Covert Manipulation	Overt Manipulation
Nonaversive procedures	
1. Desensitization (Wolpe, 1958)	1. Contingency contracting (Homme, *et al.*, 1963)
2. Emotive imagery (Lazarus & Abramovitz, 1962)	2. Relaxation (Jacobson, 1938)
3. Coverant control (Homme, 1965)	3. Shaping (Barlow, Agras, Leitenberg, & Wincze, 1970)
4. Covert positive reinforcement (Cautela, 1970c)	4. Prompting (Lovaas, Frietag, Nelson, & Whalen, 1967)
5. Covert modeling (Cautela, 1971b)	5. Fading (McCrady, 1973)
6. Guided imagery (Wolpin & Pearsall, 1966)	6. Use of tape recorder (Schwitzgebel, 1963)
	7. Record-keeping (Watson & Tharp, 1972)
	8. Modeling (Bandura, 1971)
	9. Behavioral rehearsal (Wolpe, 1973, pp. 91–94)
	10. Bio-feedback (Shapiro, Barber, DiCara, Kamiya, Miller, & Stoyva, 1972)
	11. Social reinforcement (Agras, Leitenberg, & Barlow, 1968; Krasner, 1962).
	a. verbal (Meichenbaum, 1971)
	b. nonverbal (Ayllon & Michael, 1959)
	12. Contingent reinforcers (Ayllon & Azrin, 1968a)
	a. tokens (Ayllon & Azrin, 1968a; Krasner & Atthowe, 1968)
	b. food (Ayllon, 1963)
	13. Assertive training (Wolpe, 1970)
	14. Self-reinforcement (Rehm & Marston, 1968)
	15. *In vivo* desensitization (Wolpe, 1973)
	16. Reinforcement sampling (Ayllon & Azrin, 1968b)

(*continued*)

they are primarily aversive or nonaversive. Some procedures, such as contingency contracting (Homme, deBaca, Devine, Steinhorst, & Rickert, 1963) or covert modeling (Cautela, 1971b), involve either aversive or nonaversive stimulation, and these appear in more than one category. In the interest of simplicity, some procedures have been labeled as "aversive" even though they may increase response probability (e.g., negative reinforcement) or

TABLE II (*Continued*)

Aversive procedures	
1. Covert sensitization (Cautela, 1966)	1. Punishment a. electrical aversion (Lovaas, Schaeffer, & Simmons, 1965) b. chemical aversion (Revusky, 1973) c. social aversion (Ayllon & Michael, 1959)
2. Covert negative reinforcement (Cautela, 1970b)	2. Negative reinforcement (Wolpe, 1973, p. 214)
3. Covert extinction (Cautela, 1971a)	3. Timeout (Sachs, 1973)
4. Covert response cost (Cautela, 1974)	4. Response cost (Kazdin, 1973)
5. Covert modeling (Cautela, 1971b)	5. Shame therapy (Serber, 1970)
6. Thought-stopping (Cautela, 1969; Taylor, 1963; Wolpe, 1973)	6. Extinction (Ayllon & Michael, 1959)
7. Implosive therapy (Morganstern, 1973; Stampfl & Levis, 1967)	7. Contingency contracting (Homme *et al.*, 1963)
8. Flooding (Baum, 1970; DeMoor, 1970)	8. Negative practice (Dunlap, 1932)
	9. Aversion-relief (Thorpe, Schmidt, Brown, & Castell, 1964)
	10. Satiation (Ayllon, 1963)

when the presentation of a noxious stimulus is not involved (e.g., extinction), since the withholding of positive reinforcement may be experienced as unpleasant by the client. Some of the more general procedures (e.g., contingency contracting) may subsume specific procedures, such as social reinforcement and response cost (Kazdin, 1973).

V. ASSESSING THE EFFICACY OF THE TREATMENT STRATEGY

The therapist must constantly assess the efficacy of the treatment procedures being employed by obtaining behavioral feedback from the client, by directly observing the client, and by listening to the verbal reports of the client and of others. In some cases, direct feedback on the effectiveness of the procedures is relatively easy to obtain, as in the case of weighing a client who is being treated for obesity. But in many cases the therapist must rely upon the client's verbal reports. If there is any reason to doubt the client's report, there are a number of ways in which the therapist can test its validity. For example, if the client is being treated for fear of elevators, the therapist can accompany the client to a place which has an elevator and can observe the client's behavior directly. He can also obtain reports from family members or friends. In situations in which there are discrepancies between the reports of a client and another observer, the therapist should check other sources of information.

Before deciding that a particular treatment is not effective, the therapist must ensure that enough time has elapsed for new learning to have taken place. The treatment choice may be correct, but the client may not be following directions properly or may not be engaging in the necessary practice. There is no easily applied rule to help decide how long a procedure should be continued without producing a noticeable change in behavior. Variables such as the degree of severity of the client's problems, as well as the nature of the treatment procedure, must be considered. For example, covert sensitization may require fewer trials than covert extinction, and aversive electric shock may require fewer trials than covert sensitization in eliminating a certain behavior.

VI. MODIFICATION OF THE TREATMENT STRATEGY

After formulating a treatment strategy and attempting to implement it through the application of specific procedures, the therapist may find that conditions arise that necessitate modification of the treatment program. For example, the client may find the procedure distasteful or may have difficulty in accepting the rationale for its use. If the therapist cannot reduce the client's reluctance to use a particular procedure (by repeating the rationale and by giving examples of its effective use), it may be necessary to consider other procedures. A good indication that something is wrong either in the choice of a procedure or its implementation is that progress (i.e., the degree of change from the client's pretreatment rate of behaving) is lacking or minimal. When this occurs, it is necessary to reassess the behavioral antecedents and consequences and to examine the ways in which the treatment procedure is being employed. The therapist may find that, although the client is cooperating when the technique is applied in the treatment setting, he/she does not implement the procedure between sessions. This may necessitate modifying the procedures, reinforcing the client for better cooperation, or adopting other techniques.

Overcoming Problems in Cooperation

As was mentioned above, often it is necessary for the client to work on his problems between sessions with the therapist, in order to make therapy more efficient in terms of time, to teach self control, and to increase the probability of generalization to the natural environment (see Table III for an instrument for assessing the client's motivation). Among the specific

TABLE III

Motivation for Behavior Change Scale (MBCS)

Date ______________________________

Name ______________________________

1. Frequency of verbal behavior indicating the client wants treatment.
   a. Not at all. ( )
   b. A little. ( )
   c. A fair amount. ( )
   d. Much. ( )
   e. Very much. ( )
2. Intensity of desire for treatment as expressed by verbal behavior.
   a. Not at all; e.g., I really don't want to change. ( )
   b. A little intensity; e.g., I don't want to change but my (wife) (husband) (children) (parents) want me to so I might as well try. ( )
   c. A fair amount of intensity; e.g., I'm ambivalent about it, sometimes I want to stop (change) and sometimes I don't. ( )
   d. Much intensity; e.g., I guess I really should change. ( )
   e. Very much intensity; e.g., I really want to change, believe me. ( )
3. Number of appointments missed.
   a. Cancels or fails to show up for appointments over 60% of the time. ( )
   b. Cancels or fails to show up for appointments around 40% to 60% of the time. ( )
   c. Cancels or fails to show up for appointments around 20% to 40% of the time. ( )
   d. Cancels or fails to show up for appointments around 10% to 20% of the time. ( )
   e. Cancels or fails to show up for appointments around 5% to 10% of the time. ( )
   f. Rarely, and then with good reason. ( )
4. Record keeping.
   a. Never keeps records as required. ( )
   b. Keeps records occasionally and omits some data. ( )
   c. Keeps records occasionally and includes all relevant data. ( )
   d. Keeps records consistently but omits some data. ( )
   e. Keeps records consistently and includes all relevant data. ( )
5. Does homework assignments.
   a. Not at all. ( )
   b. Occasionally and incomplete. ( )
   c. Occasionally and completes assignment. ( )
   d. Regularly but does not complete assignment. ( )
   e. Regularly and completes assignment. ( )
6. During the therapy session the client:
   a. Refuses to answer any questions. ( )
   b. Refuses to answer some of the questions with evasion. ( )
   c. Tries to answer some questions without evasion. ( )
   d. Tries to answer most of the questions without evasion. ( )
   e. Answers all the questions without evasion. ( )
7. Pays attention (looks at therapist, answers questions promptly, follows directions easily, etc.).
   a. Not at all. ( )
   b. A little. ( )
   c. A fair amount of the time. ( )
   d. Most of the time. ( )
   e. All the time. ( )

Total Score ____

situations that require this kind of cooperation from the client are the following:

1. While learning the technique of progressive relaxation, the client usually is asked to practice relaxing at least twice a day between sessions.

2. After being taught how to do thought-stopping, the client is told to use the technique whenever unwanted thoughts occur.

3. As part of a program of assertive training, the client may be required to assert himself whenever possible between visits to the therapist, or to show more assertive behavior whenever he finds himself in a particular type of situation (e.g., when he is being unfairly criticized by his parents).

4. Contingency contracting requires the performance of certain adaptive behaviors (e.g., completing homework) before other behaviors (e.g., turning on the television) may be performed, and the client may be asked to behave according to certain response-reinforcement contingencies.

5. For many of the behaviors to be modified, it is desirable for the client to keep accurate daily records of behavioral frequency, antecedents, consequences, etc.

6. When covert conditioning procedures are used, the client is asked to practice every day the scenes that were developed during the therapy session—it also is useful if the client (particularly if he is being treated for a maladaptive approach behavior such as overeating) runs through a series of covert sensitization or covert extinction scenes as soon as possible following any behavioral "slips" (i.e., instances in which he performs the target maladaptive behavior).

Frequently, the client's maladaptive behaviors are so reinforcing that he/she experiences difficulty in changing them. This is particularly true in the case of addictive behaviors, such as smoking or drug use. If the maladaptive behavior results in consequences that are a main source of reinforcement for the client, it may be desirable for the therapist to increase the general sources of reinforcement for the client. This can be done by encouraging reinforcer sampling (Ayllon & Azrin, 1968b), by helping the client to restructure his environment so that it is more reinforcing, and by training the client to engage in more positive scanning of his environment.

In addition to increasing the client's overall level of reinforcement, a number of specific procedures can be used to increase his cooperation. It may be necessary to use shaping procedures in order to elicit cooperation in record keeping. It is helpful for the therapist to show the client how to fill out record-keeping forms and to provide forms that make recording easy. It is useful to develop a schedule for practicing homework, and to instruct the client to record how frequently he has practiced the required procedures as well as how often the maladaptive behaviors have occurred. The importance of behavioral feedback of this type in determining the efficacy of the treatment procedures being employed should be stressed.

Another method that has been found useful for increasing cooperation is to tape-record scenes used in therapy sessions, relaxation instructions, or even instructions concerning the homework to be practiced. The client can play the tapes at first while practicing, and then gradually fade out the use of the tapes in order to increase self-control.

The therapist can reinforce the client's cooperation not only socially (e.g., by praising him for practicing between sessions), but also through the use of covert reinforcement. This procedure involves instructing the client to imagine that he/she is practicing the required behaviors and then having him/her imagine a pleasant scene when the therapist says, "Reinforcement!" In general, the use of reinforcement procedures in therapy has the nonspecific effect of increasing the likelihood that the client will perform the required behaviors between sessions with the therapist.

It usually is nonproductive to attribute a client's lack of cooperation to "resistance." The client's behaviors in carrying out his treatment program are governed by the same laws that govern other adaptive or maladaptive behaviors. Thus, the therapist can increase cooperation by employing the same methods he uses to change the client's problematic behaviors.

VII. DECISIONS ABOUT TERMINATION

If the client has shown a rapid decrease in the frequency of his/her maladaptive behaviors, the therapist and client may decide that the goal of treatment has been accomplished and they may begin to discuss the termination of treatment. If the therapist is reinforced by accomplishing rapid behavioral changes or quick "cures," he may be too hasty in terminating clients who do well initially. A number of therapists (Cautela, 1968) contend that the results of treatment are more likely to be maintained if treatment is continued for at least 6 weeks after a behavior change has stabilized at the required level. This is in keeping with the empirical observation that the overlearning of one behavior decreases the likelihood of spontaneous recovery of a competing behavior (Pavlov, 1927).

Another factor in determining when to terminate treatment is the environmental situation in which the client presently is residing or to which he will be returning after termination. If his/her environment is likely to provide reinforcement for maladaptive behaviors, self-control procedures which then will reduce the likelihood of his/her being reconditioned in a maladaptive manner are needed. If the client is planning to move to a more congenial environment in the near future, termination should be delayed until after he/she has relocated.

Termination can be a gradual process, with the therapy sessions being spaced out from once a week to once every 2 weeks, to once a month, to once every 3 months. This is an especially useful procedure if there has been little opportunity for the client to test the efficacy of the behavioral change procedures in his own environment (e.g., if the client has been hospitalized during treatment and is being discharged to his usual environment). The process of increasing the interval between therapy sessions allows him/her to obtain feedback on the efficacy of the treatment techniques.

Many therapists find it useful to readminister the structured behavior assessment instruments given initially, in order to evaluate both the degree of change during therapy and to identify any new problems that might have developed during the intervening time. Occasionally, clients find the therapy situation so rewarding that they do not wish to terminate, even after the initial problematic behaviors have been successfully modified. These clients may present a variety of new "problems" as a justification for continuing treatment longer than necessary. In these cases (when the therapist feels that there is no significant reason for continuing treatment), it often is helpful if the client is told that he/she has developed sufficient skills to handle new problems on his/her own and that he/she should attempt to apply these skills before embarking on a course of further therapy. The therapist may even recommend that the client take a "vacation" from therapy for a month or so in order to evaluate his ability to deal with new problems on his own. In most cases, the client will decide that further therapy is not warranted and will have been positively reinforced for solving his own problems without the therapist's help.

It is interesting to note that clients often will apply techniques that are learned to deal with one kind of problem successfully to change other problematic behaviors. For example, a client who has learned to use thought-stopping when he has homosexual urges may report success in using the same technique to control his desire to overeat. This suggests the utility of teaching clients prior to termination how the techniques they have learned might be applied in a variety of problem situations.

Behavior therapists convey to their clients the expectation that the object of therapy is to teach the client skills that will make it possible for him/her to solve future problems without further therapy. That is not to say that clients of behavior therapists do not sometimes return for more treatment, but rather that an important goal of behavior therapy is to teach the client to deal with his own problems, even if this requires several successive approximations.

VIII. CRITICAL ISSUES IN INDIVIDUAL BEHAVIOR THERAPY

A. Behavior Therapy and Learning Theory

Although some behavior therapists (Lazarus, 1971) hold that the basis of behavior therapy is not modern learning theory, but rather any phenomena of experimental psychology, there are a number of advantages for the therapist to conceptualize behavior therapy within a learning model. Learning theory research provides us with a body of knowledge concerning variables that affect behavior, and, although the different learning models are based upon different assumptions about behavior, empirical generalizations from learning experiments can be useful in devising new procedures or establishing parameters for existing procedures. For example, the development of a variety of covert conditioning procedures (Cautela, 1973a) was based upon overt operant conditioning research, and the implementation of a procedure such as covert reinforcement can be made more effective by manipulating parameters such as schedules of reinforcement in ways indicated by learning theory research.

B. The Use of Punishment

In some instances, the therapist must decide whether an aversive *versus* a nonaversive treatment procedure should be used. Although there has been much discussion in the literature about the efficacy and the ethics of the use of punishment (Baer, 1970; Begelman, 1971), there have been few attempts to provide guidelines for the use of punishment in individual behavior therapy.

A number of factors should be taken into account in deciding whether to use a punishment procedure:

1. *Potential harm to the individual.* Occasionally a situation may arise in which the client is engaging in severe self-injurious behavior which, if allowed to continue, may result in severe and irreversible physical damage (e.g., head-banging or eye-poking behavior). Even though it probably could be demonstrated that, in most cases, the behavior is being maintained by the social reinforcement it elicits, an extinction procedure (e.g., withdrawing attention when head-banging behavior occurs) may take too long or may be impossible to carry out owing to lack of cooperation from significant others. In these cases, an aversive procedure may be the treatment of choice, at least until the behavior has been reduced in frequency.

2. *Lack of change in treated behaviors when nonaversive procedures*

are used. If the therapist has tried nonaversive procedures with little or no result (and he feels confident that his behavioral analysis is correct), it may be necessary to try aversive procedures in an attempt to change the client's problematic behaviors. It should be stressed, however, that lack of effectiveness of nonaversive procedures is most likely due to an inadequate behavioral assessment or incorrect use of the procedures, and that the therapist and client should be continuously evaluating the implementation of treatment.

3. *The client requests the use of an aversive technique.* It sometimes happens that the client himself requests that an aversive conditioning technique be used; when this occurs, it generally is because the client has tried unsuccessfully to use other techniques and/or has heard that aversive procedures work even in difficult or "resistive" cases. If the client is adamant and the therapist agrees (after doing a behavioral analysis), then punishment, negative reinforcement, response cost, or other aversive procedures may be employed. It is explained to the client that positive reinforcement for alternative behaviors should be combined with any aversive procedure. If the client agrees, the combined procedures (e.g., covert sensitization and covert reinforcement) can be employed. It is suggested that whenever an attempt is made to decelerate a behavior with aversive stimulation, an incompatible behavior should be reinforced. Unfortunately, a review of the individual behavior therapy literature indicates that often this is not done.

The practice of obtaining the client's *informed* consent before behavioral change procedures are employed is *absolutely indispensable,* and the therapist should take great care to see that the client fully understands the rationale and details of the treatment procedure prior to initiation of treatment.

C. Transference in Behavior Therapy

According to the psychoanalytic model, the phenomenon of transference is essential to the therapeutic process. Freud advocated facilitating transference by having the therapist remain as anonymous as possible, which meant not socializing with the client, not giving information about the therapist's personal life, and even having the client look away from the therapist during their sessions together (Freud, 1912a). Behavior therapists generally have given little attention to the transference phenomenon, although it is interesting to note that some analytically oriented therapists have claimed that transference readily occurs when a client is being treated by a behavior therapist. The rationale for this is that the behavior therapist is directive and authoritative, as the client's parents were, and this fosters transference.

First of all, the behavior therapist is not directive in the sense that he tells the client what is right or wrong or what ought to be done according to a particular value system. The behavior therapist provides the client with a technology for changing the behaviors which he desires to change. This may involve presenting guidelines regarding specific responses that will increase the probability of achieving the desired result. No doubt, as was previously mentioned, the therapist can become a powerful social reinforcer for the client. It is also likely that the client will react to the behavior therapist on the basis of stimulus generalization from other individuals having characteristics similar to those of the therapist. However, this does not indicate that the transference phenomenon as outlined by Freud is operating in the therapeutic relationship.

The behavior therapist can use his/her social reinforcement value in a deliberate and planned way to shape the client's desirable behavior. The therapist generally does not hesitate to use himself/herself as a model, by discussing his/her own successful responses to situations similar to the client's, his/her attempts to control his/her own behaviors, and even, on occasion, his/her difficulties in adapting. In contrast to the psychoanalytically oriented therapist, the behavior therapist strives for visibility and involvement. This may involve socializing with the client if he feels it may be helpful to the client (e.g., the therapist and his wife may accompany the client and his wife to a social situation that usually results in anxiety for the client) or having contacts with the client outside of the usual setting for therapy (e.g., the therapist may accompany a snake-phobic client on a trip to the snake house at the zoo).

The notion of transference being a phenomenon essential to the therapeutic process is particularly difficult to support in view of the successful results produced by automatic desensitization (Lang, Melamed, & Hart, 1970), in which the "therapist" is a machine, and do-it-yourself desensitization (Kahn & Baker, 1968), in which the client follows a set of programmed instructions in order to desensitize himself.

D. The Problem of Insight

Behavior therapists are often accused of proceeding mechanically without helping the client to develop insight into his/her problems, even though there is no evidence that achieving insight consistently leads to desired behavior change (Paul, 1966). This statement is partly accurate if "insight" refers to making conscious the unconscious factors that are influencing the behavior of the client. The statement is not accurate if "insight" refers to helping the client become aware of the present antecedents and consequences that influence the target behaviors. Procedurally, the "insight therapist" decides that insight has been achieved if the following criteria are met: (a) the client at some particular point makes a statement about the relationship between his feelings and particular individuals and situations; (b) the statement of the relationship agrees with the hypothesis of the therapist; (c) the client reports a covert or overt behavior change.

There are a number of difficulties with the analytic concept of insight. First of all, there is no hard-core evidence that the concept of the unconscious as developed by Freud is a valid one. Second, it is probable that an agreement with the therapist's hypotheses is gradually shaped by the therapist (Wolpe & Rachman, 1960). Third, a case can be made for the just as likely assumption that "insightful" statements follow or are concurrent with behavior change rather than causally related (Cautela, 1965; Hobbs, 1962).

E. Motivation for Therapy

When behavior therapists describe their successful cases, they are often asked such questions as: "How motivated was your client?" or "Don't your clients have to be highly motivated to cooperate with your procedures?" These questions imply that treatment effects are due primarily to some vague behavior called "motivation."

If "motivation" refers to the degree to which a client expresses a desire to change his behavior, there is no reason to assume that the clients of behavior therapists are more "motivated" than clients engaged in any other form of therapy. The client's verbal statements regarding his willingness to change do not affect treatment outcome. The only important motivational variable is the extent to which the client engages in tasks (procedures) inside and outside of the office. In other words, the amount of drive a client has does not affect learning—only, the number of reinforced trials does (Hull, 1952, pp. 6–7).

If the behavior therapist has any advantage over other therapists in this regard, it is the use of the behavior modification procedures previously outlined in the discussion on how to achieve cooperation.

IX. CONCLUSION

The standardization of a behavioral therapeutic strategy is difficult for a number of reasons. Both the therapist's and the client's behavioral repertoires influence the therapeutic style used. The progress of therapeutic endeavors has not reached the state in which there is agreement on the evaluation of established procedures. When dealing with human beings, it is not uncommon to find that similar maladaptive behaviors in different individuals are under the control of different antecedents and consequences.

In spite of all the above conditions, however, a presentation of guidelines for therapists can accelerate progress toward more efficient treatment of clients.

REFERENCES

Agras, W. S., Leitenberg, H., & Barlow, D. H. Social reinforcement in the modification of agorophobia. *Archives of General Psychiatry,* 1968, **19,** 423–427.

Arthur, A. Z. Diagnostic testing and the new alternatives. *Psychological Bulletin,* 1969, **72,** 183–192.

Ayllon, T. Intensive treatment of psychotic behavior by stimulus satiation and food reinforcement. *Behaviour Research and Therapy,* 1963, **1,** 53–61.

Ayllon, T., & Azrin, N. *The token economy: A motivational system for therapy and rehabilitation.* New York: Appleton, 1968. (a)

Ayllon, T., & Azrin, N. H. Reinforcer sampling: A technique for increasing the behavior of mental patients. *Journal of Applied Behavior Analysis,* 1968, **1,** 13–20. (b)

Ayllon, T., & Michael, J. The psychiatric nurse as a behavioral engineer. *Journal of Experimental Analysis of Behavior,* 1959, **2,** 323–334.

Baer, D. M. A case of the selective reinforcement of punishment. In C. Neuringer & J. L. Michael (Eds.), *Behavior modification in clinical psychology.* New York: Appleton, 1970. Pp. 243–249.

Bandura, A. Psychotherapy based upon modeling principles. In A. E. Bergin & S. L. Garfield (Eds.), *Handbook of psychotherapy and behavior change: An empirical analysis.* New York: Wiley, 1971. Pp. 653–708.

Barlow, D. H., Agras, W. S., Leitenberg, H., & Wincze, J. P. An experimental analysis of the effectiveness of shaping in reducing maladaptive avoidance behavior. *Behaviour Research and Therapy,* 1970, **8,** 165–173.

Baum, M. Extinction of avoidance responding through response prevention (flooding). *Psychological Bulletin,* 1970, **74,** 276–284.

Beech, H. R. Some theoretical and technical difficulties in the application of behavior therapy. *Bulletin of the British Psychological Society,* 1963, **16,** 1–9.

Begelman, D. A. The ethics of behavioral control and a new mythology. *Psychotherapy: Theory, Research and Practice,* 1971, **8,** 165–169.

Benassi, V., & Lanson, R. A survey of the teaching of behavior modification in colleges and universities. *American Psychologist,* 1972, **27,** 1063–1069.

Cahoon, D. D. Symptom substitution and the behavior therapies. *Psychological Bulletin,* 1968, **69,** 149–156.

Cautela, J. R. Desensitization and insight. *Behaviour Research and Therapy,* 1965, **3,** 59–64.

Cautela, J. R. Treatment of compulsive behavior by covert sensitization. *Psychological Record,* 1966, **16,** 33–41.

Cautela, J. R. Covert sensitization. *Psychological Reports,* 1967, **20,** 459–468.

Cautela, J. R. Behavior therapy and the need for behavioral assessment. *Psychotherapy: Theory, Research and Practice,* 1968, **5,** 175–179.

Cautela, J. R. Behavior therapy and self-control: Techniques and implications. In C. M. Franks (Ed.), *Behavior therapy: Appraisal and status.* New York: McGraw-Hill, 1969. Pp. 232–340.

Cautela, J. R. Behavioral analysis history questionnaire. Unpublished questionnaire, Boston College, 1970. (a)

Cautela, J. R. Covert negative reinforcement. *Behavior Therapy and Experimental Psychiatry,* 1970, **1,** 273–278. (b)

Cautela, J. R. Covert reinforcement. *Behavior Therapy,* 1970, **1,** 33–50. (c)

Cautela, J. R. Covert extinction. *Behavior Therapy,* 1971, **2,** 192–200. (a)

Cautela, J. R. Covert modeling. Paper presented at the Association for Advancement of Behavior Therapy, Washington, D.C., 1971. (b)

Cautela, J. R. Reinforcement survey schedule: Evaluation and current applications. *Psychological Reports,* 1972, **30,** 683–690.

Cautela, J. R. Covert processes and behavior modification. *Journal of Nervous and Mental Disease,* 1973, **157,** 27–36. (a)

Cautela, J. R. *Cues for tension and anxiety scale.* Unpublished questionnaire, 1973. (b)

Cautela, J. R. Covert response cost. In preparation, 1974.

Cautela, J. R., & Kastenbaum, R. A. A reinforcement survey schedule for use in therapy, training, and research. *Psychological Reports,* 1967, **20,** 1115–1130.

Cautela, J. R., & Upper, D. A behavioral coding system. Paper presented at the Association for Advancement of Behavior Therapy, Miami, December 1973.

Davison, G. C. Systematic desensitization as a counterconditioning process. *Journal of Abnormal Psychology,* 1968, **73,** 91–99.

DeMoor, W. Systematic desensitization versus prolonged high intensity stimulation (flooding). *Journal of Behavior Therapy and Experimental Psychiatry,* 1970, **1,** 45–52.

Dunlap, K. *Habits: Their making and unmaking.* New York: Liveright, 1932.

Ferster, C. B. Classification of behavioral psychology. In L. Krasner & L. P. Ullmann (Eds.), *Research in behavior modification.* New York: Holt, 1966. Pp. 6–26.

Franks, C. M. (Ed.) *Behavior therapy: Appraisal and status.* New York: McGraw-Hill, 1969.

Freud, S. The dynamics of transference (1912a). In E. Jones (Ed.), *Collected papers: Sigmund Freud.* Vol. II. London: Hogarth Press, 1956. Pp. 312–322.

Freud, S. Recommendations for physicians on the psychoanalytic method of treatment (1912b). In E. Jones (Ed.), *Collected papers: Sigmund Freud.* Vol. II. London: Hogarth Press, 1956. Pp. 323–333.

Gelder, M. G. Desensitization and psychotherapy research. *British Journal of Medical Psychology,* 1968, **41,** 39–46.

Goldfried, M. R., & Kent, R. N. Traditional vs. behavioral personality assessment: A comparison of methodological and theoretical assumptions. *Psychological Bulletin,* 1972, **77,** 409–420.

Goldfried, M. R., & Merbaum, M. *Behavior change through self-control.* New York: Holt, 1973.

Goldiamond, I. Self-control procedures in personal behavior problems. *Psychological Reports,* 1965, **17,** 851–868.

Hobbs, N. Sources of gain in psychotherapy. *American Psychologist,* 1962, **17,** 741–747.

Homme, L. E. Perspectives in psychology: XXIV. Control of coverants, the operants of the mind. *Psychological Record,* 1965, **15,** 501–511.

Homme, L. E., Csanyi, A. P., Gonzales, M. A., & Rechs, J. R. *How to use contingency contracting in the classroom.* Champaign, Ill.: Research Press, 1969.

Homme, L. E., deBaca, P. C., Devine, J. V., Steinhorst, R., & Rickert, E. J. Use of the Premack principle in controlling the behavior of nursery school children. *Journal of Experimental Analysis of Behavior,* 1963, **6,** 544.

Hull, C. L. *A behavior system: An introduction to behavior theory concerning the individual organism.* New Haven, Conn.: Yale University Press, 1952.

Jacobson, E. *Progressive relaxation.* Chicago: University of Chicago Press, 1938.

Kahn, M., & Baker, B. Desensitization with minimal therapist contact. *Journal of Abnormal Psychology,* 1968, **73,** 198–200.

Kanfer, F. H. Assessment of behavior modification. *Journal of Personality Assessment,* 1972, **36,** 418–423.

Kazdin, A. E. The effect of response cost and aversive stimulation in suppressing punished and nonpunished speech disfluencies. *Behavior Therapy,* 1973, **4,** 73–82.

Krasner, L. The therapist as a social reinforcement machine. In H. H. Strupp & L. Luborsky (Eds.), *Research in psychotherapy.* Vol. 2. Washington, D.C.: American Psychological Association, 1962. Pp. 61–94.

Krasner, L. Reinforcement, verbal behavior, and psychotherapy. *American Journal of Orthopsychiatry,* 1963, **33,** 601–613.

Krasner, L. Behavior modification research and the role of the therapist. In L. A. Gottschalk (Ed.), *Methods of research in psychotherapy.* New York: Harper, 1966. Pp. 292–311.

Krasner, L., & Atthowe, J. M., Jr. *Token economy bibliography.* New York: State University of New York, Stony Brook, 1968.

Kushner, M., & Sandler, J. Aversion therapy and the concept of punishment. *Behaviour Research and Therapy,* 1966, **4,** 179–186.

Laing, R. D. *The politics of experience.* New York: Ballantine Books, 1967.

Lang, P. J., Melamed, B. G., & Hart, J. Psychophysiological analysis of fear modification using an automated desensitization procedure. *Journal of Abnormal Psychology,* 1970, **76,** 220–234.

Lazarus, A. A. Crucial procedural factors in desensitization therapy. *Behaviour Research and Therapy,* 1964, **2,** 65–70.

Lazarus, A. A. *Behavior therapy and beyond.* New York: McGraw-Hill, 1971.

Lazarus, A. A., & Abramovitz, A. The use of "emotive imagery" in the treatment of children's phobias. *Journal of Mental Science,* 1962, **108,** 191–195.

Lomont, J. F. The ethics of behavior therapy. *Psychological Reports,* 1964, **14,** 519–531.

Lovaas, O. I., Frietag, L., Nelson, K., & Whalen, C. The establishment of imitation and its use for the development of complex behavior in schizophrenic children. *Behaviour Research and Therapy,* 1967, **5,** 171–181.

Lovaas, O. I., Schaeffer, B., & Simmons, J. Q. Building social behavior in autistic children by use of electric shock. *Journal of Experimental Research in Personality,* 1965, **1,** 99–109.

McCrady, R. E. A forward-fading technique for increasing heterosexual responsiveness in male homosexuals. *Journal of Behavior Therapy and Experimental Psychiatry,* 1973, **4,** 257–261.

Meichenbaum, D. H. Cognitive factors in behavior modification: Modifying what clients say to themselves. Paper presented at the Association for Advancement of Behavior Therapy, Washington, D.C., September 1971.

Meyer, V., & Crisp, A. H. Some problems in behavior therapy. *British Journal of Psychiatry,* 1966, **112,** 367–381.

Mischel, W. *Personality and assessment.* New York: Wiley, 1968.

Monroe, B. D., & Ahr, C. J. Auditory desensitization of a dog phobia in a blind patient. *Journal of Behavior Therapy and Experimental Psychiatry,* 1972, **3,** 315–317.

Morganstern, K. P. Implosive therapy and flooding procedures: A critical review. *Psychological Bulletin,* 1973, **79,** 318–334.

Paul, G. L. *Insight vs. desensitization in psychotherapy.* Stanford, Calif. Stanford University Press, 1966.

Pavlov, I. P. *Conditioned reflex.* London and New York: Oxford University Press, 1927.

Phillips, L., & Draguns, J. G. Classification of the behavior disorders. *Annual Review of Psychology,* 1971, **22,** 447–482.

Rehm, L. P., & Marston, A. R. Reduction of social anxiety through modification of self-reinforcement: An instigation therapy technique. *Journal of Consulting and Clinical Psychology,* 1968, **32,** 565–574.

Revusky, S. Some laboratory paradigms for chemical aversion treatment of alcoholism. *Journal of Behavior Therapy and Experimental Psychiatry,* 1973, **4,** 15–17.

Sachs, D. A. The efficacy of time out procedures in a variety of behavior problems. *Journal of Behavior Therapy and Experimental Psychiatry,* 1973, **4,** 237–242.

Schwitzgebel, R. Delinquents with tape recorders. *New Society,* January, 1963, 14–16.

Serber, M. Shame aversion therapy. *Journal of Behavior Therapy and Experimental Psychiatry,* 1970, **1,** 213–215.

Shapiro, D., Barber, T. X., DiCara, L. V., Kamiya, J., Miller, N. E., & Stoyva, J. (Eds.) *Biofeedback and self-control.* Chicago: Aldine, 1972.

Stampfl, T. G., & Levis, D. J. Essentials of implosive therapy: A learning theory-based psychodynamic behavioral therapy. *Journal of Abnormal Psychology,* 1967, **72,** 496–503.

Taylor, J. G. A behavioral interpretation of obsessive compulsive neurosis. *Behaviour Research and Therapy,* 1963, **1,** 237–244.

Thorpe, J., Schmidt, E., Brown, P., & Castell, D. Aversion-relief therapy: A new method for general application. *Behaviour Research and Therapy,* 1964, **2,** 71–82.

Upper, D., Cautela, J. R., & Brooke, J. M. Behavioral self-rating checklist. In preparation, 1974.

Watson, D. L., & Tharp, R. G. *Self-directed behavior: Self-modification for personal adjustment.* Monterey, Calif.: Brooks/Cole, 1972.

Weinberg, N. H., & Zaslove, M. "Resistance" to systematic desensitization of phobias. *Journal of Clinical Psychology,* 1963, **19,** 179–181.

Wolpe, J. *Psychotherapy by reciprocal inhibition.* Stanford, Calif.: Stanford University Press, 1958.

Wolpe, J. *The practice of behavior therapy.* Oxford: Pergamon, 1969.

Wolpe, J. The instigation of assertive behavior: Transcripts from two cases. *Journal of Behavior Therapy and Experimental Psychiatry,* 1970, **1,** 145–151.

Wolpe, J. *The practice of behavior therapy.* (2nd ed.) Oxford: Pergamon, 1973.

Wolpe, J., & Lang, P. J. A fear survey schedule for use in behavior therapy. *Behaviour Research and Therapy,* 1964, **2,** 27–30.

Wolpe, J., & Rachman, S. Psychodynamic evidence: A critique based on Freud's case of Little Hans. *Journal of Nervous and Mental Disease,* 1960, **131,** 135–148.

Wolpin, M., & Pearsall, L. Rapid deconditioning of a fear of snakes. *Behaviour Research and Therapy,* 1966, **41,** 25–37.

DRUGS AND BEHAVIOR ANALYSIS[1]

ROBERT PAUL LIBERMAN AND JOHN DAVIS[2]
Camarillo-Neuropsychiatric Institute (UCLA) Research Program
Camarillo State Hospital
Camarillo, California

I. INTRODUCTION

The clinical and research integration of practitioners and scientists in behavior modification and psychopharmacology has been retarded by traditional divergencies in their basic assumptions about causes of behavior. The field of behavior analysis and modification grew out of an optimistic and idealized belief that most of man's behavior could be understood and controlled as a function of environmental variables. On the other hand, psychopharmacology was developed with the conviction that the most important sources of influence on human behavior were chemical and physiological events within the nervous system. Investigators in both fields, however, share a vital interest in the measurement of the behavioral outcomes of drug and environmental interventions. Despite an early and influential penetration

[1] The opinions stated in this chapter are those of the authors only and should not be construed as official policy of the California Department of Health or the Regents of the University of California. The writing of this chapter was supported in part by NIMH Research Grant No. MH19880-01A1MHS.

[2] The authors acknowledge the important contributions made to their research in this area by Charles Wallace, Ph.D. and the nursing staff of the Clinical Research Unit at Camarillo State Hospital. The support and encouragement of Robert Coombs, Ph.D. (Chief of Research, Camarillo State Hospital), John Darmer (Hospital Administrator, Camarillo State Hospital), Harry Jones, M.D. (Medical Director, Camarillo State Hospital), and Louis Jolyon West, M.D. (Medical Director, Neuropsychiatric Institute-UCLA) are appreciated.

into basic animal psychopharmacology by psychologists trained in an experimental analysis of behavior (Laties & Weiss, 1969), there has been only a small amount of research using behavior analysis in applied, clinical psychopharmacology. This chapter will hopefully call attention to this neglected interface between the environmental and biological causes of behavior and spur research and clinical studies in important clinical domains.

The authors will survey and summarize findings from four areas where drug research and applied behavior analysis intersect. These areas include (1) drugs as adjuncts that facilitate behavior therapy; (2) environmental interventions that increase the reliability of drug usage by chronic psychotics; (3) experimental analysis of clinical drug effects using direct behavioral observation; (4) drugs as reinforcers, aversive stimuli, or agents of extinction.

II. DRUGS AS ADJUNCTS TO FACILITATE BEHAVIOR THERAPY

Behavior therapists have frequently used relaxation-eliciting psychotropic drugs to facilitate systematic desensitization. Anxiolytic agents have also been used alone to produce sufficient reduction of anxiety, enabling the patient to approach a feared object or enter a feared situation (Silverstone, 1970). Some of the major anti-anxiety drugs that have been used are listed in Table I with their generic and trade names. The bulk of the evidence from studies on the effects of these drugs, alone or in combination with systematic desensitization, indicates that they are significantly more effective than placebo in reducing subjectively rated symptom distress and behavioral avoidance of feared situations (Brady, 1969, 1971; Klein & Davis, 1969; Silverstone, 1970).

Lipsedge, Hajioff, Huggins, Napier, Pearce, Pike, and Rich (1973) reported that an antidepressant drug of the monoamine oxidase inhibitor class, iproniazid, was effective in reducing anxiety but not effective in reducing phobic avoidance. In the same study, they found that methohexitone-assisted desensitization and standard desensitization both produced significant reductions in self-rated anxiety and avoidance, but the drug-assisted procedure was more effective. Brady (1966) has reported the effective use of methohexitone-assisted desensitization with sexually frigid women. Using multiple measures and a control group receiving brief, insight-oriented therapy, Brady found that the group receiving methohexitone-assisted desensitization achieved significantly greater improvement in their sexual functioning. There were no differences between the groups in other areas of social, emotional, or work functioning (Brady, 1972).

TABLE I

Generic and Trade Names for Psychotropic Drugs

	Generic Name	Trade Name
I. Anti-anxiety agents used to facilitate desensitization	Methohexital	Brevital
	Amobarbital	Amytal
	Pentobarbital	Pentothal
	Chlordiazepoxide	Librium
	Diazepam	Valium
	Oxazepam	Serax
	Meprobamate	Miltown, Equanil
	Tybamate	Tybatran
	Benactyzine	Deprol
II. Stimulants used for hyperactivity in children	Methylphenidate	Ritalin
	d-Amphetamine	Dexedrine
III. Antipsychotic drugs	Thioridazine	Mellaril
	Chlorpromazine	Thorazine
	Trifluperazine	Stelazine
	Fluphenazine	Prolixin, Permitil

A recent study by Lader and Mathews (1970) found no differences among methohexitone-assisted relaxation and relaxation induced by tape or "live" instructions. Physiological measures of relaxation were used as the dependent measures, not clinical changes in phobias. Likewise, an unpublished study by Serber and Goerwitz (1974) did not find any incremental benefit of tybamate over placebo in eliciting relaxation in normal subjects. Relaxation was measured by both polygraph and self-report. Since anxiolytic drugs are used by therapists in desensitization primarily with individuals who cannot achieve deep muscle relaxation in response to instructions, the above studies reporting negative results should be replicated with subjects who experience difficulty in relaxing to instructions.

The role of drugs in desensitization can be conceptualized in two ways. In the classical conditioning paradigm the unconditioned stimulus is the drug, whereas the conditioned stimuli are verbalizations presented by the therapist (i.e., instructions to relax and description of scenes from a fear hierarchy). The unconditioned and conditioned responses are the drug-induced and therapist-induced relaxation responses, respectively. An operant paradigm may be a more experimentally fruitful conceptual framework for studies on drug-assisted desensitization. In the operant approach, the administration of the drug is a cognitively and physiologically mediated prompt which assures that relaxation responses are emitted. Relaxation responses include both physical relaxation and verbal relabeling of his affective state by the patient. These responses can be measured by physiological monitoring and self-report. Once the drug produces the desired relaxation responses, it can be gradually faded so that the therapist's verbal prompts can begin to assume control over the responses as discriminative stimuli. Gradual fading or withdrawal of the drug is a naturally occurring element in methohexitone-assisted desensitization and may help to account for its effectiveness.

Legally prevented from administering psychotropic drugs, psychologists have used attribution theory to challenge the use of drug-assisted desensitization. Davison and Valins (1968) state that patients undergoing drug-assisted desensitization probably attribute their relaxed condition to the drug, rather than to self-control. According to these authors, if a patient "has no reason to re-evaluate his attitudes or behavior vis-à-vis the phobic stimulus," little generalization should be expected to occur into the natural life setting. Since drug-assisted desensitization has been empirically demonstrated to be effective repeatedly with the effects transferring to natural settings, the argument based on attribution theory may be little more than an academic polemic delivered by psychologists to medical psychiatrists. On the other hand, reference to attribution theory may add to the operant paradigm's explanatory power in desensitization. Fading of the methohexitone occurs both within each treatment session as the effects wear off, and also across sessions as the therapist gradually diminishes the dose and relies more and more on instructions. Thus, both within and across sessions, the patient becomes aware that continued relaxation can be maintained even in the relative absence of the drug. Reevaluation or relabeling of his feelings and behaviors in relation to the phobic situation can occur, thereby promoting generalization.

In a study using rats, Sherman (1967) found that punishment-induced suppression of lever-pressing extinguishes faster when amobarbital is administered. Furthermore, when the amobarbital is gradually withdrawn, extinction occurs more readily than when it is rapidly withdrawn. It is unfortunate that the animal studies which have demonstrated drug-state dependent learning with its consequential limitations on generalization have not employed gradual fading of the drug (Baum, 1971). Gradual withdrawal of diazepam has been reported to facilitate desensitization (Pecknold, Raeburn, & Poser, 1972). Marks, Viswanathan, Lipsedge, and Gardiner (1972) assessed the effects of flooding (implosion) on phobias in combination with diazepam or placebo. Flooding was efficacious when it occurred during waning diazepam effects. Flooding administered during the peak effects of diazepam was less effective but better than flooding carried out under placebo conditions.

Gradual withdrawal of drugs used to facilitate desensitization will also prevent therapists from falling into the pitfall of equating generalized reduction in behavioral responsiveness from specific reduction in symptomatic behavior. Drugs should be used as adjuncts to behavioral interventions in a highly selective and specific manner—not as chemical "straitjackets." When drugs are to be used to assist desensitization, the therapist should carefully instruct the patient that the drug is used only as a temporary prompt which will be gradually faded out.

III. MOTIVATING MEDICATION USE

There is an impressive body of evidence which indicates that schizophrenia has a genetic component (Gottesman & Shields, 1972; Wender, 1969) and that drugs affect behavior (Klein & Davis, 1969). Despite the well demonstrated efficacy and widespread clinical use of psychotropic drugs, few authors reporting the effects on behavior by psychosocial therapies describe the medication status of their subjects. Much valuable information on the interaction between drugs and socioenvironmental interventions has been lost because of this deficit in journal reporting (Spohn, 1973). Almost 20 years after their introduction, there is no doubt that phenothiazine drugs beneficially alter the deviant behaviors of schizophrenics and that lithium reduces the excessive motor and verbal behaviors of manic patients. It is the contention of the authors that withholding these psychotropic drugs when clearly indicated by the patient's behavioral disturbance is tantamount to unethical clinical practice.

With clear evidence showing the profound therapeutic effectiveness of phenothiazines and lithium on psychotic behaviors, there should be research and demonstration projects mounted by behaviorists to increase the likelihood that chronic mental patients will take their medications. The failure of chronic psychotics to regularly ingest their medications is a major contribution to the high rate of readmission to psychiatric hospitals (Goldberg, DiMascio, & Chaudhary, 1970). The wasted resources and human misery produced by the revolving-door, discharge-readmission phenomenon in mental hospitals presents a public health problem of great magnitude. Patients enter the hospital in a psychotic state and are rapidly medicated. Within a few weeks to a month they are sufficiently, behaviorally compensated to be able to return to their homes and families in the community. They are discharged with a supply of medication or a prescription and strong urgings by nurses and doctors to "take your medicine." For a variety of reasons the ex-patient soon stops taking his medication—medicine labels him as "crazy," sick, or weak; produces distressing side effects; is a bothersome routine; and costs a significant amount of money (Goldberg *et al.,* 1970; Mumford, 1973). For a while the person continues to feel well since the antipsychotic effects are longer-lasting than the side effects. This "honeymoon period" only serves to reinforce the cessation of the medication. Within 1 to 12 months, the psychotic behavior returns as the medication is slowly metabolized and excreted. Once again the patient requires hospitalization and the revolving-door keeps turning.

An array of behavioral interventions could be studied to assess their effects on medication taking. Azrin and Powell (1969) showed how a simple mechanical time alarm could be used to prompt chronic psychotics to take their medication. Their device was never submitted to a systematic evaluation with psychiatric patients, however. A. J. Turner (1972) has described a community-based reinforcement program which aims at increasing the reliability of medication-taking among ex-mental patients. Thirty ex-patients were visited on a regular, time-interval schedule by rehabilitation workers who tested their urine for the presence of phenothiazine metabolites. Positive urine tests resulted in the receipt of credits which could be used immediately or saved toward the purchase of desirable items from a reinforcement menu. After the individual is "hooked" on the reinforcers, the visits are faded to a variable interval schedule with greater and greater durations between visits. This change in the schedule of reinforcement has produced more reliable and durable taking of medication and a decrease in rehospitalization. After one year of evaluation, A. J. Turner (1973) has reported a savings of $15,000 based on a cost-effectiveness study comparing the community incentive program with a more conventional medical check by a physician.

At the Oxnard (California) Mental Health Center, plans are underway to develop and evaluate a demonstration program for delivering medication services to the approximately 500 chronic psychotics living in the Center's catchment area. The program will include a means of supplying medication and prescriptions other than by conventional medical check-ups. A registry of all chronic psychotics will be constructed which will "preventively" prompt the mental health center staff to regularly monitor the social and vocational status of these individuals. A community-based reinforcement system similar to the one suggested by A. J. Turner (1972) will be developed. Prescriptions will be dispensed by a physician at a sumptuous banquet provided by the mental health department in a local social hall. The psychiatrist can observe the patient's "mental status" in a naturalistic setting where cues for sick role behavior are not present. In addition, the receipt of a prescription, and hopefully the subsequent use of medication, will become paired with a pleasant, nonstressful social event replete with primary reinforcers.

The next 10 years should see the implementation of a variety of behavioral interventions aimed at increasing the medication-taking behavior of chronic psychotics as well as strengthening their use of birth control methods (Duncan, Hilton, Kraeger, & Lumsdaine, 1973). Interventions such as therapeutic instructions, fading of prompts, classical conditioning, covert conditioning, self-monitoring, and community-based reinforcement systems can make major contributions to primary and secondary prevention in public health.

IV. EXPERIMENTAL ANALYSIS OF DRUG EFFECTS

The criteria for assessment of drug effects in clinical populations using single case designs should include: (a) continuous direct and reliable observations of behavior with enough observations to establish a clear trend within any condition; (b) controlled experimental designs, such as ABAB, BAB, or multiple baseline; and (c) double blind administration of the drug(s) and placebo. The first studies to meet these criteria were controlled laboratory experimental analyses of infrahuman behavior. Reviewing of these animal studies is beyond the scope of this chapter. The interested reader is referred to Dews (1963, 1965), Laties and Weiss (1969), and Ferster and Appel (1963) for applications of operant techniques and drug assessment with animals. Lindsley (1956, 1961, 1962) was the first to apply an experimental analysis of behavior to drug effects in clinical subjects. In his 1961 report, he described a procedure for determining when a surgical anesthetic has reached an effective level. The patient was fitted with earphones held in place by a surgical cap through which was presented an aversive noise. The patient could avoid the noise by tapping together two electrodes, one on the index finger and one on the thumb. The faster the patient tapped, the less noise was presented and a high tap rate completely avoided noise. Using direct, continuous, cumulative records, the rate of avoidance responding reflects the level of anesthetic. The technique allowed the anesthesiologist to set the precise dosage required to fully anesthetize the patient, but yet allow for rapid recovery with minimal side effects.

Lindsley (1962) used operant techniques with psychiatric inpatients to assess the effects of drugs on reinforced operant behaviors. In a small laboratory chamber, electromechanical programming equipment automatically recorded a single patient's lever pulling for candy on a VI schedule and vocalizations, in an A-B-A design. When a stable rate of lever pulling was established, the patient was given benactyzine, a drug believed to have antipsychotic properties. Lever pulling responses declined markedly with a

20-minute latency. A concomitant rise in psychotic vocalizations occurred during the drug condition, but vocalizations returned to the baseline, 4 hours post-ingestion.

The lowered frequency of lever pulling during the drug condition began to increase 3 hours post-ingestion and completely returned to baseline at 4 hours post-ingestion. During a second session in which a lactose placebo was administered, lever pulling remained at a high rate with low levels of psychotic vocalizations. This study meets the criteria of (a) continuous records of directly observed behavior, (b) controlled design, and (c) double blindness, since mechanical records were kept and presumably the subject did not know what medication he was receiving. Thus Lindsley demonstrated that an "antipsychotic" drug was really "hallucinogenic."

McPherson and Le Gassicke (1965) described a single case experiment in which they assessed the effects of oxazepam on a patient's response to a questionnaire dealing with symptoms and side effects. The experimenters utilized a 6-day, no drug pretrial plus a PPXDDXPDXPD time series design, where: P = 3-day block of placebo, D = 3-day block of oxazepam, X = 1 treatment-free day. In behavior analysis literature, this translates to an A^1-A-B-A-A^1-B-A-A^1-B design, where: A = no treatment, A^1 = placebo, B = active drug. Measures were taken on the second and third days of each 3-day block. A double-blind code was maintained throughout the experiment. The results indicated that oxazepam had a significant effect in reducing symptoms. All eight drug scores were lower than the nine placebo and no-drug, pretrial scores. There were no side effects and the drug was fast-acting. The method employed in this experiment was easy to mount, conclusive, and significant in improving this patient's symptomatology.

Mefford, Moran, and Kimble (1960) used an A-B-BC-A research design to assess changes in urinary creatinine and psychological test responses (perceptual speed) of three psychotics as a function of placebo (A^1), chlorpromazine (B), and chlorpromazine plus electroconvulsive (ECT) therapy (BC). For 2 cases, perceptual speed and creatinine was increasing during the first placebo condition, declined with chlorpromazine, more substantially declined when ECT was added to chlorpromazine, and returned to the higher initial level when the placebo was reinstated. The third patient showed a decline in perceptual speed and creatinine output only when ECT was added to chlorpromazine.

Using single-subject designs, Grinspoon, Ewalt, and Shader (1967) studied the effects of psychotherapy and a phenothiazine drug in chronic schizophrenics. Continuous records were collected in the form of retrospective weekly ratings by nursing staff who were "blind" to the drug. The systematic provision and withdrawal of intensive, analytic psychotherapy was arranged in an A-B-A-B design. The drug, thioridazine, and an active placebo (atropine), used to mimic the autonomic side effects of thioridazine, were administered sequentially in an A-B-A^1-B-A^1-B design. The results indicated that changes from phenothiazine to placebo conditions produced considerable regression in the patient's clinical status as measured by the behavioral rating forms. Improvements occurred when the drug was reinstituted. No effects were found for psychotherapy. Systematic replications with long washout periods were important aspects of this study. A drawback, however, was a lack of reported reliability for the ratings.

Chassan (1967) termed the use of a single subject as his own control an "intensive design" strategy. A statistical method, based on within-subject averages was suggested for analysis of drug-placebo differences.

> Thus an intensive design for the purpose of testing drug effects with respect to a given patient will consist of a sequence of treatment weeks and corresponding observations over a period of perhaps several months. Within the duration of such a study there will be several alternations between, say, test medication and placebo on a double-blind basis. A rating or a set of ratings or evaluations is made on the patient for each week or day of treatment. The ratings while on the test medication are then compared with those on placebo, and statistical analysis—including tests for significant differences between test-medication and placebo scores—is performed on these data [Chassan, 1967, pp. 180–181].

Researchers in the field of behavior modification and psychotherapy have developed strategies for single case analysis (Barlow & Hersen, 1973; Chassan, 1967; Gottman, 1973; Risley & Wolf, 1972). Sulzbacher (1973) suggests that the problem of great individual differences in dose-response can be best resolved by an intensive study of single subjects, exposing each to several dosage levels of the drug. A recent study that employs the three criteria set forth earlier attests to the precision in dose response relationships that can be obtained using single cases. Hollis and St. Omer (1972) tested the effects of graded doses of chlorpromazine on the motor behavior of retarded children using continuous, direct, and automatic recording. They found that chlorpromazine decreases the rate of motor responding and that graded increases in dosage corresponded to graded decreases in motor behavior. This study is a refinement of Lindsley's earlier work and represents a model for similar clinical studies.

From a behavior analysis background, clinical researchers have developed techniques to obtain reliable, direct, and continuous records of clinically significant behaviors without the use of automatic recording and cumulative records. Hall (1971) outlined a set of techniques for measuring behaviors in the natural environment. Through a handy flow chart, Alevizos, Berck, Callahan, and Campbell (1974) provided guidelines for deciding on the kind of observation and recording method to use with various target behaviors. Callahan, Alevizos, Teigen, Newman, and Campbell (1974) investigated the behavioral effects on chronic, institutionalized, schizophrenic women of changing from twice-per-day administration of phenothiazine medication to a once-per-day schedule. The Behavior Observation Instrument (Liberman, DeRisi, King, Eckman, & Wood, 1974) was used to directly assess behavioral changes in the ward setting. The authors found that a once-per-day administration did not increase behavioral disruptions and led to more alertness. The authors further point out how direct observations taken during program changes in clinical settings can offset opinionated conclusions reached anecdotally by biased staff. In this study, nursing personnel attributed behavioral disruptions to the change to a once-per-day schedule of drug administration. When the observational data were analyzed, no increase in disruptions was noted. A closer analysis revealed that the patient population had increased while staffing had decreased; thus, an increased work load created the "appearance" of more frequent behavioral disruptions.

Essential when using observational techniques is the use of double- or triple-blind experimental procedures. The need for a double-blind code is documented in an article by Sulzbacher (1973). Sulzbacher reviews procedural biases in 756 evaluative studies of drug effects with children up to 1972. Several elements, he concludes, are important in the reduction of procedural bias. The first essential element is the use of a placebo. Second is employment of a double-blind code where both the subject, administrators, and observer-raters are unaware of active medication states or a triple-blind regimen where subject, administrators, observer-raters, and experimenter are all unaware of potent conditions. Third, response specification and direct measurement reduce bias. Where any of these elements are missing, significant drug effects may represent a reflection of procedural bias.

Sulzbacher (1972) reports data on drug effects for three boys, 7–8 years old, in a special class for the learning disabled. d-Amphetamine sulfate (Dexedrine) and methylphenidate (Ritalin) were studied in two and one cases, respectively. One of the reasons for choosing these medications is their rapid metabolic turnover. Seventy percent of each drug is metabolized within 24 hours. In each case, a placebo and at least two drug dosages were employed. A triple-blind (ordering physician, data-collectors, and subject unaware) procedure was used in conjunction with an A-B-A withdrawal design with multiple replications (Sulzbacher, 1972). On each day of the study the subject was randomly assigned to either one of the two drug doses or placebo. Direct observations were taken throughout the studies on clinically significant and well-defined behaviors such as being "out-of-seat," talking out in class, and academic performance measures of reading and arithmetic. The results of the study showed that both the subjects who were receiving d-amphetamine sulfate improved while the one case receiving methylphenidate showed a placebo effect. In spite of the rapid washout, the last case may have represented a drug effect if there was carryover from the drug conditions to the placebo condition. An idiosyncratic, slow, metabolism of the drug may have accounted for such an effect. Reliability measures taken throughout all phases of the study would have eliminated some sources of observer bias and helped to tease out the cause of the "placebo" effect. The results of all cases might have been more striking and more easily interpreted if longer washout periods had been used. Hollis and St. Omer (1972) successfully used longer washout periods in their A-B-A design studying the behavioral effects of drugs on retardates. As it is commonly used, the A-B-A design requires that a stable trend be established before a change in experimental conditions is made.

In an experimental school in a hospital setting, Zike (1972) recorded "jump-ups," "talk-outs," and attention to task to measure the effects of methylphenidate on one case and deoxyephedrine on a second. Well defined aggressive and depressive responses were used to gauge the effects of chlorpromazine and chlorpromazine + trifluoperazine on a third child. Although the observation methods are not detailed, acceptable reliability data are presented and coupled with a consistent double-blind procedure for all cases. Three design strategies were used: A-B-A, A-A^1-B, and A-B-BC. While A-A^1-B and A-B-BC design strategies do not necessarily lend themselves to easy interpretation, a 5-day treatment condition for each period allowed for washout and stabilization of trends. Methylphenidate was highly effective in decreasing talk-outs and jump-ups with concurrent increases in attention to task. Experimental control was well demonstrated in the case with an A-B-A design. The second case (A-A^1-B strategy) demonstrated less conclusively the effect of deoxyephedrine in reducing talk-outs and jump-ups while increasing attention to task. In the third case, the experimenter broke the double-blind code to respond to immediate clinical and ethical considerations in dealing with the life-endangering behaviors of a young boy. The results of the A-B-BC strategy showed that aggression was reduced during the chlorpromazine condition (B) while the effects of chlorpromazine + trifluoperazine (BC) on "depressive" behaviors were questionable.

Liberman, Davis, Moon, and Moore (1973) described three cases illustrating the effects of phenothiazines on clinically meaningful behaviors. The first patient, John O., a 21-year-old high school graduate, was admitted to the Clinical Research Unit because of social withdrawal from peers and a high rate of describing somatic delusions and hypochondriacal preoccupations. He complained that his "head was like a piece of wood" and that he felt that "his body was a hollow tube filled with a vacuum." At every opportunity he would accost a staff member and pour out his complaints, frequently asking for reassurances that he would soon be "cured." He also spoke in a moaning, whining manner of how hopeless he was and how his previous pleasures were now devoid of interest to him.

John was a tall, well developed young man who lived at home with his parents and had gradually decompensated over a 3-year period. He had a negligible work history with some brief interludes in sheltered workshops. He had no friends and no social life outside of his family. He had been hospitalized at a community mental health center twice in the past 2 years and was receiving maintenance trifluperazine (Stelazine) 20 mg/day at the time of his admission.

Two behavioral measures were recorded by the CRU staff, during 18 daily, randomly time-sampled 30-second conversations held 6 days/week. John was approached on the unit by a member of the nursing staff and was politely asked to join in an informal chat. The staff member noted whether or not John agreed and followed through with the conversation. The rate of compliance with this socal interaction became a measure of John's social participation. Noncompliance was operationally considered to be an asocial response. The more he refused these chats, the more withdrawn and autistic he was assessed. The entire CRU staff rotated in social approaches to John and a semistandardized verbal format was used to prompt his participation.

The second measure was the presence or absence of delusional or hypochondriacal verbal content in these time-sampled chats. When John did engage in conversation with a nurse or technician, any expression of "sick talk" was noted for that 30-second segment. Multiple expressions were counted the same as a single occurrence. Thus, two all-or-none measures were recorded for each of 18 daily observations: (1) compliance or noncompliance to prompts for conversations; and (2) presence or absence of "sick talk" during any conversation actually held. The inter-rater reliability for these two observations exceeded 90%.

During all phases of the experiment, John was also on a token economy wherein he earned tokens by grooming himself and carrying out ward jobs and exchanged these tokens for cigarettes, meals, bed, and ground privileges.

An A-A^1-B-A^1-B, within-subject, experimental design was used to assess the effect of the phenothiazine on John's social withdrawal and content of conversation. During the first 14 days, John was without medications, having been taken off his trifluperazine on day 1. After this baseline period (A), he was placed on a placebo for 8 days (A^1). The professional and nursing staff described the placebo as a powerful drug and highly touted its alleged potency to John. John himself had been requesting that he be placed again on medication, and he was pleased and excited to receive the placebo.

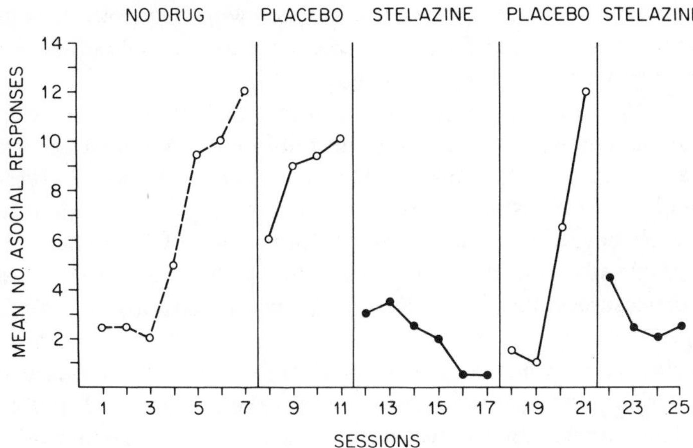

Fig. 1. Average number of refusals to engage in a brief conversation. (Reprinted from Liberman, R. P., Davis, J., Moon, N., & Moore, J. Research design for analyzing drug-environment-behavior interactions. *Journal of Nervous and Mental Disease,* 1973, **156,** 432–439. By courtesy of the Williams & Wilkins Co., Baltimore, Maryland.)

The drug treatment phase consisted of 12 days (B) in which John received 60 mg/day of Stelazine in a single dose. A withdrawal to placebo conditions occurred for 8 days and then reinstitution of the drug was made.

The data in Fig. 1 show clearly the significant impact of the drug on social participation. When John was taken off medication he became extremely withdrawn, refusing two-thirds of his chats with nursing staff by the end of the baseline (A) period. Institution of the placebo resulted in a temporary increase in socializing, but this effect was lost after the first 2 days. It should be noted that John became increasingly mute during the baseline and placebo periods, and his grooming and token earnings all sharply decreased.

Addition of Stelazine led to a rapid decrease in social withdrawal, with John participating in all 18 daily chats during the final 4 days of the treatment period. Return to the placebo led to another increase in autistic withdrawal. The final reinstitution of the phenothiazine again produced more social responsiveness. Periods during which John received the drug were also associated with much improved grooming and work behavior.

The effects of the drug on the content of conversation were less marked. However, the administration of the phenothiazine was correlated with observational periods with more consistently rational speech. When the drug was removed during the withdrawal period, John's rate of rational talk plunged from 72 to 17%. Reinstitution of the drug produced an increase in rational talk to 56%. It should be noted, however, that the presence or absence of the drug was not correlated with frequency of delusional or hypochondriacal talk. These behaviors occurred in about 20% of all chats throughout all phases of the study.

Case 2 represented an attempt to assess the interaction of fluphenazine with an on-going operant program reinforcing interpersonal eye contact in a chronic schizophrenic, mute patient. The presence or absence of motor and verbal self-stimulation were noted during 18 one-minute observations each day. Eye contact was reinforced on a CRF schedule in six daily therapy sessions. Reliability measures were acceptable for each of the three measures taken. An A-B-A design was used to assess the effects of the drug.

During the placebo (A) phase of this experimental analysis, the patient showed verbal and motor self-stimulation on the average of 2 and 49% of the 18 observations, and an average eye contact rate of 3.7 per minute. It should be noted that reinforcing eye contact with the therapist was the first step in a systematic speech training program for the patient.

The drug phase (B) of the analysis indicated that fluphenazine had facilitating effects on both verbal self-stimulation which occurred at an average of 22% of observations and rate of eye contact, which rose to an average of 4.5 per minute. Motor self-stimulation showed no change except to become more variable across days.

Reversed trends in the data were not obtained when there was a return to placebo (A). Verbal self-stimulation continued to rise to an average of 55% of observation, motor self-stimulation remained constant, and rate of eye contact continued to rise to a mean of 5.6 per minute. These data are summarized in Fig. 2. The failure to obtain reversed trends suggests a drug-initiated response facilitation which is seen most clearly in the increase of verbal self-stimulation, and less so in rate of eye contact.

The results suggest that eye contact and verbal self-stimulation are closely related to one another while motor self-stimulation is independent of both. In the placebo phase all baselines were stable. When the drug was instituted a rise in eye contact and verbal self-stimulation is noted while motor self-stimulation stays constant. Interestingly, verbal self-stimulation which is not being systematically consequated with tangible rewards rises much more than frequency of eye contact. If eye contact and verbal self-stimulation represents an interaction between closely related parts of a total response chain, then the facilitation of verbal self-stimulation may be explained.

In the third case presented by Liberman *et al.* (1973), chlorpromazine was found to contribute little or nothing to the reduction in delusional speech of a psychotic woman produced by time-out from reinforcement.

It is important to employ research designs that tease out the separate

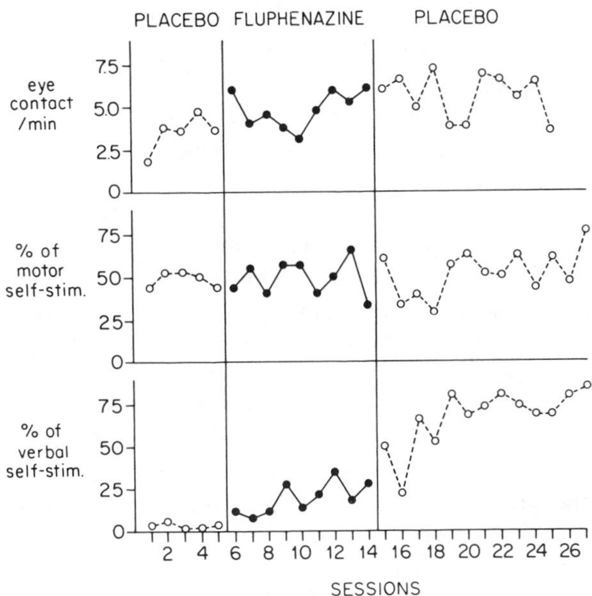

Fig. 2. Interpersonal eye contact, motor and self-stimulation in a schizophrenic young man during placebo, and fluphenazine (20 mg daily) conditions. Each session represents the average of a 2-day block of observation. (Reprinted from Liberman, R. P., Davis, J., Moon, N., & Moore, J. Research design for analyzing drug-environment-behavior interactions. *Journal of Nervous and Mental Disease,* 1973, **156,** 432–439. By courtesy of the Williams & Wilkins Co., Baltimore, Maryland.)

effects of environmental contingencies and drugs on the behavior of psychotic patients. The within-subject withdrawal design common to behavior modification research provides a means of assessing environment-drug-behavior interactions.

In the case studies reported by Liberman *et al.* (1973), phenothiazines were shown to be the causal factor in decreasing autistic withdrawal (case 1), a contributing factor to the increase in orienting eye-contact (case 2), and of little importance in reducing delusional speech (case 3). In case 2, it is possible that the increase in rate of eye contact during the placebo phase was in part related to residual phenothiazine stored in Billy's tissues. It is established that phenothiazines and their active metabolites are still found in the body up to 6 months after discontinuation of medication (Ban, 1969). Without concurrent monitoring of blood and urine levels of phenothiazines, and long washout periods between experimental conditions, it is impossible to assess the real interaction between drug and environmental effects on behavior.

It is likely that more intensive and comprehensive employment of reinforcement contingencies will decrease the effect of drugs on behavior. In a landmark triple-blind, between-group study by Paul, Tobias, and Holly (1972) maintenance phenothiazine chemotherapy failed to contribute to the responsiveness of hard core, chronic psychotics when active environmental programs were utilized.

Combined single case and group designs were used to evaluate the effects of diazepam in eight anxious outpatients (D. A. Turner, Purchatzke, Gift, Farmer, & Uhlenhuth, 1974). Multiple response measures were utilized: rating scales, self-report instruments, and three types of direct observations. The most interesting aspect of this study lies in its detailed analysis of group and individual differences for placebo vs. drug states. When statistically analyzed, the mean diazepam-placebo differences for the group of eight patients was significant ($P < 0.05$) for two of the ratings scales, five self-report measures, and two directly observed behaviors. However, analysis of the within-subject data revealed considerable individual differences in patterns of differential responding to placebo and diazepam. Two patients had statistically significant ($P < 0.05$) placebo-diazepam differences on only one response measure, while one patient showed significant differences on 13 of the measures. Single case methods provided greater individual specificity of responses to drugs, a reduction in time and sample size, and greater discriminative power between drug and placebo conditions.

V. DRUGS AS AGENTS OF PUNISHMENT, REINFORCEMENT, AND EXTINCTION

The first interfacing of drugs and behavior therapy occurred in aversion therapy for alcoholism (Lemere & Voegtlin, 1950; Thimann, 1949). To suppress the intake of alcohol, patients were given repeated trials of being exposed to the sight, odor, and taste of alcoholic beverages (conditioned stimuli) at the same time that they were experiencing the noxious effects (unconditioned responses) of apomorphine or emetine (unconditioned stimulus). These noxious effects included nausea, vomiting, sweating, chills, dizziness, and other disagreeable, autonomic symptoms. With sufficient trials pairing the CS with the UCS, the CS alone theoretically elicited similar noxious effects (conditioned responses) resulting in avoidance of drinking alcoholic beverages. While these early studies were not well controlled, the clinical results indicated that approximately 50% of the patients who completed aversion therapy remained abstinent for 3–5 year periods of follow-up. The patients who received this treatment were highly selected for their voluntary interest and desire for abstinence, their willingness to remain in the hospital for several weeks and submit to an extremely disagreeable treatment, and their relatively high socioeconomic status.

Chemical aversion therapy has also been applied to fetishism, transvestism, homosexuality, drug addiction (Liberman, 1968), cigarette smoking, and overeating. These studies have been adequately reviewed by Brady (1971), Silverstone (1970), Franks (1966), Bandura (1969), Ditman (1966), and Yates (1970). The use of drugs in aversion therapy has yielded to the more efficient and specific application of electrical aversive stimuli and the less noxious and more convenient technique of covert sensitization. However, it should be noted that experimental evidence with animals suggests that in the presence of cues mediated by interoceptive pathways, chemically induced aversive stimuli may be more effective suppressants of behavior (Garcia, McGowan, Ervin, & Koelling, 1968). For instance, the odor and taste of alcoholic beverages may develop better CS properties in suppressing drinking if they are paired with an UCS that elicits noxious gustatory and gastric responses than if paired with peripheral shock. The probability of establishing associated learning depends in part on central integration of the particular afferent channels through which the conditionally paired stimuli are presented.

While much clinical research has been reported on the use of drugs as aversive stimuli, few experimenters have evaluated the use of drugs as positive reinforcers. Thompson (1968) and Schuster and Thompson (1969) have outlined research strategies for testing drugs as positively valenced stimuli in infrahumans. These authors suggested that studies with animals might help in the understanding of drug addiction in humans. Narcotics, barbiturates, marijuana, amphetamines, and other psychotropic drugs that produce euphoria or other pleasant affects may be conceptualized as positive reinforcers for the instrumental behaviors that precede their use. In addicted individuals, the absence of positively valenced drugs constitutes an operational definition of withdrawal. In turn, behaviors that produce relief from the noxious symptoms of the withdrawal syndrome—seeking and self-administration of drugs—are negatively reinforced. Interpersonal and task-oriented behaviors which maintain an individual in an addicted state are conditioned by avoidance of withdrawal. From another vantage point, "abused" drugs may be conceptualized as positive reinforcers for behaviors that sustain their use (Liberman, 1968; Schuster & Johanson, 1973; Wikler, 1973). Drug dependence, thus, is maintained by negative and positive reinforcement. The positively valenced drugs do not by themselves provide an inclusive source of reinforcement for drug-seeking behaviors since manifold social and material rewards consequate such activities.

A recent therapeutic application of the positively reinforcing effects of drugs has been the LSD treatment of alcoholics and heroin addicts. Intensive preparatory interviews during which verbal commitments were made for adaptive vocational and interpersonal behaviors in the future preceded a day-long session with a high dose of LSD. The LSD produces a psychedelic or mystical experience with abreaction, catharsis, and pleasurable sensory stimuli. While one year follow-ups of double-blind studies indicate that LSD-treated substance abusers show twice as much abstinence as control groups given placebos, the effects would theoretically be greater if the experimenters utilized more carefully elementary principles of behavior (Kurland, Unger, Shaffer, & Savage, 1967; Pahnke, Kurland, Unger, Savage, & Grof, 1970; Soskin, Grof, & Richards, 1973). For example, more than one administration of the psychedelic drug should be given contingent upon more overtly practiced, adaptive behaviors in the social and instrumental dimensions. LSD also has been used to mobilize motor and verbal behaviors in depressed, terminal cancer patients (Pahnke, Kurland, Goodman, & Richards, 1969).

Another example of the use of drugs as positive reinforcers in treatment is the methadone maintenance programs for heroin addicts. While methadone serves as a central "blockader" of the effects of heroin or other narcotics, it also produces a calm, steady emotional state and prevents the addicted individual from experiencing the unpleasant symptoms of withdrawal (Senay, Jaffe, diMenza, & Renault, 1973). Patients who are enrolled in a methadone maintenance clinic receive their doses of methadone contingent upon their abstaining from other drugs. Abused drugs obtained on the "street" can be detected in the urines of patients which are collected on a variable ratio basis. Presumably, then, methadone serves as a reinforcer for behaviors which are alternatives to seeking and self-administering of drugs. Studies have shown that patients receiving methadone with only minimal psychosocial therapy do as well as those receiving methadone in combination with an intensive, therapeutic and rehabilitative program (Senay *et al.,* 1973).

One clinical research effort involves investigating the use of marijuana to positively reinforce regular clinic attendance and acceptance of disulfiram (Antabuse) among alcoholics. Disulfiram and marijuana would be given under supervision to ensure their proper use. Marijuana has been described by alcoholics to produce similar effects on mood as does alcohol but does not impair intellectual and sensorimotor performance as does alcohol (Rosenberg, 1973).

Methadone and nonaddicting narcotic antagonist drugs (Cyclazocine, Naloxone, Naltrexone) have marked effects as "blocking" agents for self-administered heroin. An addict who is saturated with methadone or a narcotic antagonist will not experience the euphoric effects of heroin; hence, these agents can be used to extinguish illicit heroin-seeking and using behaviors. Theoretically, to extinguish the operantly and classically conditioned drug-seeking behaviors, the narcotic addict should be permitted to engage in drug-using behavior, but gain no reinforcement. Administering methadone or a narcotic antagonist on a chronic, maintenance basis can produce an opportunity for extinction. Because methadone is an addicting narcotic itself, individuals maintained on it do not experience psychological or physiological "drug cravings." Thus, extinction is less likely to occur under methadone treatment because the maladaptive drug-seeking and self-administering behaviors are not elicited by "drug-cravings" and other aspects of "conditioned abstinence." On the other hand, narcotic antagonists allow "drug-cravings" to occur, go unsatisfied, and potentially to disappear because of nonreinforcement. The addict's chances for remaining abstinent when the narcotic antagonist is discontinued should be improved because "conditioned abstinence" and "drug-cravings" can extinguish. The effectiveness of narcotic antagonists as well as their limitations have been described (Fink, 1973; Kleber, 1973); however, the role of specific exposures to opiates in the treatment process and a validation of the extinction hypothesis has not been clarified.

VI. CONCLUSIONS

Behavior analysis and psychopharmacology are unlikely partners that, combined, have begun to generate interesting and heuristic research and clinical experimentation. These two fields derive from disparate basic assumptions about the major sources of influence on behavior, but hold in common an adherence to the scientific and reliable measurement of behavior and experimental methodology. Research stemming from the interaction between behavior analysis and psychopharmacology has been productive in four general areas: (1) drugs as facilitators or adjuncts to behavior therapy; (2) behavioral and environmental strategies for prompting and reinforcing the appropriate and prescribed use of antipsychotic drugs; (3) single-case experimental designs using direct and continuous observations of behavior to assess the effects of psychotropic drugs; (4) drugs as agents of punishment, reinforcement and extinction of clinically important behaviors.

Each of these areas of practical interaction lead to benefits in clinical practice. The yield from mixing the seeds of behavior analysis and psychopharmacology can be substantially improved if the results of basic research with infrahumans are integrated into applied efforts. Much is now known about the behavioral mechanisms of drug action, including how the frequency of responding and schedules of reinforcement interact with drug effects. For example, pigeons emitting 18 responses per minute were slowed by amobarbital, but not when pecking at 6 responses per minute. Pigeons that make perfect discriminations between two stimuli through an errorless training procedure were unaffected by chlopromazine or imipramine. The same drugs totally disrupted the performance of pigeons trained to make the discrimination in the more conventional method. The responding of animals on an FI 15-minute schedule of reinforcement is almost completely suppressed by pentobarbital whereas responding on a FR 50 schedule is hardly affected at all (Laties & Weiss, 1969). Research on the effects of drugs on behavior should attempt to understand how drugs interact with the behavioral and environmental variables that control the behavioral effects. Basic research with animals has isolated some of these variables, such as the experimental history of the subject, the current and past schedules of reinforcement, the pattern and rate of responding, and the nature of the discriminative stimuli available. These variables can now be studied in a clinical psychopharmacology that is embedded in an adequate experimental analysis of behavior.

Experimental research designs, using a single subject as his own control, has several unique advantages for clinical psychopharmacologists over the better known group designs (Barlow & Hersen, 1973):

1. It enables the researcher to assess effects of drugs on specific, clinically relevant problems.

2. It enables the researcher to assess a drug's potency for the individual subject in question, avoiding the pitfalls of individual variation.

3. It allows for the assessment of drug specificity on a range of behaviors within the single case; that is, the drug may affect only one of a number of behavioral responses.

4. For an individual case it allows the researcher to assess interactive effects of chemotherapy and other modes of therapy.

5. It is inexpensive to employ and can be carried out in any clinical setting.

6. It permits the precise measurement of latency, peak potency, and duration of effects.

7. It avoids the ethical problems inherent in withholding treatment from control groups.

A collaboration between researchers in behavior analysis and clinical psychopharmacology also promises to lead to a more reliable, valid, and comprehensive classification of behavior disorders based upon differential response to environmental and chemical interventions. The identification of various subgroups within the large, clinical populations referred to as schizophrenic, hyperkinetic, and depressed would promote behavioral-biological research and contribute to the state of the art when we will be closer to predicting what treatment in which setting is most effective for a specific individual.

REFERENCES

Alevizos, P. N., Berck, P. L., Callahan, E. J., & Campbell, M. D. An instructional aid for staff training in behavioral assessment. *Journal of Applied Behavior Analysis,* 1974, **7,** 472.

Azrin, N. H., & Powell, J. Behavioral engineering: The use of response priming to improve prescribed self-medication. *Journal of Applied Behavior Analysis,* 1969, **2,** 39–42.

Ban, T. *Psychopharmacology.* Baltimore: Williams & Wilkins, 1969.

Bandura, A. *Principles of behavior modification.* New York: Holt, 1969.

Barlow, D. H., & Hersen, M. Single-case experimental designs: Uses in applied clinical research. *Archives of General Psychiatry,* 1973, **29,** 319–325.

Baum, M. Avoidance training in both alcohol and non-drug states increases the resistance-to-extinction of an avoidance response in rats. *Psychopharmacologia,* 1971, **19,** 87–90.

Brady, J. P. Brevital-relaxation treatment of frigidity. *Behaviour Research and Therapy,* 1966, **4,** 71–77.

Brady, J. P. Drugs in behavior therapy. In D. H. Effron (Ed.), *Psychopharmacology: A review of progress 1957–1967.* Publ. No. 1836. Washington, D.C.: Public Health Service, 1969. Pp. 271–280.

Brady, J. P. Drugs in behavior therapy. In J. H. Marserman (Ed.), *Current psychiatric therapies.* Vol. 2. New York: Grune & Stratton, 1971. Pp. 86–93.

Brady, J. P. Behavioral treatment of sexual frigidity. Paper presented at the fourth annual Southern California Conference on Behavior Modification, Los Angeles, October 1972.

Callahan, E. J., Alevizos, P. N., Teigen, J., Neuman, H., & Campbell, M. D. Behavioral effects of reducing the frequency of phenothiazine administration. *Archives of General Psychiatry,* 1975, in press.

Chassan, J. B. *Research design in clinical psychology and psychiatry.* New York: Meredith, 1967. Pp. 180–216.

Davison, G. C., & Valins, S. On self-produced and drug-produced relaxation. *Behaviour Research and Therapy,* 1968, **6,** 401–402.

Dews, P. B. Behavioral effects of drugs. In S. M. Farber & R. H. L. Wilson (Eds.), *Conflict and creativity.* New York: McGraw-Hill, 1963. Pp. 138–153.

Dews, P. B. Pharmacology of positive reinforcement and discrimination. In M. Y. Mikkel'son & V. G. Longo (Eds.), *Pharmacology of conditioning, learning, and retention.* New York: Macmillan, 1965. Pp. 91–96.

Ditman, K. S. Review and evaluation of current drug therapies in alcoholism *Psychosomatic Medicine,* 1966, **28,** 667–677.

Duncan, D., Hilton, L., Kraeger, P., & Lumsdaine, J. *Fertility control methods: Strategies for introduction.* New York: Academic Press, 1973.

Ferster, C. B., & Appel, J. B. Interpreting drug-behavior effects with a functional analysis of behavior. In Z. Votava, M. Horvath, & O. Vinar (Eds.), *Psychopharmacological methods.* Oxford: Pergamon, 1963. Pp. 170–181.

Fink, M. Questions in cyclazocine therapy of opiate dependence. *Psychopharmacology Bulletin,* 1973, **9,** 38–39.

Franks, C. M. Conditioning and conditioned aversion therapies in the treatment of the alcoholic. *International Journal of the Addictions,* 1966, **1,** 61–98.

Garcia, J., McGowan, B. K., Ervin, F. R., & Koelling, R. A. Cues: Their relative effectiveness as a function of the reinforcer. *Science,* 1968, **160,** 794–795.

Goldberg, H. L., DiMascio, A., & Chaudhary, B. A clinical evaluation of prolixin enanthate. *Psychosomatics,* 1970, **11,** 173–177.

Gottesman, I. I., & Shields, J. *Schizophrenia and genetics: A twin study vantage point.* New York: Academic Press, 1972.

Gottman, J. M. N-of-one and N-of-two research in psychotherapy. *Psychological Bulletin,* 1973, **80,** 93–105.

Grinspoon, L., Ewalt, J. R., & Shader, R. Long term treatment of chronic schizophrenia. *International Journal of Psychiatry,* 1967, **4,** 116–128.

Hall, R. V. *Managing behavior. Book 1. Behavior modification: The measurement of behavior.* Lawrence, Kansas: H & H Enterprises, 1971.

Hollis, J. H., & St. Omer, V. V. Direct measurement of psychopharmacologic response: Effects of chlorpromazine on retardate behavior. *American Journal of Mental Deficiency,* 1972, **76,** 397–407.

Kleber, H. D. Therapeutic approaches combined with narcotic antagonists. *Psychopharmacology Bulletin,* 1973, **9,** 39–40.

Klein, D. F., & Davis, J. M. *Diagnosis and drug treatment of psychiatric disorders.* Baltimore: Williams & Wilkins, 1969.

Kurland, A. A., Unger, S., Shaffer, J. W., & Savage, C. Psychedelic therapy utilizing LSD in the treatment of the alcoholic patient: A preliminary report. *American Journal of Psychiatry,* 1967, **123,** 1202–1209.

Lader, M. H., & Mathews, A. M. Comparison of methods of relaxation using physiological measures. *Behaviour Research and Therapy,* 1970, **8,** 331–337.

Laties, V. G., & Weiss, B. Behavioral mechanisms of drug action. In P. Black (Ed.), *Drugs and the brain,* Baltimore: Johns Hopkins Press, 1969. Pp. 115–133.

Lemere, F., & Voegtlin, W. L. An evaluation of the aversion treatment of alcoholism. *Quarterly Journal of Studies in Alcohol,* 1950, **11,** 199–204.

Liberman, R. P. Aversion conditioning of drug addicts: A pilot study. *Behaviour Research and Therapy,* 1968, **6,** 229–231.

Liberman, R. P., Davis, J., Moon, W., & Moore, J. Research design for analyzing drug-environment-behavior interactions. *Journal of Nervous and Mental Disease,* 1973, **156,** 432–439.

Liberman, R. P., DeRisi, W., King, L. W., Eckman, T., & Wood, D. Behavioral measurement in a community mental health center. In P. O. Davidson, F. Clark, & L. Hamerlynck (Eds.), *Evaluation of behavioral program in community residential, and school settings.* Champaign, Ill.: Research Press, 1974. Pp. 105–140.

Lindsley, O. R. Operant conditioning methods applied to research in chronic schizophrenia. *Psychiatric Research Reports,* **5,** 1956, 118–139.

Lindsley, O. R. Operant behavior during anesthesia recovery: A continuous and objective method. *Anesthesiology,* 1961, **22,** 937–946.

Lindsley, O. R. Operant techniques in the measurement of psychopharmacologic response. In J. H. Nadine, & J. H. Moyer (Eds.), *Psychosomatic medicine: The first Hahnemann symposium on psychosomatic medicine*. Philadelphia: Lea & Febiger, 1962. Pp. 373–383.

Lipsedge, M. S., Hajioff, J., Huggins, P., Napier, L., Pearce, J., Pike, D. J., & Rich, M. The management of severe agoraphobia: A comparison of iproniazid and systematic desensitization. *Psychopharmacologia* 1973, **32,** 67–80.

McPherson, F. M., & Le Gassicke, J. A single patient, self-controlled and self-recorded trial of WY 3498. *British Journal of Psychiatry,* 1965, **111,** 149–154.

Marks, I. M., Viswanathan, R., Lipsedge, M. S., & Gardiner, R. Enhanced relief of phobias by flooding during waning diazepam effect. *British Journal of Psychiatry,* 1972, **121,** 493–505.

Mefford, R. B., Jr., Moran, L. J., & Kimble, J. P., Jr. Chlorpromazine-induced changes in blood constituents in schizophrenia. In C. Lindley (Ed.), *Transactions of the fourth research conference on chemotherapy and psychiatry*. Washington, D.C.: Veterans Administration, 1960. Pp. 241–245.

Mumford, E. The noncompliant patient. *Medical Dimensions,* 1973, **3,** 18–22.

Pahnke, W. N., Kurland, A. A., Goodman, L. E., & Richards, W. A. LSD assisted psychotherapy with terminal cancer patients. *Current Psychiatric Therapies,* 1969, **9,** 144–152.

Pahnke, W. N., Kurland, A. A., Unger, S., Savage, C., & Grof, S. The experimental use of psychedelic (LSD) therapy. *Journal of the American Medical Association,* 1970, **212,** 1856–1863.

Paul, G. L., Tobias, L. L., & Holly, B. L. Maintenance psychotropic drugs in the presence of active treatment programs. *Archives of General Psychiatry,* 1972, **27,** 106–115.

Pecknold, J. C., Raeburn, J., & Poser, E. G. Intravenous diazepam for facilitating relaxation for desensitization. *Journal of Behavior Therapy and Experimental Psychiatry,* 1972, **3,** 39–41.

Risley, T. R., & Wolf, M. M. Strategies for analyzing behavior change over time. In J. Nesselroade & H. Reese (Eds.), *Life-span developmental psychology: Methodological issues.* New York: Academic Press, 1972. Pp. 1–13.

Rosenberg, C. M. Marijuana reinforcement of disulfiram use in the treatment of alcoholism. *Psychopharmacology Bulletin,* 1973, **9,** 25.

Schuster, C. R., & Johanson, C. E. Behavioral analysis of opiate dependence. In S. Fisher & A. M. Freedman (Eds.), *Opiate addiction: Origins and treatment.* New York: Winston, 1973.

Schuster, C. R. & Thompson, T. Self-administration of and behavioral dependence on drugs. *Annual Review of Pharmacology,* 1969, **9,** 483–502.

Senay, E. C., Jaffe, J. H., diMenza, S., & Renault, P. F. A 48-week study of methadone, methadyl acetate, and minimal services. In S. Fisher & A. M. Freedman (Eds.), *Opiate addiction: Origins and treatment.* New York: Winston, 1973.

Serber, M., & Goerwitz, K. Effects of tybatranon: Physiological indices of relaxation. Unpublished manuscript, 1974.

Sherman, A. R. Therapy of maladaptive fear-motivated behavior in the rat by the systematic gradual withdrawal of a fear-reducing drug. *Behaviour Research and Therapy,* 1967, **5,** 121–129.

Silverstone, T. The use of drugs in behavior therapy. *Behavior Therapy,* 1970, **1,** 485–497.

Soskin, R. A., Grof, S., & Richards, W. A. Low doses of dipropyltryptamine in psychotherapy. *Archives of General Psychiatry,* 1973, **28,** 817–821.

Spohn, H. E. The case for reporting the drug status of patient subjects in experimental studies of schizophrenic psychopathology. *Journal of Abnormal Psychology,* 1973, **82,** 102–106.

Sulzbacher, S. I. Behavior analysis of drug effects in the classroom. In G. Semb (Ed.), *Behavior analysis and education.* Lawrence: University of Kansas Support and Development Center for Follow Through, Department of Human Development, 1972. Pp. 37–52.

Sulzbacher, S. I. Psychotropic medication with children: An evaluation of procedural biases in results of reported studies. *Pediatrics,* 1973, **51,** 513–517.

Thimann, J. Conditioned reflex treatment of alcoholism. *New England Journal of Medicine,* 1949, **241,** 368–370, 408–410.

Thompson, T. Drugs as reinforcers: Experimental addiction. *International Journal of Addictions,* 1968, **3,** 199–205.

Turner, A. J. Bird in the box approach to community mental health. Paper presented at the Association for Advancement of Behavior Therapy, New York, October 1972.

Turner, A. J. Programs and evaluations. Annual Report, Huntsville-Madison County Community Mental Health Center, Huntsville, Alabama, 1973.

Turner, D. A., Purchatzke, G., Gift, T., Farmer, C., & Uhlenhuth, E. H. Intensive design in evaluating anxiolytic agents. Unpublished manuscript, Univ. Chicago School of Medicine, 1974.

Wender, P. H. The role of genetics in the etiology of the schizophrenics. *American Journal of Orthopsychiatry,* 1969, **39,** 447–458.

Wikler, A. Dynamics of drug dependence: Implications of a conditioning therapy for research and treatment. In S. Fisher & A. M. Freedman (Eds.), *Opiate addiction: Origins and treatment.* New York: Winston, 1973.

Yates, A. J. *Behavior therapy.* New York: Wiley, 1970. Pp. 305–323.

Zike, K. Drugs in maladaptive school behavior. Unpublished manuscript, obtainable from author at Harbor General Hospital, Los Angeles, Ca., 1972.

AUTHOR INDEX

Numbers in italics refer to the pages on which the complete references are listed.

T

SUBJECT INDEX

A

B

O

P

R

S

B
C 7
D 8
E 9
F 0
G 1
H 2
I 3
J 4